Europe After Maastricht
An Ever Closer Union?

München 1994
Law Books in Europe

1118592/9

Die Deutsche Bibliothek – CIP-Einheitsaufnahme

Europe after Maastricht : an ever closer union? / Ed.
by Renaud Dehousse. - München : Beck, 1994 ˋ
  (Law books in Europe)
  ISBN 3 406 38342 4
NE: Dehousse, Renaud [Hrsg.]

Printed in Germany
© 1994, C. H. Beck'sche Verlagsbuchhandlung, München

for Law Books in Europe:
Editorial Aranzadi, Pamplona (ISBN 84-7016-968-8);
C. H. Beck, Munich (ISBN 3-406-38342-4);
Bruylant, Brussels (ISBN 2-8027-0884-8);
Giuffrè Editore, Milan (ISBN 88-04744-8);
Kluwer, Deventer (ISBN 90-6544-821-7);
Manz, Vienna (ISBN 3-214-05659-X);
Stämpfli + Cie, Bern (ISBN 3-7272-9097-8);
Sweet & Maxwell, London (ISBN 0-421-52170-8).

Contents

List of Contributors

Brian Bercusson
is Professor of Law at the European University Institute, Florence, Italy

Renaud Dehousse
is Assistant Professor of Law at the European University Institute

Hans Ulrich Jessurun d'Oliveira
is Professor of Law at the European University Institute

Christian Joerges
is Professor of Law at the University of Bremen and at the European University Institute

Roger Morgan
is Professor of Political Science at the European University Institute

Emile Noël
is the Principal of the European University Institute and Honorary Secretary General of the Commission of the European Communities

Francis Snyder
is Professor of Law and Head of the Law Department at the European University Institute

Joseph H.H. Weiler
is Professor of Law at Harvard Law School and Director of the Academy of European Law at the European University Institute

List of Principal Abbreviations

AEL	Collected Courses of the Academy of European Law
AÖR	Archiv für öffentliches Recht
BIS	Bank of International Settlements
Bull.EC	Bulletin of the European Communities
CEEP	Centre Européen des Entreprises Publiques
CEPR	Center for European Policy Research
CFSP	Common Foreign and Security Policy
CLR	Commonwealth Law Reports (Australia)
CML Rev.	Common Market Law Review
CMLR	Common Market Law Reports
COM	Commission of the EC Documents
COREPER	Committee of Permanent Representatives
CSCE	Conference on Security and Cooperation in Europe
DJT	Deutscher Juristentag
EC	European Community
ECB	European Central Bank
ECHR	European Convention on Human Rights
ECJ	European Court of Justice
ECR	European Court Reports
ECSC	European Coal and Steel Community
ECU	European Currency Unit
EEA	European Economic Area
EEC	European Economic Community
EFTA	European Free Trade Association
EJIL	European Journal of International Law

ELRev.	European Law Review
EMI	European Monetary Institute
EMS	European Monetary System
EMU	Economic and Monetary Union
EP	European Parliament
EPC	European Political Cooperation
ERM	Exchange Rate Mechanism
ERTA	European Road Transport Agreement
ESCB	European System of Central Banks
ETUC	The European Trade Union Confederation
EuGRZ	Europäische Grundrechte Zeitschrift
EUI	European University Institute
EUR	Europarecht
EuZW	Europäische Zeitschrift für Wirtschaftsrecht
FRG	Federal Republic of Germany
GDR	German Democratic Republic
MEP	Member of European Parliament
MNS	Migration News Sheet
NATO	North Atlantic Treaty Organization
NJW	Neue Juristische Wochenschrift
OJ	Official Journal
RabelsZ	Rabels Zeitschrift für auslandisches und internationales Privatrecht
RdC	Recueil des Cours de l'Académie de droit international
RIIA	Royal Institute for International Affairs
RMC	Revue du Marché Commun
SEA	Single European Act
SEC	Commission of the EC Documents
TEU	Treaty on European Union

UNICE	Union des Industries de la Communauté Européenne
WEU	Western European Union
Yale L.J.	Yale Law Journal
ZLR	Zeitschrift für Lebensmittelrecht

Preface

'Europe after Maastricht' is the outcome of some collective reflection done at the European University Institute after the conclusion of the Treaty on European Union. On the initiative of Professor Renaud Dehousse, legal scholars and political scientists took part, each dealing with aspects of the Treaty closest to their own specialization, while maintaining contact and benefitting from the exchange and confrontation of ideas. This resulting collective work is a good example of what can be done in a multi-national, interdisciplinary Institute like this one in Florence.

The study thus done yields no grounds for complacency. A number of imperfections or weaknesses in the Maastricht Treaty are familiar today, and have been well chewed over in the public or parliamentary debates surrounding ratification of the Treaty. Others are less obvious, and have had to be flushed out with subtlety and rigour: for instance, in social policy or in connection with European citizenship. The Florence Institute is a European institute and proud of it, but that in no way affects its academic independence. It is the combination of a high level of competence, quality research and a critical spirit that gives its work value – and it is certainly this set of qualities that has led the European institutions to seek the benefit of the advice of its professors or the findings of their research.

Eighteen months of discussions and votes won with difficulty (in Denmark and France), along with the war of attrition in Britain (where it is has been more the government than the Treaty's opponents that have been worn down), have caused the positive aspects of the Maastricht Treaty to be forgotten: the ambitious objective of economic and monetary union, the significant progress (despite all the limitations) towards a less technocratic Community more under the control of elected representatives, and the considerable innovation of a differentiated approach (in relation to Denmark and Britain), which will be the only way to make further progress possible in a Europe in course of enlargement. It will accordingly be necessary, once the groundswell of the ratification debates has subsided, to take up the Treaty again, set its machinery in motion and test the reality and solidity of the commitments it embodies. The analysis presented here may provide considerable help with preliminary thinking towards the decisions to be taken over the coming months.

In this connection, keeping to the first deadline set, namely 1 January 1994 for the move to the second stage of economic and monetary union, is bound to take on a symbolic quality. It will acquire a political value that has no common measure with the rather modest content of the measures it involves. Let us hope that secondary quarrels (for instance, over the siting of the European Monetary Institute) do not come along to spoil its potential. New initiatives towards economic recovery, a closing of the ranks in monetary terms, and institutional innovations, if coordinated with that deadline, might lead to the beginning of a relaunching of Europe by meeting some of the expectations of the European peoples.

The long economic crisis of 1992 and 1993 has highlighted the divergencies in Europe – divergencies in political objectives, in economic performance and in monetary policies. But it has also, something insufficiently noted, brought salutary reactions of return to monetary realism, return to budgetary disciplines, and mobilization for employment. In the medium term, in several of our countries, the growing awareness of the needs of the economy and the reforms introduced will have fall-out that the new mechanisms introduced following Maastricht ought to lend further strength to. Will that be enough to ensure the success of the Treaty? The question remains open. As Joseph Weiler rightly writes in his conclusion, as this century draws to its close the construction of Europe can advance only if it remains a bearer of hope and of progress.

Emile Noël
June 1993

Part I

The Institutional Framework

Chapter 1

From Community to Union

Renaud Dehousse

European union is by no means a new concept. The preamble to the EEC Treaty spoke as early as 1957 of 'creating an ever closer union among the peoples of Europe', and the abstract notion of European union was widely used in Community circles from the 1970s onwards. The Werner plan, the Tindemans report, the Solemn Declaration adopted by the Stuttgart European Council in 1983 all made use of it, as did the Single European Act.[1]

In spite of this recurrent use – or maybe because of it – it is fair to say that the exact meaning of the expression has remained hazy. The concept of 'Union' did not refer to any clear form of government. It was generally accepted that establishment of the Union might involve a development of the supranational features of the European Community, as well as an extension of cooperation among the Member States to new areas. But exactly which form these changes would take remained unclear.

Léontin-Jean Constantinesco eloquently underlined the *raison d'être* of this situation:

> L'intégration européenne n'est pas un *être* mais un *devenir*; elle n'est pas une situation acquise mais un processus; elle n'est pas un résultat, mais l'action devant mener à ce résultat.[2]

Yet this uncertainty did not deter the contracting parties to the Maastricht Treaty. Both the official name of the Treaty – 'Treaty on European Union' – and the substance of its provisions suggest that the establishment of a European Union was its primary institutional objective. Indeed, the very first provision of the Treaty states that

> By this Treaty, the High Contracting Parties establish among themselves a European Union, hereinafter called 'the Union'.[3]

Article A.

---

1   See on this issue the reflections of Wellenstein, 'Unity, Community, Union – What's in a Name?', 29 *CML Rev.* (1992) 205.

2   'La nature juridique des Communautés européennes', *Annales de la Faculté de droit de Liège* (1979) 151.

3   Article A.

The purpose of this chapter is to analyse the kind of structure that was given to the Union and, in a second stage, the political scope of the decisions made by the intergovernmental conferences in which the Treaty was negotiated.

I. The Structure of the Union

The course of the negotiations rapidly showed that the structure of the Union was one of the most delicate points to be solved by the Member States' representatives. Much time was spent debating whether the Union should be given a unitary structure, governed by Community discipline occasionally tempered by significant adjustments, or whether new areas of joint action, like the common foreign and security policy or justice and home affairs, should rather be governed by *ad hoc* rules. The discussions culminated in November 1991 with the rejection of the unitary model suggested by the Dutch Presidency and the adoption of the three-pillar structure proposed in the draft Treaty prepared by the Luxembourg Presidency.[4]

Underlying this sometimes esoteric discussion was a confrontation between radically divergent approaches to European integration. On one side were those who advocated a form of political integration based on the existing communities, the supranational features of which would be reinforced and gradually expanded to new areas. On the other side stood those who defended a more intergovernmental approach in order to avoid any undue erosion of their national sovereignty.

The tension between these two approaches is nothing new; it has characterized the history of European integration from the outset.[5] Yet recent developments – the revival of the Community in the wake of the Single Market programme and the collapse of communist regimes in Eastern Europe – have given new vigour to an old quarrel.

The Single European Act had struck a compromise between these two trends. It was based on the idea, advanced for the first time in the Tindemans report, that European Political Cooperation and the Community were two distinct pillars on which European Union would one day be constructed.[6] Although the institutional bridges between the European Community and existing EPC mechanisms were reinforced, their being governed in a single instrument did not entail an extension of Community methods to political cooperation. Article 3 of the Single Act clearly stated that each retained its own set of rules, contained in separate titles of the Act.

---

4   The various stages of the negotiations are reported in Durand, 'Le traité sur l'Union européenne (Maastricht, 7 février 1992) – Quelques réflexions', in *Le droit de la CEE – Commentaire Mégret*, Vol. 1 (2nd ed. 1992) at 359-364.
5   This continuity is well shown in Jacqué, 'Cours général de droit communautaire' *AEL* (1990), Vol. I, Book 1, 237-360, especially at 247-256. See also de La Serre, 'Le traité d'Union européenne', 180 *La documentation française – Regards sur l'actualité* (1992) 3.
6   De Schoutheete, 'Le rapport Tindemans dix ans après', *Politique étrangère* (1986) 527.

The Maastricht Treaty is based on a similar compromise. The supranational character of the Community has been reinforced, although with some reservations.[7] Existing mechanisms of intergovernmental cooperation, such as European Political Cooperation and cooperation among Ministers for Justice and Home Affairs, have been structured or reinforced. Yet although the European Union is endowed with a single institutional framework, more integrated than the structure established by the Single Act, these areas have not been integrated into the Community framework. The newly created Union thus rests on three separate pillars, each governed by its own set of rules. As we shall see, however, this does not mean that the system established by the Maastricht Treaty is one of watertight compartments.

A. A More Integrated Structure

The Union established by the Maastricht Treaty has often been depicted as a hybrid creature.[8] According to Article A, the new body is founded on the existing Communities, which each retain their separate existence, flanked by two intergovernmental pillars, the common foreign and security policy (CFSP) and cooperation in the fields of justice and home affairs. The Union is assigned its own objectives, which are – broadly stated – those of each pillar. Broad principles – subsidiarity,[9] respect for national identities, for human rights and democracy[10] – govern its action. Citizenship of the Union is also established, though the relevant provisions oddly appear in the EC Treaty.[11] Common provisions govern the revision of the Treaty and the admission of new members;[12] membership of the Community cannot therefore be dissociated from membership of the Union.

More importantly, the Union is to be 'served by a single institutional framework'.[13] The meaning of this somewhat elliptic statement is made clear in later parts of the Treaty, which indicate that some Community institutions – Parliament, Council and Commission – are 'graciously put at the disposal of the Union'.[14] The other institutions are denied any role in the functioning of the Union – explicitly in the case of the European Court of Justice,[15] implicitly in the case of the Court of Auditors. Formally speaking, the European Council – which sees its guidance mission confirmed – appears as the only institution that is solely of the

---

7   See Chapter 2.
8   See, e.g., 'Editorial Comments, "Post-Maastricht"', 29 *CML Rev.* (1992) 199.
9   Article A states that 'decisions are taken as closely as possible to the citizen', while Article B explicitly refers to the subsidiarity principle.
10   Article F.
11   Articles 8 to 8e.
12   Articles N and O, respectively.
13   Article C.
14   C. Timmermans, in *L'Union européenne après Maastricht* (1992) at 51. See Articles J.11(1) (common foreign and security policy) and K.8(1) (justice and home affairs).
15   Article L.

Union. This notwithstanding, the solution that has prevailed, while legitimizing the recent practical evolution, has put an end to the artificial and at times rigid separation that existed between Community matters and foreign policy issues dealt with in the EPC framework: from now on both should be dealt with by the Council, albeit according to different rules.

Be that as it may, institutional unity is far from complete. In addition to the exclusion of the Court of Justice, to which I shall return in a moment, the Treaty explicitly states that decisions pertaining to each pillar are to be prepared in distinct *fora*. Whereas in theory the role of COREPER in Community policies is not challenged, the Political Committee, which has always been at the core of the EPC process, will retain its role as regards common foreign and security policy,[16] and a committee of senior officials will play a similar role in the fields of justice and home affairs.[17] Moreover, decisions adopted in the field of security policy may, if necessary, be implemented by the Western European Union, which will further reinforce institutional fragmentation. Given the insistence by some Member States on the necessity of retaining distinct decision-making processes, coordination among these various bodies is likely to be a delicate task. This probably accounts for the greater profile given in the Maastricht Treaty to the Secretary-General of the Council,[18] on whose shoulders this burden will primarily fall.

Consistency in the various policies pursued by the Union will not be the only problem. When reading the relevant provisions of the Treaty, one cannot avoid the impression of institutional weakness. This impression is generated by two elements. First, the Union lacks any financial autonomy: all expenditure incurred in the framework of the two intergovernmental pillars must be borne either by the Community budget or by the Member States.[19] Second, the Union as such enjoys no legal personality.

Both elements seriously restrict the Union's capacity to act. It may of course be able to act through the Communities, which retain their separate legal existence,[20] or by means of international agreements among the Member States, as envisaged for instance in the fields of justice and home affairs.[21] But solutions of this kind are always full of problems and uncertainties. The following example has been suggested: imagine that damages are caused by an observers' mission sent to a third country by some Member States, on the basis of a decision by the Council of

---

16 Article J.8(5).
17 Article K.4(1). This Committee will also occasionally intervene in the preparation of Council decisions concerning visas to be required from nationals of third countries; see Article 100d.
18 See new Article 151 of the EC Treaty. A declaration included in the Final Act of the intergovernmental conference states that the European Political Cooperation Secretariat should be merged with the General Secretariat of the Council.
19 Articles K.8(2) and J.11(2).
20 This possibility is contemplated for economic sanctions against third states; see Article 228a.
21 Article K.3(2)(c). Decisions taken in the framework of the common foreign and security policy might take a similar form. Article J.3(4) stipulates that 'joint actions shall commit the Member States in the positions they adopt and in the conduct of their activity'.

Ministers of the European Community, taken in the framework of the CFSP but financed in part by the Community budget. Who would be internationally responsible?[22]

Legal constructs always have symbolic value, and the three-pillar structure is no exception to the rule. It clearly reflects the reluctance shown by some Member States towards the development of the Community as a political body. At the same time, the stakes are far from being merely symbolic. I have indicated above that the two intergovernmental pillars remain governed by their own sets of rules.[23] Although these rules occasionally differ, common elements dominate, and they all point in the same direction: supranational institutions like the Commission or the European Parliament – not to mention the European Court of Justice – play a far lesser role than they do in the Community framework.

The Commission now enjoys a right of initiative in common foreign and security policy, which had never been formally recognized in the past.[24] The same is true for many matters falling under the provisions on justice and home affairs[25] – the so-called 'third pillar' –, in which the status of the Commission was even weaker than in EPC. However, the upgrading of the Commission's role is limited: unlike in the Community framework, its right of initiative is shared with the Member States, and unanimity is not required to alter its proposals in the few instances where majority voting is possible.[26]

Likewise, as the European Parliament is in general only to be consulted or even merely informed of developments within the Union's intergovernmental policies, it cannot be regarded as a party to the decisions that will be made. The Council remains the main decision-maker, and Member States' prerogatives are protected by the fact that unanimity has remained the rule – a rule with very few exceptions, as majority voting is only foreseen for procedural matters and implementing decisions.[27] Thus, the supranational features that make for the institutional specificity of the European Community are largely absent from the two intergovernmental pillars.

---

22   C. Timmermans, *supra* note 14, at 51.
23   See Article E.
24   Article J.8(3).
25   See Article K.3(2).
26   Article 189A(1), which contains the unanimity rule that previously appeared in Article 149 of the EEC Treaty, is not listed among the institutional provisions applicable to the intergovernmental pillars (see *supra* note 9).
27   Articles J.8(2) and J.3(2) for the CFSP; Articles K.4(3) and K.3(2) for justice and home affairs.

B. A System of Watertight Compartments?

The originality of the structure which has been described lies in the compromise attempted between two different models: the integrated Community model and the more loosely structured world of intergovernmental cooperation. Great care has therefore been taken to avoid any risk of contamination between these two worlds.

Once again, national governments have offered evidence of their aversion to 'judicialization' of diplomatic processes.[28] The European Court of Justice, which by its pro-integration rulings has greatly contributed to the strengthening of the Community's legal system, has seen its jurisdiction confined to the European Communities and to the final provisions of the Maastricht Treaty.[29] The only intervention foreseen in the two intergovernmental pillars is the possibility for the Court to be given competence to interpret conventions concluded by the Member States in the framework of their cooperation in the fields of justice and home affairs, and to rule on disputes regarding their application.[30] A similar exclusion had already been provided for in the Single Act.[31] It clearly suggests that in the view of the Treaty drafters, the institutional bridges set up between the Community and the intergovernmental pillars should not lead to a complete absorption of the latter into the former.

In a similar manner, the upholders of the Community system insisted throughout the negotiations on the necessity of preserving the supranational features that make for its specificity against any interference from intergovernmental cooperation. As a result, preservation of the *acquis communautaire* has been raised to the level of 'objective of the Union'[32] – which would appear to be a fairly conservative approach for a newly established body, if it were not for the above-mentioned fears! More concretely, Article M excludes any possibility that the provisions governing the intergovernmental pillars might be read as amendments of the Community treaties. This is confirmed by several provisions scattered throughout Titles V and VI of the Treaty, which explicitly state that they are 'without prejudice to the powers of the European Community'.[33]

However, it cannot be said that the Treaty has set up a system of watertight compartments. Matters dealt with in the framework of the intergovernmental pillars are too closely connected to Community matters for a rigid separation to be maintained.

---

28 See Stein, 'European Foreign Affairs and the Single European Act', 23 *International Lawyer* (1989) 977, at 987.
29 Article L. As a result, Article F, which assimilates fundamental rights to general principles of Community law, cannot be read as a formal recognition of the Court's jurisdiction to protect these rights.
30 Article K.3(2)(c).
31 Compare Dehousse and Weiler, 'EPC and the Single Act: From Soft Law to Hard Law?' in M. Holland (ed.), *The Future of European Political Cooperation – Essays on Theory and Practice* (1991) 121, at 135.
32 Article B.
33 See, e.g., Articles J.8(5), K.1, K.3(2)(c), K.4(1).

In the past, it had already emerged that drawing a clear line between international economic policy, which falls in the realm of Community competences, and foreign policy matters, dealt with in the framework of European Political Cooperation, was not always possible. Similarly, the conditions of residence by nationals of third countries on the territory of Member States, which is one of the areas covered by the new provisions on cooperation in the fields of justice and home affairs, has already been touched by Community directives.[34]

Clearly, the Treaty drafters were aware of this kind of interdependence, which was often mentioned as one of the *raisons d'être* of the setting up of a single institutional structure. Specific provisions occasionally attempt to regulate the relationships between the two worlds – the Community one and the intergovernmental one. Thus for instance the new Article 228a, dealing with economic sanctions, establishes a two-step procedure: the resort to sanctions must be decided upon by common position or joint action – which, according to the provisions on the common foreign and security policy, require a unanimous decision of the Council – while the actual sanctions must be adopted according to standard Community procedures for commercial policy matters, i.e. by the Council acting by a qualified majority on a proposal from the Commission.

Such a solution clearly aims at preserving the spirit of both worlds.[35] But it also suggests that from a legal point of view, a clear-cut separation between matters dealt with within the three pillars is not always possible. This in turn makes it difficult to exclude any intervention by the Court of Justice in matters dealt with in the framework of the two intergovernmental pillars.[36] To return again to the example of economic sanctions: suppose that a decision to sever all economic relations with a third state is adopted in the framework of the CFSP, and implemented by the Member States irrespective of the Community's exclusive competence as to commercial policy. Even if, by virtue of Article L, the Commission is prevented from challenging the legality of such a decision on the basis of Article 173 of the EC Treaty, it could use the infringement procedure provided by Article 169, and sue the Member States jointly for having violated their Treaty obligations.[37] The same

---

34   See the symposium on 'The Status of Non-Community Nationals in EC Law', 3 *EJIL* (1992) 36.
35   In doing so, the Treaty on European Union actually did no more than confirm prior practice, for the Commission had indicated in the past that a consensus within EPC was a prerequisite to the adoption by the Community of economic sanctions. See the statement by Commissioner De Clercq before the European Parliament on 11 September 1985 cited by Nuttall, 'Interaction between European Political Cooperation and the European Community', 7 *Yearbook of European Law* (1987) 211, at 233.
36   The following remarks draw on Dehousse and Weiler, *supra* note 31 at 135-136.
37   As is known, a somewhat similar situation was at the basis of the celebrated *ERTA* case (Case 22/70), *Commission v. Council* [1970] ECR 263. See also Everling, 'Reflections on the Structure of the European Union', 29 *CML Rev.* (1992) 1053, at 1063, who suggests a possibility of indirect review of European Council decisions, in case the validity of Community decisions based on the latter is challenged before the Court.

would be true of a decision on customs cooperation adopted in the framework of the third pillar,[38] if it purports to ignore the existence of the common customs tariff.

Questions concerning the demarcation between intergovernmental cooperation and matters of Community competences are of equal relevance to both legal orders. By way of consequence, any possibility of judicial scrutiny of decisions adopted in the framework of intergovernmental cooperation cannot be excluded.

II. An Evaluation

The first comments on the Maastricht Treaty have displayed some scepticism. European Union has been described as a hybrid structure, a 'house half-built ... suddenly abandoned by its builders'.[39] Several commentators have stressed the inelegant character of the pillars structure established by the Treaty.[40] The dividing lines are at times difficult to draw, and coexistence between the various elements might prove difficult.

Even if correct, this form of evaluation is of little help in making sense of the intricate structure set up in the Treaty. I have tried to show above that this complexity is intrinsically linked to a confrontation between two approaches to integration matters: the Community approach, with its emphasis on supranationalism, and the intergovernmental one, which aims at preserving the Member States' autonomy. This compromise explains why the Union, although it has been given a single institutional structure, still operates under two distinct regimes.

It is difficult to say why exactly the establishment of the European Union took this strange form. Clearly, belonging to a common group – be it called community or union – necessarily entails a degree of cohesion *vis-à-vis* the outside world. Seen in this light, the establishment of a common foreign and security policy or a common immigration policy – for this is what the third pillar is about – makes sense in these times of rapid changes, where many of the scars of the Second World War have been healed by history. But in doing so the core of national sovereignty has been touched. This may explain both the insistence of some on maintaining such delicate themes outside of the Community framework, and the reactions provoked by the Treaty in many countries.

Thus, Maastricht did not put an end to the debate between supranationalists and intergovernmentalists, which has been going on for decades. The antagonistic visions of the institutional future of the European continent which were defended by the participants in the intergovernmental conference still remain. In many respects,

---

38 Article K.1(8).
39 'Editorial Comments', *supra* note 8, at 202.
40 See, e.g., Louis, 'Les accords de Maastricht – Un premier bilan', 4 *Revue du marché unique européen* (1991) 5; Everling, *supra* note 37, at 1059-64.

the transitory character of many decisions represented a way around a difficult debate.

It is even difficult to determine which of the two camps actually prevailed at this stage. The very existence of the pillars structure, imposed by a determined minority among the Member States, has largely been viewed as a victory for the intergovernmentalists. Conversely, insertion of the provisions on economic and monetary union within the Community framework scored an important victory for the integration camp.

For all its complexity, the birth of a European Union should not be seen as an end, but rather as 'a new stage in the process of creating an ever closer union between the peoples of Europe', as described in Article A. Several bones of contention, such as the scope of the co-decision procedure or the Commission's proposal to modify the hierarchy of norms provided by the EC Treaty,[41] have been put aside with a pledge that they would be reconsidered by an *ad hoc* intergovernmental conference, to be convened by 1996 at the latest.[42] Naturally, further provisions could be reconsidered in the light of internal and external developments.

What will then become of this 'Union without unity', as it has been called?[43]

Giving a clear answer to such a simple question is a difficult exercise. One might note that the Member States have subscribed to a language that would seem to announce a further strengthening of the Community pillar. I have already mentioned the many statements which aim to preserve Community methods against any undue intergovernmental interference. One might also mention that whereas the Treaty foresees the possibility of a 'communitarization' of many matters debated in the framework of cooperation in the fields of justice and home affairs,[44] no mechanism is provided whereby Community matters could be re-transferred to the less integrated world of intergovernmental cooperation. Moreover, even if the reference to the 'federal vocation' of the Union which existed in the draft of the Luxembourg Presidency has eventually been omitted, a combined reading of Articles N(2) and B would suggest that the revision to come should not limit itself to a mere consolidation of existing forms of cooperation, but rather build on the *acquis communautaire*.

However, formalist references of this kind are clearly unable to make such changes become reality. The manifold difficulties that have emerged in the

---

41   See respectively Article 189b(8) of the EC Treaty and the declaration on the hierarchy of Community acts in the final act of the intergovernmental conference. Similar commitments were made as regards the common foreign and security policy (Articles J.4 and J.7), as well as for a possible extension of Community competences to include matters of civil protection, tourism and energy policy, which are covered by an *ad hoc* declaration.
42   Article N(2).
43   De La Serre, *supra* note 5, at 21.
44   Article K.9, which provides a two-steps procedure (unanimous decision by the Council, ratified by the Member States in accordance with their respective constitutional requirements). A similar mechanism is contemplated in Article 8e for provisions strengthening European citizenship.

ratification process should warn us against the dangers of basing any kind of prediction on such a thin basis.

One possible scenario would be that the pillars structure established by the Treaty will lead to a situation of 'dynamic imbalance': being institutionally better equipped, and thus able to operate more efficiently, the Community pillar will be able to play a more active role than the intergovernmental ones. Functional needs could then lead to the gradual taking over of an increasing number of tasks at Community level.

However, this scenario suffers from a major weakness: for such a prospect to materialize, Member States would have to accept the prospect of a further development of the Community, whereas recent developments have provided ample evidence that several among them are no longer willing to accept similar spillovers.

True, several national governments have indicated that in their view, the current consensus-based system would not be viable if membership of the Union were to increase significantly. This amounts to an indirect criticism of the pillars structure, which was conceived to preserve national sovereignties. Yet the view which holds that an enlargement limited to a few EFTA countries should not entail drastic institutional changes has gained ground in the face of the many difficulties encountered during the ratification debates. Alternatively, one should not lose sight of the fact that in the institutional debates to come, the European Parliament will play a far more important role than it has in the past, as it will have to give its assent to any enlargement of the Community.[45] It could therefore condition its approval to a curtailing of intergovernmental cooperation, in which its powers are kept to a minimum.

The power play will therefore be complex, and its outcome should not be taken for granted.

There is, for instance, a widespread tendency to regard the pillars structure as an anomaly, imposed due to a lack of consensus on what the proper structure of the Union should be, and which is bound to be superseded when the time is ripe. Because of its complexity, intergovernmental cooperation is often viewed as a kind of second best alternative to a more ordered structure, decentralized though the former might be.

This kind of consideration often stems from a misunderstanding of the reality of federalism, which is often viewed – at least in Europe – as a system of centralized decision-making.[46] It might therefore be worth pointing out that federalism and intergovernmentalism are not mutually exclusive.

In our world of interdependence, elements of intergovernmentalism can be discerned even in truly federal systems, where the component units and the federal authorities are called upon to collaborate in areas of joint interest. Both the

---

45   Article O.
46   See in this respect the remarks of L. Cohen-Tanugi, *L'Europe en danger* (1992) at 75-83.

structures and the processes through which such cooperation takes place – ministerial meetings in which a large majority or unanimity is required for a decision to be made – are reminiscent of a situation familiar to the observers of the Community scene.

This is not to say that the current pillars structure should or will remain but rather that, even if it were to be altered, intergovernmental cooperation would not altogether disappear: the functional reasons which have brought about its growth in federal systems would *a fortiori* justify its continued existence in the framework of European Union.

Chapter 2

A New Institutional Balance?

Emile Noël

Strengthening the democratic legitimacy of the Union and making its institutions more effective were two of the objectives proposed by President Mitterrand and Chancellor Kohl in their letter of 19 April 1990 to the President of the European Council, requesting the commencement of preparatory work for an intergovernmental conference on political union. At the European Council in Rome (13 and 14 December 1990), the conference's attention was principally drawn to 'democratic legitimacy', as was indicated by the Presidency Conclusions. The role and powers of the European Parliament drew the bulk of discussion on institutional arrangements, including during the final negotiations in Maastricht. A few steps, albeit modest, were however also taken towards greater efficiency of the system.

The outcome of the negotiations is a complex set of new rules. As was the case for the Single European Act, the final implications of the Maastricht Treaty will be the product of interpretations given to it by the institutions and the new ways of 'acting' that the institutions pursue. I wish here to consider, in the light of past experience, what these actions might be, so as to better assess the political scope of these institutional changes. In so doing, I shall also seek to take account of one of the special features of the new Treaty. On a number of points of prime importance it contains political signals for the future, rather than specific commitments. The provisions on a future common defence or 'European defence' are an outstanding example. Some of these new institutional provisions ought also, as we shall see, to be interpreted as political signals announcing tomorrow's developments. Indeed, a new intergovernmental conference is already scheduled for November 1996.

Without underestimating the importance of other institutional innovations (e.g., in respect of the Court of Justice, the Court of Auditors, the Economic and Social Committee or the new Committee of the Regions) I wish here to confine myself to the main provisions concerning the three specifically political institutions (i.e., Parliament, Council and Commission) and their mutual relationships, without considering in detail the special features or anomalies (legal or political) that pervade the texts of the Treaty and its annexes.

I. Legislative Powers of the European Parliament

Parliament's major demands were (i) the introduction of 'co-decision' into the Community's legislative process and (ii) the extension of the circumstances in which Parliament's assent is required before the Council decides. These measures were prominently mentioned in the conclusions of the Presidency after the Rome meeting of the European Council. They remained sensitive points throughout the negotiations, right up to the final decisions taken by the heads of State or government.

These arduous discussions are responsible for the astonishing complexity of the final compromise and the formal caution or reticence that surrounds it. 'Co-decision' is indeed introduced,[1] but without retaining the term itself. The Treaty refers only to the 'procedure of Article 189 B'. Similarly, the cooperation procedure introduced by the Single Act is no longer explicitly mentioned by name. The texts now refer only to the 'procedure of Article 189 C'. This seems rather an odd way to capture the citizens' attention and facilitate their understanding of the Community process!

As to the substance, the core of the co-decision procedure is the establishment, after a first reading (proposal by the Commission, opinion by Parliament, adoption of a 'common position' by the Council), of a Conciliation Committee in which Parliament and the Council have equal representation whilst the Commission participates. The Committee will be charged with the task of reaching 'agreement on a joint text', by qualified majority of Council members and majority of the Parliament representatives; this joint text is then to be approved by an absolute majority of votes cast in the Parliament and a qualified majority in the Council.

This balanced procedure was readily accepted by Parliament. With a view to limiting the risks of blockage, the Conference burdened it – largely distorting it – by stipulating that in the event of the Conciliation Committee's failure to agree, the Council could still confirm its joint position (possibly with amendments from the Parliament) by qualified majority. The act in question is then definitively adopted unless Parliament rejects it by an absolute majority of its members. This 'third reading' met with resolute opposition from Parliament, of which the Conference did not take account.

By contrast, Parliament secured partial satisfaction in respect of the field of application of the new procedure, which covers some fifteen Treaty provisions, among them in particular those relating to the creation and operation of the internal market[2] and the new powers assigned to the Community.[3] Co-decision is also

---

1   New Article 189B.
2   Articles 100A, 49, 54, 56 and 57.
3   Education (Article 126), culture (Article 128), health (Article 129), consumer protection (Article 129A), trans-European networks (Article 129D).

introduced for the research and development framework programme,[4] and to a limited extent in the environmental sphere.[5]

This advance is reinforced by the extension of the number of cases where assent from Parliament is required. The Single Act had introduced this procedure, though confining it to accessions and association agreements. Parliament had made wide use of it to put forward its foreign-policy views (e.g. with regard to agreements with Israel, Morocco and Syria). The Maastricht Treaty extends the procedure to new fields, such as the exercise of the right of residence in the Community,[6] the structural funds,[7] the procedure for election of members of Parliament,[8] and amendments to the statute of the European Central Bank.[9] Additionally, in relation to international agreements, Parliament's assent will be required in a considerable number of cases over and above those contemplated in Article 238.[10] However, Parliament did not secure the assent requirement for Treaty amendments[11] or for provisions relating to the Community's own resources.[12]

Despite the complexity of the procedures established by the provisions on assent and co-decision, they undoubtedly give Parliament genuine legislative power for the first time. A significant number of important Community acts can henceforth be taken only with the explicit agreement of Parliament, or at the very least where it expresses no opposition. This is a qualitative leap by comparison with both the Treaty of Rome and the Single Act, where the Council retained the last word. The fact that acts adopted by the co-decision procedure[13] must be signed by both the President of the Parliament and the President of the Council[14] sanctions this innovation.

Does this institutional advance actually improve the Community's 'democratic legitimacy'? While one can only welcome increased involvement of the people's elected representatives in the legislative process, it is also obvious that transparency of procedure is an essential feature of the control of these representatives by their electors. Yet, contrary to all expectations, the Maastricht Treaty has made the process still more opaque by introducing complex procedures (only very briefly described here) and creating exceptions or special rules for certain areas (research or the environment).

Parliament will therefore have much to do to make European citizens aware of what its role and impact in the drafting and adoption of a Community Act has been.

---

4   Article 130I.
5   Article 130S(3).
6   Article 8A(2).
7   Article 130D.
8   New Article 138(3).
9   Article 106(5).
10   Cf. new Article 228(3).
11   Article N(1).
12   Article 201.
13   Article 189B.
14   Article 191B(1).

It is the 'third reading' cases that give the greatest cause for concern here. MEPs, with some justification, complain that they will in practice be facing a *fait accompli* in cases where the Council confirms its 'joint position'. Not only will it be difficult to secure an absolute majority in order to reject the Council's conclusion, but the Parliament's 'brand image' will be adversely affected, making it look like the institution that blocks or rejects legislation, as opposed to the one that drafts and amends it.

The ingenuity Parliament has displayed in implementing the Single Act provides some hope that it may at least partly overcome these obstacles. At present, MEPs are advocating the conclusion of an inter-institutional agreement between the Council and Parliament, in order to secure an interpretation of the new rules which would favour a greater role for Parliament, e.g. by extending the sphere of application of the co-decision and assent procedures: the Council would commit itself to resort to such measures to an extent greater than that explicitly dictated by the Maastricht Treaty. The chances for the success of such an approach seem to be very limited. Arrangements have certainly been made with the Council in connection with the Single Act, but their scope has been limited to procedural questions. It is more than doubtful whether governments will in the near future accept any lifting of limitations that were deliberately placed on the Parliament's role, in order to arrive at a difficult compromise.

On the contrary, Parliament is likely to strengthen its internal rules so that its authorities (the President, the Bureau, the Enlarged Bureau, political groups, etc.) can keep tight control over the course of the co-decision procedure. The committee on rules of procedure has commenced studying these changes. The strict discipline already introduced for running the cooperation procedure following the Single Act has been effective: limitation on amendments that can be submitted in second reading, sittings restricted to voting, referrals back to committee to put pressure on the executive, etc. Today it is the proper functioning of the Conciliation Committee that should be its chief objective.

Finally, Parliament would like to limit or even eliminate cases of 'third reading'. The Commission will undoubtedly be subjected to vigorous pressure to make a formal commitment to withdraw its proposals in the absence of agreement in the Conciliation Committee (which would paralyse the Council), or at least to make such withdrawals case by case. The new relationships the Maastricht Treaty establishes between Parliament and Commission[15] should induce the Commission to take much greater account of Parliament's requirements than had been the case in the past.

Whatever improvements Parliament may be able to secure in applying the texts, all their imperfections cannot be overcome. In order to assess their real scope it is better to treat them as a political signal, indeed a strong political signal. When they accepted direct elections to the Parliament in the 1970s, the Member States

15   *Infra* section II.

specified that this development would not entail any change in Parliament's role or powers. Ten years later, with the assenting opinion and the cooperation procedure introduced by the Single Act, Parliament became closely involved in the legislative process. Five years later, it is to attain legislative power. This dynamic of the strengthening of Parliament's powers is likely to continue in the next revision of the Treaties, set to take place in 1996 or even before.

II. Parliament and Commission

The Maastricht Treaty introduces a major change in relationships between Parliament and the Commission. Here too, it took action by the European Council itself to give full force to provisions which had been the object of pressing demands by Parliament.

As regards the procedure for appointing the Commission. The Treaty provides that the President of the Commission be appointed by the governments following consultation with the full Parliament.[16] Once Parliament became a directly elected body a practice emerged which called for Parliament's Enlarged Bureau to hold a hearing with the President-designate to discuss his political approaches. The changes are considerable. In the first place, consultation is to come *before* formal designation of the President, and is to include a debate in plenary session, no doubt after the Bureau or a special committee has heard the President-designate. In any case, even though consultation alone is called for, governments are hardly likely to appoint a President 'designate' on whom Parliament has given an unfavourable opinion.

The rest of the procedure confirms this interpretation. It is stipulated,[17] that the President-designate and the other members of the Commission (designated in consultation with the President) 'shall be subject as a body to a vote of approval by the European Parliament'. In the past, Parliament had managed to persuade the Commission to present itself to Parliament to set forth its main policy lines. This, however, only took place once the Commission had taken up its duties. This meant a 'vote of confidence' of sorts. Though not devoid of political significance, this procedure retained a fairly formal character. The vote of approval, the foregoing debate and the accompanying motion will have an entirely different scope. Approval by Parliament will be the decisive factor in appointing the Commission, even though the formal decision is to be taken afterwards, by common accord of the Member States.

Parliament's involvement in the appointment procedure is considerably strengthened by another, apparently technical, measure that has substantial practical implications. As from January 1995 (that is, after the five-year renewal of

16   New Article 158(2), first subparagraph.
17   Article 158(2), third subparagraph.

Parliament due in June 1994), the Commission's term of office is to coincide with Parliament's term, staggered by a few months. This results from a combination of articles and measures: the Commission's term of office is extended to five years,[18] but the term of the present Commission, which began in January 1993, will be limited to two years, until 6 January 1995.[19] In the event of censure, the new Commission's term is limited to the time remaining from the censured Commission's mandate.[20]

A genuine political framework for the Commission is thereby created, and will have important consequences, perhaps even more for the Commission than for Parliament. The 'vote of approval' by Parliament has the nature of election. This means a break with the present position of an 'appointed' Commission, the political nature of which is often questioned. The Commission will have been 'elected' on the basis of a programme, and for the whole length of its term (apart from the last six months), the Parliament that elected it will be able to check on its actions, that is, the performance of commitments made. In these circumstances, a vote of censure would have full significance. Further, with Parliament now involved in appointing the Commission, such a vote would have to lead to appointment of a new Commission in harmony with Parliament's policies. The prospect of having more or less the same people re-appointed by the governments following a censure, was one of the factors underlying the fact that for forty years no recourse to censure has been taken. That risk is now ruled out.

After 1995, when all of the above provisions (co-decision, assent, appointment of the Commission) will be in full use or application, the renewed Parliament (June 1994) and the Commission will both have much higher political stature than we are familiar with today. The political nature of the appointment (or rather election) of the Commission and the granting of genuine powers to Parliament will lead to the establishment between the European Parliament and the Commission of a new type of relationship, more closely resembling relationships between a parliament and a government. This transformation will be associated with the transformation in relationships between the European Parliament and the Council resulting from the co-decision procedure. The dialogue between Parliament and Council will thus take on growing importance, at the expense of the Commission-Council dialogue that today characterizes the Community's functioning.

---

18   New Article 158(1).
19   Article 158(3).
20   Supplement to Article 144.

III. The Commission

Throughout the intergovernmental conference, the Commission was on the defensive, and sought to maintain its almost exclusive right of proposal. It had to accept adjustments which, without completely undermining it, have limited its scope.

This is especially true in relation to economic and monetary union, where for a number of measures the Council is no longer to decide on a proposal, but on a *recommendation* by the Commission (this right of 'recommendation' being sometimes shared with the European Central Bank). This applies to major, sensitive decisions such as the economic policies of Member States and the Community,[21] measures to be taken in the event of a Member State's excessive budget deficit,[22] changes in the ecu central rates,[23] and the meeting of the conditions for the move to a single currency,[24] etc. This procedure was already provided for in the Treaty of Rome, but in very limited circumstances.[25] In the case of a mere recommendation, the Council's freedom of manoeuvre is much greater as, unlike proposals, which are protected by the unanimity rule contained in Article 189a, recommendations can be amended by a qualified majority. The position of the Commission is thus significantly weaker in such a context.

In relation to Parliament, the Commission has seen the prerogatives it had secured in the cooperation procedure eroded in the co-decision procedure. As is known, in the cooperation procedure, at second reading, the Council can adopt by qualified majority only those amendments by Parliament taken up by the Commission.[26] In the co-decision procedure, the amendments adopted by the Conciliation Committee are submitted directly to to the Council and Parliament, and the Council can decide by a qualified majority whatever the Commission's position might be.

By contrast, the Commission was able to prevent the creation of a right of initiative for Member States or Parliament on issues of Community relevance. The provisions of Article 152 (possibility for the Council to ask the Commission to put a proposal to it) remained unchanged, and a similar right was granted to Parliament.[27] For some of the areas pertaining to economic and monetary union, this request may also be made by a Member State. The Commission was also able to hamper such proposals limiting its right to alter (and therefore to withdraw) a proposal at any point in the legislative process. This right is confirmed in Article 189A(2).

---

21 New Article 103(2) and (4).
22 Article 104C.
23 Article 109.
24 Article 109J and K.
25 E.g. for measures of mutual assistance to be adopted in case a Member State's balance of payments is in difficulty (Article 108) or for negotiations on commercial policy (Article 113).
26 Article 189C(e).
27 Article 138B.

Accordingly, the only significant changes in the Commission's institutional position are to be found in its new relationship with Parliament. One should not, however, ignore the indications that relations between Commission and Council are beginning to deteriorate, as was illustrated by doubts that several delegations at the Conference seemed to have about the Commission's impartiality or sense of responsibility in exercising its right of proposal. It was symbolic that the Conference saw fit to set forth in the Treaty itself[28] the position of Secretary-General of the Council, hitherto defined only in the internal rules. The outstanding merits of the present Secretary-General justified this decision. But this decision also consecrates the Secretary-General's increasing role in supporting the Council Presidency's efforts to develop and formulate compromises that permit Council decisions. The more media-oriented Presidency thus 'stands in' for the Commission, often with the latter's complicity.

The personality of the Commission's President or members may lead to a reversal of this drift in Commission-Council relations. The new relationship between Parliament and Commission will also, from 1995 onward and perhaps even before, influence the traditional relationship between Commission and Council. These trends deserve attentive consideration by the Commission in looking toward the 1996 revision.

IV. The European Council

The present extent of the Council's powers is such that any institutional revision might only entail a transfer of powers to other institutions or the introduction of more binding procedures in the exercise of the Council's powers. This is indeed the consequence of the changes that concern Parliament (co-decision, assenting opinion). In this connection, the limitation of the Commission's right of proposal is a highly noteworthy exception.

The most interesting innovation is the legalization of the European Council's role. Although it had been expressly mentioned in the Single European Act,[29] this reference merely confirmed its membership and the timing of its meetings. The Maastricht Treaty makes the European Council an organ of the Union,[30] and specifies its function: to 'provide the Union with the necessary impetus for its development and ... define the general political guidelines thereof'. It further explicitly assigns several decisions of prime importance to the European Council, notably the adoption of general foreign policy and common security guidelines[31] and the broad guidelines of the economic policies of both Member States and the

28   New Article 151(2).
29   Article 2.
30   Article D.
31   Article J3(1) and J8(1).

Community.[32] Occasionally, reference is made to decisions of the Council 'meeting in the composition of Heads of State or of Government', for instance for the move to the third stage of economic and monetary union[33] or for admission to the monetary union of Member States that initially had derogations.[34] The appointment of members of the Board of Governors of the European Central Bank and of the President of the Board of the European Monetary Institute are to be made by Member State governments at the level of 'Heads of State or of Government'. The Conference did not seek to establish any coherence between this procedure and the one applying to the President and Members of the Commission.

Some of these decisions appear to be politically based. Others are more anecdotal in nature. Neither variety substantially changes what has until now been the European Council's practice at decisive moments in the Community's life. At most, they codify that practice.

V. Improvement in Efficiency of Institutions

The harvest is meagre in this area. The Commission and Parliament have called for a sharp reduction in cases where the Council would still have to decide unanimously in Community matters, so as to confine them only to constitutional or quasi-constitutional questions (Treaty amendments, accession of new members, own resources, etc.). No attention was paid to this view. It is only in a few of the new areas (e.g. education, health, consumers, trans-European networks) that majority decision by the Council is provided for, sometimes with recourse to the co-decision procedure. No change in the Council's internal procedures and working methods is therefore to be expected.

With a view to efficiency, the Commission had also called for the Council to abandon its practice of having committees of Member State representatives assist (or rather control) the Commission after conferring powers on it, or at least to favour recourse to simple consultative committees. It was unable to secure satisfaction. The provisions concerned[35] remain unchanged.

Likewise, the Conference postponed a decision on reducing the number of members of the Commission. With seventeen members today, the functioning of the Commission has become rather cumbersome, and an increase in the number of commissioners following the accession of new countries would further hamper its efficiency. This question should be reconsidered after the entry into force of the Maastricht Treaty, and in the light of the prospect of forthcoming enlargements. The number of countries concerned (even if only the countries of the European Free

32   Article 103(2).
33   Article 109J(3) and (4).
34   Article 109K(2).
35   Article 145.

Trade Association are considered at the first stage) should make a review of the operating rules and even the very structure of the institution essential. The European Parliament has already forcibly expressed itself on this point, while the reticence shown by governments is evident.

VI. Conclusion

In conclusion, the Maastricht Treaty, despite its complexities and shortcomings, substantially changes a large part of the Community's institutional landscape. In 'normal' circumstances (i.e., those prevailing before 1989) it could have been hailed as a major advance on the road to union or the European federation.

Is this conclusion still tenable today, now that the Community and its Member States are confronted with the immense challenge of the collapse of the Soviet Union, the freeing of the countries in its former defensive bulwark and the re-structuring of the whole of that part of the world? One of the aspects of that challenge is the surge of applications to join the Community. Another, much more important, aspect is the contribution that Europe ought to be able to make towards establishing democratic structures that respect human rights (particularly of minorities) and are economically viable in a vast area extending as far as the Pacific Ocean. The Maastricht negotiators deliberately decided to ignore these problems. Were they really right to endeavour, as in the past, to 'let time take its time'?

Part II

The Europeanization of Economic and Monetary Policy

Chapter 3

European Economic Law, the Nation-State and the Maastricht Treaty

Christian Joerges[*]

I. Introduction: A Framework of Analysis

It might seem misplaced or, at best, evasive that this paper concentrates on the Europeanization of economic *law* in the context of an analysis of the Maastricht Treaty for at least two reasons. First, although the text of the new Treaty certainly contains important new economic law provisions,[1] its explosive core in terms of integration policy undoubtedly lies in the perspective of a Monetary Union;[2] second, the provisions on the Economic Union[3] are primarily concerned with a 'soft' coordination and supervision of economic *policy* rather than the completion of the Community's economic *law*. Yet, paradoxically, the difficulties, embarrassments and uncertainties provoked by the Danish vote of 2nd June 1992, the close outcome of the French referendum and the rejection of the Single

---

[*]   A prior version of this paper which related to the Draft Treaty prepared by the Luxembourg Presidency in June 1991 (Conf-UP-UEM 2008/91) was submitted to the annual colloquium of the Arbeitskreis Europäische Integration on 'Die Entwicklung der EG zur Politischen Union und zur Wirtschafts- und Währungsunion unter der Sonde der Wissenschaft' (The EC's Development towards Political, Economic and Currency Union under Scientific Scrutiny) on 14-16 November 1991 in Bonn. An updated version of this paper was presented at the European University Institute, Florence. Following many helpful comments, especially from Anita Bernstein, Renaud Dehousse, Giandomenico Majone, and the particularly constructive critique of Michelle Everson who translated the German version, I started to revise and ended up rewriting the whole piece. This third version was then presented at the seminar on 'Democratic and Legal Problems of the European Community', organized jointly by the Institute of Public Law, Oslo University, and the Institute of Legal Science (Section B), Copenhagen University, on 18-19 January 1993 in Copenhagen. I again received extremely helpful comments from Niklas Bruun, Francis Snyder, Joseph Weiler, Henrik Zahle and many other participants at the Copenhagen seminar. There is now every reason to write a fourth version; and this will follow in time. The questions discussed in this paper follow on from reflections which have already been published; cf. esp. Joerges, 'Markt ohne Staat? Die Wirtschaftsverfassung der Gemeinschaft und die regulative Politik' in R. Wildenmann (ed.), *Staatswerdung Europas? Optionen für eine politische Union* (1991), 225 as well as Joerges, 'Social Regulation and the Legal Structure of the EEC', in B. Stauder (ed.), *La sécurité des produits de consommation* (1992) 31.

1   Such as Articles 73a-73h on capital and payments; for a more comprehensive account cf. *infra* part III A 1.
2   Articles 3a, 105-109m together with the two Protocols on the Statute on the European System of Central Banks and of the European Central Bank and the Statute of the European Monetary Institute.
3   Articles 102a-104c and the Protocol on Excessive Deficit Procedure.

European Space in Switzerland on 6th December 1992 justify a so-to-speak conservative approach to Maastricht for quite different reasons.

As a closer look will reveal,[4] the integration strategy of the Maastricht Treaty does not break with, but instead rests upon, the politics pursued so far. The disillusionment of the proponents of a further deepening of European integration with the behavior of a substantive part of the European electorate on the one hand, and the mistrust of European voters of their pro-community minded political leaders on the other, does not just concern the agreements reached in Maastricht; it also affects the *acquis communautaire* and the future course of European legal policy.[5] The Maastricht crisis has revealed integral problems of the integration process which are likely to remain on the Community's agenda regardless of the final outcome of ratification procedures.

It is almost impossible to overestimate the complexities of the integration process. We simply do not know of any grand theory that would enable us to fully understand the present course of European integration and provide us with a coherent and normatively attractive model of the future shape of a European republic. But such uncertainties do not exclude analytical and theoretical efforts. What we can do is identify problems that need to be taken into account when analysing the impact of European integration, and examine the ability of various integration strategies to cope with the problems we have identified.

This introductory section provides a theoretical framework for the analysis of what may provisionally be called the ongoing process of the Europeanization of economic law. The following section examines various legal theories of integration that attempt to explain and guide that process. The problems and perspectives thereby identified will then serve as a guide through the pertinent provisions of the Maastricht Treaty. Do the new provisions answer, or at least address, our queries with regard to the transformation of economic law in Europe?

A. Starting Point: Notions of Economic Law

The first difficulty which any enquiry into the Europeanization of economic law must take into account stems from this term itself. 'Economic law' (*Wirtschaftsrecht*) is a concept embedded within historical contexts and political and theoretical controversies. It is neither possible nor advisable to dissociate oneself from such intricacies. On the contrary, we should be aware that the process of integration concerns historically specific legal arrangements, that it is perceived

---

4   Cf. *infra* part III.
5   Among the many documents indicating a search for new directives, see the speech of Delors, 'Die Europäische Union verständlich machen' *EG-Informationen* (V/1992) 1; Delors , 'Le principe de subsidiarité: contribution au débat', in *Institut Européen d'Adminstration Publique, Subsidiarité: défi du changement* (1991) 7 and the Report to the EEC Commission by the High Level Group on the Operation of Internal Market 'The Internal Market After 1992. Meeting the Challenge' (1992).

and evaluated on the basis of different traditions of legal thought and also that historical contingencies affect our understanding of European economic law.

It is nevertheless possible to agree upon a range of legal fields which the term 'economic law' comprises: framework regulations providing for the administrative supervision of entire sectors of the economy; the organizational law of public, corporative and private actors; the protection of competitive structures and the control of anti-competitive practices; the legal institutions and instruments of macroeconomic control of economic processes. Any more substantial statement going beyond that taxonomy becomes more risky. What exactly are the objectives of the legislative activities just mentioned? If regulatory objectives are decisive, can mandatory contract law or product liability law be excluded from our concept? Does it make sense to include within this field modern regulatory techniques as they are practised by institutions and agencies operating in the fields of industrial policy, social regulation and the control of risks?

There is both a European and an international debate on all of these issues.[6] It seems safe to summarize the state of this debate as follows: there is no agreement as to the normative content and functions of economic law. But we do at least know why there is no consensus: the core problem of economic law always has been and continues to be to respect and to guarantee 'justified' demands through economic juridification processes. The theoretical contexts within which this juridification problem is addressed have changed and continue to evolve. Today, theoretical guidance is provided by neo-liberal legal theories (in Germany: *Ordnungstheorie*)[7] and economic analyses of law, system sociologies and their followers in legal theory,[8] interventionist approaches to regulation (in Germany: *Sozialstaatstheorien*) and, last but not least, 'proceduralized' versions of critical theories.[9]

The economic law of the European Community results from political processes, their transformation into law and further implementation. The legal, even the academic, discourse on European economic law has quite successfully avoided any theoretical and methodological pitfalls. It has been characterized as non-ideological, formalistic, purely doctrinal, strictly pragmatic and so forth.[10] However, neither is European economic law and its impact on national legal systems simply theoretically neutral, nor should we assume that abstract debates on the social functions and normative commitments of economic law do not relate to any

---

6   See, e.g., G. Rinck (ed.), 'Begriff und Prinzipien des Wirtschaftsrechts' 17 *Landesberichte zu einem internationalen Symposion* (1971); T. Daintith (ed.), *Law as an Instrument of Economic Policy: Comparative and Critical Approaches* (1987); G. Teubner, *Recht als autopoietisches System* (1989).
7   For a recent restatement cf. Mestmäcker, 'Wirtschaftsrecht', 54 *RabelsZ* (1990) 409.
8   See Teubner, 'Steuerung durch plurales Recht. Oder: Wie die Politik den normativen Mehrwert der Geldzirkulation abschöpft', in W. Zapf (ed.), *Die Modernisierung moderner Gesellschaften. Verhandlungen des 25. Deutschen Soziologentages in Frankfurt am Main 1990* (1991) 528.
9   For an abstract recent summary cf. J. Habermas, *Faktizität und Geltung, Frankfurt a.M.* (1992) 516-537.

practical problem. It therefore seems more adequate to interpret the formalism of European law as reflecting a specific way of coping with integration problems. [11] Be that as it may, there are many reasons to expect that it will no longer be possible to avoid a more overt debate on those fundamental problems and potential conflicts which have to date been kept hidden.

B. First Concern: the Selectivity of EC Economic Law and its Disintegrative Effects

The framers of the Treaty did not seek to design a comprehensive institutional framework for economic policy. Rather, they agreed upon competences ('albeit in limited fields'), [12] rules and principles, which can at best be interpreted as elements of a legal order. At the core of this legal order are the Four Freedoms and the rules on competition. Only a few policy sectors – with agriculture, however, among them – were assigned to the Community. 'Economic policy' responsibilities continued to rest with the Member States. And yet, 'economic law' powers of legislation were established more or less accidentally wherever existing laws conflicted with the freedoms guaranteed by the EEC Treaty, wherever they resulted in trade restrictions (Article 30), where national regulations seemed irreconcilable with rules of competition and the resulting duties of the Member States (Articles 85 ff. and 5 paragraph 2), where the differences between legal orders affected the establishment or the functioning of the Common Market (Article 100) and where Community action appeared to be required in order to achieve one of its objectives (Article 235).

So far, all Community law measures based on these provisions have affected the economic laws of the Member States and their political responsibility only partially and selectively. Despite the rapid growth of European law during the last decade, its provisions merely concern fragments of national legal systems and do not totally transform national legal orders. Inevitable incoherences and coordination problems result from this selective expansion; an adoption of rules on competition may affect mandatory rules of contract law; [13] the harmonization of certain mandatory rules of contract law needs to be coordinated with existing bodies of legislation and case law. [14]

This dynamic expansion of European economic law had begun even prior to the adoption of the SEA in 1987. The European Court of Justice used Article 30 of the

10   Cf. the protests of Bengoetxea 'Institutions, Legal Theory and EC Law', 77 *Archiv für Rechts-und Sozialphilosophie* (1989) 195; but see also *infra* part II A.
11   Cf. F. Snyder, *New Directions in European Law* (1990) at 30 ff.
12   Case 6/64 *Costa* v. *ENEL*, [1964] ECR, 585.
13   For a more detailed analysis cf. Joerges, 'Contract and Status in Franchising Law', in C. Joerges (ed.) *Franchising and the Law. Theoretical and Comparative Approaches in Europe and the United States* (1991) 11 and especially at 60 ff.
14   Cf. Müller-Graff, 'Europäisches Gemeinschaftsrecht und Privatrecht', 46 NJW (1993) 13 ff.; Brüggemeier and Joerges, 'Europäisierung des Vertrags- und Haftungsrechts' in P.-C. Müller-Graff (ed.), *Gemeineuropäisches Privatrecht* (1993 forthcoming).

EC Treaty to increase Community control over national legislation. European competition law has been consolidated and used as an additional control standard for national regulations. We have witnessed an ever more extensive interpretation of the freedom to provide services. Articles 100 and 235 of the EC Treaty have served to open up one new policy sector after the other.

This gradual intrusion of the Community into areas of national competence has been both criticized and praised.[15] Harmonization policy in particular, which originally appeared to have a clear functional meaning and found its legitimacy and its limits within the definitions contained in Article 100 of the Treaty, has virtually transcended all conceivable boundaries. It is important to realize that each step towards harmonization does not only remove differences between legal orders, but similarly has to be understood as an act of 'positive' legislative policy. It would be unreasonable to expect the Community simply to follow pre-existing national models even should they seem outdated. Even if the Community were 'only' entitled to ensure equal competitive conditions, its powers of action in economic law would potentially be comprehensive since it could thus concern itself with all provisions affecting economic conditions.

Following the adoption of the SEA, the sphere, intensity and speed of the Community's legislative activities again increased dramatically.[16] To be sure, the Community was to promote a specific objective, i.e. bring about the Internal Market, while the political competences granted to the Community were to remain limited. But the Internal Market programme has proved so successful that attention is now drawn to the follow-up problems resulting from this success story.

Despite the ingenious jurisprudence of the European Court of Justice, which has redirected and intensified integration policy, important issues of primary law remain unsettled. For one thing, the application of Article 30 of the EC Treaty shows ever more clearly that the assignment and limitation of rights of market access need some more general guidance which can only be gained from a comprehensive understanding of the integration process and its objectives. It is apparent that the jurisprudence of the European Court of Justice which is based upon economic freedoms at times touches upon fundamental questions of legislative policy which have not been pre-decided by Community law.[17]

The Community's competition law has systematically been expanded into a comprehensive regulatory scheme through the adoption of the Merger Control Regulation. It is applied to control anti-competitive regimes within the Member

---

15   For a particularly thoughtful recent evaluation cf. Steindorff, 'Quo vadis Europa? Freiheiten, Regulierung und soziale Grundrechte nach den erweiterten Zielen der EG-Verfassung', in Forschungsinstitut für Wirtschaftsverfsssung und Wettbewerb e.V. (ed.), *Weiterentwicklung der Europäischen Gemeinschaften und der Marktwirtschaft* (1992) 11.

16   For an informative and systematic survey see Falke, 'Föderalismus und rechtliche Regulierung der Wirtschaft in der Europäischen Gemeinschaft', in G. Stuby (ed.), *Föderalismus und Demokratie* (1992) 195; Steindorff, ibid. at 19 ff.

17   See, e.g., Case C-362/88, Judgment of 7 March 1990, *GB-Inno*, [1990-I] ECR 667.

States through Article 5.[18] However, the systematic expansion of competition law is no guarantee that there is agreement on the objectives of competition policy. The debate on industrial policy and other 'non-competitive' considerations in appraising mergers and in exempting restrictive practices continues. The commitments of the Member States to the 'Economic Constitution' of the EC remain as disputed as the legal content of this constitution itself.

Article 100a of the Treaty has been designed and interpreted as a booster to the new Internal Market policy and as a means of protecting advanced legislative standards. By now, however, two unforeseen effects of this provision have become apparent: first, the Community now obtains access to more and more policy fields because of their connections with the Internal Market objective. Second, Article 100a, paragraph 4 grants protection against 'deregulation' but not against more stringent regulation. Debates on the reasonableness and legitimacy of regulatory objectives are settled by majority vote. It was inevitable that this should rekindle the discussion on the 'Limits of EC Competences'[19] which had long seemed a rather dry academic debate. It was equally inevitable that ways and means were sought to ensure that national constitutional law not be superseded by secondary Community law.[20]

More examples could be added to these. But it already seems safe to conclude that it is the very success and the new dynamism of integration policy, together with the widening and deepening of the Community's involvement in regulatory tasks, which now provokes new criticism as to the quality and legitimacy of Community law. When the Commission launched its Internal Market programme, these effects were not foreseeable. This strategy seemed to be solidly backed by the whole history of European integration. The Europeanization of economic law had been brought about gradually through the step-by-step adoption of legal frameworks aiming at the integration of markets. The vision of a single European market put new emphasis on this 'traditional' objective and it brought consensus. But once the machinery implementing that objective was set in motion, its 'interventionist' implications became apparent.

Such implications are twofold. Where the logic of market-building requires a common European legal framework, national regulatory traditions must be replaced; this type of interventionism is usually perceived as a move towards deregulation. However, market building may also require or be supplemented by new regulatory activities at the European level. This type of interventionism has proven to be much stronger than was anticipated. Such consequences will be examined somewhat more

---

18 For a comprehensive recent analysis cf. A. Bach, *Wettbewerbliche Schranken für staatliche Maßnahmen nach europäischem Gemeinschaftsrecht* (1992).

19 This is the title of E. Steindorff's monograph *Grenzen der EG-Kompetenzen* (1991); cf. also Huber, 'Bundesverfassungsgericht und Europäischer Gerichtshof als Hüter der Gemeinschaftsrechtlichen Kompetenzordnung' 116 *AöR* 1991, 210 see also *infra* part II 2 c.

closely in the next section.[21] It is, however, already possible to relate the two sides of market-building interventionism to the current debates on European economic law. These controversies are always about both the contents of EC economic law *and* the tension between market integration and national regulatory concerns; they tend to question both the competences of the Community *and* the legitimacy of interference by Community law. To put it slightly differently: the new debate is no longer confined to the gradual substitution of national by European law. It has instead revealed the interventionist implications of legal integration. It has highlighted the disintegrationist consequences of legal integration within national legal systems in their entirety.

C. Second Concern: the Nation-State and Democracy

It seems tempting to invoke the nation-state as a guardian against Community interventionism. Legal integration not only undermines the coherence and regulatory functions of national legal systems. It equally concerns the autonomy of national policy-making. It threatens the capability of national communities to pursue their own objectives. The tension between legal integration and national legal systems implies tension not only between European and national law but between supranational regimes and national democracies as well.

And yet, one should be cautious in playing the legitimacy of the nation-state off against the democratic deficiencies of European institutions. The nation-state is not inherently democratic or legitimate. European history has witnessed fundamentally different modes of nation-building. Nowhere has the merging of national identities with the principles of democracy been an easy task.[22] In Germany, to take a particularly worrying example, it was the defeat and the division of the nation-state that initiated the postwar move towards the *Staatsbürgernation*, i.e. the building up of a 'national' identity based upon constitutional rights and democratic political practices rather than on ethnic criteria and cultural heritage.[23]

The history of economic law is inextricably linked with the history of the modern nation-state. From its beginnings, economic law has been conceived as a

20 Cf. among the many voices enunciating such concerns K.H. Friauf and R. Scholz, *Europarecht und Grundgesetz* (1990) (pleading, inter alia, for a commitment from the German Government to defend rights guaranteed by the Basic Law when voting at European level).
21 *Infra* part II B.
22 For a historically rich comparative assessment cf. N. Elias, *Studien über die Deutschen, Machtkämpfe und Habitusentwicklung im 19. und 20. Jahrhundert*, (1990) 159-222 ff.; see also the analyses of K.H.F. Dyson, *The State Tradition in Western Europe*, (1980) especially at 33-58 ff. and P. Wagner, *Sozialwissenschaften und Staat. Frankreich, Italien, Deutschland 1870-1980* (1990).
23 Cf. Lepsius, 'Ethnos und Demos' in R.M. Lepsius, *Interessen, Ideen und Institution* (1990) 247; P. Glotz, *Der Irrweg des Nationalstaats* (1990); Habermas, 'Staatsbürgerschaft und nationale Identität', in J. Habermas, *Faktizität und Geltung* (1992) 632, and the remarks by Touraine, 'Existe-t-il encore une société française?', in D. Schapper and H. Mendras (eds.), *Six manières d'être Européen* (1990) 143, 152.

response to economic instability and the social problems of market economies. But this response has always had its parochial ingredients. In his famous inaugural lecture of 1895, Max Weber[24] named these elements with all his merciless analytical clarity. The economic policy of the nation-state, Weber explained in his critique of German idealism and the Historical School, must neither be mystified as representing some common higher morality nor be conceptualized as a nation-specific response to historically determined conditions. And yet, economic policy is bound to define national priorities and objectives. Economic law shares this in-built parochialism. It reacts to economic and social problems of capitalist market societies; but its reactions will tend to be one-sided definitions of the 'common good'. To be sure, the taming of the nation-state through democratic constitutions has the potential of ensuring that the common good will be defined in a legitimate way and will respect basic rights and freedoms. But the legitimacy which the economic law of the democratic nation-state can claim, rests upon processes in which only the members of the national community can participate. This holds true for statutory as well as for judge-made law. There is no built-in protection against one-sided definitions of economic objectives and the common good.

On the other hand, the logic of European integration cannot claim *a priori* superior legitimacy where it dismantles national concerns in the name of market integration. It is one thing to ensure free trade and to thereby overcome the 'state of nature' in international economic relations. It is quite another project to restructure national societies according to the logic of market integration.

II. Conceptual Traditions and New Challenges

These tensions between Europe's supranational regimes and the democratic legitimacy of national legal orders have preoccupied academic debate on the Community from its beginnings. Even though the discourse on European law and the legal reasoning of the European Court of Justice often appear to be overly technical and formalistic, there is a broad range of legal theories of integration which do not content themselves with ordering the positive law of the Community. Such theories of legal integration do, of course, respond to and reflect the respective extents of integration. It would be unfair to criticize concepts developed in the 60s – or even in the early 80s – for their inability to provide answers to all post-1985 concerns. But it is instructive to recall their fundamental assumptions and principles which might aid their adaptation to changing circumstances. Just as the drafters of the Maastricht Treaty built upon past practice and experience, its commentators and critics tend to remain faithful to principles and ideas that they have relied on in the past.

---

24 Weber, 'Der Nationalstaat und die Volkswirtschaftspolitik (1895)', in M. Weber, *Gesammelte Politische Schriften* (3rd ed, 1971) 1.

A. Legal Theories of Integration

The following brief sketch of important strands within legal theories of integration cannot be comprehensive. But neither are these theories selected randomly. They represent options and partially irreconcilable perspectives that continue to affect our present discussions.

1. Ordnungspolitik (Neo-liberal Economic Policy) as European Economic Constitutional Law

The first tradition I refer to is particularly difficult to explain to a non-German audience. Despite its dominant role in German economic law theory, its influence upon so many important advisory boards and its impact on official pronouncements concerning governmental policies, the German *Ordnungstheorie* seems hardly known or accessible.[25]

German theory on the Community's Economic Constitution has never been content with merely positivist or pragmatic interpretations of the EC Treaty, but has instead always striven to find a functional understanding of European law and a normatively consistent overall perspective on the integration process. The integration of the Member States together with the consequential renunciation of national sovereignty set the scene for the creation of a 'Law' which would dictate the substantive process and the substantive results of integration. This 'Law' is at its core *'economic'* constitutional law since integration should be based on open markets and should aim for the creation of one common market; at the same time this 'Law' is economic *'constitutional'* law as it envisages that the opening up of markets should follow through the competitive process and that this common market should take the form of a system of undistorted competition.

The foundations of this interpretation were laid down during the construction phase of the EEC and were further refined during the debates of the late 1970s.[26] That this theory did not accurately portray the construction phase of the EEC and the historical 'intent' of the Member States was well known amongst its

---

25   Among the few 'external' presentations of this tradition I have detected are Nicholls, 'The Other Germany – The "Neo-Liberals",' in R.J. Bullen and H. Pogge von Strandmann and A.B. Polonsky (eds.), *Ideas into Politics. Aspects of European History* (1984) 164, (a historical account); Hutchinson, 'Notes on the Effect of Economic Ideas on Policy: The Example of the German Social Market Economy', 135 *Journal of Institutional and Theoretical Economics* (1979), 426; Contantinesco, 'La constitution économique de la C.E.E.', 13 *Revue trimestrielle de droit européen* (1977) 244 (a sympathetic but independent presentation). For a recent comprehensive presentation by one of the leading representatives among German economists cf. Streit, 'Economic Order, Private Law and Public Policy', 148 *Journal of Institutional and Theoretical Economics* (1992) 675.

26   See J. Scherer, *Die Wirtschaftsverfassung der Europäischen Gemeinschaft* (1970) and D.W. Rahmsdorf, *Ordnungspolitischer Dissens und Europäische Integration* (1980).

supporters.[27] But nevertheless the fact that the agreement made among the founder States resulted in the growth of a Treaty dominated by very strong anti-interventionist policies, and thus favoured the establishment of a liberal economic regime, has been interpreted as 'the cunning of reason' (*List der Vernunft*).[28] The interpretation of the EC Treaty as an Economic Constitution committed to the advancement of market integration and the achievement of the principles of a market economy, then yielded a theoretical evaluation of this 'cunning of reason'. This brought two results: on the one hand, the Community, through its interpretation as an order constituted by law and committed to economic freedoms, acquires a legitimacy which protects it against attacks based upon democracy theory or constitutional policy.[29] On the other, the restriction of Community powers has the effect of blocking social policy moves which are illegitimate from the point of view of neo-liberal order theory.[30] This argument is neither weakened by references to the contingencies of the unification process, nor by the indeterminacies of the Treaty text,[31] and not even by the fact that a 'mixed economy' would be the only conceivable common denominator in the various constitutional traditions of the Community's Member States,[32] since its purpose is to transcend the unclear or even contradictory compromise formulas of the Treaty in a theoretically consistent manner.

2. The Communities as 'Special Purpose Associations (Zweckverbände) of Functional Integration'

In identifying the communities as 'special purpose associations (*Zweckverbände*) of functional integration',[33] Ipsen, in common with the neo-liberal interpretation of the

27 Von der Groeben, 'Zur Wirtschaftsordnung der Europäischen Gemeinschaft (1981)', in *Die Europäische Gemeinschaft und die Herausforderungen unserer Zeit. Aufsätze und Reden 1967- 1987* (1987) 201, 217.

28 Müller-Armack, 'Die Wirtschaftsordnung des Gemeinsamen Marktes', in *Wirtschaftsordnung und Wirtschaftspolitik. Studien und Konzepte zur sozialen Marktwirtschaft und zur europäischen Integration* (1966) 401, 405 ff.; See also Mestmäcker, 'Wettbewerbsregeln oder Industriepolitik: Nicht nur in diesem Punkt verstößt der Vertrag von Maastricht gegen bewährte Grundsätze des Vertrages von Rom', *Frankfurter Allgemeine Zeitung* of 10 October 1992, 15.

29 Mestmäcker, 'Macht-Recht-Wirtschaftsverfassung' (1973) reprinted in E.-J. Mestmäcker, *Die unsichtbare Hand des Rechts* (1978) 9, 23 ff.

30 Mestmäcker, 'Politische und normativ-funktionale Legitimation der Europäischen Gemeinschaften', in E.-J. Mestmäcker, *Recht und ökonomisches Gesetz* (1972) 82.

31 See P. Ver Loren van Themaat, 'Die Aufgabenverteilung zwischen dem Gesetzgeber und dem Europäischen Gerichtshof bei der Gestaltung der Wirtschaftsverfassung der Europäischen Gemeinschaften', in E.-J. Mestmäcker (ed.), *Eine Ordungspolitik für Europa. Festschrift Hans von der Groeben* (1987) 425.

32 Cf. P. Häberle, ''Wirtschaft' als Thema neuerer verfassungstaatlicher Verfassungen', *Jura* (1987) 577.

33 H.P. Ipsen, *Europäisches Gemeinschaftsrecht* (1972) at 176 ff. The first presentation of his concept dates back much further; see Ipsen, 'Der deutsche Jurist und das Europäische Gemeinschaftsrecht', 45 *DJT* (1964) II, L 14. Its explanatory strength again became visible in Ipsen's critique of the Draft Treaty of a Political Union of 14 February, 1984, 17 *Bull. of the EC* (1984), 2 (see 'Zum Parlamentsentwurf einer Europäischen Union', 24 *Der Staat* (1985) 325 f.), and in his subsequent

Community as a market-oriented economic legal constitution, referred explicitly to extra-legal assumptions. But in contrast to neo-liberal theory, Ipsen does not view the law as the centre of a concept that envelops both an economic and a legal order. The term '*Zweckverband*' defines a commitment to specific functions of 'technical realization', i.e. to administrative tasks that can be and need to be assigned to a supranational bureaucracy.[34] Technical bureaucratic rationality thus replaces the neo-liberal legal order of the market.

With this theory – its political and constitutional elements gleaned from Forsthoff,[35] its integrational elements owing to American neo-functionalism – Ipsen rejected both constitutionalist-federalist perspectives of integration and a reduction of the Community to an organizational body in international law. Community law represents a *tertium* between the law of fully-fledged federal systems and the law of international organizations. According to Ipsen, it is inadequate to view those areas in which the four freedoms and market principles operate as the 'normal' Community regime and to qualify policy areas where the Community itself acts in a 'regulatory' fashion as exceptional or irregular. Ipsen therefore uses the expression 'Economic Constitution' merely to describe the relevant elements of primary law – a customs union committed to principles of competition, the four freedoms, the ban on discrimination in Article 7 EEC, and also planning that respects competitive and economic freedoms. All this may be compatible with the neo-liberal programme as well as with a 'mixed' economy; the integration process is thus not based upon a principled constitutional commitment to competitive structures. The social functions of law in the integration process instead remain contingent.[36]

3. Legal Structures and Decision-Making Processes

The neo-liberal concept and Ipsen's theory of integration can be read as representing two different types of rationality – the logic of market building and the logic of technocratic regulation. Both conceptions betray their dependence on phases in the Community's history. So does the third conception I refer to, namely

analysis of the SEA (see 'Europäische Verfassung – Nationale Verfassung', 22 *EuR* (1987) 195; see also Ipsen, 'Die Bundesrepublik Deutschland in der Europäischen Gemeinschaft', in P.-C. Müller-Graff and M. Zuleeg (eds.), *Staat und Wirtschaft in der EG* (1987) 9 and, most recently, Ipsen, 'Zur Exekutiv-Rechtsetzung in der Europäischen Gemeinschaft', in P. Badura and R. Scholz (eds.), *Wege und Verfahren des Verfassungslebens. Festschrift für Lerche* (1993), 425.

34   The terms he uses vary ('independent agencies' in the American sense; 'emancipated' as envisaged by D. Mitrany) but the message always remains the same; non-political expertise (*politikfreie Sachrationalität*) was to guide Community actions.

35   E. Forsthoff, *Der Staat der Industriegesellschaft* (2nd ed. 1971). Again, my presentation has to be extremely brief. A more thorough analysis would have to deal with the impact of Carl Schmitt on constitutional concepts trying to justify the exemption of public functions from democratic controls. For an analysis confronting Ipsen's concepts with the actual development of the Community cf. Everling, 'Vom Zweckverband zur Europäischen Gemeinschaft', in R. Stödter and W. Thieme (eds.), *Hamburg – Deutschland – Europa. Festschrift für Hans Peter Ipsen* (1977), 595.

36   H.P. Ipsen, *Europäisches Gemeinschaftsrecht*, *supra* note 33 at 995 ff., and 1054-55.

Joseph Weiler's theory of the supranational and intergovernmental dual structure of the Community.[37]

Weiler developed his theory many years after Ipsen, and therefore against a different background of experience. The starting point for his analysis is an apparent paradox: while European law, in a continuing process of evolution, erected truly constitutional structures, the Community underwent one political crisis after another. This contradiction between legal evolution and political erosion was resolved by Weiler in his discovery of mutual dependencies between the presumably divergent legal and political processes. He saw the decisive step in the establishment of these interdependencies in the concepts of direct effect[38] and supremacy[39] of European law,[40] set forth by the European Court of Justice as early as the 1960s. These claims to validity were accepted by the courts of Member States, even if in part hesitantly and unwillingly. But the European Court of Justice's leading decisions of the 1960s were followed by de Gaulle's empty chair policy which in 1966 led to the Luxembourg compromise. The Member States' veto rights laid down in this compromise brought a radical reshaping of Community decision-making processes. At all levels – from the formulation of political objectives through to the preparation, adoption and implementation of Community law – the Member States were able to secure extensive rights of participation.[41] It is just this development, which may appear to those favouring integration to be a retrograde step, that Weiler interprets as a recipe for success. He sees the influence of Member States on Community decision-making processes as legitimate in accordance with its overall structure as a combination of sovereign States. In practical political terms this influence amounts to an indispensable counterweight to the construction of a supranational structure of constitutional law, thus ultimately securing the stability of the European system.

In my understanding of Weiler's conception, it is important not to equate his references to the role of Member States with the role of nation-states in international law. To be sure, the Member States are described as sovereign actors when transferring powers to the Community and when acting as the Community legislator. But they are conceived as constitutionally bound actors. Their 'sovereign' acts rest upon the autonomy or, more emphatically, dignity of democratic communities. This is why one must in principle regard their exercise of sovereignty as an expression of the concerns of politically accountable governments. Weiler would also hardly deny that governmental definitions of interests do not necessarily reflect upon the interest of society as a whole. His *legal* reconstruction of the

37   Of Weilers's earlier writings see esp. J.H.H. Weiler, 'The Community System. The Dual Character of Supranationalism', 1 *Yearbook of European Law* (1981) 267.
38   Case 26/62 *van Gend en Loos* v. *Nederlandse Administratie der Belastingen* , [1963] ECR 1.
39   Case 6/64, *Costa* v. *Enel*, [1964] ECR 585.
40   J.H.H. Weiler, *Supranational Law and Supranational System: Legal Structures and Political Process in the European Community*, Ph.D. Thesis EUI Florence (1982) at 69 ff.
41   For details J.H.H. Weiler, ibid. 117 ff., and 409 ff.

Community, however, rests upon the assumption that each Member State has an 'interest' in defining its identity and that such national concerns are to be respected in principle as the outcome of democratically legitimate political processes.

B. Practices and Institutional Innovations

These various answers to the Community's legitimacy problem differ quite substantially from one another. According to the neo-liberal conception, it is thus the juridification of the market economy that constitutes and delimits the Community's legal order; Ipsen's notion of the Community as a 'special purpose association' comprises a broader range of regulatory activities. What both concepts have in common, however, is the search for, and recognition of, supranational structures that cannot and need not be legitimized by any notion of democratic government. In that respect, both approaches differ significantly from Weiler's insistence upon the role of the Member States in the Community. The apparent weakness of supranationalism – its dependence on intergovernmental cooperation and consensus between *all* the Member States – is the price to be paid for the acceptance of Community regimes by the Member States and their electorates.

All legal theories of European integration refer to non-positive normative premises, theoretical assumptions, and empirical conditions. This is why we must understand the various responses to the legitimacy problem as alternative options for the Community's development. The validity of such options cannot be 'falsified' by legal practices which simply disregard the guidance offered by theories. On the other hand, such unexpected events or practices may reveal shortcomings in theoretical reconstructions of the integration process which as a result may at least require some conceptual refashioning.[42] The following sections will therefore once more address the problems raised in present debates on European economic law.[43] They will examine the potential of legal theories to cope with the dynamics of integration, to reflect the reasons for and the challenges posed by recent developments.

---

42   An explanation of this assertion would have to touch upon a whole series of abstract issues such as the critique of legal formalism and the differences between organicist-irrational and sociological traditions in German jurisprudence. Suffice it to say that the following argument proceeds on the assumption that the law is both distinct from and depending upon theoretical reconstructions of 'reality', that legal debates must reflect upon the 'Faktizität und Geltung' of law. It even assumes that any meaningful discussion of important legal developments needs to take these interrelationships into account. For a particularly enlightening confirmation of this view cf. F. Snyder's analysis of the compliance problem in European law, 'The Effectiveness of European Community Law: Institutions, Processes, Tools and Techniques' 56 *Modern L. Rev.* (1993) 19, especially at 24-27.

43   See *supra* part I 2.

1. Community Regulation of Market Integration

At first sight, the potential of the neo-liberal tradition to adapt to the new dynamics of European integration, and to provide guidance for its assessment, seems to be most promising. After all, the whole internal market programme was presented by its promoters, and perceived by its commentators, as a move towards deregulation and enhanced competition.[44] Its most ingenious institutional innovation – the principle of mutual recognition – was thought to overcome bottlenecks in the Community's harmonization procedures by rendering uniform regulatory frameworks unnecessary and by initiating processes of 'regulatory competition'. These processes were expected to provide the most beneficial legal regimes.[45] Even the turn to majority voting was apparently understood as a means of ensuring the carrying out of the neo-liberal agenda.[46] When the European Court of Justice re-discovered the potential of Article 5 of the Treaty to ensure the primacy of Community competition law over anti-competitive national regimes, the validity of the neo-liberal understanding of a Community supranational Economic Constitution seemed to be confirmed.[47]

But as we now know, the implementation of the internal market programme did not meet these expectations in various respects:

– first, the implementation of mutual recognition encountered many practical difficulties. Even in those fields where it has been carried out, the ensuing framework contains re-regulatory elements at both the Community and at the Member State level.[48] In other areas, notably in all the more recent directives concerning the harmonization of private law, the Community tends to promote relatively strict mandatory provisions which usually raise pre-existing levels of

---

44 Dehousse, '1992 and Beyond: The Institutional Dimension of the Single Market Programme', *Legal Issues of European Integration* (1989) 109. It is important to add, however, that political scientists underline the importance of another factor. The internal market programme was intended to strengthen the position of the European economy *vis-à-vis* its international competitors. Cf. Keohane and Hoffmann, 'Institutional Change in Europe in the 1980s', in R.O. Keohane and S. Hoffmann (eds.), *The New European Community. Decisionmaking and Institutional Change* (1991) 1; W. Streeck and P.C. Schmitter, *From National Corporatism to Transnational Pluralism: Organized Interests in the Single European Market, Politics and Society* (1991) 133 ff., and at 148 ff.; Streeck, 'From Market-Making to State-Building? Reflections on the European Political Economy of European Social Policy', in S. Leibfried and P.O. Piersan (eds.), *Emergent Supranational Social Policy* (forthcoming, 1993) Neo-liberal authors would not deny the factual relevance of this aspect but would treat it as normatively irrelevant.

45 For a representative neo-liberal appraisal cf. Wissenschaftlicher Beirat beim Bundesministerium für Wirtschaft (Academic Advisory Board of the Federal Ministry of the Economy), *Stellungnahme zum Weißbuch der EG über den Binnenmarkt* (1986).

46 Cf. Keohane and Hoffmann, *supra* note 44, at 21.

47 Cf. the extensive analysis of the Court's jurisprudence and its evaluation by the German Monopolies Commission: *Achtes Hauptgutachten der Monopolkommission* (1988/1989) Bundestags-Drucksache 11/7582 of 16 July 1990, 48 f., 389 ff., 408 ff.

48 Cf. Reich, 'Competition Between Legal Orders: A New Paradigm of EC Law?', 28 *CML Rev.* (1992), 861, 872 ff. On the third generation of insurance directives. See M. Everson, *Legal Formulation in Flux. The Attempt to Create an Integrated European Insurance Market Through Law*, Typescript (European University Institute Florence 1992).

protection.[49] If mutual recognition was a strategy to enhance consumer choice – by exerting pressure on regulated economies, at the same time by improving the chances of less developed and less strictly regulated economies[50] – it has been only partially successful.[51]

– The invalidation of national regulations because of their anti-competitive effects and their subsequent replacement by Europeanized regulatory frameworks has a long-standing tradition. So have the efforts to adopt European policies beyond the boundaries of competition law. The Community's activities in the field of industrial policy provide the most prominent and most controversial example.[52] Articles 130f *et seq.*, as introduced by the SEA, have acknowledged the 'constitutional' status and the supranational character of Community measures furthering research and technological development.[53] Neo-liberal commentators take great pains to restrict the function of these provisions and realign their interpretation with the Treaty's commitment to a competitively structured economy. The logic of such interpretations rests upon the fundamental premise of neo-liberalism. If the establishment of a competitive order is to be understood as the legitimizing basis of European integration, any programming of the economy which resorts to 'politics' seems to violate the Treaty's constitutional structure.

– The neo-liberal rejection of European industrial policy is of exemplary importance. Usually, the replacement of national regulations, be it by competitive regimes or by functionally equivalent Community regulations, is perceived as an intrusion into national regulatory competences. Such arguments bring to mind the multifold objectives and implications of 'economic regulations'. Economic law concerns and their regulatory functions cannot be analysed in isolation. In general, they cannot be traced back one-dimensionally to one single objective. The maintenance of book prices protects trade, but is also understood as an instrument of cultural policy. Distribution systems for pharmaceutical products benefit pharmacists but they serve a public health purpose at the same time. The laws on legal training erect barriers to the free provision of services, but they also vouch for the quality of the legal system. These multiple functions of economic law cause the encroachment of the Community into ever more policy aspects and fields. The neo-liberal agenda requires that both the Community *and* the Member States disregard extra-competitive objectives as essential elements of economic law.

Paradoxically enough, the ongoing controversies over the Community's tendencies to include so many regulatory objectives within its market-building strategy and the resistance of Member States to any further assignment of powers to

---

49　Cf. Brüggemeier and Joerges, *supra* note 14.

50　Cf. Siebert, 'The Harmonization Issue in Europe: Prior Agreement or a Competitive Process', in H. Siebert (ed.), *The Completion of the Internal Market* (1990) 53.

51　This is more evident in the field of social regulation; see *infra* 2.

52　Cf. Frees, 'Das neue industriepolitische Konzept der Europäischen Gemeinschaft', 26 *EuR* 1991, 281 ff. (discussing the Commission's recent restatement of its policy: 'Industrial policy in an open and competitive environment: guidelines for a Community approach', COM (90) 556 final of 16 November 1990).

53　Cf. Glaesner, in E. Grabitz, *Kommentar zum EWG-Vertrag* (1988) at Art. 130f para. 1.

the European level, reveal a *common* concern for the preservation of institutional frameworks and regulatory instruments. This common concern is well founded. It would seem simply irresponsible to expose the European economy to rigid deregulatory strategies without providing the means to correct their possible failure. This is why the neo-liberal agenda is neither a realistic nor a normatively attractive programme for the Europeanization of economic law.

2. Social Regulation and Institutional Transformations

According to a terminology commonly used in the US and now beginning to be widely applied in Europe, regulatory strategies presupposing and partially correcting market processes are categorized as either 'economic' or 'social' regulation. The term economic regulation is usually reserved for interventions which relate primarily to the protection of economic interests against – real or supposed – forms of market failure.[54] The types of regulatory activities discussed so far would all fit under that heading although it should be borne in mind that the concerns which legislators promise to pursue often comprise non-economic definitions of the public interest. The term social regulation includes above all protection against risks to health and the control of environmental hazards.[55]

Although the American terminology is a relatively fresh import, the control of risks to health through all sorts of product safety legislation and safety-at-work regulation, has a long-standing tradition in Europe too. Such regulation was, however, perceived as 'social' policy, or as a special branch of administrative and labour law, rather than an activity related to market processes and economic law. The growing importance of these fields, the establishment of specialized administrative bodies and the rapid expansion of environmental legislation have, however, led to a gradual adoption of American concepts.

The EEC Treaty of 1957 did not envisage social regulation as a specific Community competence or responsibility. Nevertheless, the Community was forced to involve itself in this area even before the SEA came into force. This was inevitable, if only because mandatory national product and process regulations in the form of employment, consumer, health or environmental protection provisions are exempted in principle from Article 30 of the EEC Treaty. The resulting difficulties for the Community's free trade objectives were overcome by the European Court of Justice with an extensive application of Article 30 of the EEC Treaty, by the Commission with the propagation of the 'country of origin principle' and the principle of mutual recognition, and by the Council with the 'new approach to technical harmonization and standardization'· The emergence of these techniques

---

54 For an up-to-date survey cf. Noll, 'The Economics and Politics of Deregulation', Florence *EUI Jean Monnet Chair Papers* (1991).
55 Cf. C.R. Sunstein, *After the Rights Revolution, Reconceiving the Regulatory State* (1990) especially at 11 ff. and 47 ff.

and their integration into a comprehensive legislative policy need not to be restated here.[56] What is important to understand, however, is the relation of these activities to market integration strategies and their somewhat surprising logic.

The discrepancy between the expectations raised by the 1992 programme and the practical development of the Community's policy soon became apparent:[57] what was originally announced as a streamlining and simplification of national legislation through the new approach to European harmonization policy resulted in a huge effort to modernize and to reorganize traditional legislative techniques and to establish comprehensive schemes of social regulation within the common market.

Although this development is still in flux, some general features may already be clearly identified.

- Especially in the field of product regulation, the regulatory frameworks the Community has established tend to be more sophisticated and more comprehensive than any legislation previously in force within the Member States. They all provide for pre-market safety guarantees and establish mechanisms for the constant adaptation of established standards and post-market controls. The safety levels provided in Community legislation have superseded the original concerns of consumer organizations and trade unions.[58]

- The comprehensiveness of these legislative frameworks has necessitated ingenious institutional innovations.[59] They can all be understood as responses to constitutional constraints (especially to the lack of a genuine Community administrative competence to implement its programmes) and to the reluctance of Member States to accept new Community prerogatives.

---

56 Particulars in C. Joerges, J. Falke, H. Micklitz and G. Brüggemeier, *Die Sicherheit von Konsumgütern und die Entwicklung der EG* (1988); Joerges, 'Product Safety Law, Internal Market Policy, and the Proposal for a Directive on General Product Safety', in M. Fallon and F. Maniet (eds.), *Product Safety and Control Processes in the EC* (1990) 139.

57 Cf. Joerges, 'Paradoxes of Deregulatory Strategies at Community Level: the Example of Product Safety Policy', in G. Majone (ed.), *Deregulation or Re-regulation? Regulatory Reform in Europe and the United States* (1990) 176.

58 Cf. for an analysis of consumer product safety legislation Joerges, 'Product Safety Law', *supra* note 56; for safety-at-work legislation cf. V. Eichener, *Social Dumping or Innovative Regulation? Processes and Outcomes of European Decisionmaking in the Sector of Health and Safety at Work Harmonization*, Typescript, University of Bochum (1992); R. Baldwin and T. Daintith (eds.), *Harmonization and Hazard: Regulating Health and safety in the EC* (1992); for foodstuffs law cf. R. Streinz, 'Entwicklung und Stand der Herstellung des Binnenmarktes im Bereich des Lebensmittelrechts, *ZLR* (1992), 233 ff.; M. Welsch, Same title, *ZLR* (1992), 272 ff.; for medicinal products cf. D. Hart and N. Reich, *Integration und Recht des Arzneimittelmarktes in der EG* (1990) at 36 ff., and 199 ff.; Geddes, 'Free Movement of Pharmaceuticals within the Community: The Remaining Barriers', 16 *ELR* (1991) 295, with postscript on the regulation and guideline proposals of the Community in fn. 1.

59 Cf. for a more detailed analysis Joerges, 'Social Regulation', *supra* introductory note, and R. Dehousse, C. Joerges, G. Majone and F. Snyder in collaboration with M. Everson, *Europe After 1992. New Regulatory Strategies*, EUI Working Paper Law 92/31; F. Snyder, *supra* note 42, at 31 ff.

(a) The establishment of new European agencies has been agreed upon for environmental protection,[60] safety at work issues[61] and medicinal products.[62] These European agencies, however, do not follow the model of American Federal Agencies. They are instead confined to advisory and coordinating functions.

(b) 'Comitology' is the most widely used form of managing social regulation. Typically a threefold subdivision can be observed: a 'political' committee responsible for final policy decisions; an 'interest group' level at which producers, traders and societal actors are represented; a 'scientific' level at which experts bring in their specialized knowledge and experience.

(c) Quasi-corporatist arrangements prevail in the field of technical standardization. Here the task of specifying mandatory safety requirements has been delegated to the European standardization organizations. The Commission, with the help of an advisory ('political') committee, supervises their work. Furthermore, the recently adopted Directive on general product safety[63] has established a regulatory committee for the handling of emergency situations.

This complex structure reflects the need of European regulatory activities to mediate between the interests of economic actors and various technological, industrial and trade policy ambitions and calculations. Any assessment of its achievements and shortcomings is probably premature and certainly requires a more detailed analysis. But it is safe to conclude that the emerging structures of social regulation in the Internal Market cannot be dealt with adequately within the paradigms discussed so far.

The neo-liberal school has so far treated the topic with benign disinterest.[64] The unworkability of mutual recognition and host country control as a general substitute for European regulation has largely gone unnoticed and the ensuing institutional problems have not been acknowledged as an unavoidable ingredient of the European 'Economic Constitution'. In that respect, Ipsen's understanding of the tasks of modern States, although not yet concerned with the 'risk society', is much more sensitive to the need of the Community to engage in regulatory activities. However, Ipsen has himself precisely defined the limits to his conception. This he has done in a way which disqualifies the Community as a risk regulator: once the boundary between comprehensive competence for the States and a partial competence for the Community becomes blurred, the vital distinction between

---

60   OJ L 120/1 of 11 May 1990.
61   COM (90) 564 final of 25 September 1991; OJ C 14/20 of 20 January 1992.
62   OJ C 310/7 of 30 November 1991.
63   OJ L 228/24 of 29 June 1992.
64   This is of course not to discredit the critique of regulatory failures by economic analyses and its importance within the debate on social regulation in the EC. But the German neo-liberals, with their insistence on individual freedoms and the undeterminability of market processes, are particularly insensitive to market failures and the externality problem; cf. W. Richter, *Wirtschaft und Recht. Eine Gegenüberstellung der Wettbewerbs-Systemtheorie und der Theorie des autopoietischen Systems*, Ph.D. Thesis Hamburg (1990) at 75 ff.

'organized creation of knowledge (*Wissensbildung*)' as a neutral consensus area and 'organized creation of aims (*Willensbildung*)' in need of legitimation, can no longer be drawn; thus the realpolitik framework of his overall construction disintegrates; representation, legitimation and consensus formation must then indeed be re-considered.[65]

3. Systems Integration and Social Integration

The foregoing analysis suggests that the *approfondissement* of European integration cannot be adequately addressed within the neo-liberal paradigm and equally points beyond the conceptualization of the Community as a purely technocratic enterprise. Weiler's theorem on the mutual dependency and stabilization of supranational legal structures and intergovernmental policy-making, could be exposed to the same type of critique. Even prior to the adoption of the SEA it had become difficult to view the establishment of European regimes as resulting from consensual processes among the Member States. With the turn to majority voting, the presupposed equilibrium between supranationalism and intergovernmentalism has been overtly distorted. Weiler himself has acknowledged these challenges. The purely functional justification for the assumption of powers which is no longer tempered by the need to arrive at consensus, is bound to lead to a legitimacy crisis.[66] It is fascinating to observe how this diagnosis of the Community's present problems, as well as his vision of 'Europe as Community' as opposed to 'Europe as Unity', remain faithful to his previous insistence on the pivotal role of democratically legitimized governments and his, albeit implicit, rejection of purely economic and technocratic rationality concepts as a basis for European integration.

Weiler's vision concerns the legitimacy of the Community as a whole. The following suggestions are reconcilable with that vision in that they equally question the possibility that the Community's economic order might be legitimized by

---

65   H.P. Ipsen, *Europäisches Gemeinschaftsrecht*, *supra* note 33 at 1045. – To give just two examples: The Commission had in 1988 submitted a draft directive on the radiation of foodstuffs (COM (88) 654 final of 12 December 1988); the Council was unable to agree upon a common position on that proposal. Similar objections were provoked by the Commission's proposal on 'novel foods' OJ C 190/3 of 29 July 1992 (Doc III/3562/89). In both cases, experts seem to be able to reach an agreement on the protection of health interests. But the issues of radiation and genetic engineering raise much broader public ('political') concerns and even experts agree that such concerns should be taken into account in regulatory decisions. cf. on the radiation issue B.M. Köhler and T. Steidl, *Gesellschaftliche Regulierung kahrungsbezogener Gesundkeitsrisiken* ,Wissenschaftszentrum Berlin, Working Paper 92-212 (1992) and on the novel foods proposal the critical appraisal by Streinz and Leible 'Novel Foods', *European Food Law Review* (1992) 99.

66   Weiler, 'Problems of Legitimacy in Post 1992 Europe', 46 *Aussenwirtschaft* (1991) 179 ff.; Weiler 'The Transformation of Europe', 100 *Yale L.J.* (1991), 2403, at 2458 ff. In his first comments on the SEA, Weiler had tended to interpret the new decision-making processes as a confirmation of his analysis because the rights granted to Member States in Art. 100a (4) of the Treaty seemed to respect the equilibrium between the Community's supranational legal order and the Member States' political autonomy (cf. J.H.H. Weiler, *The European Community in Change: Exit, Voice and Loyalty*, Vorträge, Berichte und Reden aus dem Europa-Institut No. 109 (1987).

certain presupposed substantive rationality concepts. But they at the same time underline developments and configurations which Weiler's theory seems to neglect. They emphasize the 'de-nationalization' of the economy and assume both divergences and tensions between economic, political and cultural integration processes and elaborate on the problems highlighted in the introductory section on the basis of the preceding discussion of theories of legal integration. But they do not offer an alternative comprehensive 'model' for the integration process. It may be that in view of all the uncertainties about that process, jurists should take a varied and even experimental approach to institutional arrangements, decisional competences and the organization of decision-making processes.

(a) The Politicization of European Economic Law

Economic law mediates between functional imperatives and normative claims, between the autonomy of societal actors and regulatory interventions. The generation of institutional structures capable of absorbing interest conflicts and ensuring the 'public responsibility' of economic systems does not follow from the transformation of economic rationality by some invisible hand or from legislative activities alone. Courts and administrative bodies, organized interests and all sorts of societal actors participate in the formation of institutions and interest arrangements.[67] The legitimacy of economic law rests upon this very process of reconciling the autonomy of individuals with societal demands through constitutionally structured political processes. This dependency of economic law on the whole of legal and political culture is the core problem faced by the Europeanization process: European economic law faces the same type of choices as does any national legal system. The regulatory options it chooses are not distinctly European. It is not possible to shield it from 'political' debates by basing it upon preconceived economic or technocratic rationality criteria. Its true problem is the discrepancy between its 'political' substance and its 'immature' political infrastructure.[68]

(b) Consent by Governments and the Assignment of Competences

The principle of unanimity and the limitation of Community powers have been the two means used to ensure the acceptance of Community law. Attentive commentators from many quarters agree that the move to majority voting needs to be compensated for by a much more stringent observance of the 'limits of EC

---

67 For a closer analysis and for evaluation of these mechanisms I can only refer to the relevant discussion. For a good critical summary, see Schuppert, 'Grenzen und Alternativen von Steuerung durch Recht', in D. Grimm (ed.), *Wachsende Staatsaufgaben – sinkende Steuerungsfähigkeit des Rechts* (1990) 217.
68 Cf. Steindorff, *supra* note 19, at 47.

competences'.[69] Before subscribing to such views of the current legitimacy crisis and its cure, one should first more closely examine the interrelationship between the former reliance upon consensus and the issue of competence, and then consider whether the revitalization of these principles would in fact be realizable and normatively attractive.

Unanimous consent amongst governments or, more realistically, amongst government officials does not necessarily represent 'the' national interest. What we increasingly observe at the Community level is the emergence of specifically European networks of interest representation. Coalition building between Community institutions – most notably the Commission – and government officials that ensures support for a European project should not be equated with intergovernmental bargaining.[70] It is tempting – and might appear theoretically elegant – to use the analytical framework of systems theory to conceptualize this process of functionally differentiated integration and its tensions: the functionally differentiated societal subsystems seem to follow their own integrationist logic. The economy takes the lead whereas other societal subsystems (such as law, politics, culture) tend to be slower or even remain 'national'. The tensions within the integration process could then be traced back to the dissolution of interdependencies between societal subsystems. But one should be cautious. The economic subsystem is not a coherent unit. Even economic integration proceeds selectively. Its impact varies between sectors and between, for instance, large and medium-sized firms. Interest configurations and political processes vary accordingly. Unanimity of governmental decision-making can hardly be viewed as a normatively convincing basis for legislating on the complex interest configurations the integration process produces. But what about competencies?

The mediating quality of economic law within national legal systems depends on, and results from, the interdependence between economic objectives and other

---

69   Cf. E. Steindorff, *supra* note 19; Weiler, 'The Transformation of Europe', *supra* note 66, at 2450 ff.; Scharpf, 'Kann es in Europa eine stabile föderale Balance geben?', in R. Wildenmann, *supra* introductory note, 415, at 422 ff.; Scharpf 'Europäisches Demokratiedefizit und deutscher Föderalismus', 3 *Staatswissenschaften und Staatspraxis* (1992) 293 ff., 302 f.
70   Political scientists have carefully documented this process; cf. e.g., V. Schneider and R. Wehrle, *Regime oder kooperativer Akteur? Die EG in der Telekommunikationspolitik*, MPFIG Discussion Paper 88/4, (1988); Hrbek, 'Nationalstaat und Europäische Integration. Die Bedeutung der nationalen Komponente für den EG-Integrationsprozeß', in P. Haungs (ed.), *Europäisierung Europas?* (1989) 81, 104 ff. with further references. As a lawyer, I would point to the establishment of organizational structures of European standardization, to developments of European competition law (especially in the field of merger control), to the differentiated Europeanization of private law. There are many indications that the law already recognizes formally what W. Streeck and P. C. Schmitter, *supra* note 44, at 151, foresee: 'Europe's future polity ... will be composed of traditional domestic relations within countries, traditional international relations between countries, less traditional transnational relations between both individuals and organizations across national boundaries, and entirely nontraditional supranational relations between European-level public institutions on the one hand and, on the other, a European civil society consisting of domestic, international, and transnational forces and relations including both nation-states and, in manifold national and cross-national combinations, their constituents.'

policy concerns.[71] Restricting Community law to its uncontested and narrowly defined economic objective and reserving adjacent policy fields to the Member States would confront us with tragic choices: in order to carry out its project of market building, the Community would be forced to claim supremacy for its economic law projects over interlocking national legal matters and policy fields. The exclusivity of national regulatory powers would preclude the integration of broader concerns into European projects of regulation, and either expose national polities to competitive pressures or incite resistance to the integration process which might impede the development of transnational responses to common or interdependent regulatory concerns.

(c) Integration as Intervention and the Autonomy of the Nation-State

Once we have decided that a return to unanimous voting and a restriction of Community powers is not an adequate response to the legitimacy problem of European economic law, we are forced to consider further institutional innovations. Three directions, which seem not to be mutually exclusive, are conceivable:

– the legitimacy problem of European law can be rephrased in terms of an uneven pace of integration, not between 'states' but between societal subsystems. 'Economic' integration proceeds faster than the building up of institutional arrangements which ensure the social acceptability of the integration process. But even 'the economy' is not uniformly structured. The intensity of integration varies amongst, and even within, different sectors. So does *de facto* European economic law. Competition law, insurance law, energy law, transportation law all organize specific sectors of the economy and develop distinct regulatory patterns. By deliberately focusing on more confined projects and by setting corresponding priorities, the Community may be more successful in providing comprehensive policy programmes and regulatory schemes. Priority-setting, even in economic integration does not provide a magic recipe for coping with all the economic and social (disintegrative) side-effects within national economies of sectorial integration. But it may help to at least identify such consequences and to consider Community and national policies which might ease processes of adaptation.

– Another starting-point for the strengthening of the Community's legitimacy would be an alternative 'juridification' of regulatory activities. As even our cursory look at the broad variety of institutional arrangements in the field of product regulation has revealed,[72] the emerging patterns will not be strictly 'centralist', but will instead be cooperative with the Community as the coordinating actor. 'Juridification' of these patterns would have to deal with the transparence of proceedings, the nomination of experts, access for societal actors, judicial control and political accountability and 'horizontal' interaction between national agencies. Again, one has to consider the side-effects of European regulation. The impact of more stringent product standards and

---

71   Cf. *supra* part I A.

safety-at-work legislation on less developed economies is at present not systematically compensated for in industrial and technological, regional and redistributional policies. Even 'Europeanised' networks of social regulation would not be able to carry out such complementary policies. Their functional justification simply rests upon the opening up of borders and the non-territorial nature of externalities. The type of juridification advocated here only envisages institutional structures which would improve the political accountability of social regulation.

– A corollary consequence of differentiated intensities within European regulation would be the acceptance of imperfect legal integration. 'Compatibility' would be a positive term for this consequence. It would require less than detailed harmonization and more than regulatory competition through mutual recognition. In this perspective, the dichotomies between European law and national law – Community powers and national sovereignty, supremacy and national responsibility – would have to be rephrased as coordinating principles. The Community would respect in principle the legitimacy of national law. It would not try to control the evolutionary processes of economic law within national legal orders, but would only intervene where important Community interests are at stake. It would specifically justify regulatory needs for uniform legal frameworks. These suggestions are by no means European heresies and they need not invoke the new principle of subsidiarity. There are many decisions within the European Court of Justice's jurisprudence on Article 30 which thoroughly weigh Community interests against national policy choices and then arrive at workable compromises between market integration objectives and national autonomy. There are furthermore strong practical reasons militating for such caution, especially in many fields of (mandatory) private law.[73]

Neither of these possible responses to the legitimacy problem can claim to 'solve' the tensions between the present structures of the Community and the democratic constitutions of its Member States. But they at least indicate normative principles which might guide legal policy in its search for legitimacy – such guidance will be taken up again in the following discussion of the Maastricht Treaty.

III. The Role of Economic Law in a European Political Union

Treaty negotiations can never be theoretical seminars. It would be asking too much of the Maastricht text to provide unambiguous and concise information on the difficulties within the process of the Europeanization of economic law which have been highlighted in this discussion. At the same time, the future potential of

---

72   Cf. *supra* part II.
73   The perspectives sketched out here have been more fully elaborated in Brüggemeier and Joerges, *supra* note 14.

'integration through law', the substance of the Community's Economic Constitution, the interdependencies and tensions between European and national fields of policy, and the setting up of efficient infrastructures for the implementation of European law are more than abstract seminar themes. The development of Community law has been beset by very real difficulties. It is therefore not only legitimate, but also necessary to expose the Maastricht text to analytical perspectives which are not addressed or not decided upon in governmental conferences.

A. The Community's Economic Constitution

The most important new step towards a future European economic order is, of course, the establishment of a European central bank entrusted with responsibility for monetary policy. The new provisions[74] touch upon a core element of national sovereignty and the assignment of competence over monetary policy to a supranational institution is certainly of constitutional importance. Although the debate on the Monetary Union is outside the scope of this paper,[75] it is worth noting that the provisions on Monetary Union, despite the strong influence of the Bundesbank model, encountered considerable opposition in Germany. Legal provisions, goes the critique, are not a sufficient guarantee for the factual maintenance of monetary stability to which the Bundesbank has dedicated its energies for decades. This is an important argument. Not only is it doubtful whether the Community will be able to impose the stability objective (to which it has committed itself in Monetary Union) upon the Member States in the vitally interrelated fields of fiscal and economic policy,[76] it is also difficult to predict to what degree political interventions will alienate monetary decisions.[77] It seems even less likely that the broad political acceptance which has, partly for historical reasons, facilitated the Bundesbank's task can be maintained in a European environment.

The patterns of the debate on the advantages and disadvantages of Monetary Union, on the textual lacunae and factual hazards of the Maastricht Treaty are

74 Cf. *supra* note 2 and the contribution of F. Snyder to this volume.
75 For an informative account of the moves and deliberations preceding the Maastricht Treaty see von Borries, 'Die Fortentwicklung der Europäischen Wirtschaftsgemeinschaft zur Wirtschafts- und Währungsunion', in H. Rengeling and R. von Borries (eds.), *Aktuelle Entwicklungen in der Europäischen Gemeinschaft* (1992) 91. The most lucid economic analysis of the new provisions I have detected is by B. Eichengreen, *Should the Maastricht Treaty be Saved?* (Princeton Studies in International Finance No. 74) (1992). For a recent analysis of the Bundesbank's independence in Germany cf. Ladeur, 'Die Autonomie der Bundesbank – ein Beispiel fur die institutionelle Verarbeitung von Ungewissheitsbedingungen', 3 *Staatswissenschaften und Staatspraxis* (1992) 486.
76 See *infra* part 1.
77 Cf. e.g. Article 109 on the power of the Council to conclude formal agreements on an exchange rate system for the ECU in relation to non-Community currencies and Article 73f on safeguard measures on movements of capital with regard to third countries.

symptomatic. They uncover the same controversies which have always dominated academic debates on the Community's Economic Constitution, and they touch upon all the issues that have been dealt with throughout this paper. Those who insist on an unequivocal commitment to neo-liberal economic philosophy reject any institutional innovation that might endanger that commitment.[78] Those who argue in favour of Monetary Union believe that the mutual interdependency of European economies requires a supranational common responsibility for monetary policy.[79] The debate is not just on technical questions and the economic problems of monetary policy. It is also on the importance of an institutional framework for interdependent economies which formally reflects that interdependence.

1. Economic Union

The general economic policy provisions of the Maastricht Treaty draw heavily upon the familiar patterns of a merely selectively integrated Community, where the Member States will retain their general powers and Community policy will simply entail the coordination of governmental actors (Article 103). However, an economic system, where the stability objective of monetary policy is to become mandatory at the European level, would indeed be irreconcilable with unrestricted autonomy for Member States in the matter of economic policy. The Treaty deals with the resulting tensions by defining and structuring coordinative relations. The Member States and the Community are 'committed to the principle of an open market economy with free competition' (Article 3a paragraph 1, cf. Article 102a). They are to set themselves common economic policy objectives. The process through which such objectives are to be established is to begin with various recommendations from the Commission 'for the broad guidelines of the economic policies of the Member States and of the Community' which are then to be adopted by a qualified majority of the Council (Article 103 paragraph 2). Compliance with recommendations thus adopted is to be 'monitored' by the Council on the basis of Commission reports (Article 103 paragraph 3). The non-compliance of a Member State may be sanctioned through 'recommendations' (Article 103 paragraph 4).

---

78 Cf. e.g., the 'Manifest von 60 Ökonomen gegen Maastricht', documented in *Integration* 4/1992, 229. The legal version of this critique argues that the transfer of sovereignty deprives the Federal Republic of its quality as a 'State' and is therefore contrary to the ' *Ewigkeitsklausel'* (eternity clause) of Article 79 para. 3 of the Basic Law (cf., albeit in a broader context). See Murswiek, 'Maastricht und der pouvoir constituant', 11 *Der Staat (1993)* 161 and Rupp, 'Muß das Volk über den Vertrag von Maastricht entscheiden?', 46 *NJW* (1993) 38. Both the German *Bundestag* and *Bundesrat* have, however, in the meantime agreed to the proposals of the *Gemeinsame Verfassungskommission* (Common Constitutional Commission, composed of 32 representatives of the *Bundestag* and 32 of the *Bundesrat*) of 15 and 16 October 1992 on changes of the Basic Law (especially on a new Article 23). Thus German ratification of the Maastricht Treaty became possible.

79 Cf. the memorandum 'Für die Wirtschafts- und Währungsunion: Eine Stellungnahme europäischer Wirtschaftswissenschaftler', *Integration* 4/1992, 232 and Ver Loren van Themaat, 'Some Preliminary Observations on the Intergovernmental Conferences', 28 CMLR (1991) 291 at 297.

These rather vague formulas on the commitments of Member States and the soft sanctions provided for in cases of non-compliance are defined somewhat more precisely, however, in the all important field of fiscal policy. 'Member States shall avoid', per Article 104c paragraph 1, 'excessive government deficits'. This duty is further specified in Article 104c paragraph 2 and in the Protocol 'On the Excessive Deficit Procedure'. The government deficit must not exceed 3% of the gross domestic product and government debt not exceed 60% of the gross domestic product (Articles 1 and 2 of the Protocol). Budget discipline is to be monitored by the Commission. Sanctions may if necessary be imposed by a Council decision taken by a two-thirds majority on the recommendation of the Commission (Article 104c paragraph 13). This is not a strictly juridified procedure (cf. Article 104c paragraph 10) since only monetary sanctions are employed (Article 104c paragraph 11).

The transfer of sovereign monetary policy rights to the Community is therefore not complemented by an equally stringent control of fiscal and economic policy. At the present, one might only guess how effectively the new arrangement will discipline political actors.[80] The integration of monetary policy will have to carry in its wake the coordination of general economic policy, especially fiscal policy. If these expectations are not fulfilled, the very foundations of monetary union will be shaken. The Member States will then be forced either to accept a further restriction of their autonomy in matters of general economic policy – or to live with a legally autonomous but factually vulnerable monetary policy system.

Does the institutionalization of currency policy and the corollary coordination of economic policy imply a completion of the Community's Economic Constitution, insofar as the legal principles which are to guide economic policy and structure its substance have been established? To answer this question, one must first try to determine the relationship between principles of currency policy and those general Community objectives as they are outlined in Article 2 and further specified by Article 3. The very fact, however, that principles and objectives have not yet been harmonized, i.e. that it remains to be established to what extent economic policy directives restrict the pursuit of the objectives named in Article 2 or whether, on the other hand, the general objectives of the Treaty necessitate economic policy adjustments, shows clearly that the Maastricht text is not to be regarded as a legally binding directive for a specific economic policy programme.

---

80   Cf. the 1992/93 report of the German economic advisory board entitled *Jahresgutachten 1992/93 des Sachverständigenrates zur Begutachtung der gesamtwirtschaftlichen Entwicklung*, Bundestags-Drucksache 12/3774 of 19 Nov. 1992, para. 432.

2. Industrial Policy

The second focus for debate concerns the new provisions on industrial policy. This controversy may come as a surprise since industrial policy was acknowledged in principle as a 'constitutional' objective by the SEA.[81] The introduction of the new Title III, as proposed by the Luxembourg Presidency in June 1991,[82] could therefore hardly be called a revolutionary step – the more so since even that proposal obliged the Community to conduct its industrial policy in accordance with 'a system of open and competitive markets'. The revised version of this proposal as now contained in Article 130 adds further substantive and procedural provisos:

> The Community shall *contribute* to the achievement of the objectives set out in paragraph 1 through the policies and activities it pursues under other provisions of this Treaty. The *Council*, acting *unanimously* on a proposal from the Commission, after consulting the European Parliament and the Economic and Social Committee, may decide on specific measures in *support of action taken in the Member States* to achieve the objectives set out in paragraph 1. This title shall not provide a basis for the introduction by the Community of any measure which could lead to a distortion of competition (emphasis added).

These amendments have in no way assuaged the principled neo-liberal critique[83] and the neo-liberal concern is quite understandable. An explicit acknowledgement of industrial policy objectives implies a weakening of the Community's commitment to a competition-based economic system. Once this commitment becomes indeterminate, the Community cannot credibly impose principles, based on its competitive Economic Constitution, upon national policy makers. Industrial policies adopted at the Community level may even overturn national competitive regimes. Unanimous voting as provided for in Article 130 paragraph 3, moreover, may not provide effective protection against interest coalitions, particularly as in the field of research and technology policies unanimity is required only for the setting up of long-term programmes (Article 130i paragraph 1) whereas the decisions implementing those programmes allow for majority voting (Article 130i paragraph 4).

Again, the debate is repetitive and symptomatic of a deeper conflict. The neo-liberal critique rests upon the premise that the Community's economy must be integrated 'through law' and limited to the establishment of a competitive market order.[84] Those who do not subscribe to the primacy of economic rationality over

---

81 See *supra* part II B 1 (notes 52-53).
82 See *supra* introductory note.
83 Cf. Siebert, 'Die Weisheit einer höheren Instanz', *Frankfurter Allgemeine Zeitung*, 14 March 1992, 15; Streit, 'Krücken für die Champions', *Frankfurter Allgemeine Zeitung* of 20 June 1992, 13; Mestmäcker, 'Wettbewerb oder Industriepolitik', *supra* note 28; Sachverständigenrat, *supra* note 80, paras. 443-445. Equally critical, however, on different premises Steindorff, *supra* note 15, at 56 ff. On Germany's postwar political *practice* , which always included industrial policy cf. W. Abelshauser, *Wirtschaftliche Wechsellagen, Wirtschaftsordung und Staat: Die Deutschen Erfahrungen,* Typescript (European University Institute Florence 1992).
84 See *supra* part II A 1.

political choices must realize that the strengthening of policy-making powers aggravates the Community's legitimacy problem.[85] Politicians, however, tend to shy away from definite commitments and to agree upon compromise formulas. And yet, the compromise at which they have arrived, is still of fundamental importance in another sense: in the future, monetary policy will be detached from those institutional structures which the Community 'traditionally' foresaw. Economic policy will have to adjust to a radically new scenario. The Member States will formally retain their general responsibility for economic policy. They will, however, be required to formulate such policies in the face of independent monetary policy, the soft Community regulation of fiscal policy through non-legal means and the mandate of the Council to define general economic policy guidelines. These new frameworks for economic policy in Europe comprise the true institutional innovation of the Maastricht Treaty.

B. New Powers and Subsidiarity

The critical reactions to the dynamics of the Community's economic law which point to so many intrusions into the legal orders of the Member States are the most visible sign of a growing legitimacy gap.[86] Two conflicting strategies sought to cure these problems seem conceivable. First, a widening of the Community's powers would clarify its mandate to integrate broader ('social') objectives into its market-building strategies. Second, the positions of Member States could be strengthened to reflect their continued political autonomy. Paradoxically, the Maastricht Treaty seems to favour both options at once through an expansion of the Community's scope for action in a considerable number of policy fields on the one hand, and the adoption of the principle of subsidiarity on the other.

1. New Competences and Political Mandates

In response to the tensions which spring from the selectivity of Community intervention and the inevitable interdependency between EC and Member State competences, the Community has often implicitly or formally expanded its powers. Such expansion will increasingly take on a 'centralist' guise should majority voting gain in importance. The dynamic development of European economic law following the adoption of the SEA clearly indicates that the close functional relationship between economic law, market integration and the procedural rules of Article 100a of the EEC Treaty, on which this process of expansion relies, is not seriously impeded by the limitation of Community competences provided for in Article 4. The Maastricht Treaty seems to be an added impetus to this development and its inherent tensions. It complements Community powers in economic law and, by

---

85   Cf. *supra* part II B 3.
86   Cf. *supra* parts I B and C.

expressly covering related fields, forestalls criticism that the Community is encroaching upon fields of social regulation where it has no clear political mandate.

The free movement of capital will become effective on 1 January 1994 (Article 73a). With the new provisions on 'trans-European networks' (Articles 129 b-d) and the Titles XIII on industry and XV on research and technological development, the Community will open up new fields of activity bearing upon economic and integration policy. The majority principle gains in importance in the fields of transport policy (Article 75), trade policy (Article 113) and environmental policy (Article 130s). Consumer protection, only indirectly addressed by Article 100a of the EEC Treaty, is established as a new field of European policy by the new Article 129a.[87] Even public health does not escape European attention, although no 'harmonization of the laws and regulations of the Member States' is to take place in this field (Article 129). All these developments are a continuation of a familiar pattern. They will reinforce the tendency towards a 'Europeanization' of political processes, towards the strengthening of the Community as a political actor and will tend to shift political decision-making from the Member States to the Community.

2. Centralization, Implementation, and Subsidiarity

The principle of subsidiarity found in Article 3b of the Maastricht Agreements is expected to counterbalance the centralization of decisional powers. In areas which do not fall within its exclusive competence, the Community shall only take action 'if and in so far as the objectives of the proposed action cannot be sufficiently achieved by the Member States and can therefore, by reason of the scale or effects of the proposed action, be better achieved by the Community' (Article 3b). The Preamble confirms this commitment and explains it further by proclaiming that decisions be taken 'as closely as possible to the citizen' – this wording is repeated in Article A of the Common Provisions. There can thus be no doubt as to the importance of the new principle. But even the most benevolent reader of the Maastricht Treaty will have difficulties in deciphering its legal meaning with any degree of precision. It is immediately apparent, however, that the impact of subsidiarity varies according to the field under scrutiny.[88] The following brief remarks are therefore confined to economic and social regulation.[89] It is with regard to these fields that we must ask: what yardstick should we use when assessing whether some action is at all 'necessary', whether such action can be 'sufficiently achieved by the Member States' or can be performed 'better' by the Community? A

---

87 For a comprehensive analysis of this provision cf. Micklitz and Reich, 'Verbraucherschutz im Vertrag über die Europäische Union – Perspektiven für 1993', 3 *EuZW* (1992) 593.

88 See, e.g., Article 128 requiring the Community to respect national and regional diversity, and Article 129 para. 4 excluding any harmonization of laws and regulations on public health. Such concretizations of subsidiarity cannot guide the organization of, for example, product regulation.

89 For a more comprehensive analysis cf. the contribution of Renaud Dehousse to this volume.

number of possible options need to be evaluated before attempting to arrive at a conclusion:

– it seems a logical step to first draw upon the rich American debate on the proper level of regulation in federal systems, i.e., consider the externalities of diversified jurisdictions, the economies and diseconomies of scale in administration, the interests of enterprises in uniform regulation, and the like.[90] One must not lose sight, however, of the institutional differences between American regulatory federalism and the European Community. Even where Community law relies on 'centralized' legislation, it depends in its implementation upon the legislative acts and, even more important, administration of Member States.[91]

– Jacques Delors himself has, although tentatively, suggested relating subsidiarity to the principles of mutual recognition and home country control.[92] This could mean two fundamentally different things:

(i) regulatory competition which replaces legislative responsibility with market rationality;[93]

(ii) an alternative to the strengthening of Community control over implementation which would rely on trust and cooperation between national administrations.[94]

Community practice, although not uniform, certainly points in the second direction. So do the regulatory needs of market building and the institutional structures of the Community.

– The most intriguing problem of the new principle is judicial control. If Article 3b entrusts the European Court of Justice with the task of evaluating the pros and cons of Community action when assessing Community competences, the subsidiarity 'principle' would indeed be a 'non-justiciable empty formula' (*nicht justiziable Leerformel*[95]). Two fundamentally different ways to avoid, or rather to live with, that verdict can be suggested:

(i) one is to 'juridify' subsidiarity in accordance with its present status in Articles 130t and 118a paragraph 3. Subsidiarity would then be understood as excluding pre-emptive federalism; it would restrict the Community to the adoption of minimum standards.[96]

---

90 See for a recent account S. Rose-Ackerman, *Rethinking the Progressive Agenda: the Reform of the American Regulatory State* (1992) at 163.

91 Cf. *supra* part II B 1 and Joerges, 'Markt ohne Staat?', *supra* introductory note to this article, at 252 ff.

92 Delors, 'Le principe de subsidiarité: contribution au débat', *supra* note 5, at 12; in the same sense see Pipkorn, 'Das Subsidiaritätsprinzip im Vertrag über die Europäische Union – rechtliche Bedeutung und gerichtliche Überprüfbarkeit', 3 *EuZW* (1992) 697, 699.

93 Cf. *supra* part II B 1.

94 Cf. *supra* part II B 3.

95 Grimm, 'Subsidiarität ist nur ein Wort', *Frankfurter Allgemeine Zeitung*, 17 September 1992, 38.

96 See Micklitz and N. Reich, *supra* note 87.

(ii) The other is to regard subsidiarity as being a deliberate delegation of decision-making to political processes in the case of controversies concerning community or national powers.[97]

The choice between all these alternatives will inevitably depend upon the perception of the nature of the problems which the subsidiarity principle is supposed to solve. If one reads it as a response to the disquieting dynamics of European economic law – its centralist guise, its institutional constraints and legitimacy problems – one may be inclined to interpret subsidiarity as a means of bridging 'systems integration and social integration'.[98] Subsidiarity would then require the Community to organize regulation in cooperative rather than centralist patterns. Cooperation implies tensions between decentralized units and the different regulatory levels. It therefore requires rules for conflict resolution. Such rules cannot be conceptualized as predetermining the substantive meaning of subsidiarity. They must instead be understood as procedural devices which aim at resolving conflicts 'as closely as possible to the citizen'. The suggestions submitted in the preceding analysis of the Community's legitimacy problem[99] would fit into such a proceduralized understanding of subsidiarity.

C. The Production of Law and its Legitimacy

Throughout the European Community and beyond its borders, parliamentary democracy is understood as the yardstick against which the legitimacy of governments should be measured. This yardstick allows for many options.[100] And yet, whichever standard one chooses, Community institutions measure up poorly. Legislation adopted by governmental representatives (or bureaucrats of a lower level); the functional delegation of legislative political decisions to expert fora and non-governmental organizations; the powers of the European Court of Justice in the no man's land between law and politics; above all the adoption of legislation by majority voting which claims precedence over national constitutional law – all of these developments worry constitutional lawyers and to an increasing degree the public at large. The demand for a strengthened role for the European Parliament seems a quite logical response to these concerns. And although the Maastricht Treaty provides for considerable improvements of the European Parliament's institutional role (see esp. Articles 158, 189b, 206b), there remains good reason to criticize its drafters for their excessive caution.[101]

---

97   See, e.g., the contribution by Renaud Dehousse to this volume.
98   Cf. *supra* part II B 3.
99   *Supra* part II B 3(c).
100   See the contribution by Emile Noël to this volume, chapter 2, and Frowein, 'Die rechtliche Bedeutung des Verfassungsprinzips der parlamentarischen Demokratie für den europäischen Integrationsprozeß', 18 *EuR* (1983) 301; Häberle, 'Gemeineuropäisches Verfassungsrecht', 18 *EuGRZ* (1991) 261.
101   Cf. R. Bieber, 'Democratization of the European Community through the European Parliament', 46 *Aussenwirtschaft* (1991) 159.

At the same time, the appropriateness of this yardstick (parliamentary democracy) for the future shape of a European Republic raises much more complex issues.[102] The following remarks touch upon just two aspects, namely the role of legislation in the legal system and the role of law in a non-federal system of regulation.

1. Economic Law and Social Integration in the Nation-State

National economic law cannot simply be understood as a product of legislation. Independent administrative units and the delegation of regulatory tasks to experts and non-governmental organizations are by no means Community inventions but are instead well-known features of national law. Economic law is to a great extent extra-legislative, pre-elaborated and pre-discussed by societal actors. Disputes between them are brought before courts who in turn must provide legal principles for their settlement. Legislative acts are certainly an important element within this process. But neither are they the product of isolated inspiration, nor do legislative acts define the final outcome of social controversies. They need to be concretized and adapted to the whole of the legal system by administrative bodies and the courts. They are exposed to the strategies of social actors and may eventually be changed during the process of implementation.

If we look at such realities in national legal systems, the popular and plausible demand for a parliamentarization of EC economic law seems a less than comprehensive solution to the Community's legitimation problems. There are differences between the European Parliament and national Parliaments not only in their relations to electorates, but also with regard to societal actors and the public at large.[103] But even if these differences were marginal, the permanent interrelationship between the legal system and interested actors, legal experts and public debates which account for its 'quality', cannot yet be presupposed to function at the European level. The development of Community law is not embedded in discursive processes of an intensity comparable to national legal systems.

---

102 Cf. J.A. Frowein, *Verfassungsperspektiven der Europäischen Gemeinschaft*, Typescript Heidelberg (1992). The current legal debate in Germany moves between two poles; cf. – both with extensive references – Ress, 'Über die Notwendigkeit der parlamentarischen Legitimierung der Rechtsetzung der Europäischen Gemeinschaften', in W. Fiedler and G. Ress (eds.), *Verfassungsrecht und Völkerrecht. Gedächtnisschrift für W.K. Geck* (1989) 625 ff. (suggesting there be a constitutional obligation upon the Federal Republic to demand parliamentary legislation at the European level) and R. Streinz, *Der Verfassungsstaat als Glied einer europäischen Gemeinschaft, Deutsches Verwaltungsblatt* (1990) at 949 ff. (arguing that supranational parliamentary control would be irreconcilable with the German Constitution); for a useful account of non-legal contributions cf. B. Wieland, *Ein Markt – zwölf Regierungen?* (1992).

103 Cf. Lepsius, 'Nationalstaat oder Nationalitätenstaat als Modell für die Weiterentwicklung der Europäischen Gemeinschaft', in R. Wildenmann (ed.), *supra* introductory note, at 19 ff., and 25 ff.

The text of a Treaty cannot artificially reproduce the infrastructures of national law at European level and create a common European 'political culture'. But it might have paid some attention to the specifics of Community law-making: government representatives and Commission officials are subjected to demands and pressures which differ qualitatively from those affecting national actors. Frequently, only fragments of their debates reach the public at large. Even the academic community knows very little of the practice of *Comitology* which is of such great practical importance. Cooperation with non-governmental organizations is not equivalent to the participation of administration and other societal representatives common in national contexts. The Maastricht Treaty makes no attempt to open up the process of law production to public scrutiny, to improve public access to administrative procedures, to provide for formalized feedback mechanisms between European law production and national actors, or to consider more extensive opportunities for judicial review.[104] In sum, its drafters may have been preoccupied too exclusively rather than too little with the role of Parliament.

2. Political and Regulatory Networks

The Community system provides for the adoption of legal rules and decisions; its institutional design did not foresee the need to implement regulatory programmes. The Community, when monitoring the enforcement of its law, accordingly used to concentrate upon the transformation of directives into national law. These efforts have been supported by the many techniques developed by the European Court of Justice in order to ensure the authority of primary and secondary Community law *vis-à-vis* the Member States. But it seems fair to conclude that the triangle of administrative discretion, judicial control and political accountability which characterizes fully-fledged legal systems is still in its infancy at the Community level. [105]

Article 5 of the Luxembourg Presidency Draft of June 1991[106] contained a provision which at least took note of the implementation problem. The Member States and the Community were to commit themselves to close cooperation between their administrative agencies. Even this scant reminder of the need to create an administrative infrastructure for the implementation of Community policies failed to find its way into the Maastricht Treaty. The process of the Europeanization of regulatory policies and economic law, however, which prompted the emergence of subject-related policy networks existing outside the institutional framework of the EEC Treaty seems to be irrevocable. It is likewise inconceivable that Community law will be efficiently implemented without cooperative support from the administrations of the Member States. The future of the principle of subsidiarity,

---

104 Cf. *supra* part II B 3 and the suggestions of Ladeur, 'European Community Institutional Reforms', *Legal Issues of European Integration* (1990) 1.
105 See the detailed and stimulating analysis Snyder, *supra* note 42, at 40 ff., and 48 ff.
106 *Supra* introductory note to this chapter.

therefore, may well lie in the development of forms of cooperation between the Member States which benefit from and 'mutually recognize' their expertise. This development might lead to a constructive differentiation between the regulatory functions and the coordinatory competences of the Community and national administrative units.

Do these observations and remonstrances plead for or against Maastricht? They are meant to illustrate the need for a comprehensive analysis of economic law independent from the established and practised European rhetoric. The normative quality of economic law, as it has developed within western democracies, forms its potential to mediate between economic rationality and social responsibility. If the integration of economic law within the European Community or a future European Union is not to jeopardize these qualities of economic law it must address the difficulties of basing systems integration on processes of 'social' integration. The Maastricht Treaty is certainly a less-than-perfect framework for such a project.[107] But the Maastricht Treaty did not itself invent the problems inherent to the integration process. Its mere rejection would even aggravate the tensions between national sovereignty and economic interdependency; it would not identify any constructive forward-looking response to the erosion of national autonomy. It is vital to remember that Maastricht, just because of its ambiguities and potentially contradictory perspectives, keeps many options open. This openness will incite continuous debate on the future architecture of the European Community. This debate may very well pave the way to a common European political culture on which the further development of European institutions could rely.

---

107 Especially if one considers the many fields not addressed in this paper, such as social policy, social cohesion and transfer payments.

Chapter 4
EMU – Metaphor for European Union?
Institutions, Rules and Types of Regulation

Francis Snyder*

I. Introduction

Economic and monetary union (EMU) is usually viewed as the centrepiece of the Maastricht Treaty on European Union (TEU).[1] It is also the Treaty's most controversial aspect. After being negotiated and agreed by representatives of the Member States, EMU provoked strong reactions, both positive and negative. For once in the European Community's history, the debate was not restricted to national governments and politicians. Instead, as demonstrated in the referenda in Denmark[2] and France, it attracted wide attention. Not only did it contribute directly to the gradual development of a real European political and legal culture. As a symbol of potential European unity, it also engaged the imagination of people throughout the world.

Whether judged favourably or not, EMU represents an attempt to put in place a major institutional innovation, and also an effort to envisage and shape the Europe of the future. It is a type of legal innovation which draws frequently on existing forms. It uses them in novel ways, however, and also combines them with new elements. It is also a conjunction of diverse strands. This is partly because of the inherent complexity of economic and monetary policy, and partly because EMU itself resulted from bargaining and compromise.

In addition to its specific significance, EMU can be understood as a metaphor for European Union. Metaphor is used here to mean 'a figure of speech in which one thing is described in terms of another', with the comparison usually being implicit.[3] Viewed from this perspective, many aspects of EMU remain ambiguous, uncertain or even obscure. This should not, however, be surprising. On one level a metaphor may be a clear expression, say of political determination to reach a

---

* The author wishes to thank Jason Coppel, Renaud Dehousse, Nathalie Habbar, Christian Joerges, Jean-Victor Louis and John Usher for their contributions to this paper. He alone of course is responsible for the contents.
1 Hereinafter referred to as the Treaty on European Union, the Maastricht Treaty or the TEU.
2 At the December 1993 Edinburgh summit, the European Council made special arrangements for Denmark, including the agreement that Denmark would not participate in the final stage of EMU: see *Agence Europe*, no. 5878, Sunday, 13 December 1992.
3 See J.A. Cuddon, *The Penguin Dictionary of Literary Terms and Literary Theory* (3rd edition 1992) 541.

compromise. Yet it may appear singularly opaque if one seeks its more profound significance.[4]

This chapter advances three specific hypotheses. First, EMU as a whole can be envisaged as an attempt to reconcile supranationalism and intergovernmentalism, rather than to choose between them. Second, it consists of two distinct but interrelated parts: economic policy-making (economic union) which tends towards intergovernmentalism, and monetary policy-making (monetary union) which tends towards supranationalism. Third, each of the two parts in itself is a complex mixture of supranational and intergovernmental elements. Supranationalism and intergovernmentalism may refer either to contrasting organizational models or to different decision-making methods.[5]

If EMU is considered as a metaphor, what kind of Union does EMU stand for? What does it express with regard to relations between the Community and the Member States? What legal or other normative instruments does it involve, and how are they deployed? Does it elaborate any new forms of regulation? What perspective does EMU offer on the European Community's changing constitution? On the basis of the Maastricht Treaty, this chapter tries to suggest some answers to these questions.

The remainder of the chapter consists of three main parts. The next part, Part II, gives a brief overview of EMU. It considers EMU as a means to an end; surveys its guiding principles, timing and institutions; and then identifies some of the compromises embodied in the Maastricht Treaty provisions. Parts III and IV then focus on institutions, rules and forms of regulation, in particular as they are proposed to be developed during the three stages of EMU. Part III treats the institutions of economic union and monetary union separately in three stages: intergovernmentalism, the move toward supranational institutions, and the development of economic discipline and the European Central Bank. Part IV first identifies two distinctive legal forms and techniques of EMU; then it analyses the evolution of rules and forms of regulation, which, according to the Maastricht Treaty, are to lead eventually to a differentiated, legally binding system of economic and monetary regulation. Finally, some general points are made in the conclusion.[6]

---

4   In this respect it is similar to political and legal symbols, which, resembling many fundamental constitutional principles, are often – if not always – ambiguous.

5   This does not of course grant any *a priori* or objective status to the concept of national interests: see F. Snyder, *New Directions in European Community Law* (1990), chapter 2: '"Interests" and the Legislative Process'. Nor does it mean that the Community has no influence on how the Member States defined their interests: see Sandholtz, 'Choosing Union: Monetary Politics and the Maastricht Treaty', 47 *International Organization*, (1993) 1-39 at 2-4.

6   This chapter forms part of a series of related papers, which together try to elaborate some general ideas on the development of Community law and institutions. See also (in chronological order) F. Snyder (with R. Dehousse, C. Joerges and G. Majone), *Europe after 1992: New Regulatory Strategies*, EUI Working Paper in Law No. 92/31 (1992); Snyder, 'The Effectiveness of European Community Law', 56 *Modern Law Review* (1993) 19-54; F. Snyder, *European Community Law and International Economic Relations: The Saga of Thai Manioc*, EUI Working Paper in Law 93/2 (1993); and F. Snyder, *Soft Law and Institutional Practice in the European Community*, EUI Working Paper in Law 93/5 (1993).

II. An Overview of EMU

A. EMU as a Means to an End

According to the Maastricht Treaty, EMU is not an objective in itself but rather a means to an end.[7] The objectives of the European Union are stated in Article B of Title I Common Provisions. This Article provides, among other things, that the objectives of the Union shall include the promotion of economic and social progress which is balanced and sustainable, in particular through the strengthening of economic and monetary cohesion and through the establishment of economic and monetary union, ultimately including a single currency. This formulation, though ostensibly concerned only with objectives, also sets out in specific terms the means for achieving these ends. Read as a 'constitutionalization' of EMU, it suggests that to some extent the means has become an end in itself.

These general provisions are elaborated in Title II of the Maastricht Treaty. This Title encompasses the articles of the Treaty on European Union that amend the EEC Treaty. It is with these latter articles that we are mainly concerned.[8]

The Maastricht Treaty provisions retain the structure of the EEC Treaty, in particular by distinguishing among objectives, means and activities. Article 2 EEC previously stated the EEC objectives and the principal means for achieving them. These provisions are modified by the Maastricht Treaty. Article G of the TEU provides for a new Article 2 EC.[9] The new objectives include 'sustainable and non-inflationary growth respecting the environment' and a high degree of convergence of economic performance'. Together with other objectives, they are to be achieved by three means: the establishment of a common market, the implementation of common policies or activities, and the establishment of an EMU.

Article 3a EC, which together with Article 3 concerns the Community activities, deals with economic union and monetary union in two separate paragraphs. As will be shown later, this conception reflects a basic distinction between the two related policies.

With regard to economic union, Article 3a(1) states that, for the purposes set out in Article 2, the activities of the Member States and the Community shall include the adoption of an economic policy which is based on the close coordination of Member States' economic policies, on the internal market and on the definition of

---

7   For an excellent introduction to EMU, see B. Eichengreen, *Should the Maastricht Treaty be Saved?*, Princeton Studies in International Finance, No. 74, December 1992.
8   For more detailed legal analysis, see Durand in *Commentaire Mégret: Le Droit de la CEE*, Vol. 1 (1992) 399-406; F. Dehousse, *L'Union économique et monétaire*, Le Traité de Maastricht 1, C.E.E.I./Centre F. Dehousse, Université de Liège (1992). On the legal and institutional aspects, see Louis, 'L'Union économique et monétaire', 28 *Cahiers de Droit Européen* (1992) 253-305.
9   Article G (A) provides that throughout the 1957 EEC Treaty [of Rome] the term 'European Economic Community' shall be replaced by the term 'European Community'. This usage is followed here.

common objectives, and which is conducted in accordance with the principle of an open market economy with free competition. [10]

With regard to monetary union, Article 3a(2) provides that, according to the set timetable and procedures, the activities of the EC shall also include the irrevocable fixing of exchange rates leading to the introduction of a single currency, the ECU. It is also to embrace the definition and conduct of a single monetary policy and exchange rate policy. The primary objective of both is to be to maintain price stability, and, without prejudice to this objective, to support the general economic policies in the Community. These objectives are to be achieved in accordance with the principle of an open market economy with free competition.

These legal provisions set EMU firmly in the framework of economic integration and the internal market: EMU is an integral part of the Community project. They also, however, presage a major distinction between economic union and monetary union. Economic union is to be achieved through the activities of both the Community and the Member States, but monetary union involves the establishment of a single policy. The former, at least within limits, tolerates diversity; the latter, even if subject to checks and balances, demands uniformity. Together they suggest not only that EMU is central to the internal market; it also forms a distinctive configuration of institutions, rules and types of regulation in the Community system. [11]

B. Guiding Principles, Timing and Institutions

The activities comprising EMU are ideally to take place according to specific principles and a fixed schedule. The guiding principles are stable prices, sound public finance and monetary conditions and a sustainable balance of payments. [12] For the first time in the industrialized world, the objectives of economic policy thus are stated explicitly in a constitution.

EMU is to be established in three stages. The first stage began in July 1990. The second stage is to start on 1 January 1994. [13] The third stage is to begin on 1 January 1999 if a prior date has not been set by the end of 1997. [14]

The EC's objectives, including those for the achievement of which EMU is established, are to be accomplished within 'a single institutional framework'. [15] Though the expression of 'a single institutional framework' may be merely a fiction

---

10   On the constitutional status of the principle of an open market economy with free competition, see Joerges, 'European Economic Law, The Nation-State and the Maastricht Treaty', in this volume at 29; and Snyder, 'L'Economia mista e la nuova costituzione economica dell'Unione Europea', in F. Merloni (a cura di), *L'Economia mista, oggi* (1993, in press).
11   The question as to whether these two aspects of EMU are entirely consistent deserves to be posed, even though it cannot be answered here.
12   Article 3a(3) TEU.
13   Article 109e TEU.
14   Article 109j(4) TEU.
15   See Article C TEU.

if it is applied to the EC as a whole,[16] the provisions for the establishment of EMU are among the major institutional innovations of the Maastricht Treaty. A European System of Central Banks (ESCB) and a European Central Bank (ECB) are to be established in accordance with procedures laid down in the Treaty.[17]

Neither the ESCB nor the ECB are institutions in the strict sense of Article 4 EEC;[18] for example, their powers are restricted to the specific domain of monetary policy. But if we take the term 'institution' in a broader sense, we can distinguish three sets of institutional arrangements which, though having different roles, form the core of EMU. Classified roughly according to function, they are regulatory institutions, advisory institutions and systemic (or framework) institutions. The institutions in each of these sets are destined to be modified substantially during the three stages of EMU. The set of regulatory institutions currently comprises the Committee of Governors of the Central Banks of the Member States (Committee of Governors). This Committee is to be replaced at the second stage by the European Monetary Institute (EMI), which in turn is to be replaced at the start of the third stage by the European Central Bank (ECB). The set of advisory institutions now includes the Monetary Committee; at the start of the third stage it is to become the Economic and Financial Committee. Currently there are no systematic institutions, except to the extent that the Council fulfils this role; the third and final stage of EMU is to be marked by the establishment of the European System of Central Banks (ESCB), the 'common set of rules' within which the ECB is to operate.

These institutions are to act within the limits of the powers conferred upon them by the Treaty and by the Statute of the ESCB and of the ECB.[19] More generally, they are bound, as are the principal EC institutions, to act within the limits of the powers conferred upon the EC by the Treaty and also of the objectives assigned to it by the Treaty. This now includes the principle of subsidiarity, as stated in the new Article 3b EC.[20] It is worth noting also that, in their relations with these institutions, and in particular in implementing the Treaty provisions and EC secondary law concerning EMU, Member States are bound by the 'fidelity clause' expressed in Article 5 EEC.

16 See Curtin, 'The Constitutional Structure of the Union: A Europe of Bits and Pieces', 30 *Common Market Law Review* (1993) 17-69 at 27-30.
17 Article 4a EC.
18 See Louis, 'L'Union économique et monétaire', *supra* note 8, at 279-280.
19 Statute of the ESCB, annexed to the Treaty: see Article 4a EC.
20 On the application of the principle of subsidiarity to economic and monetary union, see European Institute of Public Administration (ed.), *Subsidiarité: défi du changement* (1991) 71-94.

C. EMU as Compromise

The main elements of EMU are the result of bargaining and compromise, especially among the representatives of the twelve Member States, but also between the Commission and the Member States.[21] Consequently the overall shape of EMU may seem difficult to discern, and its details impossible to grasp. For this reason, it is useful to keep in mind that EMU is a combination of supranationalism and intergovernmentalism.[22] On the one hand, both as organizational models and methods of decision-making, supranationalism and intergovernmentalism are interwoven throughout EMU. On the other hand, the distinction between them underlies the structural division within EMU between economic policy and monetary policy.

The Maastricht Treaty provisions emphasize the functional linkage between the 1992 project and EMU. This represents a position held strongly by the Commission. According to this view, the internal market in goods and services and the complete liberalization of capital movements required a system of fixed exchange rates and a single monetary policy.[23]

The constitutionalization of the aims of economic and monetary policy reflects the influence of Germany. It has been argued,[24] however, that the statement of the aim of price stability as a constitutional principle represents a more unambiguous ranking of the aims of monetary policy than is found even in Germany. Especially since it is expressed clearly in the Community's constitution, this marks an important shift in the conception of monetary policy.

The choice of a fixed timetable for EMU represents a negotiating victory for those countries, such as Belgium and the Netherlands, which favour a more federalist approach to monetary policy. Such discipline may pose problems for other countries, such as Italy, Portugal or Greece; it also caused difficulties during the elaboration of the 1993 budget in Belgium.

---

21 For the argument that EC governments favoured monetary union for different reasons, at different times, see Sandholtz, *supra* note 3. For further details on national positions, see Carini, 'Le scommesse del dopo-Maastricht', *La Repubblica*, Affari & Finanza, 25 September 1992, 2; Butler, 'The Way Ahead', *The Economist* (London), January 30th 1993, 21-23.

22 See the general alternatives sketched in the Christophersen Report: *Agence Europe*, 1604/1605, 23 March 1990; 1606, 24 March 1990. With regard to supranationalism, I mean what Weiler has called 'decisional supranationalism': see Weiler, 'The Community System: The Dual Character of Supranationalism', 1 *Yearbook of European Law* (1981) 267-306; reprinted in F. Snyder (ed), *European Community Law*, Vol. I (1993).

23 See Commission of the European Communities, 'One Market, One Money', *European Economy*, 44, October 1990, special issue, 18. See also Padoa-Schioppa, 'The European Monetary System: A Long-Term View', in F. Giavazzi, S. Mossi and M. Miller (eds), *The European Monetary System* (1988) 373-376.

24 Thygesen, 'Economic and Monetary Union in the 1990s', in A. Pijpers (ed), *The European Community at the Crossroads* (1992) 142.

In addition, the institutional framework of EMU follows mainly the German model, at least so far as the autonomous status and political independence of the ECB is concerned.[25]

EMU thus represents both a shift in the conception of monetary policy and a major institutional innovation. Its implementation in practice, however, is likely to prove problematic. This is so not only because of the breakdown of the European Monetary System beginning in September 1992, when Italy and then the United Kingdom withdrew from the Exchange Rate Mechanism.[26] It is also due to other compromises embodied in the Maastricht Treaty itself.

For example, economic theory does not posit the absolute priority of either economic policy or monetary policy, in the sense that the integration of one must be achieved first as a precondition for the integration of the other. Yet, as the stages for achieving EMU make clear, EMU is based on the so-called 'coronation theory', according to which monetary union cannot occur in the absence of economic convergence, rather than the reverse.[27] This represented the German position. It was a concession by France, counterbalancing to some extent the German concession to allow the Deutschmark to be replaced by the ECU.

In addition, as already noted, in both form and content Article 3a TEU distinguishes sharply between the integration of economic policy and the integration of monetary policy. Thus Article 3a(1) refers to the activities of the Community as including *inter alia* 'the adoption of an economic policy which is based on the close coordination of Member States' economic policies ...' Article 3a(2) provides that these activities shall include 'the definition and conduct of a single monetary policy and exchange-rate policy...' This formulation leaves economic policies mainly to the Member States, though within a Community framework, while it assigns the conduct of monetary policy to the Community. The provisions on economic union thus tend toward intergovernmentalism, and those on monetary union toward supranationalism. The latter reflect the German concern to insulate monetary policy from the influence of countries, especially in southern Europe, which have not adopted a strict macroeconomic discipline.

The convergence of economic policies thus is a precondition to the achievement of monetary union, yet the former remain largely under the control of the Member States and can be influenced by the Community mainly by coordination. Partly because of specific compromises which are crystallized in this arrangement, and partly in order to cope with the potential disjunction between economic and monetary policies, the programme for achieving EMU was expressed legally in

---

25 See, e.g., Carini, *supra* note 21; A. Giovannini, *Central Banking in a Monetary Union: Reflections on the Proposed Statute of the European Central Bank*, CEPR Occasional Paper No. 9 (1992) at 7-19.
26 See 'The Implications and Lessons to be Drawn from the Recent Exchange Rate Crisis' (Report by the Committee of Governors) *Agence Europe*, 1837, 28 May 1993.
27 See also Louis, 'L'Union économique et monétaire', *supra* note 8, at 258-259. In the context of the EMS, see M. Emerson and C. Huhne, *The ECU Report* (1991) 140.

terms of stages. Whether this complex compromise strategy will work in practice is another matter.

The resulting conundrum places a special weight on the detailed institutional arrangements specified in the Maastricht Treaty. Consequently, the following discussion focuses specifically on relations between the Community and the Member States, the use of different types of rules, and different forms of regulation. The ways in which social, political and economic factors relating to EMU may enhance, undermine or completely bypass the neatly formulated legal provisions are of equal, if not greater, importance. In the medium and long term these factors are unknown, however, and even in the short term they are better left to those more qualified to discern their combined influence on future developments.

III. Institutions

A. The Stage of Intergovernmentalism

1. Introduction

EMU involves the development and operation of specific institutions. They emerge gradually, however, in three stages. The process of institutional development is most striking in the case of monetary union. The institutional developments concerning economic union, as will be seen, are more diffuse.

The first stage, which began on 1 July 1990, makes use of existing institutions within and outside the formal Community system. They are mainly inter-governmental institutions, in which the Member States play a dominant role.

2. Economic Union: Using the Existing System

This is especially the case with regard to economic policy. The central institutions during the first stage are the Member States and the Council. On the one hand, Member States are during the first stage to regard their economic policies as a matter of common concern and to coordinate them within the Council.[28] On the other hand, as a result of Council Decision 90/141 of 12 March 1990,[29] the Council can undertake multilateral surveillance of all aspects of Member States' short-term and medium-term economic policy.

Other Community institutions are also involved, using procedures and inter-institutional links which are classic in the Community system. This institutional network serves partly to knit together the actions of the different Member States, and also to link those of the Member States as a group with those of the

28   Article 103(1) EC.

Community. For example, the Council is to adopt an annual economic report after consulting the European Parliament and the Economic and Social Committee.[30] Regular reports on the results of multilateral surveillance are to be made by the Council President and the Commission to the European Council and the European Parliament. When the Council makes political recommendations, the Council President can be invited to appear before the competent committee of the European Parliament. In addition, governments are to bring the results of the multilateral surveillance to the attention of their national parliaments so that they can be taken into account in national policy-making.

3. Monetary Union: Incorporation of Previously Peripheral Institutions

The Member States, the Council and the other well-known Community institutions operate during the first stage almost entirely in the realm of economic policy. With regard to monetary policy, other more specialized, less public and less directly accountable institutions hold the floor. From an institutional perspective, the first stage of EMU serves to bring into the centre of the Community system several institutions which, though always important, were previously on the periphery.

The most important is the Committee of Governors of the Central Banks of the Member States. The Committee of Governors was constituted legally by EEC Council Decision 64/300 of 8 May 1964.[31] It consists of the governors of the central banks of the Member States and the Director-General of the Luxembourg Monetary Institute. It is not a Community institution in the sense of Article 4 EEC.

The role of the Committee of Governors during the first stage of EMU is five-fold. First, the Committee holds consultations concerning the general principles and broad lines of monetary policy. Second, it is to exchange information regularly about the most important measures within the competence of the central banks and to examine these measures; the Committee is normally to be consulted before national authorities take decisions on the course of monetary policy, such as the setting of annual money supply and credit targets. Third, it is to promote the coordination of the monetary policies of the Member States, with the aim of achieving price stability as a necessary condition for the proper functioning of the EMS and the realization of its objective of monetary stability. In addition, it can express opinions, a matter to be discussed later. The chair of the Committee of Governors is invited to participate in the relevant meetings of the Council.

The Committee of Governors meets at regular intervals, normally ten times each year. It meets in Basel, usually on the same dates as the meetings of the

---

29 Council Decision 90/141/EEC of 12 March 1990 on the attainment of progressive convergence of economic policies and performance during stage one of economic and monetary union, OJ L78/23 of 24 March 1990.
30 Acting on a Commission proposal: see Council Decision 90/141, *supra* note 29.
31 OJ 77 of 21 May 1964, as amended by Council Decision 90/142/EEC of 12 March 1990, OJ L78/25 of 24 March 1990. This measure was adopted on the basis of Articles 105(1) and 145, first indent, EEC.

administrative council of the Bank of International Settlements (BIS). Formerly the BIS provided the secretariat for the Committee of Governors, but since 1990 the Committee of Governors has had a separate secretariat.[32]

In addition to the Committee of Governors, another key institution in the first stage of EMU is the Monetary Committee. The establishment of a Monetary Committee was envisaged by Article 105(2) EEC. This Article provided that, in order to promote coordination of the policies of Member States in the monetary field to the full extent needed for the functioning of the common market, a Monetary Committee with advisory status was to be set up. It was to have two tasks. The first was to keep under review the monetary and financial situation of the Member States and of the Community and the general payments system of the Member States and to report regularly thereon to the Council and to the Commission. The second was to deliver opinions at the request of the Council or of the Commission or on its own initiative for submission to these institutions. The Member States and the Commission were each to appoint two members of the Monetary Committee.

Subsequently, on the basis of Article 153 EEC, the Monetary Committee was created by Council Decision of 18 March 1958.[33] Since then the Monetary Committee has played an important role, particularly in relation to monetary policy and the free movement of capital. Until recently it was relatively unknown, but the ERM debacle has brought it into the public spotlight.

The Maastricht Treaty expands the role of the Monetary Committee. Article 109c(1) EC provides[34] that, in order to promote coordination of the policies of Member States to the full extent needed for the functioning of the internal market, a Monetary Committee with advisory status is to be set up. The Member States and the Commission are each to appoint two members of the Committee.[35]

According to the Maastricht Treaty, the Monetary Committee has four tasks. The first is to keep under review the monetary and financial situation of the Member States and of the Community and the general payments system of the Member States and to report regularly thereon to the Council and to the Commission.[36] The second is to deliver opinions at the request of the Council or of the Commission, or on its own initiative for submission to those institutions.[37] These tasks are identical to those provided in Article 105(2) EEC.

32　See Rules of Procedure of the Committee of Governors of the Central Banks of the European Economic Community (1990), Article 9.
33　Comité Monétaire de la Communauté Européen, *Compendium des textes communautaires en matière monétaire* (1989), 155.
34　In the same wording as the previous Article 105(2) EEC.
35　Article 109c(1), 3rd para. EC.
36　Article 109c(1), 2nd para., 1st indent EC.
37　Article 109c(1), 2nd para., 2nd indent EC.

In addition, however, the Monetary Committee is to contribute to the preparation of the work of the Council.[38] Finally, at least once a year it is to examine the situation regarding the movement of capital and the freedom of payments, as they result from the application of the Treaty and of measures adopted by the Council. The examination is to cover all measures relating to capital movements and payments. The Committee is to report to the Commission and to the Council on the outcome of this examination.[39] As a result of these new functions in particular, the Monetary Committee is in a position to play a linking role between economic policy integration and monetary policy integration, or in other words between decision-making and regulatory processes in diverse locations and at different levels of the Community system.

B. Toward Supranational Institutions

1. Introduction

The second stage for achieving EMU is to begin on 1 January 1994.[40] It involves a move toward more centralized institutions, and supranational institutions assume greater significance.

2. Economic Union: Towards A Supranational Umbrella

With regard to economic policy, the Council is joined by the Commission as the main institution. In addition to the continuing coordination of their economic policies, the Member States become subject to a variety of prohibitions.[41] They are also required to endeavour to avoid excessive government deficits.[42] They must, as appropriate, start the process leading to the independence of their respective central banks.[43]

With the beginning of the second stage, Member States are also subject to Commission monitoring of their budgetary situation and the stock of government debt 'with a view to identifying gross errors'.[44] If a Member State does not fulfil the requirements under set criteria, the Commission must prepare a report; in certain other circumstances, the Commission is not required to prepare such a report but nevertheless may do so.[45] The Monetary Committee is required to formulate an

---

38 That is, to the work of the Council referred to in Articles 73f, 73g, 103(1), (3), (4) and (5), 103a, 104a, 104b, 104c, 109c(2), 109f(6), 109h, 109i, 109j(2) and 109k(1): Article 109c(1), 2nd para., 3rd indent EC. This is to be without prejudice to Article 151.
39 Article 109c(1), 2nd para., 4th indent EC.
40 Article 190e(1) EC.
41 See Article 109e(3) EC.
42 Article 109e(4) EC.
43 Article 109e(5) EC.
44 See Arts 109e(3), 104c(2) EC.
45 Article 104(3) EC.

opinion on this report.[46] The Commission then may address an opinion to the Council, which may take measures to be discussed later.[47] In other words, the matter may end with the preparation of the report by the Commission and the opinion of the Monetary Committee; Council action does not necessarily follow.

3. Monetary Union: New Bottle, but Old Wine?

With regard to monetary union, the intergovernmental institutions of the first stage are to be partly restructured according to a more centralist mould. At the start of the second stage the Committee of Governors is to be dissolved.[48] A new institution, the European Monetary Institute (EMI), is to be established and take up its duties.[49] It is to have legal personality.[50]

During the 1991 Intergovernmental Conference some Member States, together with the Commission, favoured the establishment of a European System of Central Banks at the beginning of the second stage of EMU. Others preferred the creation of a transitional body during the period when the final responsibility of monetary policy still remained with the Member States. The resulting compromise, proposed by Belgium, was the structure, composition and powers of the EMI.[51]

The organization of the EMI is a mixture of intergovernmental and supranational elements. The members of the EMI are the central banks of the Member States.[52] The EMI is to be directed and managed by a Council, consisting of the Governors of the national central banks and of a President.[53] The President is to be appointed by common accord of the Governments of the Member States at the level of Heads of State or Government.[54] He or she is to be selected from among persons of recognized standing and professional experience in monetary or banking matters. Only nationals of Member States may be President of the EMI. From the standpoint of the organization of institutions, the creation of the role of the President of the EMI is the most significant innovation of the second stage, since to some extent at least it represents a supranational element at the apex of what would otherwise be an entirely intergovernmental institution.

---

46 Article 104c(4) EC.
47 See Article 104c(5)-(12) EC.
48 Article 109f(1), 4th para. EC.
49 Article 109f(1), 1st para. EC. All assets and liabilities of European Monetary Cooperation Fund are to pass automatically to the EMI (Protocol on the Statute of the EMI: Article 1 (1.3) EC).
50 Article 109f(1), 1st para. EC. The Statute of the EMI is laid down in a Protocol annexed to the Treaty: Article 109f(1), 3rd para. EC.
51 See Louis, 'L'Union économique et monétaire', supra note 8, at 273. As described by the former British Permanent Representative, '[t]he Germans having resisted all attempts by the French, British and others to have an evolutionary stage 2, the EMI's new functions will be only to make procedural preparations for stage 3': Butler, supra note 21, at 22.
52 Protocol on the Statute of the EMI, Article 1(1.2).
53 Article 109f(1), 1st para. EC. One of the Governors is to be Vice-President, to be appointed by the EMI Council: Article 109f(1), 2nd para. EC.
54 Acting on a recommendation from, as the case may be, the Committee of Governors or the Council of the EMI, and after consulting the European Parliament and the Council.

The objective of EMI is to contribute to the realization of the conditions necessary for the transition to the third stage of EMU.[55] The tasks of the EMI are numerous.[56] Its first task is to strengthen cooperation between the national central banks. Second, the EMI is to strengthen the coordination of the monetary policies of the Member States, with the aim of ensuring price stability. Third, it is to monitor the functioning of the European Monetary System. Fourth, it is to hold consultations concerning issues falling within the competence of the national central banks and affecting the stability of financial institutions and markets. Fifth, it is to take over the tasks of the dissolved European Monetary Cooperation Fund. Sixth, it is to facilitate the use of the ECU and oversee its development, including the smooth functioning of the ECU clearing system..

In addition, the EMI is to prepare the instruments and the procedures necessary for carrying out a single monetary policy in the third stage. It must also promote the harmonization, where necessary, of the rules and practices governing the collection, compilation and distribution of statistics in the areas within its field of competence. The EMI is also to prepare the rules for operations to be undertaken by the national central banks in the framework of the ESCB; to promote the efficiency of cross-border payments; and to supervise the technical preparation of ECU bank notes.[57]

At the latest by 31 December 1996, the EMI is required to specify the regulatory, organizational and logistical framework necessary for the ESCB to perform its tasks in the third stage. This framework is to be submitted for decision to the ECB at the date of its establishment.[58]

The EMI has also potentially significant powers with regard to relations with other EC institutions and the Member States. It must be consulted by the Council regarding any proposed Community act within its field of competence.[59] Within certain conditions, the EMI is also to be consulted by the authorities of the Member States on any draft legislative provision within its field of competence.[60]

Also during the second stage, the EMI and the Commission prepare the way for the Council to take the essential decision regarding movement to the third stage. With the approach of the third stage, the EMI and the Commission are to report to

---

55 Protocol on the Statute of the EMI, Article 2.
56 Article 109f(2) EC.
57 Article 109f(3), 1st para. EC
58 Article 109f(3), 2nd para. EC. The Council may also confer upon the EMI other tasks for the preparation of the third stage: see Article 109f(7) EC.
59 Article 109f(6), 1st para. EC.
60 Article 109f(6), 2nd para. EC. This consultation is to take place within the limits and under the conditions set out by the Council, acting by a qualified majority on a proposal from the Commission, and after consulting the European Parliament and the EMI: see Article 109f(6), 2nd para. EC. Where the Treaty provides for a consultative role for the ECB, references to the ECB are to be treated as referring to the EMI before the establishment of the ECB: Article 109f(8), 1st para. EC. Where the Treaty provides for a consultative role for the EMI, references to the EMI are to be read, before 1 January 1994, as referring to the Committee of Governors: Article 109f(8), 2nd para. EC. During the second stage, the term 'ECB' used in Articles 173, 175, 176, 177, 180 and 215 is to be read as referring to the EMI: Article 109f(9) EC.

the Council on the progress made in the fulfilment by the Member States of their obligations regarding the achievement of economic and monetary union.[61]

Despite the significant procedural role of the EMI, however, it is for the Council to assess the fulfilment by the Member States of the conditions for movement to a single currency.[62] It is also for the Council to take any necessary action, including setting a date for the start of the third stage; this is to be done by the Council meeting in the composition of Heads of State or of Government, that is, as a Community institution, and acting by a qualified majority.[63] In order to do so, the Council must decide, on the basis of specified procedures, whether, a majority of the Member States fulfil the necessary conditions for the adoption of a single currency.[64] These procedures include an examination of the achievement of a high degree of sustainable economic convergence among the Member States, by reference to economic and monetary criteria.[65] Despite the differences in the institutional development of economic union and monetary union up to this point, economic criteria thus constitute a frame of reference in determining the passage to the third stage of EMU. If an earlier date is not set by the end of 1997, the third stage is to begin on 1 January 1999.[66]

C. Economic Discipline and the Central Bank

1. Economic Union: Using Community Institutions Intergovernmentally

The advent of the third stage of EMU is intended to represent a shift in institutional arrangements with regard to economic policy. The second stage, as already noted, is based in this respect primarily on intergovernmental relations and coordination of national policies.[67] From the beginning of the third stage, however, the Member States become subject to strict economic policy discipline.[68] Instead of the simple coordination of actions taken by Member States individually, this discipline is the result of action by the Council, based on a Commission recommendation; a discussion and conclusion by the European Council; and the adoption of a recommendation by the Council acting by a qualified majority.[69]

In other words, the institutional arrangements for economic policy recommendations at the third stage resemble the classic Community legislative process, but with four significant exceptions, in addition to the fact that the Commission does not have full power of legislative initiative. First, the European

---

61 Article 109j(1), 1st para. EC.
62 Article 109j(2) EC.
63 Article 109j(3) EC.
64 Article 109j(3) EC.
65 For an economic criticism of the convergence criteria, see B. Eichengreen, *Should the Maastricht Treaty be Saved?*, Princeton Studies in International Finance, No. 74, December 1992, 48-52.
66 Article 109j(4) EC.
67 See Article 103(1) EC.
68 See Article 109e(3), 2nd para. EC. This discipline is discussed later.
69 See Article 103(2) EC.

Council is directly involved. Second, the European Parliament is excluded. Third, the result of the process is not hard legislation but soft law. It is precisely these exceptions, however, which raise significant questions. The first is not new,[70] and the second and third appear to be increasingly common.[71] But together they signal the distinct possibility of a Community which, though already criticized for a 'democracy deficit', runs the risk of serious problems of popular legitimacy.

2. Monetary Union: Central but not Centralized Institutions

With regard to monetary union, the Maastricht Treaty provides for the establishment at the start of the third stage of the European Central Bank (ECB).[72] When the date for the beginning of the third stage has been decided,[73] the Council is to adopt various provisions[74]; and the governments of the Member States without a derogation are to appoint the President, the Vice-President and the other members of the Executive Board of the ECB.[75] This institutional configuration is designed to consecrate formally a differentiated monetary union.

As soon as the Executive Board is appointed, the ESCB and the ECB are deemed to be established and are to prepare for their full operation. The full exercise of their powers starts from the first date of the third stage;[76] this does not apply of course to Member States which do not fulfil the convergence criteria and which have been granted a derogation. The ECB is to have legal personality.[77] As soon as the ECB is established, it will take over the functions of the EMI, and the EMI is to go into liquidation.[78] All assets and liabilities of the EMI then pass automatically to the ECB. The liquidation of the EMI is to be completed by the beginning of the third stage.[79]

The decision-making bodies of the ECB are the Executive Board and the Governing Council.[80] The Executive Board consists of a President, a Vice-President and four other members.[81] All are to be appointed by common accord of the Governments of the Member States at the level of the Heads of State or of Government. They are to be appointed from among persons of recognized standing

---

70   In practice, the European Council has often been involved more or less directly in the Community legislative process in the past: see J. Werts, *The European Council* (1992). Its role has, however, sometimes been controversial: see Case 253/84, *Groupement Agricole d'Exploitation en Commun de la Ségaude* v. *Council*, [1987] ECR 123.
71   See, e.g., Snyder, *Soft Law and Institutional Practice in the European Community*, *supra* note 6.
72   Article 109L(1) EC.
73   Either in accordance with Article 109j(3), or, as the case may be, immediately after 1 July 1998.
74   Referred to in Article 106(6) EC.
75   Article 109L(1), 1st para. EC. If there are Member States with a derogation, the number of members of the Executive Board may be smaller than provided in Article 11.1 of the Statute of the ECB, but in no circumstances is it to be less than four: Article 109L(1), 2nd para. EC. The derogation procedure is discussed later.
76   Article 109L(1), 3rd para. EC.
77   Article 106(2) EC.
78   The modalities of liquidation are laid down in the Statute of the EMI (Article 109L(2)).
79   Protocol on the Statute of the EMI, Article 23(23.1).
80   Article 106(3) EC.
81   Article 109a(2)(a) EC.

and professional experience in monetary or banking matters.[82] The term of office is to be eight years and is not renewable.[83] Only nationals of Member States may be members of the Executive Board.[84] In turn, the Governing Council of the ECB comprises the members of the Executive Board of the ECB and the Governors of the national central banks.[85]

The Executive Board represents the supranational element in the structure of the ECB, while the Governing Board is a mixed supranational and intergovernmental body. These institutions thus represent a transformation of the structure of the EMI towards a greater supranationalism, at least if one takes the procedure of appointment as an index. On the one hand, the supranational element which was represented in the EMI only by the President is enlarged to encompass the entire Executive Board. On the other hand, this supranational element is differentiated as a distinct body and then recombined with the intergovernmental element as the Governing Council. Even in the latter, however, the representatives of national authorities outnumber the members appointed by common accord of the Governments, though the relative weight of the two favours the supranational element more than did the structure of the EMI.

However, within the limits of the ECB powers, the principle of the independence of the ECB from the other EC institutions and the Member States is affirmed clearly in the Treaty. Article 107 states that, when exercising the powers and carrying out the tasks and duties conferred upon them by the Treaty and the Statute of the ESCB, neither the ECB, nor a national central bank, nor any member of their decision-making bodies is to seek or take instructions from Community institutions or bodies, from any government of a Member State or from any other body. In addition, the Community institutions and bodies and the governments of the Member States undertake to respect this principle and not to seek to influence the members of the decision-making bodies of the ECB or of the national central banks in the performance of their tasks.

It has been suggested that, formally speaking, the ECB enjoys greater independence than either the US Federal Reserve or the German Bundesbank.[86] This suggestion has two aspects, which though related need to be carefully distinguished. The first is the relation of the ECB to the Member States, a matter of the Community's quasi-federal structure. The second is the extent to which the ECB is accountable for its actions, a matter involving the issues of democracy and legitimacy. The two aspects are closely related, because, in a Community with a weak parliament, the Council and the governments of the Member States, that is, the

---

82 Article 109(2)(b), 1st para. EC. The appointment must be based on a recommendation from the Council, after it has consulted the European Parliament and the Governing Council of the ECB: ibid.
83 Article 109(2)(b), 2nd para. EC.
84 Article 109(2)(b), 3rd para. EC.
85 Article 109a(1) EC.
86 Giovannini, *supra* note 25 at 10.

intergovernmental elements, are commonly understood to embody the principle of democratic control.[87]

In both respects the ECB is distinctive. As already seen, the representatives of the Member States play a more important role in the ECB in practice than might be thought. A majority of members of the ECB Governing Council are representatives of the national central banks. In addition, the President of the Council, as well as a member of the Commission, is entitled to participate, without having the right to vote, in meetings of the Governing Council of the ECB.[88] The President of the Council may submit a motion for deliberation to the Governing Council of the ECB.[89] Conversely, the President of the ECB is to be invited to participate in Council meetings when the Council is discussing matters relating to the objectives and tasks of the ESCB.[90]

The actions of the ECB which take the form of rules or other regulatory activity are subject to certain controls, discussed later. In addition, the ECB must address an annual report on the activities of the ESCB and on the monetary policy of both the previous and current year to the European Parliament, the Council and the Commission, and also to the European Council. The President of the ECB is to present this report to the Council and to the European Parliament, which may hold a general debate on that basis.[91] At the request of the European Parliament or on their own initiative, the President of the ECB and the other members of the Executive Board may be heard by the competent Committees of the European Parliament.

The ECB, though a Community body, is therefore a complex admixture of Community and intergovernmental elements. The product of compromise, it also diverges substantially from the practice in many Member States with regard to relations between the central bank and political authorities.[92] Not surprisingly, the provisions concerning the ECB have been the subject of much criticism. Yet the ECB is knitted tightly into the Community's intricate set of inter-institutional relations, both vertically and horizontally. As a result, it enjoys a substantial

---

87 An analysis of the extent to which this common conception is justified lies outside the scope of this chapter.
88 Article 109b(1), 1st para. EC.
89 Article 109b(1), 2nd para. EC.
90 Article 109b(2) EC.
91 Article 109b(3) EC.
92 See, e.g., Goodman, 'The Politics of Central Bank Independence', 23 *Comparative Politics* (1991) 329-349; Budekin, Wihlborg and Willett, 'A Monetary Constitution Case for an Independent European Central Bank', 15 *The World Economy* (1992) 231-249; *Vers un système européen de banques centrales: Projet de dispositions organiques* (Rapport du groupe présidé par Jean-Victor Louis) (1990), Annex I.

independence, but one that is to some extent accountable.[93] It deserves to be emphasized, however, that the accountability of the ECB is due less to the (limited) extent to which it is answerable directly to Community political institutions or national governments than to the fact that it is locked into a relatively complex institutional structure and set of inter-institutional relations. In fact, it may be suggested that the ECB is *sui generis* among the institutions thus far established, or to be established, in the Community system.

The relations between the Community and the Member States in the third stage of EMU cannot, however, be evaluated on the basis of the ECB alone. The product of a gradual transformation of institutions, the ECB is also part of a broader institutional configuration, the ESCB.[94] The ESCB is a set of rules and an institutional framework, rather than an institution in itself. It is to be composed of the ECB and of the national central banks.[95] The ESCB will be governed by the decision-making bodies of the ECB, the Executive Board and the Governing Council.[96]

The primary objective of the ESCB is to maintain price stability. Without prejudice to this objective, the ESCB is to support the general economic policies in the Community with a view to contributing to the achievement of the objectives of the Community.[97] In pursuing its objectives, the ESCB is required to act in accordance with the principle of an open market economy with free competition, favouring an efficient allocation of resources, and in compliance with the principles set out in Article 3a, that is, stable prices, sound public finances and monetary conditions, and a sustainable balance of payments.[98] Within this framework, the basic tasks of ESCB are to define and implement the monetary policy of the Community; to conduct foreign exchange operations consistent with the provisions of Article 109; to hold and manage the official foreign reserves of the MS; and to promote the smooth operation of payment systems.[99]

In addition to the ECB and the ESCB, a third institutional transformation is envisaged at the third stage of EMU. The Monetary Committee is to be dissolved[100]

---

93   The expression 'accountable independence' is drawn from Lastra, 'The Independence of the European System of Central Banks', 33 *Harvard International Law Journal*, (1992), 475-519 at 481-482, 519, which discusses this issue in more detail. See also Thygesen, 'Decentralization and Accountability within the Central Bank: Any Lessons from the US Experience for the Potential Organization of a European Central Banking Institution?', in P. De Grauwe and T. Peeters (eds), *The ECU and European Monetary Integration* (1989) 91-114, plus comment by Rey, 115-118.

94   See *Vers un système européen de banques centrales, supra* note 92.

95   Article 106(1) EC. The Statute of the ESCB is laid down in a Protocol annexed to the Treaty: see Article 106(4) EC. According to the Statute of the ESCB, certain related measures remain to be adopted by the Council: see Article 106(6) EC. The Council may also amend specified articles of the ESCB Statute, acting either by a qualified majority on a recommendation from the ECB and after consulting the Comission or unanimously on a proposal from the Commission and after consulting the ECB. In either case the assent of the European Parliament is required: see Article 106(5).

96   Article 106(3) EC.

97   Article 105(1), 1st para. EC. The objectives in question are those laid down in Article 2 EC.

98   Article 105(1), 2nd para. EC.

99   Article 105(2) EC.

100   Article 109c(2), 1st para. EC.

and replaced by the Economic and Financial Committee. Despite the change of name, however, the two committees are very similar in composition and function. The principal difference between them is that the latter is adapted directly to the tasks and institutional setting of the third stage of EMU. As with the Monetary Committee, the Member States and the Commission shall each appoint no more than two members of the Economic and Financial Committee, but two members are to be appointed by the ECB.[101] However, the Council is to lay down detailed provisions concerning the composition of the Committee.[102]

The tasks of the Economic and Financial Committee are fivefold. Its first task is to deliver opinions at the request of the Council or of the Commission, or on its own initiative for submission to those institutions. The second is to keep under review the monetary and financial situation of the Member States and of the Community, and to report regularly to the Council and to the Commission, in particular on financial relations with third countries and international institutions: technically speaking, this international mandate distinguishes the Economic and Financial Committee from the Monetary Committee, but in practice this role has been fulfilled by the Monetary Committee since 1964. The third task is to help to prepare certain work of the Council,[103] as well as to carry out other advisory and preparatory tasks which the Council may assign to it.

Fourth, at least once a year, the Economic and Financial Committee is to examine the situation regarding the movement of capital and the freedom of payments, specifically as they result from the application of the Treaty and of measures adopted by the Council. This exercise is to cover all measures relating to capital movements and payments. The Committee is required to report the results of its examination to the Commission and to the Council.[104] Finally, if and as long as there are Member States with a derogation,[105] the Committee has the task of keeping under review the monetary and financial situation and the general payments system of these Member States and of reporting regularly on their situation to the Council and to the Commission.[106] This task is oriented specifically to the third stage of EMU.

---

101 Article 109c(2), 3rd para. EC.
102 The Council is to act by a qualified majority on a proposal from the Commission and after consulting the ECB and the Committee. The European Parliament is entitled merely to be informed by the President of the Council. See Article 109c(3) EC.
103 In particular, and without prejudice to Article 151, the work of the Council referred to in Articles 73f, 73g, 103(1),(3),(4) and (5), 103a, 104a, 104b, 104c, 109c(2), 109f(6), 109h, 109i, 109j(2) and 109k(2, 109(1)(4) and (5).
104 Article 109c(2), 2nd para. EC.
105 As referred to in Articles 109k and 109l.
106 Article 109c(4) EC.

IV. Rules And Forms Of Regulation

A. Introduction

1. Why is Legal Form Problematic?

EMU involves specific types of rules and forms of regulation. Their novelty and importance can be understood most easily if, by way of introduction, we consider two general issues. The first issue may be expressed as a question: Why is legal (or non-legal) form problematic? The question of legal form has long been a subject of debate in the Community system, but it is especially controversial now because of the Community's 'legitimacy crisis'. This question is discussed in this section; the next section considers the second issue, concerning legal technique.

The types of rules and forms of regulation for implementing EMU were considered in two important reports prior to the Maastricht Treaty. At the June 1988 Hanover summit, the European Council called for the creation of a committee of experts to draw up plans for EMU. The committee was composed mainly of the governors of the national central banks and chaired by EC Commission President Jacques Delors. It concluded that a balance should be struck in the implementation of EMU between reliance on binding rules and discretionary coordination.[107] It proposed 'binding rules in the budgetary field' and 'other arrangements both to limit the scope for divergences between member countries and to design an overall economic policy framework for the Community as a whole'.[108] It thus proposed that binding rules would be used to impose upper limits on national budget deficits, to exclude access to direct central bank credit and other forms of monetary financing, and to limit recourse to external borrowing in non-Community currencies.[109]

The second report was a working document drawn up under the direction of Commission Vice-President Hennig Christophersen. It was a background paper for the pre-Maastricht Intergovernmental Conference on EMU.[110] It noted that, since the publication of the Delors Report, there had been a substantial debate about the part which national budgetary policies should play in achieving a convergence of economic and monetary policies. In its view, the main concern about the possible need for binding rules was the threat to monetary stability due to excessive public deficits and national debts.[111] The latter, as is well known, was of particular concern to Germany. However, the Christophersen Report rejected the idea of binding Community rules concerning ceilings on national budget deficits. It

---

107 Committee for the Study of Economic and Monetary Union, *Report on Economic and Monetary Union in the European Community* (1989) at 17, and 19-20.
108 Ibid., 24.
109 Ibid., 20; see also 24.
110 The main part of this report may be found in *Agence Europe*, 1604/1605, 23 March 1990; the annex to the report is published in *Agence Europe*, 1606, 24 March 1990.
111 See *Agence Europe*, 1604/1605, 23 March 1990, 10.

proposed to rely instead on binding procedures and policy coordination.[112] It also advocated the use of indirect sanctions: for example, a country exceeding agreed limits might be denied automatic access to certain Community aid.[113] In its view, binding rules were justified in only two cases. The first was to prohibit privileged access of national authorities to financial markets. The second was to prevent the guaranteed 'bailing-out' by the Community of countries in budgetary difficulty.[114]

Though focusing of course on EMU, both reports thus dealt with fundamental issues regarding the Community's constitution and institutional structure. Both concerned the nexus of relations between the Community and the Member States, on the one hand, and the relationship between binding rules and market discipline, on the other hand. In other words, both sought to resolve simultaneously the dilemma of how to allocate power in the Community system and the dilemma of how to achieve an acceptable balance between state and market.[115] It is the intersection of these two concerns which, in large part, underlies the intricate combination of supranational and intergovernmental elements in EMU.

Since the Maastricht Treaty was signed, the institutional, economic and political implications of different types of rules and forms of regulation have assumed even greater prominence. The Danish and French referenda raised questions concerning the meaning of 'subsidiarity', not only in the sense of Article 3b of the Maastricht Treaty,[116] but also in the more general sense of the distribution of political power and regulatory authority between the Community and the Member States. The Sutherland Report on the future operation of the internal market, which was presented to the Council in autumn 1992, reconsidered the relationship between legally binding norms and instruments which were not legally binding.[117] Then, in October 1992 the Commission made a communication to the Council and the European Parliament. It stated that subsidiarity involved not only the concept of subsidiarity *stricto sensu*, namely the question as to who should exercise legislative power. It also embraced the concept of proportionality, that is, the question as to whether and how the power should be exercised.[118]

---

112   See *Agence Europe*, 1603/1605, 23 March 1990, 10. The distinction between binding substantive rules and binding procedures, as well as the distribution of political power which is involved in each alternative, is indicated neatly in Joined Cases 281, 283-285, 287/85, *Germany, France, the Netherlands, Denmark and the United Kingdom* v. *Commission*, [1987] ECR 3203.

113   See also *La Libre Belgique*, 21 March 1990, 13; compare the report in *Les Echos*, 21 March 1990, 2.

114   In other words, the Community would not guarantee such aid, but this would not exclude *ad hoc* assistance: *Agence Europe*, 1604/1605, 23 March 1990, 10. See also *Les Echos*, 21 March 1990, 2.

115   That is, acceptable to the twelve Member States.

116   See Constantinesco, 'Who's Afraid of Subsidiarity?', 11 *Yearbook of European Law* (1991) 33-55; R. Dehousse, *Does Subsidiarity Really Matter?*, EUI Working Paper in Law No. 92/32 (1992); Emiliou, 'Subsidiarity: An Effective Barrier against "the Enterprises of Ambition"', 43 *European Law Review* (1992) 383-407; Toth, 'The Principle of Subsidiarity in the Maastricht Treaty', 29 *Common Market Law Review* (1992) 1079-1105.

117   See 'The Internal Market after 1992: Meeting the Challenge Report to the EEC Commission by the High Level Group on the Operation of the Internal Market' (1992).

118   See Commission of the European Communities, 'The principle of subsidiarity: Communication of the Commission to the Council and the European Parliament', SEC(92)1990 final, Brussels, 27 October 1992.

The Commission interpreted the concept of proportionality as meaning that priority should be given to measures which are not legally binding, that is, to soft law.[119] While the use of soft law is of course only one way of implementing the concept of subsidiarity, this general interpretation has been accepted by the European Parliament, the Member States and the European Council.[120] The proposal by the Commission for an inter-institutional agreement with the Council and the European Parliament on this basis has also been accepted by the European Parliament and the Member States.[121] The priority to be given to soft law thus appears to form one of the guidelines for the application of the subsidiarity principle and Article 3b of the Maastricht Treaty.[122]

The principle of subsidiarity was intended initially as a response to calls for greater democracy in Community decision-making.[123] As expressed in the Maastricht Treaty, and as now commonly understood, it is designed in principle to allocate more decision-making power to the Member States.[124] In both respects, however, its practical implementation in EMU may have perverse, unintended consequences. Hence the paradox of subsidiarity.[125] On the one hand, the increasing use of soft law may lead to the implementation of EMU by means of singularly untransparent Community instruments. On the other hand, it may mean in practice that Community action, when taken, is increasingly discretionary and is subject only with difficulty to legal controls. The choice of soft law as a (legal) form may give priority to efficiency at the expense of legality and legitimacy.

2. Phased Obligations

A second general issue concerns legal technique. The implementation of EMU involves a specific legal technique that is unusual, if not unknown, elsewhere in the Community system. This technique can be called 'phased obligations'.[126] The

---

119   See Commission of the European Communities, *supra* note 119, at 4, 5, 14.
120   See Conclusions of the Presidency, European Council in Edinburgh, 11-12 December 1992, Annex I to Part A, 'Overall Approach to the Application by the Council of the Subsidiarity Principle and Article 3b of the Treaty on European Union, esp. 9: 'The form of action should be as simple as possible, consistent with satisfactory achievement of the objective of the measure and the need for effective enforcement. The Community should legislate only to the extent necessary. Other things being equal, directives should be preferred to regulations and framework directives to detailed measures. Non-binding measures such as recommendations should be preferred where appropriate. Consideration should be given where appropriate to the use of voluntary codes of conduct.'
121   See Conclusions of the Presidency, European Council in Edinburgh, 11-12 December 1992, Annex I to Part A, 'Overall Approach to the Application by the Council of the Subsidiarity Principle and Article 3b of the Treaty on European Union', 9. On the Commission proposal for an inter-institutional agreement, see Commission of the European Communities, *supra* note 119.
122   See also 'Subsidiarité: Nouveau code de conduite pour construire l'Europe', 172 *EURinfo* (1993) 12-13.
123   See, e.g., M. Wilke, H. Wallace, *Subsidiarity: Approaches to Power-sharing in the European Community*, RIIA Discussion Papers 27 (1990).
124   This in itself represents a substantial change from the original principle.
125   See further Snyder, *Soft Law and Institutional Practice in the European Community*, *supra* note 6, at 6-9, on which this paragraph is based.
126   The question of potential parallels with obligations in international law is intriguing but lies outside the scope of this chapter.

expression 'phased obligations' refers to two or more different legal obligations which require distinct types of compliance at different times, but which, when seen as part of a series in the graduated (or phased) implementation of regulatory policy, constitute an integrated whole. From the legal standpoint each obligation can be analysed separately, but the social, economic or political meaning of each obligation becomes apparent only when the obligations are considered together. If we consider the obligations as a series, and it is only from this perspective that they really make sense, it is apparent that each obligation is merely a step toward the achievement of a single objective.

The technique of phased obligations can be illustrated briefly by the evolution of Community controls on privileged government access to national financial markets and institutions. In the first phase of EMU Member States are obliged merely to make any necessary changes in their national laws.[127] The prohibition under Community law on any measure, not based on prudential considerations, establishing privileged relations between public authorities to financial institutions comes into effect only at the beginning of the second stage.[128] Each of these two steps involves a different legal obligation, but each makes sense only if the two are considered as a whole and as part of the implemention of a single regulatory policy.

The technique of phased obligations represents a relatively pure form of law in the service of policy. We can clarify this assertion by imagining a scenario which perhaps is close to the reality of EMU. Suppose that the policy-maker sets a goal, but decides that the achievement of the goal in one fell swoop is politically impossible. The policy-maker therefore divides the gap to be bridged between present reality and future goal into numerous small steps. It identifies a series of policies which, when added together, would reach the goal. Then it asks the drafters of the legislation to express the series of policies in legal terms. The result is a series of phased obligations. Each obligation is legally discrete, but a single obligation does not really make sense on its own, at least if it is viewed, as it is intended to be, teleologically or in terms of regulatory policy. The series of phased obligations thus is a relatively direct reflection in legal terms of the evolution of policy. The integrity of the former mirrors that of the latter: the legal obligations must be grasped by means of a teleological analysis, and their significance only appears clearly when the parts are viewed as a whole.

The novelty of this technique may be highlighted by a brief comparison to a technique in the Rome Treaty which, on a superficial view, may appear similar. The Rome Treaty provided for the progressive abolition of customs duties on imports. The relevant provisions encompassed an obligation to abolish progressively customs duties on imports and a fixed timetable for specific and progressive reductions.[129] These provisions were oriented toward a specific goal, constituted a

---

127 See Article 109e(1), (2)(a), 1st indent EC.
128 See Articles 104a(1), 109(3).
129 See, respectively, Articles 13(1) and 14 EEC. Two closely related provisions are Articles 12 and 15, which, respectively, contain a standstill clause and provide the possibility of partial or total

whole, and only made sense when viewed as such. They can be analysed either as a single legal obligation or as a series of discrete obligations. On the one hand, they may be said to involve only one legal obligation, namely to abolish progressively customs duties on imports; Article 14 thus simply states a timetable for fulfilling this obligation. On the other hand, the general obligation and each of the steps in the timetable may be considered as a discrete obligation, so that, taken together, they constitute a series. On either analysis, however, this legal technique differs from the technique of phased obligations in EMU. If one accepts the first analysis, there is a single obligation, not a series. If one accepts the second, the obligations, though differing in degree, are essentially of the same type. In contrast, the phased obligations involved in EMU are a series of discrete obligations of different types: only when viewed as the expression of policy do they constitute a whole.

The use of phased obligations in the implementation of EMU, it may be suggested, is related directly to two broader factors. On the one hand, EMU concerns matters of great technical complexity, upon which the various Member States hold very different views. On the other hand, it involves an intricate distribution of power between the Member States and the Community. Consequently, the design and implementation of EMU are inevitably the result of compromise. The agreed legal provisions create different types of obligations, established by various institutions and involving action at different levels of the divided-power system, which ideally are to be combined to form a coherent agreed policy over a specified period of time. The technique of phased obligations provides a means by which the law can express, channel and crystallize the gradual evolution of a negotiated complex policy. In the circumstances, just as the choice of legal form, it aims to reconcile the demands of supranationalism and intergovern-mentalism.

suspension of customs duties. In my view, however, they are separable. First, not only are they distinct legal obligations; they are also potentially discrete in terms of economic policy. Second, they do not necessarily form part of a series which also includes Articles 13(1) and 14.

B. Stage One: New Legal Techniques for a New Context

1. Hard National Adaptation and Community Soft Law

During the first stage of EMU, the principal normative instruments with regard to economic policy are twofold: first, the requirement to adapt national legislation to Community norms; and, second, types of soft law.

With regard to economic policy, the Maastricht Treaty to some extent adopted the view of the Delors Committee concerning legally binding rules regarding national budgetary discipline, but in a highly differentiated way. The basic technique for ensuring minimum convergence of national law within a Community framework is that of phased obligations.[130] The Treaty provisions establish a prohibition. This provides a legal framework, in which policy objectives are expressed more or less directly in Community law. During the first stage, however, Member States are required to adapt their national legislation or take other measures if necessary to comply. Only at the second stage does the prohibition itself become legally binding.

An example is the prohibition on overdraft or other credit facilities in favour of public authorities.[131] During the first stage of EMU Member States are required, again by express Treaty provisions, to adapt their national legislation or take other appropriate measures to comply with the prohibition. The decision as to whether such measures are necessary is left to the individual Member States. It is subject to their obligations, under Article 103(1), to regard their economic policies as a matter of common concern and to coordinate them within the Council, and also to the Article 5 fidelity clause. It is also to be taken within the general economic discipline of the Council and the European Council and monitoring by the Commission.[132] The prohibition itself applies only in the second stage. However, the Member States tend to consider, at least in this instance, that they need take no action until the second stage.[133] This suggests that the effectiveness of the technique of phased obligations may be open to question.

A second normative instrument is soft law. For example, Member States are required to regard their economic policies as a matter of common concern and to coordinate them within the Council.[134] Broad guidelines of the economic policies of the Member States are to be formulated by the Council, acting by a qualified majority on a recommendation from the Commission. These guidelines are to be reported to the European Council, which is to discuss a conclusion. On the basis of this conclusion by the European Council, the Council (of the European

---

130 Note the similarity to Community directives. The difference between phased obligations and directives is, of course, that phased obligations involve two or more different obligations established by Community law, while the temporal sequence envisaged by directives involves first Community legislation and then national transposition.
131 See Articles 104(1), 109e(2)(a), 1st indent EC.
132 As set out in Article 103(2)-(5).
133 Personal communication from Professor Jean-Victor Louis.
134 Article 103(1) EC.

Communities) is to adopt a recommendation setting out these broad guidelines. It must inform the European Parliament of these guidelines.[135]

The types of norms with regard to monetary policy during the first stage of EMU are similar, though less transparent. According to its earlier rules of procedure,[136] the Committee of Governors could issue opinions, present communications or make reports. These acts were not however formal acts within the EC legal system. They were rarely published and were generally not available to the public. The current rules of procedure of the Committee do not specify types of acts.[137] However, Council Decision 90/142 provides that the Committee may formulate opinions on the overall orientation of monetary and exchange rate policy as well as on the respective measures introduced in individual Member States; express opinions to individual governments and the Council of Ministers on monetary policies and the functioning of the EMS; and prepare an annual report.[138]

Similarly, the Monetary Committee may deliver opinions, either at the request of the Council or the Commission or on its own initiative for submission to those institutions.[139] As in the past, these opinions may concern the overall orientation of monetary and exchange rate policy as well as the respective measures introduced in individual Member States. The Committee may also express opinions to individual governments and the Council of Ministers on policies which might affect the internal and external monetary situation in the Community and, in particular, the functioning of the EMS.[140] Thus even prior to Maastricht this form of soft law was used in the Community system.[141]

2. Policy Coordination and Multilateral Surveillance

The main forms of regulation during the first stage of EMU are policy coordination and multilateral surveillance. The phased obligations and soft law in this stage both employ the coordination of national policies as a form of regulation. In addition, however, the Council, acting on the basis of reports by the Commission, is to

---

135 See Article 103(2) EC.
136 Règlement intérieur du 12 octobre 1964 du Comité des Gouverneurs des Banques centrales des Etats membres de la Communauté économique européenne, in Comité Monétaire de la Communautée Européenne, *Compendium des textes communautaires en matière monétaire* (1989).
137 See Rules of Procedure of the Committee of Governors of the Central Banks of the European Economic Community (1990).
138 Council Decision 90/142/EEC of 12 March 1990, *supra* note 31.
139 Article 109c(1) EC.
140 Council Decision 90/142, *supra* note 31.
141 Though the opinions of the Monetary Committee are sometimes reported in the specialist press, there is no specific requirement that they be brought to the attention of the European Parliament, for example. However, the Committee is required to prepare an annual repport on its activities, which is transmitted to the European Parliament, the Council of Ministers and the European Council. The President of the Committee may also be invited to appear before the European Parliament on this occasion and also before the competent European Parliament committee where the circumstances so justify: see Council Decision 64/300, Article 3, 3rd para., as replaced by Council Decision 90/142 of 12 March 1990, *supra* note 31.

monitor economic developments in the Member States and assess their consistency with the broad guidelines. This form of regulation is premised on the idea that

> [t]hrough learning by doing, multilateral surveillance should increasingly result in compatible policies, with precise and appropriate commitments by the Member States.[142]

If the economic policies of a Member State are not consistent with these broad guidelines, or if they risk jeopardizing the proper functioning of economic and monetary union, the Council[143] may issue recommendations to the Member State concerned. This multilateral surveillance is usually to be undertaken by the Council meeting in restricted session. However, the Council President may also be authorized by the Council[144] to make the recommendations public. The President is to report on the results to the European Parliament. The procedure of multilateral surveillance, as already noted, is not new in the Community system.[145] What is new, however, is that this procedure is to be used to ensure respect for the broad guidelines, a form of soft law adopted by the Council in the form of a recommendation following a conclusion by the European Council.[146]

It is worth emphasizing that the European Parliament has no role in either the formulation of the guidelines or in their application. It is simply informed by the European Council, at a stage when the guidelines have already been formulated by the Council and a recommendation adopted by the European Council. It also receives a report from the President of the Council and the Commission on the results of multilateral surveillance. Broadly similar procedures apply in the event that a Member State finds itself in economic difficulty.[147]

C. Stage Two: Strange Admixtures and Curious Conjunctions

1. Economic Union: Phased Obligations and Supranational Monitoring

In the second phase of EMU Member States are subject to stronger obligations, though these are highly differentiated, phased in their application or couched in the form of soft law. These norms are put into practice by means of forms of regulation which sometimes blur any distinction between supranational and national forms.

The technique of phased obligations assumes special prominence in the second phase. One example is the prohibition on overdraft or other credit facilities with national central banks. While previously the Member States were required simply to adjust their national legislation if necessary, the prohibition itself comes into force at the beginning of the second stage.[148] However, the best example of the use of

---

142 Council Decision 90/141/EEC of 12 March 1990, *supra* note 29.
143 Acting by qualified majority on a Commission recommendation.
144 Acting by a qualified majority on a Commission proposal.
145 See Council Decision 90/141/EEC of 12 March 1990, *supra* note 29.
146 See also Louis, *supra* note 8, at 263.
147 See Article 103a EC.
148 See Articles 104(a, 109(e)(2), 1st indent EC.

phased obligations concerns the extremely sensitive matter of national budget deficits; here it is used in conjunction with differentiated types of norms and regulatory techniques.

During the second stage Member States are required merely to endeavour to avoid excessive government deficits.[149] The outright prohibition on excessive deficits, expressed in Article 104c(1), does not apply until the beginning of the third stage.[150]

In the second stage the use of phased obligations with regard to budget deficits is accompanied by recourse to supranational institutions, in particular the Commission, rather than simply Member State action or coordination by the Council. During the second stage the government deficits of Member States are subject to Commission monitoring. In the event of national non-compliance with specified criteria,[151] the Commission must (or, in certain other circumstances, may) prepare a report. On the basis of this report the Monetary Committee is to formulate an opinion. In addition, if the Commission considers that an excessive deficit in a Member State exists or may occur, the Commission is required to address an opinion to the Council.

The sanctions which may be used by the Council depend on the particular stage of EMU. During the second stage, the Council, acting by a qualified majority on a Commission recommendation, and after hearing the Member State, must decide whether an excessive deficit exists. If the decision is affirmative, the Council must make recommendations to the Member State concerned. Subsequently, if the Council considers that there has been no effective action in response to its recommendations during the period laid down, it may make the recommendations public.[152] In the third stage, however, the Council may decide on much more severe sanctions; these are discussed later.

2. Monetary Union: 'Official' Soft Law

Concerning monetary policy, only soft law measures are used, as in the first stage. During the second stage, however, these measures are taken by a different institution, that is, the EMI rather than the Committee of Governors. Moreover, the EMI is now mandated to take acts within the meaning of Article 189 EEC, even though these acts are not legally binding.

Acting by a majority of two-thirds of the members of its Council, the EMI may formulate opinions or recommendations. These concern the overall orientation of monetary policy and exchange rate policy, as well as on related measures introduced

149   Article 109e(4) EC.
150   See Article 109e(3) EC. The prohibition is expressed in Article 104c(1) EC.
151   On the criteria, see Article 104c(2), first para. (a) EC. The reference values for determining compliance with the budgetary procedure are provided in the Protocol on the Excessive Deficit Procedure, annexed to the Treaty: see Article 104c(2), 2nd para.
152   See Article 104c(6)-(8) EC.

in each Member State.[153] The EMI may also submit opinions or recommendations to governments and to the Council on policies which might affect the internal or external monetary situation in the Community and, in particular, the functioning of the European Monetary System. These powers restate almost verbatim those which can be exercised by the Committee of Governors of the Central Banks during the first stage.[154] In addition, however, the EMI can make recommendations to the monetary authorities of the Member States concerning the conduct of their monetary policy.[155] Acting unanimously, the EMI may decide to publish its opinions and its recommendations.[156]

With regard to the types of rules, this stage thus represents a 'routinization' or 'juridicization' of soft law, in that soft law is officially recognizsed as a regular form of normative act. The EMI acts in a way which begins to approach that of other main Community institutions, though for the latter the use of rules which are not legally binding still remains the exception. This stage of EMU gives birth to a public rule-making institution that is quite different from the much less public, more specialised roles of the Committee of Governors (or the Monetary Committee) in the first stage.

C. Stage Three: Toward Hard Law in a Differentiated Regulatory System

1. 'National' Economic Policies within a Community Framework

With the beginning of the third stage of EMU, Member States will be subject with regard to economic policy to a variety of obligations expressed in hard legal form.[157] For example, they will be required to avoid excessive government deficits,[158] whereas in the second stage they were required simply to endeavour to avoid such deficits.[159] Though Member States continue to be responsible for economic policy, they are now required to exercise their powers within a framework established in large part by means of Community procedures and often involving Community institutions.

To take the example of budgetary discipline: not only is the obligation expressed to be one of hard law; it may also be enforced by means of sanctions imposed by Community institutions, namely the Council, and without a unanimous vote. In the event of a persistent refusal by a Member State to put into practice Council recommendations to end a situation of an excessive government deficit, the Council

---

153 On the legal effects of recommendations, see Case C-322/88, *Grimaldi* v. *Fonds des Maladies Professionnelles*, [1989] ECR 4407.
154 See Council Decision 90/142/EEC of 12 March 1990, *supra* note 31, amending Decision 64/300/EEC with a new Article 3(4),(5).
155 Article 109f(4) EC.
156 Article 109f(5). The analogous provision regarding the Committee of Governors during the first stage was couched in less direct terms: see Council Decision 90/142/EEC, *supra* note 31, amending Decision 64/300/EEC by a new Article 3, para. 3.
157 See Article 109e(3) EC.
158 Article 104c(1), Article 109e(3), 2nd para. EC.

may decide to give notice to a Member State to take necessary measures to remedy this failure. It may request the Member State to submit reports according to a specific timetable.[160] Enforcement actions by the Commission under Article 169 or by Member States under Article 170 cannot, however, be brought in the event of failure to comply with the notice or with less stringent measures.[161]

As long as a Member State fails to comply, the Council may also decide to apply or intensify a variety of more serious measures.[162] It may require a Member State to publish specified additional information before issuing bonds and securities; invite the European Investment Bank to reconsider its lending policy with regard to the Member State; require the Member State to make a non-interest-bearing deposit of an appropriate size with the Community until, in the view of the Council, the excessive deficit has been cured; or impose fines of an appropriate size. Such measures are to be taken by the Council, on a Commission recommendation, by a two-thirds majority vote, weighted in accordance with Article 148(2) but excluding the votes of the Member State concerned.[163] If any of these severe sanctions were ever to be taken, however, the Council President would be required only to inform the European Parliament.[164]

2. Centralized Institutions and Hard Law in a Monetary Union

In the third stage the developing centralized institutions for monetary policy will also be able to use hard law. The ECB will have the power to make legally binding acts within its sphere of activity. Article 108a(1) provides that in order to carry out the tasks entrusted to the ESCB, the ECB shall (a) make regulations to the extent necessary for the conduct of monetary policy or for its regulatory tasks and in cases which shall be laid down in the specified acts of the Council[165]; (b) take decisions necessary for carrying out the tasks entrusted to the ESCB; and (c) make recommendations and deliver opinions. The acts of the ECB have the same legal force as similar acts of other Community institutions.[166] They are also subject to the same requirements concerning the duty to state reasons, publication and enforcement. The legally binding acts of the ECB are subject to judicial review.[167] Conversely, the ECB may seek judicial review on the same footing as the European Parliament, namely for the purpose of protecting its prerogatives.[168]

National central banks are an integral part of the ESCB. They are legally required in the third stage to act in accordance with the guidelines and instructions

---

159 Article 109e(4) EC.
160 Articles. 104c(9), 109e(3) EC.
161 Article 104c(10) EC.
162 Article 109e(3). EC.
163 Article 104c(13) EC.
164 Article 104c(9) EC.
165 Those referred to in Article 106(6) EC.
166 See Article 108a(2), which is identical to Article 189.
167 Article 173(1) EC.
168 173(3) EC.

of the ECB. The Governing Council of the ECB is empowered to take the necessary steps to ensure compliance with the guidelines and instructions of the ECB, and to require that any necessary information be given to it.[169] The ECB is entitled to invoke against national central banks the special enforcement procedure, according to which the Court of Justice has jurisdiction in disputes concerning the fulfilment by national central banks of obligations under the Treaty. In this respect, the powers of the ECB in respect of national central banks are to be the same as the Commission's Article 169 powers in respect of Member States.[170] In addition, the ECB is entitled, within certain limits, to impose fines or periodic penalty payments on undertakings for failing to comply with obligations under its regulations and decisions.[171] By these provisions, the ECB is assimilated functionally into the category of major Community institutions.[172]

3. The Role of Member States, In and Outside EMU

The regulation of monetary policy in the third stage thus occurs by Community institutions or within a framework established by Community institutions. Nevertheless, Member States continue to play a role, though mainly through the Council, that is, within a Community institution rather than individually or within a non-Community, intergovernmental framework.

The most significant aspect concerns exchange rates and external monetary policy. The Council may conclude formal agreements on an exchange-rate system for the ECU in relation to non-Community currencies.[173] It may also adopt, adjust or abandon the central rates of the ECU within the exchange-rate system.[174] In the absence of such an exchange-rate system, the Council may formulate general orientations for exchange-rate policy in relation to these currencies.[175] Finally, the Council is also to decide the arrangements for the negotiation and conclusion of agreements concerning monetary or foreign-exchange regime matters with third

---

169 Protocol on the Statute of the ESCB and the ECB, Article 14.3.
170 Article 180(d) EC. If the Court of Justice finds that a national central bank has failed to fulfil an obligation under the Treaty, the bank is required to take the necessary measures to comply with the decision of the Court of Justice: ibid.
171 See Article 108a(3) EC.
172 It is not however included legally in the category of Community institutions in the sense of Article 4 EEC.
173 See Article 109(1) EEC. This requires unanimity in the Council, and the Council must act on a recommendation from the ECB or from the Commission. It must also consult both the European Parliament and the ECB, the latter in particular to try to reach a consensus consistent with the objective of price stability.
174 Article 109(1) EC. This may be done by the Council acting by a qualified majority on a recommendation from the ECB, or on a recommendation from the Commission and after consulting the ECB.
175 Article 109(2). In this case, the Council may act by a qualified majority, either on a recommendation from the ECB or on a recommendation from the Commission and after consulting the ECB. These general orientations must be without prejudice to the primary objective of the ESCB to maintain price stability.

countries or international organizations.[176] These agreements are binding on the EC institutions, the ECB and the Member States.[177] Thus, even within EMU, the Member States retain an important role with regard to exchange rate policy.[178]

With regard to monetary union, however, the implications of the third stage differ fundamentally according to whether a given Member State has met the convergence criteria or has been granted a derogation. The Maastricht Treaty sets forth in Chapter 4 various transitional provisions concerning Member States which do not fulfil the necessary conditions for the adoption of a single currency. The basic provision is Article 109k(1). If the decision has been taken to set the date for movement to the third stage, the Council must decide whether any Member States are to have a derogation. The decision is to be taken by qualified majority, following a Commission recommendation.[179] If a date has not been set, however,[180] and the Council has confirmed which Member States fulfil the necessary conditions for the adoption of a single currency, the Member States which do not fulfil the conditions are to have a derogation.[181]

This derogation entails the exclusion of the Member State concerned, and its national central bank, from rights and obligations within the ESCB.[182] Most importantly, the central banks of Member States with a derogation retain their powers in the field of monetary policy according to national law.[183] In addition, certain articles of the Maastricht Treaty do not apply to these Member States,[184] and the voting rights of these Member States are suspended with regard to related Council decisions.[185]

The Maastricht Treaty provides for the eventual abrogation of the derogation. At least once every two years, or at the request of a Member State with a derogation, the Commission and the ECB are to report to the Council. Following specified procedures, the Council is to decide which Member States with a derogation fulfil the criteria set down in Article 109j(1) and abrogate the derogation.[186]

---

176 Article 109(3), 1st para. In this case the Council may act by a qualified majority on a recommendation from the Commission and after consulting the ECB.
177 Article 109(3), 2nd para. EC.
178 For a criticism of this role, see Eichengreen, *supra* note 7, at 58-59, 62.
179 Article 109k(1), 1st para. EC. The nature of the derogation is defined in the 3rd paragraph of this Article. The decision to set the date is to be taken as provided in Article 109j(3).
180 In which case Article 109f(4) applies.
181 See Article 109k(1), 2nd para. EC. In either event, such Member States shall be referred to as 'Member States with a derogation': Article 109k(1), 1st and 2nd paras. EC.
182 Article 109k(3) EC. The exclusion of these Member States and their national central banks from rights and obligations within the ESCB is laid down in Chapter IX of the Statute of the ESCB: see Article 109k(3) EC. Numerous articles of the ESCB Statute do not confer any rights or impose any obligations on the Member States concerned: see Protocol on the Statute of the ESCB, Article 43(43.1).
183 Protocol on the Statute of the ESCB, Article 43(43.2).
184 Article 109k(3) EC.
185 See Article 109k(5) EC. The provisions in question are Articles 104c(9) and (11), 105(1),(2) and (5), 105a, 108a, 109 and 109a(2)(b): Article 109k(3) EC.
186 Article 109k(2) EC.

The institutional implications of the third stage are also potentially distinctive for two other countries, the United Kingdom and Denmark.[187] From the institutional standpoint, provisions which are broadly similar to those concerning Member States with a derogation apply to these two Member States if they notify the Council that they do not intend to move to the third stage.[188] In this event, they will not participate in the institutional arrangements for EMU, and their relevant national laws will continue to apply. However, both Member States retain the right to change their notification.[189] Under the compromise agreed at the European Council in Edinburgh in December 1992, Denmark gave notice that it will not participate in the third stage. It also stated, however, that it may inform other Member States that it no longer wishes to avail itself of this decision.[190] These provisions, perhaps more than any other, illustrate the extent to which EMU is the result of compromise as well as the potential institutional complexity of the European Union.

V. Conclusion

This paper has aimed neither to give a systematic description of the Maastricht Treaty provisions concerning EMU, nor to evaluate the likelihood of the implementation of EMU, either according to the Treaty provisions or in another way. Instead its purposes were twofold. The first was to illuminate the gradual development of institutions, rules and forms of regulation during the three stages of EMU. The second, based on these selected aspects, was to conceive of EMU as a metaphor for the new European Union. Any conclusion of such an exercise is bound to be partial, if only because of the difficulty of generalizing about the Community on the basis of one, albeit an important one, of its component parts.

On the one hand, EMU is the result of compromises between different interests and different conceptions, first with regard to the appropriate relationship between market and state, second with regard to the allocation of power within the

---

187 Portugal, France and Denmark retain certain powers with regard to monetary policy in overseas regions or territories or in territories which are not part of the Community: see Protocol on Portugal, Protocol on France and Protocol on Denmark annexed to the TEU.
188 See Protocol on Certain Provisions relating to the United Kingdom of Great Britain and Northern Ireland; Protocol on Certain Provisions relating to Denmark.
189 On the United Kingdom, see Protocol on Certain Provisions relating to the United Kingdom of Great Britain and Northern Ireland, Article 10.
190 See Annex I, Decision of the Heads of State and Government, Meeting within the European Council, concerning 'Certain Problems Raised by Denmark on the Treaty on European Union', Section B(1), (2), Section E(2), in 'Denmark and the Treaty on European Union', *Agence Europe*, 5878 (spec.ed.), Sunday, 13 December 1992. In the former case, Denmark will not participate in the single currency, will not be bound by the rules concerning economic policy which apply only to the Member States participating in the third stage of economic and monetary union, and will retain its existing powers in the field of monetary policy according to its national laws and regulations, including the powers of the National Bank of Denmark in the filed of monetary policy. In the latter case, Denmark will apply in full all relevant measures then in force taken within the framework of the European Union: ibid.

Community's divided-power system, and third with regard specifically to economic and monetary union. These compromises are embodied in the detailed provisions of the Maastricht Treaty. Their most striking reflection is the attempt in EMU to reconcile supranational and intergovernmental organizational models and methods of decision-making. This is illustrated especially in the structural distinction between economic policy-making (economic union) and monetary policy-making (monetary union).

The institutions to be developed in the course of achieving economic union and monetary union, respectively, reveal this distinction clearly. Table I shows the institutional aspects of economic union. Table II shows the institutional development in monetary union.

Table I

Institutional Development in Economic Union

(main institutions only)

Stage	National Level	Community Level
I	Member States	Council
II	Member States	Council, Commission
III	Member States	Council, Commission European Council

Table II

Institutional Development in Monetary Union

Stage	Regulatory Institutions	Advisory Institutions	Systematic Institutions or Arrangements
I	Committee of Governors of Central Banks of the Member States	Monetary Committee	[Council]
II	European Monetary Institute	Monetary Committee	[Council]
III	European Central Bank	Economic and Financial Committee	European System of Central Banks

Table III

Rules and Forms of Regulation during the Stages of EMU

Stage	Types of Rules and Forms of Regulation	
	Economic Policy	Monetary Policy
I	soft law policy coordination phased obligations multilateral surveillance	intergovernmental soft law
II	soft law phased obligations supranational surveillance	mixed 'official' soft law
III	phased obligations hard law community framework, procedures and sanctions	hard law

As a comparison of these tables indicates, economic union is designed primarily to make use of existing institutions, while monetary union envisages the creation of new institutions.

Francis Snyder

The types of rules and forms of regulation are also expected to change substantially during the implementation of EMU. Table III indicates the main changes.

It delineates clearly the development of Community hard law concerning monetary policy. It also shows that, while Member States remain responsible for economic policy, they are increasingly subject to a Community framework, including legally binding rules. [191]

On the other hand, envisaged as a metaphor, EMU suggests a new European Community of almost bewildering variety. It means a new division of labour between the Community, the Member States, other levels of government, and other organizations. Using these categories, it is relatively easy to distinguish between the main loci of power with regard to economic policy and monetary policy. Even within each of these areas, however, EMU involves a complex allocation of power and decision-making authority. As other chapters in this book indicate, the development of an increasingly complicated division of legal labour in the Community system is not unique to EMU.

An example of this phenomenon within EMU is the tendency to draw into the Community system institutions which were established originally on the periphery of the four main institutions. First, they are endowed with specific tasks but in a new context, and eventually they are transformed into bodies which, like the main institutions, must be politically accountable and supervised by the courts. This process raises special difficulties with regard to the openness and transparency of decision-making processes and the accountability and legitimacy of these institutions.

Another example is the potential which is inherent in EMU for the development of a two-speed Europe. The distinction at the third stage between Member States which are included and those with a derogation at least presumes a common goal. The special provisions for the United Kingdom and Denmark, however, are of a different nature. They provide expressly for the possibility that, for reasons other than economic criteria, a Member State may choose not to participate in common institutional arrangements. The compromise reached at Edinburgh concerning Denmark is especially complex, first because the legal nature of the instrument in which it is expressed is not entirely clear, and second because of the provisions themselves express an eventual recognition of a purely political decision.

The emerging institutional configuration involves new types of rules and forms of regulation. EMU represents a logical extension of existing trends in the Community system toward a complex admixture of rules, including guidelines and other forms of soft law, more or less binding expert opinions, and the production of

191 In the words of the Christophersen report, '[t]here does not have to be one economic policy in EMU in the same way as there has to be one monetary policy': supra note 22 at 8. On other models, see ibid., at 4-6, which concludes [at 6] that 'Credibility and stability demand that there is a single monetary policy... On the economic side, considerably fewer economic powers are needed at the centre than is the case in any existing economic and monetary union.'

hard law by new institutions. It also stands for the development of new hybrid forms of regulation, involving complex networks of relations between Community institutions and between the Community and the Member States. It is important, however, that these not only be workable in practice but also that they be legally coherent. Only time will tell whether the Maastricht Treaty provisions regarding EMU are sufficient for these purposes.

One final point emerges if one considers EMU as a metaphor. In a Community which long has been dominated by instrumentalist logic, EMU represents both a means and an end. Does this suggest that the constitutional structure of the Community/Union is not just becoming more complex but also tending toward confusion? [192] An analysis of the institutions, rules and forms of regulation involved in EMU indicates the importance of reconsidering European Community constitutional law. This is especially the case when one takes into account the increasing diversity of matters within the ambit of both the Community and the Member States. It is accentuated by the tendency to express in the Community's constitution many matters which in national legal systems would be left in part to secondary legislation. The relationship between a written constitution and civil society is frequently controversial. But it is one thing for a political and legal system to develop in ways which differ substantially from the views of the founders. This process is surely unavoidable. It is quite another for a system which is concerned to enhance its legitimacy and democratic character to tend toward constitutional incoherence. Envisaged as a metaphor, however, instead of evaluating the merits of either the end or the means EMU suggests that it is time for a fundamental rethinking of the nature and role of the Community's constitution.

Consequently, if we think of EMU as a metaphor for European Union, it seems clear that our conception of the European Union needs to be substantially revised. EMU may present a vision of a future European Union, but it provides a lens that resembles a kaleidoscope more than a telescope. By looking into it, we can see that EMU as set out in the Maastricht Treaty is the result of many, often highly technical compromises. One should not be surprised, therefore, that the metaphorical meaning of EMU is partial, incomplete and sometimes inconsistent. Precisely because of the central significance of EMU in the European Union, however, it is essential to begin to draw the emerging elements of the Community's constitution together. We need to elaborate a new vision of the totality of the Community's structure. Though this task is far beyond the scope of this paper, its significance lies in the fact that the European Community is not merely a special-purpose association (*Zweckverband*), a legal and administrative machine. As the debate about EMU has demonstrated, the Community is becoming a political system with a European political and legal culture.

---

192   On the historical development, see Weiler, 'The Transformation of Europe', 100 *Yale Law Journal* (1991) 2403-2483.

Part III

Beyond Market Integration

Chapter 5

Community Competences: Are there Limits to Growth?

Renaud Dehousse[*]

In federal systems, which constitute an obvious reference point for the European Community, power is distributed along two axes: between federal institutions on the one hand, and between the centre and component units on the other. Chapter 2 has focused on the first, horizontal, axis and tried to identify the changes in the relationships among Community institutions. As regards the vertical axis, the central questions in most ratification debates have been the following. First, how much power will the Treaty take away from the Member States of the Community? And second, are there limits to the gradual erosion of States' prerogatives, and the correlative growth of Community powers? This chapter will attempt to answer these two basic questions.

Before entering into the merits of the discussion, it is useful to first define a few parameters whereby change can be measured. Conceptually, it can be said that powers are taken away from the Member States in three kinds of situations. First, when the Community is granted new competences: even if these are not exclusive, the supremacy principle implies that whenever the Community acts, the margin of discretion enjoyed by the Member States will be reduced by Community discipline. Second, Member States' prerogatives are also reduced when the Treaty provides for a majority vote, as this makes it possible to bypass the opposition of one or more of them when adopting a given Community provision. Third, further powers are taken away from the Member States whenever there is an increase in the powers of the European Parliament, since this result is normally achieved at the expense of the Council, which is the main representative of national governments within the Community system.

At all three levels, the Single European Act had already prompted significant change. Constitutional recognition has been given to the capacity of the Community to act in fields such as economic and social cohesion, research and development and environmental protection. Majority voting was introduced in a number of areas in order to allow the implementation of the single market programme. Subsequently, the rules of procedures of the Council were even modified to facilitate the resort to

* I am indebted to a number of persons for their comments and suggestions on some parts of this work. I wish to thank in particular Mr. Emile Noël, Principal of the European University Institute, Professors Brian Bercusson, Luis Díez-Picazo, Christian Joerges and Giandomenico Majone from the EUI, and Professor Joseph Weiler from Harvard Law School. Not all of them share the views expressed in this piece; I alone am responsible for any shortcomings.

voting.[1] Lastly, against every expectation – including Parliament's – the establishment of the cooperation procedure has significantly increased Parliament's say in the legislative process. All these changes have considerably speeded up the Community decision-making process.[2] By the same token, however, Member States' powers in the Community system have suffered a first reduction – which demonstrates that there exist close links between the vertical and horizontal axes referred to earlier.

I. Maastricht: Widening *cum* Deepening?

Turning to the Maastricht Treaty, the changes appear even more impressive.

Formal Treaty recognition has legitimized Community intervention in no less than nine new areas, some of which had hardly been touched by the Community in spite of the generous wording of Article 235, which empowers the Council to act in order to 'attain ... one of the objectives of the Community'. These new competences include fields as diverse as European citizenship,[3] visa policy,[4] education,[5] culture,[6] public health,[7] consumer protection,[8] the creation of trans-European networks in the areas of transport, telecommunications and energy infrastructures,[9] industry,[10] and development cooperation.[11] In addition, fields of activity which were already envisaged by the EEC Treaty have been substantially expanded. This applies of course primarily to economic and monetary union which, although formally mentioned, was only loosely structured in the past. The same is also true for economic and social cohesion,[12] as well as for vocational training.[13]

Thus, the spectrum of Community competences has been spectacularly enlarged. The scope of the phenomenon is further reflected in two small changes: the overall

---

1 The voting procedure can now be initiated at the request of one Member State or of the Commission, provided a simple majority of the Council's members agrees. See Article 5 of the Council's Rules of Procedure, OJ L 291 of 15 October 1987.
2 There is no shortage of works on the Single Act and its implications for the European Community. The most exhaustive analysis is to be found in J. De Ruyt, *L'Acte unique européen* (1988). For an analysis of the dynamics of institutional change see Dehousse, '1992 and Beyond: The Institutional Dimension of the Single Market Programme', *Legal Issues of European Integration* (1989-I) 109; for an assessment of the impact of the Single Act on the decision-making process see Ehlermann, 'The "1992 Project": Stages, Structures, Results and Prospects', 11 *Michigan Journal of International Law* (1990) 1097.
3 Articles 8 to 8e.
4 Articles 100c and d.
5 Article 126.
6 Article 128.
7 Article 129.
8 Article 129a.
9 Articles 129b to 129d.
10 Article 130.
11 Articles 130u to 130y.
12 Articles 130a to e.
13 Article 127.

catalogue of Community activities contained in Article 3 has jumped from 11 to 20 items, and the old EEC has been renamed 'European Community' *tout court* by the Maastricht Treaty. This latter change has a clear symbolic meaning: in the presence of such diverse spheres of interest, it was difficult to argue that the Community remained exclusively concerned with economic integration.

This widening of Community competences has been supplemented by institutional changes which have contributed to a loosening of the Member States' grip over the Community decision-making process.

Even if the Commission's desire to see majority voting become the rule has been partly frustrated, the opportunities for such voting have been greatly increased. Majority voting is envisaged for the adoption of at least some measures in most of the new Community competences. In only two areas – culture and industry, where the legitimacy of Community intervention was the object of heated debate, albeit for different reasons – is any possibility of voting excluded. Likewise, in the case of environmental policy majority voting, which was exceptional under the Single Act, will now become the rule. The same is also provided for highly sensitive decisions, such as determining those countries whose nationals should be in possession of a visa in order to enter the Community,[14] or whether the conditions for adopting a single currency are met.[15]

As the increase in the powers of the European Parliament is addressed elsewhere in this contribution,[16] I shall therefore limit myself here to mentioning that the newly established co-decision procedure will be used in most new fields of Community competence[17] and that provision has also be made for it in areas ranging from internal market policy[18] to environmental protection.[19] The assent of Parliament is also required for a series of measures having a quasi-constitutional nature. Lastly, the cooperation procedure has been extended to no less than 13 new areas: broadly speaking, it is envisaged for the implementation of general programmes[20] or for the adoption of legislative acts in the framework of economic and monetary policy.[21]

---

14   From 1 January 1996 only; see Article 100c(3).
15   Such a decision will be made by the Council 'meeting in the composition of Heads of State or of Government'. See Article 109j(3).
16   See Chapter 2.
17   Industry and visa policy being the only fields where this procedure is not foreseen.
18   Article 100a.
19   For the adoption of general action programmes; see Article 130s(3).
20   See, e.g., Articles 129d(3) (European networks), 130e (economic and social cohesion), 130o(2) para. 2 (research and development) and 130s(1) (environmental protection).
21   See Articles 103(5) (adoption of rules for the multilateral surveillance of Member States' economic policy), 105a(2) (harmonization of rules governing the circulation of coins in the Community), 104a(2) (rules prohibiting credit facilities to public institutions) and 104b(2) (rules prohibiting certain financial commitments to the European Central Bank, the Community, or Member States).

II. Growth or Freeze?

All these elements point in the same direction. Never in the past had the Community seen such a far-reaching expansion of its competences, nor such a sharp development of its supranational features. On all counts the Maastricht Treaty goes much further than any prior institutional reform, Single Act included.

However, such a statement must be immediately qualified. For never in the past had the Member States' reluctance to accept the growth of Community powers been so palpable. Both the pillars structure described in Chapter 1 and the special agreement on social policy owe their existence to the unwillingness of some governments to accept the development of Community action in the areas involved. Similar reservations are also apparent in the provisions governing the exercise by the Community of its new competences, sometimes at the expense of style. Thus, for example, the Community is given the power to contribute to the development of education, but its action must respect 'the responsibility of the Member States for the content of teaching and the organization of education systems and their cultural and linguistic diversity';[22] Community cultural policy must respect the national and regional diversity of the Member States;[23] consumer protection policy 'supports and supplements action by the Member States',[24] development cooperation policy 'shall be complementary to the policies pursued by the Member States',[25] and so on. Means of action granted to the Community also bear the mark of similar concerns: the Community is often invited to 'encourage' or 'promote' cooperation between the Member States or to adopt incentive measures, but many new provisions explicitly prohibit any kind of harmonization of national laws and regulations.[26]

In strict legal terms such provisions are as much limiting as they are enabling. A whole range of activities which were previously possible under Article 235 or other general heads of competence are now explicitly excluded: a text like directive 89/662, which imposed uniform labelling requirements for cigarette packets in order to protect human health, could not be adopted under the new Article 129. In other words, one cannot help but conclude that the aim of the Treaty drafters was not only to make Community intervention possible beyond the sphere of economic integration, but also to ensure that such intervention will not exceed certain limits.

The coexistence within one single document of such contradictory intents should not be viewed as an inconsistency, but rather as one more reflection of the clash between the different visions of the Community's *raison d'être* that permeated negotiations at the intergovernmental conference.[27] Similarly, at the time of the Single Act, a significant *quantum leap* had been made possible only at the price of

---

22 Article 126. A similar formulation appears in Article 127 as regards vocational training.
23 Article 128.
24 Article 129a(1)(b).
25 Article 130u(1).
26 See, e.g., Articles 126(4) (education), 127(4) (vocational training), 128(5) (culture), and 129(4) (public health).

the insertion into the Treaty of a number of derogation clauses, which were severely criticized.[28] Although the technique used in the Treaty on European Union differs, the spirit has remained unchanged.

III. Subsidiarity and its Limits

A. From Subsidiary to Principal: The Rise of the Subsidiarity Principle

Member States' reluctance to accept a growth of Community competences is not only apparent in the provisions governing the Community's new policies; it has also led to the formal recognition of the subsidiarity principle in the Treaty.

The emergence of this principle, which has rapidly gained fame in Community circles, is a story worth telling, if only in a few words.[29] As is now widely known, the concept of subsidiarity has ancient roots in European political philosophy. It is primarily invoked – by the Catholic church among others, – as a general principle of social organization protecting the private sphere against any undue interference from the state, the latter being called upon to intervene only when action by private parties was unable to reach certain objectives. In some federal systems the same principle is used as a 'rule of reason',[30] to draw a line between the respective competences of the centre and the component units: preference is to be given to action at a level as close as possible to the citizen.[31]

Although some elements of the Community's institutional structure bore some resemblance to this approach,[32] the concept was not used as such in reference to the

27   See *supra* Chapter 1.
28   See for example Pescatore, 'Observations sur l'Acte unique européen', in *L'Acte unique européen* (1986) 39.
29   See V. Constantinesco, *La distribution des pouvoirs entre la Communauté et ses Etats membres: l'équilibre mouvant de la compétence législative et le principe de subsidiarité*, report presented at the conference on 'The Institutions of the European Community after the Single European Act: The New Procedures and the Capacity to Act. Balance Sheet and Perspectives in View of the Intergovernmental Conferences', Bruges (1990); M. Wilke and H. Wallace, *Subsidiarity: Approaches to Power-sharing in the European Community*, RIIA Discussion Paper No. 27 (1990).
30   Constantinesco, 'La subsidiarité comme principe constitutionnel de l'intégration européenne', *Aussenwirtschaft* (1991) 439-459, at 447.
31   Article 72(II) of the German Basic Law, for instance, provides that
       'The Federation shall have the right to legislate in ... matters [of concurrent competence] to the extent that a need for regulation by federal legislation exists because:
         1. a matter cannot be effectively regulated by the legislation of individual *Länder* , or
         2. the regulation of a matter by a Land law might prejudice the interest of other *Länder* or of the people as a whole, or
         3. the maintenance of legal or economic uniformity, especially the maintenance of uniformity of living conditions beyond the territory of any one Land, necessitates such regulation.' Translation in A. Blaustein and G. Flanz (eds.), *Constitutions of the Countries of the World* (August 1991) 110.
32   See Kapteyn, 'Community Law and the Principle of Subsidiarity', *Revue des affaires européennes* (1991) 35-43, at 38-39, who cites *inter alia* Article 235 of the EEC Treaty, the use of directives which 'leave to the national authorities the choice of forms and methods' whereby their objectives should be achieved (Article 189), and the principle of proportionality. See also Constantinesco,

Community until very recently. Given the Member States' near total control over the decision-making process, it was difficult to argue that their sovereign powers were really endangered by European integration. However, things were to change with the Single European Act, which provided simultaneously for a broadening of the Community's sphere of competence, and for a more systematic use of majority voting: not only was the Community increasingly to intervene in areas such as culture or environmental protection, where subnational bodies have traditionally been active but, equally importantly, it was now at times able to bypass the opposition of one or a few Member States. This combined development[33] offers a good illustration of the links existing between the vertical and the horizontal dimensions of federalism, discussed above. For the first time in the history of the Community the fear of a centralist drift, occasionally inflamed by the behaviour of Community institutions,[34] became more than a rhetorical statement in the mouths of a handful of politicians.

Centre-periphery problems of this kind are common in federal systems. Yet at Community level, the problem is made somewhat more acute by the fact that the Community enjoys a *functional* competence: the Community has been empowered to perform certain tasks which are necessary to achieve the general objectives listed in Article 2 of the Treaty. Moreover, some provisions drafted in broad terms enable it to take whatever measure needed to establish a common market (Articles 100 and 100a) or simply to achieve 'objectives of the Community' (Article 235). This has allowed a number of incursions into fields where the Community had not been granted an explicit competence – hence the gradual extension of Community activities that was noted from the 1970s onwards.

In this context the idea of assigning clear limits to the growth of Community powers gradually gained ground. Not surprisingly, the Single Act contained a first reference to the subsidiarity principle: in the field of environmental policy, the Community was to act only 'to the extent that the objectives [of environmental policy] can be attained better at Community level than at the level of the individual Member States'.[35] Representatives of European regions subsequently claimed that subsidiarity should be enshrined within the treaty, while they should be granted the

---

supra note 29 and the report on the subsidiarity principle prepared by Mr. Giscard d'Estaing for the Institutional Committee of the European Parliament, Doc. PE A3-163/90 of 22 June and 4 July 1990. For a radically opposed view, see Toth, 'The Principle of Subsidiarity in the Maastricht Treaty', 29 *CML Rev.* (1992) 1079-1105, at 1080-86.

33   The importance of which is stressed in Weiler, 'The Transformation of Europe', 100 *Yale Law Journal* (1991) 2403-83, at 2462-63.

34   See the criticisms of Hailbronner, 'Legal Institutional Reform of the EEC: What can we Learn from Federalism Theory and Practice?', *Aussenwirtschaft* (1991) 485-496. The fears of the German *Länder* were expressed forcefully in the *Bundesrat* at the time of ratification of the Single Act. See Hrbek, 'The German *Länder* and the European Community. Towards a Real Federalism?', in W. Wessels and E. Regelsberger (eds.), *The Federal Republic of Germany and the European Community: The Presidency and Beyond* (1988) 215.

35   Article 130r(4).

power to initiate proceedings against Community acts adopted in violation of this principle.[36]

In the course of the intergovernmental conference, the idea of formal recognition of subsidiarity was supported both by the Commission, eager to give evidence of its own moderation, and by some Member States, alarmed by the seemingly endless growth of Community powers. For a majority of actors in the Community process, subsidiarity had thus become a principal concern. This broad consensus was not flawless, and occasionally led to curious contrasts: the implications of subsidiarity in the field of monetary policy, for example, were radically opposed, depending on whether they were identified by the United Kingdom or by the Commission.[37] Be that as it may, the convergence of divergent interests once again had a strong impact on the negotiations, as is apparent from the agreement reached in Maastricht.

B. Subsidiarity as a Regulatory Principle

The very first provision of the Maastricht Treaty states that decisions are to be taken 'as closely as possible to the citizen'. How this result is to be achieved is explained in Article 3b, which formally establishes two rules which up to then had enjoyed the status of general principles of Community constitutional law: the principle of attributed powers[38] and the principle of proportionality.[39] Subsidiarity proper is defined in paragraph 2 of the same provision, which is worth quoting in full as the wording is of some importance:

> In areas which do not fall within its exclusive competence, the Community shall take action, in accordance with the principle of subsidiarity, only if and in so far as the objectives of the proposed action cannot be sufficiently achieved by the Member States and can therefore, by reason of the scale or effects of the proposed action, be better achieved by the Community.

The redundancies in these few lines hint at just how eager national governments were to protect their prerogatives against any undesired Community intrusion. This concern is also reflected in the wording of Article 3b. In theory, subsidiarity could have been used as a double-edged sword: negatively, to protect Member States' prerogatives against undue Community interference; but also positively, to allow

---

36 See the motion adopted by the Assembly of European Regions in December 1990, *Regions of Europe* (2/1990) 56.

37 See F. Dehousse, 'La subsidiarité, fondement constitutionnel ou paravent politique de l'Union européenne?', *Liber Amicorum E. Krings* (1990) 51.

38 'The Community shall act within the limits conferred upon it by this Treaty and of the objectives assigned to it therein.'

39 'Any action by the Community shall not go beyond what is necessary to achieve the objectives of this Treaty.'

the Community to act should such action appear necessary.[40] Yet, only the negative formulation was retained in the final version: as it stands, Article 3b might be invoked to regulate the use the Community makes of its competences, but not to grant it additional powers.[41] This, it is submitted, is a precise *résumé* of the political objectives this provision is meant to achieve.

The scope of Article 3b confirms the above interpretation. First, although subsidiarity has been raised to the level of general principle of the European Union, Article 3b appears in the EC Treaty rather than in the common provisions, which suggests that Community competences were the primary target. Second, the use by the Community of its exclusive competences is not governed by the subsidiarity principle. This seems logical: whenever the Community is under an obligation to act and the Member States are deprived of the necessary powers, there can be no question of subsidiarity. In contrast, subsidiarity will play an important role only in areas in which powers are shared between the Community and the Member States. This will be the case *inter alia* in relation to the so-called 'flanking policies', i.e. in fields such as consumer protection, environmental policy or economic and social cohesion, which although not belonging to the core of market integration, cannot be fully dissociated from the latter.[42]

It therefore appears that subsidiarity – at least as it is defined in the Treaty – is not really a problem of competence, as one is often inclined to believe. The demarcation of competences is operated by other provisions of the Treaty, on top of which one finds the principle of attributed powers – reaffirmed in the first paragraph of Article 3b – which is designed to protect the Member States against a too generous reading of Community powers.[43] The primary aim of the subsidiarity

40 Such is, after all, the spirit of Article 235, as underlined among others by President Delors in an address at the European Institute of Public Administration. See 'Le principe de subsidiarité: contribution au débat' in *Subsidiarité: défi du changement* (1991) 7.

41 This negative overtone was reinforced during the intergovermental conference. The conclusions of the Rome European Council acknowleged that subsidiarity could justify an extension of Community competence (see *Bull. EC* (12-1990) at 11). The draft circulated by the Luxembourg Presidency contained a milder version of Article 3b, according to which the Community could act 'if and insofar as those objectives can be better achieved by the Community than by the member States acting separately'. The Luxembourg draft has been reprinted in *Europe Documents* No. 1722/1723 of 5 July 1991.

42 See however Toth, *supra* note 32, at 1091, who argues that 'the principle of subsidiarity as defined in the Maastricht Treaty *cannot* apply to matters covered by the original EEC Treaty', for 'the Community's competence is necessarily exclusive over all matters pertaining to the pursuit of Community objectives'. Such a view, I submit, rests on a confusion between the idea of exclusive competence and the supremacy principle. Clearly, even in fields in relation to which the Community has not been granted exclusive competence, the Member States' capacity to act is limited by the supremacy principle once a Community act has been adopted. However, it does not necessarily follow that the Community will always completely occupy the relevant field, thereby preventing the Member States from acting: supremacy and pre-emption are two distinct, though clearly related, concepts. A similar point has been made in the Commission's communication on 'The Principle of Subsidiarity', SEC(92) 1990 final of 27 October 1992, at 9 of the annex.

43 A similar argument has been made in the Commission's communication on the subsidiarity principle, ibid. at 3 of the annex. In the Commission's view, the fact that 'national powers are the rule and the Community's the exception ... explains why it would be pointless ... to list the powers

principle is rather to regulate the use made by the Community of its non-exclusive competences. Lacking such a competence, any discussion of the respective merits of national and Community action would be deprived of meaning. We shall see further that this remark has important implications regarding the manner in which Article 3b is to be implemented.

What are the criteria to be used to assess the need for Community action? At first sight, Article 3b seems to envisage a twofold subsidiarity test:

–   in the first place, attention must be paid to the means available at national level, to see whether they might suffice to attain the objectives of the measure which is envisaged at Community level. This may entail a review of financial resources as well as legal instruments, of potential as well as existing measures.

–   the second test entails an evaluation of the envisaged Community action, in order to determine whether 'by reason of the scale or the effects of the proposed action', its objectives can be 'better achieved' at Community level. This is what the Commission has labelled a 'value added test'.[44]

These two tests seem to refer to two different types of operation. The first appears closer to a mere *effectiveness* test: if action at national level is capable of producing the desired result, it should be given preference. In contrast, the second test is more concerned about *efficiency* matters: the reference to the fact that the objective has to be 'better achieved' at Community level can be seen as an indication that a comparative evaluation of the costs and benefits of action at Community and at national level is required.

It has been suggested that each of these two conditions are to be satisfied before the Community might act.[45] But the two tests cannot be combined in a mechanical fashion. If one opts for the effectiveness test, two things are possible: either action at national level can be effective, and the Member States should act, or it is not. In this latter case, adding a separate efficiency condition does not really make sense: provided it is itself effective, Community action is likely to be more efficient than ineffective national measures.

The legislative history of Article 3b may aid in understanding how this ambiguous result was reached. The Luxembourg draft referred to 'objectives ... better achieved by the Community than by the Member States acting separately'.[46] This suggests that the Member States had in mind a comparative assessment of national and Community measures, which can only be done through an evaluation of their respective efficiency. As indicated above, some felt it necessary to strengthen this wording by indicating that if national action proved 'sufficient' to

---

reserved to the Member States', as suggested for instance in the Giscard d'Estaing report, *supra* note 32.

44   Commission communication on subsidiarity, *supra* note 42, at 10 of the annex.

45   See the memorandum on subsidiarity presented by the Federal Republic of Germany, reported in *Agence Europe* of 12-13 October 1992, at 13-14, and Toth, *supra* note 32, at 1097-98.

46   See *supra* note 41.

attain the pursued objective (read: where it would be as efficient as the proposed Community action), it should be given preference.

Thus, rather than two distinct conditions, what we have here are but two facets of the same problem, effectiveness being but a necessary component of the efficiency assessment which subsidiarity entails. Naturally, the complexity of the exercise has clear implications for the way the subsidiarity principle is to be implemented.

C. Implementing Subsidiarity

Article 3b has already given rise to some debate on the implementation of the subsidiarity principle. Is it 'justiciable', i.e. could the European Court of Justice annul a Community act on the basis of an infraction against the subsidiarity principle? Should it assume such a delicate duty? Are there any alternatives to judicial implementation? I shall deal with these three questions in succession.

Before doing so, however, a word of caution is necessary, for law is rarely as neutral as it claims to be and the answers that most naturally come to mind are often inspired by political-institutional preferences. Hidden normative statements then tend to obfuscate the discussion. In my view, the best way to facilitate the debate is to eschew a supposedly 'neutral' viewpoint, according to which problems are treated as if they were essentially technical ones, and rather to spell out as clearly as possible the kinds of considerations that underlie our reasoning. This is what I shall try to do in the following pages.

1. Is Subsidiarity Justiciable?

That subsidiarity could be invoked in annulment proceedings against Community acts is beyond doubt. During the intergovernmental conference, thought had been given to the idea of referring to subsidiarity in the preamble of the Treaty. Yet, as we saw, another solution prevailed and subsidiarity, being mentioned in the body of the Treaty, is to be regarded as binding on all Community institutions. Any violation of the principle could therefore serve as a basis for an annulment proceeding based on Article 173 of the EC Treaty. A Member State that unsuccessfully opposed the adoption of a given measure which it deemed to be in conflict with the subsidiarity principle could thus subsequently bring the matter before the Court on this basis.

However, it is far from certain in my view that private parties could do so, for the Court might find it difficult to regard Article 3b as sufficiently clear and precise to enjoy direct effect. In the past, it has denied direct effect to Treaty provisions that leave a wide discretion to Community institutions.[47] Such is undoubtedly the case of Article 3b, the ambiguities of which are discussed above.

In spite of this reservation, it seems likely that the Court will one day be confronted with a subsidiarity problem. How will the Court tackle this?

The difficulty is twofold. From a functional viewpoint, it is not clear that the Court is equipped to answer the question it would be asked. From a political viewpoint, a ruling on the compatibility of a given measure with the subsidiarity principle could create a legitimacy problem. Although the two problems are closely intertwined, it is better to treat them separately.

(a) The Functional Issue

As noted above, subsidiarity as defined by the Treaty goes beyond classical competence problems, in relation to which courts must rule on the compatibility of a measure with rules governing the division of powers between the centre and the periphery. Rather, what would be required of the Court is a ruling on the adequacy of the means used to reach a given end: Was Community action really necessary to achieve the objectives of the challenged measure, or would action at national level have represented a valid alternative?

The answer to such a question involves a delicate qualitative assessment, and the parameters to be used are far from clear. Suppose for instance that the Council were to set up a programme providing for financial assistance for projects aiming to increase the mobility of school teachers. At first sight, such a measure would seem to fall squarely within the limitative framework of Article 126. Assume further, however, that the validity of this programme were to be challenged by one Member State, arguing that Community action was not necessary since the same objective could equally have been achieved by the Member States, either acting individually or pooling their resources to finance specific programmes, and that the Community had therefore violated the subsidiarity principle.

How could the Court assess the merits of such claim? This would differ greatly from traditional litigation on the demarcation of competences, which the Court is used to dealing with.[48] Here, it would be unable to refer to a superior norm, against which the validity of Community action could be checked.

Article 3b seems to suggest that the Court should attempt to determine whether national action would have been sufficient. But what sort of parameters should it use in order to ascertain the efficiency of national measures, some of which might even exist in project form only?

---

47   See for instance Case 74/76, *Iannelli* v. *Meroni*, [1977] ECR 557 as regards state aids. While admitting the difficulty, Sir Leon Brittan, Vice-President of the EC Commission, has expressed the hope that Article 3b will one day be held directly applicable. See the text of his Robert Schuman lecture at the European University Institute, *Europe Documents* No. 1786 of 18 June 1992, 3.

48   As exemplified by its growing jurisprudence on the use of legal bases. See for a recent example Case 300/89, *Commission* v. *Council* (titanium dioxide), [1991] ECR 2869.

113

Even assuming that the Court were able to overcome this first difficulty, on what basis would it then further decide whether national actions would be 'sufficiently' efficient to attain the objectives of the measure under scrutiny? Obviously, this involves more than an effectiveness assessment. What would be required is a careful weighing up of the costs and benefits of the proposed Community measure, when compared with those of national action.

Article 3b indicates that in the evaluation process, due regard should be paid to 'the scale or effects of the proposed action'. The first criterion may be understood as a reference to the transfrontier dimensions of a given problem. As regards the second one, the Commission has suggested also considering such factors as the costs of inaction, or the need to reach a critical mass.[49] But leaving these attempts to provide objective criteria aside, what will ultimately be needed is a ruling on the compared efficiency of both types of measure.

Is this really a task which can be fulfilled by a judicial body? Will the Court have at its disposal the necessary elements to provide an answer? It would, of course, be able to rely on the submissions of parties, but these are likely to contain considerations informed by political opportunism rather than by scientific evidence. And the problem is made even more complex by the relativity of the efficiency concept: costs and benefits might be different for all interested parties. Suppose for instance that the costs of the proposed Community action are found to be evenly distributed among the Member States, while its benefits accrue only to some of them. Will the fact that inaction would entail even greater costs be deemed sufficient to justify Community action?

In other words, a subsidiarity assessment appears to involve delicate policy choices, which go beyond the tasks traditionally assigned to judicial bodies.[50]

Vigorously pleading in favour of justiciability, Jacqué and Weiler have invoked an analogy with the proportionality principle to suggest that the European Court of Justice had already touched upon similar issues on other occasions.[51] The similarity is indeed striking: both principles are used in order to regulate the use of Community competences, with a view to limiting any encroachment upon certain elements which are given a 'superior' value: fundamental rights and basic freedoms contained in the Treaty in the case of the proportionality principle, Member States' competences in the case of the subsidiarity principle. Both principles also require an assessment of the appropriateness of the means used to reach a given end.

Yet, the parallel is by no means complete. Proportionality problems are essentially limited to a question of means and ends: could not other measures, equally effective but less detrimental to superior interests, have been used? In

---

49   Communication on the subsidiarity principle, *supra* note 42, at 10 of the annex.
50   See however Kapteyn, *supra* note 32, at 40, who argues that criteria such as a 'more effective attainment' or the 'cross-boundary dimension or effect' or a given problem 'can be the subject of a discussion based on more objective criteria of an economic, social, technical or legal nature'.
51   Jacqué and Weiler, 'On the Road to European Union – A New Judicial Architecture', 27 *CML Rev.* (1991) 185-207.

contrast, as I have tried to show, subsidiarity problems involve a difficult efficiency assessment. Moreover, the efficiency of Community measures is to be assessed *relatively*, in comparison with that of alternative national measures. The Commission has even suggested that proportionality is but one dimension of any subsidiarity assessment;[52] it is indeed likely that a Community intervention going beyond what is necessary to achieve one objective of the Treaty would not be found to be efficient. All this makes the subsidiarity review a far more delicate exercise – politically as well as functionally.

Despite this important difference, the Court's jurisprudence on the proportionality principle is highly instructive.[53] Two elements are worthy of particular attention. First, although the scope of the principle has gradually been expanded to cover the entire field of Community law, including rules adopted by the Council and the Commission as well as individual administrative decisions, the vast majority of legislative measures subjected to review have been Commission regulations, 'which can be said to straddle the border between the creation of legal rules and the adoption of administrative measures'.[54] The primary focus has thus been on the Community's administrative action.

Second, the way the proportionality review has been carried out is equally interesting. In assessing whether a Community measure was suited to the purpose of achieving the objective pursued, the Court has always shown great caution when the Treaty provided the Community legislator with a wide margin of discretion; it has generally confined itself to examining whether the measure at issue was 'obviously inappropriate for the realization of the desired objective'.[55] This clearly suggests that the Court, being aware of the difficulty involved in determining the effectiveness of a given measure, was reluctant to substitute its own appreciation for that of the Community legislator, except in cases of blatant unsuitability.

The Court has shown a similar reticence on other occasions. In the notorious *ERTA* case,[56] the Court ruled that it was for the Council, when acting on the basis of Article 235, to determine when Community action was in fact 'necessary' to attain one of the Community's objectives. Likewise, in Case 276/80,[57] it was asked to rule that by establishing quotas to combat the steel crisis of the late 1970s, the Commission had infringed Article 58(1) of the ECSC Treaty, which provides that quotas should be used as an *ultima ratio*. The plaintiff argued that Article 57, which invites the Commission to give preference to 'the indirect means of action at its disposal, such as ... cooperation with Governments to regularize or influence general consumption' or intervention in regard to prices, provided sufficient means to deal

---

52 Communication on the subsidiarity principle, *supra* note 32, at 5 of the annex.
53 See J. Schwarze, *European Administrative Law* (1992) at 708-866 for a detailed review.
54 Ibid. at 861.
55 Case 40/70, *Schroeder* v. *Germany*, [1973] ECR 138, 142.
56 Case 22/70, *Commission* v. *Council*, [1971] ECR 263.
57 *Ferriera Padana* v. *Commission*, [1982] ECR 517.

with the crisis. In other words, the Court was confronted with a kind of subsidiarity challenge *ante litteram*. In its ruling, it simply noted that

> [i]n the event of a manifest crisis Article 58 of the ECSC Treaty confers upon the Commission a wide power of appraisal which it exercised in adopting Decision No. 2794/80/ECSC. The Commission has set out the reasons for which it considered that the means of action provided for in Article 57 were not sufficient to deal with the crisis. It considered that it could not take steps to influence general consumption in the present economic situation... The Commission accordingly concluded that the indirect means of action at its disposal had proved insufficient and that it was necessary to intervene directly in order to restore the balance between supply and demand. In arriving at this conclusion the Commission did not exceed the limits to its power of appraisal and the submission must therefore be rejected.[58]

Thus the Court seems to have considered that, the Commission having complied with the (formal) requirement of a statement of the reasons on which its actions were based, all the Court itself could do regarding the merits of the problem was to make sure the Commission had acted within the limits of its powers.

A similar reasoning had been explicitly developed in an earlier case, where the validity of a Commission regulation modifying monetary compensatory amounts following the temporary withdrawal of the French franc from the European monetary 'snake' was questioned:

> As the evaluation of a complex economic situation is involved, the Commission and the Management Committee enjoy, in this respect, a wide measure of discretion. In reviewing the legality of the exercise of such discretion, the Court must confine itself to examining whether it contains a manifest error or constitutes a misuse of power or whether the authority did not clearly exceed the bounds of its discretion.[59]

This line of reasoning suggests that where the Treaty leaves a margin of discretion to other Community institutions, the Court is not inclined to substitute its own interpretation for theirs.

The point is worth making for, in a seminal essay on the statement of reasons requirement, Martin Shapiro has shown that Article 190 of the EEC Treaty might be construed by the Court as enabling it to review the substance of decisions adopted by European institutions, in a manner akin to the review by US Circuit Courts of decisions of administrative agencies.[60] Indeed, on a number of occasions the European Court of Justice has held that the statement of reasons was more than a pure procedural requirement and has demonstrated some propensity to assess whether the reasons given were actually correct.[61] Though the Court's moves in this

58   Ibid. at 540.
59   Case 29/77, *Roquette* v. *France*, [1977] ECR 1835, recitals 19 and 20. See also Case 42/84, *Remia - Nutricia*, [1985] ECR 2545, recital 43.
60   'The Giving Reasons Requirement', *The University of Chicago Legal Forum* (1992) 179-220.
61   See, e.g., Case 24/62, *Germany* v. *Commission*, [1963] ECR 69.

direction have been somewhat ambiguous, it might in theory use this avenue to review the subsidiarity assessment carried out by Community institutions.

Yet the above evidence suggests that the Court is not eager to do so. If such a line is maintained, it will approach with great caution any discussion on the conformity of Community measures with the subsidiarity principle, and leave a large measure of discretion to the institutions that are required to decide on the matter. Only in exceptional circumstances would its scrutiny lead to a negative judgment.[62]

(b) The Legitimacy Issue

The Court's decision will in the last instance depend on how it conceives of its institutional mission. In this respect, the fact that the subsidiarity principle has been enshrined in the body of the Treaty is likely to carry some weight. In doing so, did not the Member States implicitly invite the Court to come to grips with the problem? Alternately, enforcing the subsidiarity principle might prove difficult for a Court that has systematically construed Treaty provisions in a broad manner, having regard to their purposes and to the overall objectives of the Treaty.[63] Clearly, teleological interpretation and subsidiarity are inspired by diametrically opposed considerations, and will be difficult to reconcile.

Moving now from the analytical to the more delicate level of normative considerations, I submit that the Court would be well advised to stick to the cautious approach it has followed in the past. Such a view is of course influenced by the above analysis: if subsidiarity is primarily a political problem, as I believe it is, judicial solutions may create a legitimacy problem. Assuming that a majority of Member States – or even all of them – have assessed the relative efficiency of various modes of action and decided upon the course to be followed, would it be legitimate for the Court to impose a different evaluation of such action?

The upholders of justiciability have stressed that there have been many examples of courts having been called upon to exert a creative role when implementing general principles to politically delicate issues. After all, deciding when life begins in matters of abortion is no less difficult a task than deciding at which level a given measure is more effective; yet, courts have often been entrusted with the power to make such decisions.[64]

This is of course true, but the analogy is not entirely convincing. First, it would be easy to show that the legitimacy of such decisions has been questioned, at times vehemently. Second, European states have strongly contrasting views as to the role

---

62   See Kapteyn, *supra*, note 32, at 41. See also Mischo, 'Un nouveau rôle pour la Cour de Justice?', *RMC* (1990) 681.

63   For an recent example of this trend, see opinion 1/91 of 14 December 1991 (EEA Agreement), not yet reported, and the comments of Brandtner, 'The Drama of the EEA. Comments on Opinions 1/91 and 1/92', 3 *EJIL* (1992) 300.

64   This is the example used by Jacqué and Weiler, *supra* note 51, at 205.

of the judiciary. Several of them were powerfully influenced by the political philosophy of the Enlightenment, which insisted on keeping judges away from politics in the name of the separation of powers. Even if constitutional justice has made considerable headway in post-World War II Europe, judicial review of the constitutionality of legislative acts remains limited in several Member States of the Community. Third, and perhaps more importantly, even assuming that when national courts undertake such delicate tasks their own legitimacy is well established, it is far from sure that the intervention of the European Court of Justice would be regarded with equal benevolence. Recent evidence suggests that many Irish citizens had more faith in their own High Court than in the Luxembourg Court when it came to dealing with the abortion issue. There is, in other words, a serious risk that by intervening in discussions of a clearly political nature, the European Court of Justice would awaken the ghost of a *gouvernement des juges* in a Community which is already under strong attack for its legitimacy deficit. The subsidiarity debate is but one aspect of this larger legitimacy crisis; solutions that might aggravate this crisis should therefore be avoided.

Turning to federal systems, one notices that courts have often showed great caution in deploying the legal instruments put at their disposal to protect the prerogatives of component units. This is all the more interesting as some of these instruments would have appeared to be easier to handle than is Article 3b. The Tenth Amendment of the United States' Constitution, for instance, states that

> [t]he powers not delegated to the United States by the Constitution, nor prohibited by it to the States, are reserved to the States respectively, or to the people.

Although clearly attuned to the subsidiarity principle, this provision might have been more readily used by courts, as it does not entail any efficiency assessment. Yet after having hesitated for a while, the Supreme Court of the United States has refused to see in this clause an instrument delineating 'islands of sovereignty'[65] protected against any kind of federal interference.[66]

The reasons which led the Supreme Court to reject this possibility are worth noting. Reporting for the majority, Justice Blackmun recalled that defining *a priori* the nature and content of limitations on federal authority under the Commerce clause had proven problematic for courts. He then added:

> It is no novelty to observe that the composition of the Federal Government was designed in large part to protect the States from overreaching by Congress. The Framers thus gave the States a role in the selection both of the Executive and the Legislative Branches of the Federal Government ... In short, the Framers chose to rely on a federal system in which special restraints on federal power over the States inhered principally in the workings of the National Government itself, rather than in the discrete limitations on the objects of federal authority. *State sovereign interests, then, are more properly protected by*

---

65   L. Tribe, *Constitutional Choices* (1985) 137.
66   *Garcia* v. *San Antonio Metropolitan Transit Authority*, 469 US (1985) 528.

procedural safeguards inherent in the structure of the federal system than by judicially created limitations on federal powers.[67]

This, however, should not be seen as undermining the constitutional position of the States:

Of course, we continue to recognize that the States occupy a special and specific position in our constitutional system and that the scope of Congress' authority under the Commerce Clause must reflect that position. But the principal and basic limit on the federal commerce power is that inherent in all congressional action – the built-in restraints that our system provides through state participation in federal governmental action. The political process ensures that laws that unduly burden the states will not be promulgated.[68]

The Australian High Court had reached a similar conclusion – although for different reasons – early in its jurisprudence in 1920.[69] In Germany, the Federal Constitutional Court has refused to give too strict an interpretation to Article 72 (II) of the Basic Law, which governs federal intervention in areas of concurrent competences.[70]

Such a convergence would seem to give some credit to those who hold that in divided-power systems, the most effective defences against centralizing pressures are to be found in the political process, rather than in the judiciary.[71] If this is true for federal systems, should it not be so *a fortiori* in the Community system, where Member States enjoy greater powers? Defining at what level a task is better accomplished is primarily a political problem; it should therefore be left to the political process.

2. Alternatives to Judicial Implementation

Rejecting justiciability does not necessarily imply that subsidiarity is condemned to remain an empty concept. Implementing the (binding) guidelines contained in Article 3b requires an effort on the part of all institutions. Thus, if one accepts Justice Blackmun's view that protecting States' rights is primarily a matter of *process*,[72] the impact of this provision on the Community legislative process is potentially more important than the justiciability issue.[73]

The Commission should play a central role in this respect, because it still holds a monopoly of initiative in most fields of Community competence and is, of all Community institutions, by far the best equipped to fulfil the evaluation task which

---

67 Ibid. at 551-552 (emphasis added).
68 Ibid. at 556.
69 *Amalgamated Society of Engineers* v. *Adelaide Steamship Co. Ltd.* , 28 CLR (1920) 128.
70 See the analysis in Constantinesco, *supra* note 29.
71 See Wechsler, 'The Political Safeguards of Federalism: The Role of the States in the Selection and Composition of the National Government', 54 *Columbia Law Review* (1954) 543.
72 *Garcia* v. *San Antonio*, *supra* note 66, at 554.
73 See Brittan, *supra* note 47, at 3.

is needed. One might therefore envisage the establishment within the Commission of a specialized unit, attached to the Secretariat-General, which would act as a clearing house and review all draft measures prepared by Commission services in order to assess their conformity with the subsidiarity principle.[74]

Procedures can play a useful role in ensuring the rationality of decision-making. Requiring that each Commission proposal be accompanied by a specific subsidiarity assessment will provide a strong incentive to address the questions raised by Article 3b.[75] It might even be argued that the statement of reasons imposed by Article 190 should lead the Commission to include in the recital of its proposals an indication of the efficiency considerations that have led to their adoption.[76] Conformity with this formal requirement could of course be subjected to the Court's scrutiny, as indicated above.

Specific safeguards for Member States' interests might also be useful. They could be placed within specific procedures. The European Parliament's Draft Treaty on European Union envisaged for example that any intervention in fields previously untouched by the Community would be possible only through enactment of an organic law, with more stringent voting requirements.[77] Such is also the spirit of 'old' Article 235, which requires unanimity for the Community to act when the necessary powers are not provided by the Treaty. Additional mechanisms of this kind could provide the Member States with means to resist unwelcome interference in their sphere of activity. They would also provide evidence of the Community's unwillingness to tolerate a creeping centralization.

As hinted above, the most immediate threat to the subsidiarity principle lies in majority voting. There have been in the past instances of measures adopted by the Council (generally in the framework of internal market policy, where one can rely upon the generous wording of Article 100a) against the opposition of one or more Member States, who argued that the action envisaged went beyond what subsidiarity required.[78] No matter how rare they may be, situations of this kind feed the fear of an ever-growing Community. Obviously, the current rules of procedure of the Council, which provide that voting is possible when a majority of members of the Council so decide, did not suffice to prevent this from happening. Some sort of remedy should therefore be found.

---

74 This proposal is developed at greater length in R. Dehousse, C. Joerges, G. Majone and F. Snyder, *Europe after 1992 – New Regulatory Strategies*, EUI Working Papers in Law, No. 92/31, at 38-41.
75 This possibility is contemplated in the Commission's communication on subsidiarity, *supra* note 42, at 21 at the annex.
76 A commitment to this effect has been taken by the Commission at the Lisboa meeting of the European Council, in June 1992. See *Bull. EC* (6.9.92) at 12.
77 See Article 12 of the Draft Treaty. According to Article 38, organic laws would have required a qualified majority both in Council and in Parliament, whereas 'normal' provisions required an absolute majority only.
78 This was the case for Directive 89/662 on cigarette labelling (OJ L 359 of 8 December 1989), adopted in spite of the opposition of the British Government.

One could conceivably argue that, as unanimity represents the best possible guarantee for Member States' interests, all one should do in order to avoid this kind of problem is return to the spirit of the Luxembourg agreement, and provide that whenever one Member State deems subsidiarity to have been ignored by a proposed measure, no vote should be taken until a satisfactory compromise can be found on this point. This institutional approach would even find support in the works of some economists, who argue that unanimity is the most appropriate rule for decisions on the efficiency of public policies.[79] Yet, as no control of the use made by the Member States of this prerogative would be possible, the costs of such a solution would be likely to greatly outweigh its benefits: Community decision-making could experience anew the *lourdeur* of the pre-Single Act years, and the Community would find it more or less impossible to tackle the many problems it is now faced with.[80] Effective remedies should therefore steer away from the Charybdis of inaction and the Scylla of Luxembourg.

One possible solution would be to provide that when a significant minority in the Council (say, three Member States, possibly representing a minimum number of votes in the Council[81]) deems a proposed measure to be in conflict with the subsidiarity principle, any decision on this point is deferred for a limited period, after which the matter will be examined by the 'General Affairs' Council, which will then decide according to normal procedures, i.e. by majority vote in fields where this is possible. Such a mechanism could even be made binding through its insertion into the rules of procedure of the Council. Similar mechanisms exist in some federal constitutions where, in order to protect their own interests, minorities are given the right to render certain decisions more difficult by increasing the level of consensus needed for their adoption.[82]

In the Community context, this solution could be viewed as an acceptable compromise by all interested parties.

On the one hand, it would provide additional guarantees to those who fear an uncontrolled growth of Community power. It has often been argued that some

---

79 This point is developed in Majone, 'Le scelte pubbliche e le nuove tecnologie', XX *Amministrare* (1990) 255-292.

80 Unsurprisingly, the Commission has indicated that it did not favour a separate treatment of the subsidiarity issue: 'there must be no question of separating the issue of subsidiarity from the substance of the matter in hand and in this way obstructing by degrees the decision-making process. Subsidiarity is part of decision-making, not a pre-condition for it. It must be considered with all the other aspects (legal basis, substantive provisions, etc.) in accordance with the voting conditions applying to a proposal.' (Communication on the subsidiarity principle, *supra* note 42, at 20 of the annex.)

81 This number should however remain below the threshold needed for a blocking minority, otherwise the guarantee would be merely illusory.

82 This is for instance the case of the so-called 'alarm bell procedure' established by Article 38bis of the Belgian Constitution. This procedure enables three quarters of the members of one of the linguistic groups in each Chamber to prevent the adoption of a draft bill which might 'have a serious effect on relations between the communities'. In such a case, the procedure is suspended and the matter referred to the Council of Ministers, which comprises Flemish and French-speaking members in equal number.

overregulatory tendencies were simply due to attempts by national officials to secure in Brussels decisions which they were unable to force through in their own country. Resort to a more politicized body might make this more difficult, by ensuring that the institutional dimensions of the problem are duly considered.

On the other hand, a Luxembourg-type drift would also seem less likely. Voting conditions being maintained, minority action would not entirely prevent the ultimate adoption of any measure by the Community, which would instead simply be deferred. Moreover, as several national governments would be required to concur in their evaluation of the proposed measure before this procedure might be used, the risk that the whole decision-making process be undermined by a systematic resort to this minority action would appear to be fairly limited. The expectation is rather that, given the various checks and balances entailed in such a mechanism, all parties would have an incentive to reach a compromise so that the ultimate decision may be made by consensus. [83]

Naturally, majority decisions might occasionally be more difficult, which could somewhat slow down decision-making. This, however, would be the price to pay to implement the subsidiarity principle.

Would this suffice? Some might argue that subsidiarity should be construed as a broader regulatory principle, which aims not only to preserve a certain degree of decentralization, but also to ensure the efficiency and the equity of the policy choices that will be made at Community level. Viewed in this light, the above-mentioned mechanisms might appear biased in favour of the institutional interests of the Member States. After all, states are far from being the only actors interested in efficiency matters. Should the constitutionalization of subsidiarity effected by the Maastricht Treaty not be seen as an invitation to a bolder construction?

In my view, the answer ought to be negative. Even leaving aside the question of remedies available for such a claim, I do not believe that the resort to an ultimate umpire represents an ideal solution. As indicated above, subsidiarity, because it is primarily concerned with questions of efficiency, does not lend itself to judicial treatment save in extreme cases. Policy choices are to be made by political bodies, and not hidden behind pseudo-neutral questions. The primary task of legal structures is to ensure that these choices are made on as rational and equitable a basis as possible. This result can only be achieved by an emphasis on *procedures*, which organize the policy process and preserve the rights of minorities.

The emphasis on protecting Member States' interests appears more legitimate in this light. Such was after all the rationale which led to the enshrinement of subsidiarity in the Treaty, as rightly or wrongly it was felt that the present structure contained the seeds of a centralist drift. Moreover, in subsidiarity debates national

---

83 It is worth noting that although the Belgian 'alarm bell' procedure referred to above was viewed as an important guarantee when it was established, it was used only once, in a relatively minor incident. It is therefore viewed by most commentators as having mainly a dissuasive effect. See, e.g., A. Alen (ed.), *Treatise on Belgian Constitutional Law* (1992) at 81.

governments are likely to be exposed to pressures from those who have an interest in the issue at hand, be it institutional (as in the case of subnational units) or substantive, as in the case of the interest groups. Granting a specific protection to states' rights goes therefore beyond the mere problem of preserving the specific interests of national governments in the Community system.

D. Conclusion: Does Subsidiarity Really Matter?[84]

Important as subsidiarity may be as a political issue, and stimulating as the technical problems raised by its implementation undoubtedly are, its true importance for the Community should not be exaggerated. Indeed, irrespective of the attempt to give flesh to it in the Treaty,[85] I would argue that the subsidiarity *concept* is ill-adapted to the problems it is meant to solve.

To be understood, this remark should be viewed in relation to the overall evolution of federal systems. The traditional vision of federalism, which has for so long influenced judicial constructs, was characterized by the view that a clear line should be drawn between the respective competences of the centre and the periphery. However, this dualism has been challenged by the contemporary evolution of federal systems: the increased complexity of industrial societies and the growth of government intervention have led to a growing interpenetration between the action of both levels of government.

Institutionally, this interdependence has been reflected in the growth of intergovernmental relations. Instances of intergovernmental cooperation abound: even international relations, which are often regarded as a field of federal competence *par excellence*, are not immune from this kind of pressure.[86] Some have even analysed this shift from dualist to cooperative federalism as an evolution of the very concept of federalism.[87]

How does all this affect subsidiarity?

The answer is simple. Subsidiarity starts from the implicit assumption that one can distinguish, in the web of functions assumed by modern states, those that should remain within the purview of lower levels, and those which should be fulfilled at a higher level. This, as I have tried to show, is no easy task. If we consider culture, we will rapidly be faced with the fact that although culture is generally seen as a field where lower levels should be acting, it will not infrequently take the form of an

---

84 This section draws largely on Dehousse, 'Autonomie régionale et intégration européenne: les leçons de l'expérience communautaire', in O. Jacot-Guillarmod (ed.), *The EEA Agreement – Comments and Reflexions* (1992) 693-705.

85 In other words, the following remarks are not directly linked to the wording of Article 3b, but rather to what I regard to be the essence of the concept. This may be one of the reasons why my reading of subsidiarity is in sharp contrast with that of L. Cohen-Tanugi, *L'Europe en danger* (1992) at 157-169.

86 R. Dehousse, *Fédéralisme et relations internationales* (1991).

87 G. Sawer, *Modern Federalism* (1976).

economic good to be traded across national borders. The same is true for environmental protection: although it is often a matter of local concern, some problems – acid rain, the depletion of the ozone layer – call for action at much higher levels.

Thus one sees that at the institutional level, the main problem is not so much to determine in an abstract fashion which authority should exercise a given function, but rather to manage interdependence among related areas. A provision dealing with free movement of cultural goods will touch both the question of free movement – for which action by the centre seems needed – and culture – which often belongs to regional competences. One may of course choose to ignore the link between these various elements of the problem, but in this case any solution is likely to give rise to conflicts. Forces such as technical and economic interdependence or the growth of government intervention,[88] which often make integration necessary, also make it difficult to handle a concept like subsidiarity.

The above analysis suggests that subsidiarity is a somewhat overrated concept. Seen in this light, the line pursued by the drafters of the Maastricht treaty appears most reasonable. Far from pursuing an illusory separation of national and Community competences, they have transformed subsidiarity into a principle regulating the use of Community competences. Article 3b thus contains a set of interrelated rules: the regulatory guidelines contained in paragraph 2 supplement the principle of attributed powers recalled in paragraph 1, while the proportionality test of paragraph 3 is a logical component of any subsidiarity assessment.

Naturally, this regulatory approach leads to a greater degree of uncertainty than if the subsidiarity spirit had been used to impose a clear demarcation of competences between the Community and its Member States. This concern is at the root of many lawyers' criticisms of Article 3b.[89] Yet would it really make sense to draw clear-cut lines where reality is characterized by increasing interdependence?

Such a view has clear implications as regards the implementation of the subsidiarity principle. Even if the concept retains some political value, as a general guideline in favour of decentralization I would argue that its direct utility as a legal instrument is limited. As it currently stands in the Treaty, it will not readily nor easily be used by the Court of Justice, except in exceptional cases.

Alternative ways to implement its philosophy are therefore needed. In my view, the primary problem is one of *process*. What matters is not only who does what, but also how, and the manner in which these two decisions will be made. In other words, specific mechanisms should be set up to protect the Member States against

---

88 It is often stated that government intervention was reduced during the 1980s. This may be true as regards interventions in the realm of economic policy. At the same time, however, regulatory activities in fields like environmental policy or consumer protection have significantly increased. It could therefore be argued that, far from really withdrawing, the state has simply altered its mode of intervention.

89 See in particular L. Cohen-Tanugi, *supra* note 85 and Toth, *supra* note 32, at 1090-91.

undue interferences from the Community, and to provide cooperation among the various levels of authority interested in a given problem

Even if this view were to prevail, it remains doubtful that subsidiarity will cure all the evils of the Community, as some seem to have hoped. Be that as it may, it cannot be denied that the subsidiarity debate is symptomatic of a mood which has gained strength in response to the expanding influence of the Community. Reference to subsidiarity in the Treaty should be understood as a strong political message: the Member States are not prepared to accept an unlimited extension of Community competences. The ratification debates have provided ample evidence of the fact that this view is – rightly or wrongly – shared by large sections of the Community populace. The message seems to have been clearly received by its addressees. No matter what has been said on its actual importance, we are therefore still likely to hear much more of subsidiarity.

Chapter 6

European Citizenship: Its Meaning, Its Potential

Hans Ulrich Jessurun d'Oliveira

I. Towards Union Citizenship

According to the Treaty on European Union concluded in Maastricht, a new 'Part Two' headed: 'Citizenship of the Union' shall be inserted into the Treaty establishing the European Community. This Part Two will consist of five articles, numbered 8 – 8e. This insertion in the Treaty is the first official move of a streetcar which already started its clattering journey a long time ago. Back in 1974, at the Paris summit of the Heads of State, a working party was established to study 'the conditions under which the citizens of the ... Member States could be given social rights as members of the Community'.[1] A year later the report on a road 'Towards European Citizenship' proposed the introduction of 'special rights', to be granted by the Member States to nationals of other Member States. These 'special rights' consisted of some civil and political rights, a nucleus of elements linked with citizenship which could be extended, as preferential treatment to privileged foreigners. The Tindemans report repeated the desirability of extending special rights to nationals of other Community Member States.[2] A Common Market parlance developed in which reference was made to a 'Citizens' Europe'[3] and European citizens, without any clarity about the meaning of these admittedly suggestive terms. Still, the frequent use of the terms by the institutions of the Community indicated a consciousness that something was missing in the build-up of the new legal order: full participation by those who are subjected to its impact.

During the run-up to Maastricht many documents were to pave the way. The Dublin summit had asked

> How will the Union include and extend the notion of Community citizenship carrying with it specific rights (human, political, social, the right of complete freedom of movement and residence etc.) for the citizens of Member States by virtue of these States belonging to the Union?[4]

---

1   *Bull. EC* (12 – 1974) 7, item 11.
2   Tindemans Report *Bull. EC Supp.* 1/76.
3   See for example P. Fontaine, *A Citizen's Europe* (1991). This book features the catchy sub-title 'Europe on the Move'.
4   Sessions of the European Council, Dublin, 25 and 26 June 1990, Annex I on Political Union, in *Conclusions of the Sessions of the European Council* (1975-1990), 388.

A few months later the Council in its Rome Session established the link, missing in Dublin, between the definition of European citizenship and democratic legitimacy of the Union.[5] At the end of 1990, on the occasion of the second Rome session of the Council, although European citizenship did not appear in its conclusions concerning democratic legitimacy, which is not without significance, it mentioned European citizenship separately as an aspect of the European Union. Indeed political rights were not mentioned separately any more in this document, although they may be hidden under the heading of 'civil rights', which continues to indicate 'participation in elections to the European Parliament in the country of residence; possible participation in municipal elections.'[6]

One of the proposed answers was framed by the Spanish Government, and was examined at the Rome meeting of the group of personal representatives of the Heads of State and Government in preparation of the Maastricht Summit.[7] This Spanish document, 'Towards European Citizenship', complained that the notion that nationals of other Member States were nothing more than 'privileged foreigners' had not been overcome, and urged for a major qualitative step 'towards European citizenship'. It defined this citizenship as a

> personal and inalienable status of citizens of Member States, which, by virtue of their membership of the Union, have special rights and tasks, inherent in the framework of the Union, which are exercised and protected specifically within the borders of the Community, without this prejudicing the possibility of taking advantage of this same quality of European citizens also outside the said borders.

It indicated roughly – as to the contents of this European citizenship – five areas of rights:

1. The central core would consist of the full freedom of movement, free choice of place of residence and free participation in the political life of the place of residence.
2. Parallel to the transfer to the Community of policies in the areas of social relations, health, education, culture, environmental protection, consumers, etc., the European citizen would acquire specific rights in these domains.

---

5   Conclusions of the Sessions of the European Council, Rome, supra note 4 at 404.
6   *Conclusions of the Sessions of the European Council, supra* note 4 at 416. The whole text concerned with European citizenship reads as follows:
    The European Council notes with satisfaction the consensus among Member States that the concept of European citizenship should be examined.
    It asks the Conference to consider to which the following rights could be enshrined in the Treaty so as to give substance to this concept:
    – civil rights: participation in elections to the European Parliament in the country of residence; possible participation in municipal elections;
    – social and economic rights: freedom of movement and residence irrespective of engagement in economic activity; equality of opportunity and of treatment for all Community citizens;
    – joint protection of Community citizens outside the Community's borders.
    Consideration should be given to the possible institution of a mechanism for the defence of citizens' rights as regards Community matters ('ombudsman').
    In the implementation of any such provisions, appropriate consideration should be given to particular problems in some Member States.'
7   See *Europe Documents* no. 1653, 2 October 1990.

3. European citizens should receive a higher degree of assistance and diplomatic and consular protection by other Member States.

4. Access to Community institutions should be facilitated and reinforced, especially the right of petition to the EP, and the setting up of a European Ombudsman system could be envisaged, in order to provide the protection of the specific rights of the European citizen.

5. Other possible developments could be proposed, such as the recognition and validity of obligations of military service or alternative service.

These proposals for the introduction of this *dynamic concept* of European citizenship were echoed in the Maastricht Treaty, without however being accepted lock, stock and barrel.

We shall now try to delineate the contours of European citizenship as defined in the Maastricht document. But it may be helpful as an analytical tool, to briefly indicate two dimensions which are generally recognized, be it in different ways, as belonging to the notion of citizenship. In the first place, if a category of persons, endowed with certain rights (and duties) is created or defined, then, by the same token, other persons are excluded. The *inclusion* of certain groups implies the *exclusion* of others. Citizenship takes as its corollary non-citizens. One of the points of establishing citizenship is the exclusion of others from the rights and entitlements granted to these citizens, and from the duties attached to such citizenship. It may be useful to investigate in which ways non-citizens are excluded from those rights attached to citizenship of the Community or the Union.

The demarcation line between citizens and non-citizens, between those who 'belong' and those who do not, is formed by the criterion of *nationality*. Thus we shall have to say something about this ticket to Union citizenship, and especially approach the question about the competence of the Union or the Community to deal with the nationality laws of the Member States.

In the second place there is the matter of the *extension* of the rights and duties which form the conditions for participation in the public life of a community which may be called citizenship. Here we will be primarily interested in the question of whether the Maastricht Treaty makes a difference to the *status quo* which has already been established by the European legal order and its constituent parts – Single Act, secondary legislation, decisions by the European courts – and whether a real improvement of the status of those who 'belong' to this society or the Community has been attained.

Furthermore, insofar as the Community or the Union is something different from the Member States, and insofar as citizenship of a Member State is something different from citizenship of the Union, we may distinguish the specific rights and duties *vis-à-vis* the Union from those *vis-à-vis* the Member States. Inevitably, we will encounter in this (vertical) dimension problems of demarcation between Member States and Union, especially where Community law dictates that there be a certain status in the body politic of a Member State for nationals of other Member

States. The typical example of this troublesome definitional conundrum concerns voting rights in the political bodies of the Member States granted to non-nationals of that State. Is this a right attached to Community citizenship, or is this an extension of Member State citizenship, or both?

II. Nationality and the Union

Although the logic of EC law suggests the assumption that nationality is a Community law term, to be defined according to Community law canons and principles, this is not the case. The considerations which the European Court of Justice (ECJ) has devoted in various decisions to the concept of 'worker' as used in Article 48 of the Treaty, with the objective of establishing a Community definition of the term 'worker' in order to avoid a multitude of variations according to the laws of the Member States, are not valid for the definition of 'national of a Member State'. Although these considerations can also be applied to 'nationals', and the linkage of the term worker with that of national is exclusive and strong, nevertheless there is an overriding argument which prohibits making the term a Community term: the fact that nationality is central to the existence of the Member States. It is not an ordinary legal term, but defines both the status of the Member States and that of the Community more than any other term. As long as the Community consists of independent and sovereign Member States, the competence to define their nationals belongs to each State.[8] This is expressed in an important and revealing declaration annexed to the Maastricht Treaty, which reads as follows:

> The Conference declares that, wherever in the Treaty establishing the European Community reference is made to nationals of the Member States, the question whether an individual possesses the nationality of a Member State shall be settled solely by reference to the national law of the Member State concerned. Member States may declare, for information, who are to be considered their nationals for Community purposes by way of a declaration lodged with the Presidency and may amend any such declaration when necessary.

Such a declaration by a Member State therefore is simply an indication for the other Member States and Community institutions about which persons are considered nationals by the State concerned. It is information about the law of the State involved, and does not bind that State. The recipients of the message, however, are safe in being guided in their actions by it, as long as the declarations have not been changed. Without these declarations the other States and the Community have to delve into the nationality law of the other States at their own risk, and are obliged to accept as such nationals those who can show valid passports or other identity documents.

---

8   See also Verhoeven, 'Les citoyens de l'Europe', *Annales de droit de Louvain* (1992/3) 169.

These declarations, of which in particular those of the United Kingdom and the Federal Republic of Germany must be mentioned here, have been complied with by the other Member States and the Community. In the case of the United Kingdom, these declarations had the effect of restricting the number of United Kingdom citizens for Community purposes; in the case of the Federal Republic of Germany on the contrary, the implication has been to include some 20 million persons whose nationality of the German Democratic Republic was, to say the least, doubtful. Nevertheless the Member States have shown that they are prepared to recognize these declarations, and have accepted the expansion of the EC with some 20 million newcomers (members of the former GDR and *Aussiedler*) without audible protest. Negotiations on accession of the GDR would have caused more complications than the anodine accession of five *Länder* to the territory of the FRG. In a way, the German unification can be seen as the melting together of two nationalities. The problem whether a bipatride with a Member State nationality and a third country nationality can be considered as a Member State national for Community law purposes (so as to be entitled to take advantage, for example, of the right of establishment and freedom of movement) has recently been decided by the ECJ in the *Micheletti* case.[9] The Court held that:

> La définition des conditions d'acquisition et de perte de la nationalité relève, conformément au droit international, de la compétence de chaque Etat membre, compétence qui doit être exercée dans le respect du droit communautaire. Il n'appartient pas par contre à la législation d'un Etat membre, de restreindre les effets de l'attribution de la nationalité d'un autre Etat Membre, en exigeant une condition supplémentaire pour la reconnaisssance de cette nationalité en vue de l'exercice des libertés fondamentales prévues par le Traité.[10]

The ECJ refers to international law in holding that it is for each Member State to define the conditions for acquisition and loss of nationality. This may be taken as a reference, *inter alia*, to Article 1 of the Convention of 1930 on Certain Questions relating to Conflict of Nationality Laws, which codifies the law on the subject and states that:

> It is for each State to determine under its own law who are its nationals. This law shall be recognized by other States insofar as it is consistent with international conventions, international customs and the principles of law generally recognized with regard to nationality.

That the ECJ restricts this 'reserved domain' by the phrase that the jurisdiction has to be exercised 'dans le respect du droit communautaire' is in line with Article 1 of the Hague Convention, which mentions that its exercise must be in line with

---

9   Case C-369/90, *M.V. Micheletti and others* v. *Delegacion del Gobierno en Cantabria*, Judgment of
     7 July 1992 (not yet reported). See also d'Oliveira, 'Plural Nationality and the European Union', in
     H.U. Jessurun d'Oliveira (ed.), *Plural Nationality, New Trends* (1993 forthcoming).
10   Ibid., at para. 10.

'international conventions', of which the EC Treaty is an example. Which specific restrictions the EC Treaty would imply is not clear.[11]

In shorthand the Heads of State and Government repeated their position when deciding at the Edinburgh Summit of December 1992, on the problems raised by Denmark on the Treaty of European Union. According to the conclusions of the Presidency concerning citizenship, they stated:[12]

> The question whether an individual possesses the nationality of a Member State will be settled solely by reference to the national law of the Member State concerned.

The Member States did not adopt the European Court of Justice ruling in *Micheletti* that these national laws must be in accordance with Community law. This may indicate that they were not prepared to accept inroads upon their reserved domain, and may have been an attempt to at least humour Danish and other sensibilities.

III. Citizenship of the Union: Its Contents

The magic wand of dramatic language is waved in Article 8(1), which bravely declares: 'Citizenship of the Union is hereby established'. This feat, reminiscent of the first verses of the Gospel according to Saint John, defies the incredulity of doubting Thomasses who believe that *'ex nihilo nihil'*.

The first thing we must note about this citizenship is that it is not of the Community but of the Union, which is based on the Community but also includes forms of intergovernmental cooperation. This means that not only the legislative instruments of the Community are available for the definition of the contents of European citizenship, but agreements within the framework of intergovernmental activities as well, including the Maastricht Treaty itself. The establishment of a European Union is intimately connected with the establishment of this Union citizenship, as is borne out by one of the recitals of the preamble explicitly demonstrating the resolution of the Member States 'to establish a citizenship common to nationals of their countries'.[13] One of the objectives of the Union listed in Article B is:

> to strengthen the protection of the rights and interests of the nationals of its Member States through the introduction of a citizenship of the Union.

---

11 See d'Oliveira, 'Plural Nationality and the European Union', *supra* note 9.
12 European Council in Edinburgh 11-12 December 1992, Conclusions of the Presidency, Part B, Annex 1, 53.
13 Is it significant that this consideration does not speak of 'the nationals' but of 'nationals'? Or is this one of the many slips of the pen? Is there the possibility of a category of nationals of Member States who are excluded from Union citizenship? I would answer negatively, unless hereby it is tacitly implied that there are nationals who are not nationals 'for Community purposes'.

Citizenship is of course a very nice word indeed, but, one may ask, is it any more potent than those mirrors and beads with which natives of other continents were gratified in the colonial past? The Maastricht Treaty affirms in Article 8(2) that it is more:

> Citizens of the Union shall enjoy the rights conferred by this Treaty and shall be subject to the duties imposed thereby.

This provision gives at least a clear indication as to where to look for the bundle of rights and duties attached to the concept of Union citizenship: not only in Part Two of the Treaty, but in the *Treaty as a whole*. One would be inclined to think that these rights are listed exclusively in the Articles 8a-8d, whereas Article 8e enshrines the dynamics and procedures for a further development of the Union citizenship. This is only part of the truth. Although some important elements have found their place in the newly inserted Part Two of the Treaty establishing the European Community, there are also, scattered through this Treaty and the Maastricht document provisions which form part and parcel of the concept of European citizenship, as Article 8(2) already indicates. Let us distinguish these rights conferred by Part Two (A) and in other places of the Maastricht Treaty (B).

A. The Core of European Citizenship

From a comparative point of view it is highly interesting to note that the core and origin of European citizenship is the right to free movement. Mobility is the central element, around which other rights crystallize. Article 8a confers 'the right to move and reside freely within the territory of the Member States ...'. This is not normally considered to be a political right linked up with democratic systems of government, but forms part of the fundamental economic freedoms of the European Market: the mobility of economically active persons has now been elevated to the core of European citizenship and expanded into mobility for persons generally. In other words: the economically irrelevant people have been promoted to the status of persons.

It is only as a secondary issue that 'the right to vote and to stand as a candidate at municipal elections in the Member State in which he resides' is mentioned,[14] whereas the right to vote and stand for election in the European Parliament is conferred on every citizen, even those who reside in Member States other than their 'own'.

In Article 8d the right is given to citizens to petition the European Parliament, and to apply to an Ombudsman whose office is to be established, with complaints about instances of maladministration in the activities of the Community institutions or bodies (European courts excepted).

---

14   Article 8b.

Finally in Article 8c an 'entitlement' is bestowed on the citizen, to protection in third countries where his own country is not represented. There he is entitled to 'protection by the diplomatic or consular authorities of any Member State, on the same conditions as the nationals of other Member States'.[15]

B. Scattered Rights

The Union Treaty itself permits us, as has been mentioned earlier in this paragraph, to seek out hidden treasures concerning Union citizenship. I have referred already to Article B which states as one of the objectives of the Union the strengthening of 'the protection of the rights and interests of the nationals of its Member States through the introduction of a citizenship of the Union' of which Part Two of the EC Treaty forms an element of its implementation.

Furthermore, and at least as important is Article F(2) of the Union Treaty which explicitly states, for the first time that

> The Union shall respect fundamental rights, as guaranteed by the European Conventions for the Protection of Human Rights and Fundamental Freedoms ... and as they result from the constitutional traditions common to the Member States, as general principles of Community Law.[16]

It will be interesting to follow the development of this very general reference to the 1950 Rome convention and its common constitutional provisions; splendid surprises are not to be discounted.

Given the history of the development of the concept of European (Union) citizenship, in which fundamental rights have been mentioned regularly,[17] it is plausible that these are seen as an element of this citizenship, an intentional part of the definition. The fact that fundamental rights and freedoms are not reserved for nationals of Member States, but that others under the jurisdiction of the Member States and the Community are entitled to their exercise is not decisive. We will see[18] that this is the case for most aspects of Union citizenship.[19]

These historical and structural indications are important reasons for the statement that the boundaries of Union citizenship are not drawn by Title Two of the EC Treaty, but that rights and entitlements, appertaining to citizenship, may be found elsewhere in and around the Treaty. It ultimately depends upon the notion, the

---

15 See also Art. 138e.
16 Art. F(3) is an Article in itself and would have merited a separate lettering or numbering.
17 See, e.g., the text adopted at the Dublin meeting of the European Council, *supra* note 4.
18 *Infra*, section V.
19 Verhoeven, *supra* note 9, at 187, seems to include fundamental rights in the notion of Union citizenship as well: 'Il avait certes été fréquemment question, avant la signature du Traité de Maastricht, d'inclure les droits fondamentaux parmis les attributs de la citoyenneté européenne. Il n'en est cependant pas fait mention dans l'article G du Traité de Maastricht qui introduit celle-ci dans le Traité de Rome. Il ne s'ensuit pas toutefois que ces droits aient été écartés. Tout au contraire, leur respect par l'Union est expressément visé à l'article F, comme l'une des exigences fondamentales de celle-ci'.

concept of citizenship, a partly ideological, political, contextual concept, where the line will be drawn between rights belonging to citizenship and other rights, and where these rights (and duties) may be found.

The citizens of the Union are mentioned elsewhere in the Treaty as well, especially in the Articles 138 et seq. Thus Article 138a contains an exclusive, ideological statement to the effect that political parties at European level are important as a factor for

> integration within the Union. They contribute to forming a European awareness and to expressing the political will of the citizens of the Union.

This newly inserted provision, of which the legally binding contents are neither here nor there, has indeed been displaced from Part Two[20] to the title concerning the European Parliament. In this Part Five on Community institutions we again find articles laying down detailed provisions concerning the right to petition the EP[21] and the creation of an ombudsman system;[22] furthermore the articles concerning direct universal suffrage for the EP have been maintained as slightly amended.[23]

Finally, mention must be made of the provisions concerning such topics as social policy, education, vocational training (Title VIII), culture (Title IX), public health (Title X), consumer protection (Title XI), environment (Title XVI) which all have implications for the intentional aspects of the term citizenship. They have been mentioned in the important Spanish document mentioned earlier. This is not an exhaustive list of elements of citizenship, rather an indication that rights connected with citizenship are scattered throughout the Treaty, and that lack of formal coherence is hiding behind the declaration that it concerns a 'dynamic concept'. How dynamic is this Union citizenship, as compared with the status quo?

The question has its weight, as one of the factors accounting for Danish reluctance to ratify the Union Treaty stems from the unwillingness to accept any creeping dynamics adding to or reducing rights which exist under Community or Danish law. This aloofness is apparent from the unilateral declaration which Denmark intends to associate to the Danish Act of Ratification of the Union Treaty. Here Denmark emphatically states that:

> 1. Citizenship of the Union is a political and legal concept which is entirely different from the concept of citizenship within the meaning of the Constitution of the Kingdom of Denmark and of the Danish legal system ...[24]

> 2. Citizenship of the Union *in no way in itself* gives a national of another Member State the right to obtain Danish citizenship or any of the rights, duties, privileges or advantages

---

20 Article 8 et seq.
21 Article 138d.
22 Article 138e.
23 Article 138(3).
24 See Conclusions of the Presidency, Edinburgh, 12 December 1992, Part B, Annex 3 57-59 (emphasis added).

that are inherent in Danish citizenship ... Denmark will fully respect all specific rights *expressly provided for* in the Treaty and applying to the nationals of the Member States.

In view of this declaration the Edinburgh Summit decided that:

> The provisions of Part Two of the Treaty establishing the European Community relating to citizenship of the Union give nationals of the Member States additional rights and protection as specified in that Part. They do not in any way take the place of the national citizenship. The question whether an individual possesses the nationality of a Member State will be settled solely by reference to the national law of the Member State concerned.[25]

While Denmark is apparently afraid of blurred edges between national citizenship (and nationality) and Union citizenship, the Edinburgh Summit tries to explain that there are clear demarcation lines between the two. Whether this separation is watertight remains to be seen: where a number of rights are granted to take part in the public and political life of the Member States, the citizenship involved may not be full, but still amounts to partial citizenship in the Member States. As long as there is no agreement among the Member States on the concept of citizenship, as distinguished from nationality, Union citizenship may have the potential of becoming the sum total of the citizenships in the Member States combined, which, of course, will mean the end of the Member States.

IV. What's new?

The *word* 'citizenship' is primarily new. It gives some coherence to certain rights which are conferred upon certain categories of persons, especially those who possess a nationality of a Member State. If one looks closely, however, the Union Treaty has frozen the existing status of nationals of Member States, and has only marginally added new and relevant elements to it.

Let us take the example of the freedom of movement. This freedom, considered as the nucleus of citizenship, dealt with in Article 8a, and conferred on 'every citizen' (read: all nationals of Member States) is certainly not dramatically larger than the one existing under the SEA and secondary legislation: the citizens are told explicitly that their freedom of movement and residence is 'subject to the limitations and conditions laid down in this Treaty and by the measures adopted to give it effect'. This amounts to declaring that not every citizen has the right to move and reside freely within the territory of the Member States, given the existing limitations and conditions.[26] What is given with the one hand is taken back with the other.

It is only in the future that the freedom of movement may be developed to a fuller extent, and it is in the procedure leading to new legislation in this area that

---

25   Ibid., at 53.
26   On the present state of affairs, but not without desiderata see O'Keeffe, 'The Free Movement of Persons and the Single Market', 17 *ELRev.* (1992) 3.

something new can be detected. Although Article 8a(2) takes as its starting point that the 'Council shall act unanimously on a proposal from the Commission and after obtaining the assent of the European Parliament' to facilitate the exercise of the rights referred to in paragraph 1, which makes the road rather narrow, it allows for exceptions as well, and these seem to be the rule. In various modes the Articles 49, 54, 56 and 57 have been revised with the introduction of the famous Article 189b procedure for the issue of new directives or regulations to bring about freedom of movement of workers, freedom of establishment, freedom to take up and pursue activities as self-employed persons, and so on. In this area acting by qualified majority will then prevail, and unanimity will be the exception. It remains to be seen whether the Article 189b will yield the hoped-for results of acceleration and deepening of the decision-making process.

Although it may be regarded as a step forward that the Union Treaty has now made available, at least in principle, the freedom of movement for *all* citizens, i.e. for *all* nationals of the Member States, whether economically active as workers and self-employed or not, the road towards the fulfillment of this arcadian objective nevertheless still seems long.

On 8 May 1992, the European Commission submitted a communication on the abolition of border controls to the European Parliament and to the Council of Ministers. In this communication the Commission reaffirms that controls of persons at the internal borders must be abolished by January 1 1993.[27] At the General Affairs Council on May 11, however, the British Secretary to the Foreign Office Douglas Hurd confirmed the refusal of Great Britain to accept the abolition of controls at British borders and thus refused to accept the Commission's interpretation of Article 8a SEA.[28] The Commission takes the position that this declaration, which argues that the deadline of 31 December 1992 for establishing the internal market did not give rise to any legal consequences, cannot change the binding force of a Treaty provision. The Commission has considered taking measures against countries which have not implemented Article 8a by 1 January 1993, or that interpret the provision in such a way as to exclude third country nationals from the freedom of movement within the internal market. This will presumably take the form of placing a complaint at the Court of Justice against states that refuse to accept the consequences of Article 8a of the SEA.[29] The new European Commissioner for the Internal Market, Vanni d'Archirafi, took a more cautious stand in a meeting of the European Parliament's Committee on Civil Liberties and Internal Affairs. This was not appreciated and led to a Resolution by the EP inviting the Commission to take action against Member States that fail to fulfil their obligations under Article 8a, 100 and 235 of the Treaty. In case the Commission and Council come up with answers falling short of the demands of the

---

27 *Agence Europe*, No. 5724, 7 May 1992. See also *Agence Europe* No. 5726, 9 May 1992.
28 *List of Events ESMV*, May 1992. See also *Agence Europe* No. 5728, 13 May 1992 and *Migration News Sheet* (hereafter referred to as *MNS*) June 1992.
29 *Agence Europe*, 2 January 1992.

EP, 'it will not hesitate to use all the measures at its disposal, and in particular its right under Article 175 of the EEC Treaty to obtain that the obligations clearly driving from Article 8a are fully complied with and applied without delay'.[30] Thus the new cautiousness of the Commission is met with a collision course by the EP. Recently the new French Government issued statements to the effect that it would not abolish its internal borders as long as effective measures at the external borders of other Member States such as Italy were not put into place, and it furthermore withdrew its intention to deposit the instruments of ratification of the Schengen Implementing Agreement with the Government of Luxembourg under Article 139 of the Agreement.

The Dublin Convention on crossing external borders, one of the 'necessary' flanking measures, still has to deal with its 'stone' of contention, Gibraltar.[31]

If the effort attached to the abolition of internal borders reflects the value which the Community attaches to the freedom of movement of persons, as the core of citizenship, then the ranking of this objective leaves no doubt. The abolition of internal borders for persons is a complete failure.

Similar remarks can be made concerning the right to vote and stand for elections to the European Parliament. The *via dolorosa* of the implementation of Article 138(3) of the EC Treaty is a well-known example of the legal, technical and political barriers to a uniform procedure for elections by direct universal suffrage in all Member States. The Act concerning the elections of the representatives of the European Parliament,[32] with its Article 7(2) stating that 'the electoral procedure shall be governed in each Member State by its national provisions', bears witness to this defeat. There is no uniformity whatsoever. Since the 1976 Act, the goal of a common procedure is still out of reach. Differences of perspective and view concerning nearly all elements of such a procedure reign supreme.[33]

The Maastricht Treaty now deals with one aspect of the right to vote and stand for election in the European Parliament; the position of citizens of the Union residing in another Member State than that of which (s)he possesses the nationality. In the present situation the laws of some Member States already grant these rights to nationals of other Member States, others do not. In some Member States, such as Italy, Spain and the Netherlands, even nationals resident in third countries are entitled to vote in European Parliamentary elections.

The Union Treaty does not really *add* to the existing voting rights for the European Parliament, but specifies that the situation of Member State nationals resident in other Member States has to be dealt with. It complicates matters considerably by adding that this specific problem shall be tackled 'by the Council,

30   *MNS* March 1993.
31   See d'Oliveira, 'Expanding External and Shrinking Internal Borders: Europe's Defense Mechanisms in the Areas of Free Movement, Immigration and Asylum', in D. O'Keeffe and Twomey (eds.), *Unresolved Legal Issues of the Maastricht Treaty* (1993).
32   Annexed to Council Decision of 20 September 1976, OJ L 278 of 8 October 1976.
33   See Doc. A3 – 0152/91 of 29 May 1991 (interim report De Gucht).

acting unanimously, on a proposal from the Commission and after consulting with the European Parliament', however, 'without prejudice to Article 138(3) and to the provisions adopted for its implementation'. Thus Article 8b(2) introduces *two* procedures to arrive at a solution for one and the same problem: that of structuring a uniform procedure for European Parliament elections. How a 'prejudice' can be avoided is extremely problematic given the European Parliament's right to propose a regime for its elections. It is clear that the European Parliament will oppose all initiatives of the Commission in this area as infringing upon its own right of initiative. Whether the 'detailed arrangements' which the Council is required to adopt prior to December 31 1993 will actually be put into place before that date leaves no doubt: the answer is of course negative.[34] The deadline set is much too early and the uniformity of the arrangements is all but guaranteed, given the explicit allowance for 'derogations where warranted by problems specific to a Member State'.

Thus, Article 8b(2) not only adds nothing to the existing entitlements or rights of citizens, but is furthermore framed with a complete lack of awareness of the fact that it forms part of such a supposedly important part of the Treaty, in which the central rights of the citizens of the Union are enumerated. One might have expected that the general principles for active and passive voting rights for the European Parliament would have been mentioned, instead of appearing as a detail;[35] that *one* procedure would have been indicated, as well as a slightly more realistic deadline. Presumably an urge to create a parallel provision to Article 8b(1) concerning 'the right to vote and stand as a candidate at municipal elections in the Member State in which he resides' has led the framers of this Part Two astray: the two voting rights are very different in nature.

Certainly a new element in the Union Treaty is the introduction of 'the right to vote and stand for election as a candidate at municipal elections in the Member State where he resides, under the same conditions as nationals of that State'. There is of course a logical ambiguity in the provision. If a Member State does not allow its own nationals to take part in municipal elections if they are residing abroad, the formal equality principle of Article 8b(1) leads to the conclusion that nationals of other Member States resident in this Member State are excluded in the same way, because they are residing 'abroad'. Although I do not presume that this was indeed the intention of the framers, this interpretation nevertheless would fit into the rationale to extend voting rights to citizens resident in another Member State: the idea that the lives of these citizens are directly affected by decisions on the local level concerning housing, education, public services etc. Those resident abroad are less directly involved in the life of the municipality.

---

34   It will not only take until at least the year 1992 to ratify the Union Treaty, but changes in the constitutions of several Member States will almost certainly take some more years.
35   Compare for example a Constitution stating merely that: 'Nationals residing abroad may vote in the elections for our Parliament', instead of: 'Nationals who have been residing abroad may vote in the election of etc.'.

But there is on the theoretical level a more important issue: Can the right to participate in local elections be considered as an aspect of citizenship of the Union? Taking part in the political life in a municipality of a Member State is a far cry from *European* citizenship: exercise of voting rights for national elections would be a much more relevant aspect of European citizenship, given the involvement of (some) national bodies of representation in the framing and implementation of the European legal and political order. Again, it is on the national level that the really important basic and general policies will be developed that concern aliens. As the EP has not seen its powers substantially increased in the Union Treaty, there is a tendency in national parliaments to take back the powers which they have in practice yielded earlier in controlling governmental activities on the European level.

I submit that granting rights at local elections have more to do with unexpressed endeavours to dissolve the identities of the Member States, and indeed their statehood, than with democracy on a European level. One may question the extent to which Article F, solemnly evoking that 'the Union shall respect the national identities of its Member States', is compatible with Article 8b(1) which imposes the breaking up of those direct links, which until recently existed between the definition of the legitimation of the State in terms of the sovereignty of the people belonging to that State on the basis of nationality, and the exercise of political powers in the State concerned.[36] To my mind, the two provisions are mutually exclusive. Insofar as Article 8b(1) entails revisions of constitutions of certain Member States, as is the case in Germany, France and possibly in Luxembourg[37] as well as other States, one may conclude that the Union does not respect the national identity of the Member States; assuming that a constitution could qualify as a repository of the national identity. This remark is not to imply that the present writer is not in favour of extending voting rights to non-nationals, but simply that Article F is untrue; and that the Union Treaty speaks with at least two tongues.

The dynamics of the concept of European citizenship speeds: the right to participate in local elections shall, according to the Treaty, be put into place by arrangements to be adopted before the end of 1994, a year later than those for the European Parliament. Optimism or lack of realism? We shall see.[38]

As for the right to petition the European Parliament as laid down in Article 8d(1) and Article 138d, it must be remarked that this right already existed under the Rules of the European Parliament. Thus the Article, as the reference to Article138d shows,

---

36 See, e.g., Art. 20(2) of the German Basic Law and the recent decisions of the *Bundesverfassungsgericht* denying *Kommunalwahlrecht für Ausländer* on the basis of Article 28 *Grundgesetz.*

37 This country will probably avail itself of the derogations offered by Art. 8b.

38 Whether these voting rights, granted under Art. 8b, are indeed rights or are to be conceived as obligations or duties, as they are under the laws of some Member States, will be for the Council to decide. If they opt to construe this political participation as a duty (which I consider rather improbable) it would be one of the very few examples of duties imposed on the Union citizens, mentioned in Art. 8. If fundamental freedoms are included in the concept of Union citizenship, and one accepts some forms of horizontal effect of these rights and freedoms, there is room for construing corresponding fundamental duties or obligations (*Grundpflichte*).

has only a systematic, token value; it does not add any right which did not already exist.

The Ombudsman, however, is a new institution designed to reinforce the position of those who are 'subject to instances of maladministration in the activities of the Community institutions or bodies...'[39] However, it is to be noted that this mandate reduces the rights of Union citizens to those of Community citizens, as the Ombudsman is not empowered to conduct inquiries and to report to the European Parliament concerning complaints about the functioning of institutions or bodies, executive committees, or other pillars of the Union than that of the Community. The same goes for the right of petition to the European Parliament, which is restricted to 'a matter which comes within the Community's field of activity'. Here too only Community citizenship, which does not exist as such, is involved. There is no outlet for complaints about matters concerning the way Union bodies operate, which are not at the same time Community bodies or institutions, or are not functioning in their Community capacity. This is an especially deplorable vacuum concerning the activities of bodies such as the one set up by Article K4, a Coordinating Committee with far-reaching powers without corresponding parliamentary or judicial control.

A few words on the diplomatic protection for Union citizens.[40] This entitlement, which must be implemented by the Member States before 31 December 1993 – this is of course out of the question – is granted on the level of the Member States, not on that of the European Union or Community. In theory it would have been possible to create the competence for the Union or Community as a subject of international law, an international person, comparable to the United Nations,[41] to exercise diplomatic protection, not only as regards staff members of the EC, but also for Union citizens at large.[42] The Maastricht Treaty opted however for a more 'horizontal' form: diplomatic protection by Member State A for nationals of Member State B. Whether third countries will accept that a Member State will act on behalf of nationals of other Member States remains to be seen. There are many instances in which a country represents the rights and interest of other States, especially if diplomatic relations with the host State are strained or broken, but this protection by proxy has to be accepted by the host country. The real question therefore is whether the Member State which takes upon itself the exercise of diplomatic protection *vis-à-vis* a national of another Member State, can act unilaterally in this respect. Does the Union afford a 'genuine link' or does it constitute a 'supranationality' of the claim in such a way that the third State has to

39   Article 138e.
40   See also Verhoeven, *supra* note 9, at 185, 187.
41   See the Advisory Opinion of the International Court of Justice in the *Bernadotte* Case, 174 ICJ Reports (1949).
42   It is understandable that the Maastricht Treaty opted for a 'safe' solution: even for staff members the capacity of the EC to exercise diplomatic protection was at that time denied. See, e.g., Pescatore, *RdC* (1961-II) 219. Cf. I. Brownlie, *Principles of Public International Law* (1979) 684. See also Blumann, 'L'Europe des citoyens', *Revue du Marché Commun* (1991) at 283, who urges for the exercise of diplomatic protection by Community institutions, such as the Presidency or the troika.

accept the diplomatic protection whether it agrees or not? The Maastricht Treaty seems to start from the assumption that this type of diplomatic protection is to be negotiated for and cannot be unilaterally relied on. It is furthermore to be taken from the text of Article 8c that the details of this diplomatic protection by proxy have to be agreed upon in intergovernmental negotiations between the Member States, and that the Union as such is not to lay down rules in this respect.

Whether the Member States will be able to develop a uniform regime for the diplomatic protection for nationals of other Member States is doubtful, given the different approaches employed among the Member States. On the other hand, it is not very practical to charge the diplomatic missions of the EC with this task.[43]

Finally, an interesting but not very transparent solution has been found for the protection of fundamental rights and freedoms, which will be respected by the Union.[44] These will not be seen as fundamental principles of the Union, but as 'general principles of Community Law'. Does this imply, that the Union, insofar as it is something else or something more than the Community – and this follows from Article A – is subjected to general principles of Community Law? How are these Community principles upheld in the Union in areas where the European Courts have no competence? It is doubtful whether the respect for fundamental rights is much more than sanctimonious lip service as long as it is not accompanied by access to Union courts for citizens of this Union.

To sum up: if it is asked just how dynamic a concept this notion of Union citizenship is, the answer must be that it is for the time being nothing more than a new name for a bunch of existing rights, a nice blue ribbon around scattered elements of a general notion of citizenship. The dynamism is – apart from a few additions to existing rights – pie in the sky, the promise of future developments. Instead of bringing order to the notion of citizenship, one must look for important aspects elsewhere than in Part Two of the Treaty establishing the European Community, which is supposedly devoted to the topic. It is thus more appropriate in this area to talk about the Community legal disorder, the European disunited legal non-system.

V. Union Citizenship and Exclusion

The previous section detailed the rights, which may collectively form the ingredients for the notion of Union citizenship. This Union citizenship functions inside the Union as indicating those who are entitled to participate in the life of the Union or the collectivity which constitutes this Union. As stated earlier, it also has

---

43 There are EC missions in places such as Ankara, Athens, Caracas, Geneva, Montevideo, New York, Ottawa, Santiago, Tokyo and Washington. Cf. H. Schermers, *Inleiding tot het Internationale Institutionele Recht* (1985) 285.
44 Article F(2).

the function of distinguishing those who 'belong' from outsiders: the objective is to *exclude* others. The question must now be asked, whether the bundle of rights connected with the notion of Union citizenship indeed fulfils this function of exclusion. It is implied from the outset, that if there is only little differentiation in terms of the rights connected with citizenship as compared with the rights which are granted to various groups of non-citizens, then citizenship does not fulfil this function properly.

The question then to be asked is whether persons who do not possess the nationality of one of the Member States are excluded from the rights which are presently being bestowed upon Union citizens. Let us begin by considering local elections. This Community right must be realized on the level of the Member States, although it is introduced as an aspect of Community law. Member States, when designing the introduction of this right, will certainly be confronted with the question whether there is reason to grant similar rights to resident non-nationals of Member States. There are already several Member States who have answered this question positively and have granted this category the right to vote and to be elected in local elections.[45] The debate is premised by a whole range of factors, including the demographic set-up of each country in terms of nationalities of the resident population: if, as in Luxemburg, more than 25% of the population is non-national the readiness to accept the political influence of such a large body is less likely than in a country like Ireland or Portugal, where the foreign population does not exceed 1%. The breakdown of the foreign population under several perspectives in the various countries also plays a role in these public debates.

It is not clear whether international law permits differentiate between nationals of Member States and others when granting voting rights, and whether this does not amount to discrimination direct or indirect, either on the basis of nationality or other characteristics of the excluded groups. The reasons put forward to allow Member State nationals to participate in local elections are not exclusively linked up with the emergence of a Community or Union collectivity, or with central elements of Community Law, but refer also to principles of democracy. Article F furthermore, in a phrase which may be as normative as it looks descriptive, mentions 'the principles of democracy' on which the systems of government of the Member States are founded. One may ask whether this principle of democracy can be reconciled with the inclusion of nationals of Member States while all other residents are excluded from (local) elections, for this entails distinguishing between a group of nationalities and all other nationalities. To create first-class and second-class citizens in this respect will *prima facie* amount to discrimination and lack of

45   See generally Sieveking, Barwig, Lörchen, Schumacher (eds.), *Das Kommunalwahlrecht für Ausländer* (1989), with a large bibliography on the topic; see in particular Sieveking, 'Kommunalwahlrecht für Ausländer in den Mitgliedstaaten der EG – Ein Europäischer Vergleich', at 69-90. Ireland, Denmark and the Netherlands have introduced voting rights in local elections for all non-nationals who comply with certain criteria (age, residence, etc.); the UK and Portugal allow certain categories of foreigners to vote, whereas in other Member States sometimes very lively debates – e.g. in Germany and France – are ignited by the prospects of Community action.

democracy, unless there are very good reasons for this distinction. I do not think that the social and political ties between the Member States justify the exclusion of persons who otherwise fulfil the conditions but do not possess the nationality of a Member State. Indeed, this type of reasoning has led Denmark to extend to all foreigners the election rights which had been granted to nationals of the other Scandinavian countries on the basis of the social links between the Nordic nations. In other countries, like the Netherlands, the distinction between nationals and resident foreigners has from the outset been seen as a democratic problem, especially in view of the integration of minorities. Thus, whether or not the exclusion of non-nationals of Member States from local elections violates non-discrimination rules of international law, my forecast is that wherever these voting rights are introduced, they will sooner or later be granted to *all* foreigners, regardless of nationality, who otherwise comply with residence conditions.

Mention should here be made of the Council of Europe's Convention on the Participation of Foreigners in Public Life at Local Level.[46] Article 6 of this interesting convention is explicitly devoted to the right to vote in local authority elections; each party to the Convention undertakes 'to grant to *every foreign resident* the right to vote and to stand for election in local authority elections...'[47] It is clear that any foreign resident, not only nationals of Member States of the Council of Europe, is granted this right.

As for the right to address a petition to the European Parliament, Article 138d explicitly grants this not only to citizens, but to 'any natural or legal person residing or having its registered office in a Member State' generally, and they are furthermore entitled to petition the European Parliament 'individually or in association with other citizens or persons'. Thus, the right to petition does not differentiate between 'citizens' and other persons, although it must be noted that it seems to differentiate between these two categories as regards residence: Union citizens wherever residing, even in third countries, and others residing in a Member State, are entitled to this right. Thus, for citizens the link of nationality of a Member State seems to suffice, whereas for others residence must furnish an independent link.[48]

The same situation is to be found concerning the availability of the Ombudsman. Under Article 138e both categories of persons – 'any citizen of the Union or any natural ... person residing in a Member State' – have access to the Ombudsman. Here again there is no significant differentiation.

As far as human rights and fundamental freedoms are concerned, Article F(2) solemnly declares that the Union shall respect them as general principles of

---

46 Strasbourg, 5 February 1992, European Treaty Series 144.
47 Emphasis added. Art. 6 reduces this to the right to vote only, and Art. 7 explicitly allows States to reduce the required period of residence.
48 There are cases, concerning matters which come under the Community's (Union's?) field of activity, affecting non-Community nationals or legal persons residing outside the Community Member States. Would the European Parliament indeed deny a right of petition here?

Community law, and it refers to the European Convention on Human Rights (ECHR) and the constitutional traditions common to the Member States. Article 1 of the ECHR grants the rights embedded in the Convention to all those within the jurisdiction of the parties. This jurisdiction includes at the very least, all persons on the territories of the parties to the Convention, whether nationals or foreigners. As foreigners are humans, human rights are theirs as well, and this truism finds its enshrinement in the common constitutional traditions. In other words, the enjoyment of human rights and fundamental freedoms only marginally distinguishes between Union citizens and others; they are to be enjoyed by 'everyone'.

Similar observations can be made concerning collective rights and entitlements such as the protection of *human* health,[49] consumer protection,[50] protection of the environment, of which one of the objectives is again the protection of human health.[51]

Again, as regards the very restricted position which individual persons have under Article 173 concerning access to the European Court of Justice, no distinction is made between nationals of Member States and others.[52]

The right to participate in the elections for the European Parliament, however, is reserved for an as yet undecided category of citizens of the Union, and non-citizens are disenfranchised. Here, one finds a clear differentiation, and thus only citizens of the Union are characterized as having active and passive voting rights for the European Parliament.

It is, however, questionable whether this should be the case. If the Union, or the Community, demands of the Member States that they grant the right to take part in local elections to foreigners, or at least a category of foreigners (which will entail, if not logically then at least empirically, the extension to other groups as well), then the logical step would be to grant voting rights to the European Parliament to 'foreigners' as well. Foreigners in terms of the European Union or Community, are those who do not possess the nationality of any Member State, but who otherwise fulfil the conditions to take part in the elections; which is primarily residence in one of the Member States. It is inconsistent to use residence as the criterion for voting in municipal and European elections, but to exclude from the latter elections those who are as 'foreign' to the Community or the Union, as nationals of other Member States are in local elections in the Member States.

Apart from such logical considerations one may reflect on the desirability, in terms of democracy, of the disenfranchisement of increasingly large groups of the permanent population in the Member States of the Union, who are subject to a myriad of rules and regulations stemming from the Community, without granting

---

49   Article 129.
50   Article 129a.
51   Article 130r.
52   It is clear from this provision that the exclusion of non-resident non-citizens from the work of the Ombudsman or enquiries by the European Parliament goes too far, and indeed is more restrictive than the provision on the access to the European Court.

them representation on the level of the decision-making process. The more important the European Parliament becomes and the more involved in the communitarian legislative process, the less acceptable it seems to be to exclude millions of persons who are directly touched by this legislation. Fear of *Überfremdung* is undemocratic.

Finally, I will turn to the right to move and reside freely within the territory of the Member States, the nucleus around which all other rights crystallize to form the concept of European Community or Union citizenship. Here for sure one finds the division between citizens and non-citizens. But there are some very important groups of non-citizens who are nevertheless beneficiaries of this central right to move and reside freely. It should be borne in mind that this right has only imperfectly been realized at the present stage of the development of the Community.

The residence directives contain a right of residence for various groups of relatives of the primary beneficiaries, irrespective of their nationality. Their right of residence and right to freedom of movement is predicated upon the right of the Union citizen, but tends to emancipate itself somewhat from it. Thus spouses of 'workers' will retain their freedom of movement and residence after dissolution of the marriage by death or divorce, according to a (revised) commission proposal for amending Regulation 1612/68 and Directive 68/360.[53]

Directive 91/439/EEC[54] on driving licences, to give another example, facilitates the 'movement of persons, settling in a Member State other than that in which they have passed a driving test'. This Directive is seen as a step forward as compared with Directive 80/1263/EEC which obliges the exchange of driving licences and which 'constitutes an obstacle to the free movement of persons', which is 'inadmissible in the light of the progress made towards European integration'.[55] Article 1 allows for mutual recognition of driving licences issued by Member States. The nationality of the holder of such a driving licence, issued by a Member State, is irrelevant. In other words, *everyone* in possession of such a driving licence is entitled to its recognition in the other Member States; this contribution to the freedom of movement is bestowed upon 'holders' of driving licences, irrespective of their nationality.

In the second place, a very important inroad into the exclusivity of the freedom of movement or residence for Union citizens must be mentioned, one which involves all economically active European Free Trade Association (EFTA) Member State nationals. In the Third Part of the Agreement on the European Economic Area,[56] entitled 'The Free Movement of Persons, Services and Capitals', the freedom of movement of workers is granted in Article 28. This freedom implies the

---

53 See COM 88/815 final – SYN 185 (29 March 1989); see also the amendments proposed by the European Parliament that extend the categories of persons to e.g. persons with whom the worker lives in a de facto union recognized as such for administrative and legal purposes, OJ C 68 of 18 March 1990 .

54 Council Directive of 29 July 1991 on Driving Licences, OJ L 237 of 24 August 1991.

55 See Preamble Dir 80/1263/EEC, OJ L 375 of 31 December 1980.

56 As signed in Porto on 2 May 1992.

abolition of all discrimination based on nationality between workers of the Member States of the EC and those of the EFTA Member States (Article 28(2)), in accordance with Article 4 which is the general anti-discrimination provision. Thus the citizens of Sweden, Finland, Norway, Iceland, Austria, Switzerland and Liechtenstein will enjoy the central feature of Union citizenship as well, to the extent that they are workers, self-employed or providers or receivers of services. Part of these EFTA country nationals will already be present in the EC Member States, without having been granted these freedoms of movement and residence. After the entering into force of the Agreement on the EEA, foreseen for January 1 1993,[57] their potential mobility will equal that of Union citizens. There is, in view of this development, even less reason to refuse this freedom to other categories of non-Member State nationals legally resident in the EC territory. The more non-Member State nationals enjoy freedom of movement within the EC the stronger the case that it amounts to unacceptable discrimination to refuse this right to others who have migrated to one of the Member States and settled there.[58]

One should keep in mind that the German unification furnished 18 million new Member State nationals from one day to the next, which is a much larger figure than that of the category of resident 'foreigners'. There is a real danger that the population in the EC will be divided into 'citizens' and an underclass mostly originating from the Middle East and the African continent, primarily the Maghreb countries.[59]

---

57   Art. 129.
58   In Art. K(1) of the Union Treaty, mention is made of 'policy regarding nationals of third countries' as one of the matters of common interest which lend themselves to intergovernmental cooperation between the governments. See C. Groenendijk, *Europese Migratiepolitiek na Maastricht: uitbreiding en beperking van vrijheden in Migrantenrecht* (1992) at 76, 78.
59   I leave the Association agreements with several of these countries aside, although they contain some important provisions on entry into the EC.

VI. Conclusion

Up until now, as far as citizenship is concerned, the European Market has been a 'futures' market. Citizenship is, in other words, nearly exclusively a symbolic plaything without substantive content,[60] and in the Maastricht Treaty very little is added to the existing status of nationals of Member States. It is worth noting that, whereas in the Member States the notion of citizenship historically accrued around the *political* rights of the individual, the notion of Union citizenship is crystallizing around freedom of movement.

It is unclear which rights and duties together are connected with Union citizenship because there is no cohesive notion of this new citizenship, and because the political dimension of citizenship is underdeveloped. The instruments for participation in the public life of the Union are lacking as this public life itself, as distinguished from the public life in the Member States, is virtually non-existent: a weak Parliament, next to no direct access to the European Courts, and so forth.

Furthermore, the rights and obligations of the European citizen as granted by the Maastricht Treaty only slightly differentiate between citizens and non-citizens. Several rights, such as the freedom of movement, are granted to large categories of non-nationals, such as nationals of the EFTA countries, or even to 'everyone', or normally to those legally resident in the territory of one of the Member States. Thus, European citizenship is not only severely underdeveloped, but also insufficiently distinct. There is enormous uncertainty concerning those who 'belong' and those who do not. In this situation, and also for policy reasons, it is better to forge a Union citizenship not only for nationals of Member States, but for resident aliens as well, because of the increased rationality and cohesiveness of such a larger concept, and for reasons of democratic access to participation in the cultural, political and economic life of the Union.

One must not forget, after all, that the creation, albeit in an as yet very rudimentary form, of a concept of citizenship which is related to a community of States, marks a significant departure from the traditional link between nationality and citizenship in the nation-state. It represents a loosening of the metaphysical ties between persons and a State, and forms a symptom of cosmopolitization of citizenship. The rising concept of European citizenship is not the concept of national citizenship writ large: its quality has changed in that it does not presuppose any more a large set of common or shared values. It is a clear indication of a phenomenon which is also to be observed in the component parts of the European Community: that the Member States have to a large extent become multicultural and multiethnic societies which may be bound together not by a set of common values, but the development of a competence to deal with their differences; indeed the re-definition of political institutions in Europe reflects this mutation. It is this competence to deal with differences which may be the nucleus of modern active

---

60   In the same vein, see Groenendijk, *supra* note 58, at 79.

citizenship,[61] and European citizenship may be useful as a laboratory for this procedural concept of proto-cosmopolitan citizenship.

61   See H.R. van Gunsteren *et al.*, Eigentijds Burgerschap (Contemporary Citizenship) (1992).

Chapter 7

Social Policy at the Crossroads:
European Labour Law after Maastricht

Brian Bercusson

Developments in the European Community's social policy during the last few years have been remarkable. Two events are outstanding: the approval by eleven Member States of the Community Charter of Fundamental Social Rights of Workers at the Strasbourg summit of December 1989, and the conclusion of a Protocol to the Treaty on European Union and an Agreement on Social Policy at the Maastricht summit of December 1991. The United Kingdom was a party to neither the Community Charter nor the Agreement, but it accepted the Protocol.

The Maastricht Treaty still has to be ratified by national Parliaments, and the United Kingdom looks likely, in the medium term, to remain outside the social policy process. But the instruments are now arguably in place for a fundamental change in European social law and policy, both in their substance and in the procedures for their formulation and implementation. The United Kingdom's absence may even assist their future success. The question remains whether the actors involved are capable of putting them into effect.

The substance of these instruments is the focus of this chapter. But the procedure of their formulation and adoption is important. The key documents proposing the changes were drafted by the Member State holding the Presidency of the Council of Ministers – the Netherlands. But their final form, and most of the substance of the provisions which eventually became the Agreement between the eleven Member States were the result of negotiations between the peak organizations of employers and of workers at European level.[1] These negotiations culminated in the Agreement dated 31 October 1991 between the ETUC and UNICE/CEEP on a new draft of Articles 118(4), 118a and 118b of the Treaty of Rome.[2] With few modifications,

---

[1] The European Trade Union Confederation (ETUC), the *Union des Industries de la Communauté Européenne* (UNICE) and the *Centre Européen des Entreprises Publiques* (CEEP).

[2] *Agence Europe*, No. 5603, 6 November 1991, 12. This chapter focuses on five documentary sources:
  – the first draft of the Dutch Presidency (*Europe Documents* No. 1733/1734, 3 October 1991).
  – the accord between the ETUC/UNICE/CEEP concerning a new draft of Articles 118, 118a and 118b of the Rome Treaty (*Agence Europe*, No. 5603, 6 November 1991, 12).
  – the second draft of the Dutch Presidency (*Europe Documents* No. 1746/1747, 20 November 1991).

this Agreement was adopted by the eleven Member States as the basis for the future social law of the European Community. This remarkable success of the social dialogue at EC level provides a striking example of the fundamental change in European social law and policy which is the subject of this chapter.

The chapter begins by summarizing European Community labour law prior to Maastricht, both in terms of its content and the legal techniques for its enforcement, and, in particular, the role of collective bargaining in the implementation of Community labour law (section I). Then, the content of the Maastricht Protocol and Agreement is analysed emphasizing, in particular, the legal status of the texts and the involvement of the social partners at Community level in the formulation of Community labour law and social policy, a process which throws some light on the principle of subsidiarity (section II).

I. Community Social Law and Policy before Maastricht

A. Before the Community Charter of Fundamental Social Rights of 1989

The balance sheet of Community social law and policy at the end of the 1980s was not encouraging. The main advances had been the harmonization of directives of the 1970s on the law relating to collective dismissals and protection of workers' rights in the event of transfer of undertakings or the employer's insolvency. Even more dynamic had been the Council Directives implementing the principle of equality between men and women as regards remuneration, treatment in employment, and social security. These, together with renewed interest in Article 119 of the Treaty of Rome, guaranteeing equal pay for men and women, had given rise to a developed case law of the European Court of Justice.[3] Finally, there was an increasing amount of Community law on the health and safety of workers.[4]

European Community labour law, embodied in directives on collective labour relations, sex equality and health and safety at work, had to be implemented in Member States. A variety of methods of ensuring that the labour law of the Member States reflected Community requirements emerged. One was through a Commission

- the Protocol on Social Policy of the twelve Member States and the Agreement between the eleven Member States concluded at Maastricht on 9-10 December 1991 (*Europe Documents* No. 1750/1751, 13 December 1991).
- the Protocol of the twelve and the Agreement of the eleven Member States signed at Maastricht on 7 February 1992 (*Europe Documents* No. 1759/1760, 7 December 1991).
3   A useful collection of Treaty provisions, Directives and the case-law of the European Court of Justice which concerns them is A. Byre, *Leading Cases and Materials on the Social Policy of the EEC* (1989). It is interesting that of the 532 pages of text in this book, 297 (55%) are taken up with EC law and policy on sex equality. A detailed exposition of EC law on sex equality is to be found in *Social Europe* (3/91).
4   In a companion volume to that referred to in footnote 3, A. Byre, *EC Social Policy and 1992, Laws, Cases and Materials* (1992), the longest section is that on 'Health Protection and Safety at the Workplace' (137 of a total of 399 pages of text (34%)). An exposition of EC law in this area is to be found in *Social Europe* (2/90).

complaint to the Court under Article 189. A number of Member States introduced changes to their national law as a result of such complaints.[5]

A second method was through references by national courts to the European Court under Article 177, when a case before them raised a question of European law. Decisions by the European court require the national courts to interpret national legislation in line with Community law.[6]

A third method resulted from decisions of the Court which attributed to Community instruments – the Treaty and some provisions of Directives – 'direct effect'. This meant these provisions could be invoked, even in the absence of national legislation, as a legal basis for a claim before a national tribunal.[7] Difficulties arose from the distinction the Court made between provisions with vertical direct effect – which could be invoked only against the State – and provisions with horizontal effect as well, which could be invoked also against private employers. Decisions by the Court seemed to allow for a wide definition of the State, which allowed for individuals to rely on these provisions against a wide variety of employers in the public sector.[8]

A fourth method emerged when the Court was faced with a complaint by Italian workers that they had not been compensated for losses incurred when their employer went bankrupt. The 1980 Directive had required Member States to protect workers' rights in such circumstances.[9] The Court found that Italy had not implemented the Directive and went on to hold that compensation was owed by the State to those injured by its failure.[10] The implications of this decision are potentially enormous in light of the many alleged defects in Member States' implementation of Community labour law.[11]

B. The Community Charter and its Aftermath

The Community Charter of Fundamental Social Rights of Workers was approved by eleven Member States in Strasbourg on 9 December 1989; the United Kingdom refused to adhere. The legal quality of the Charter is secondary to its political significance. It is effectively a direction to the Commission of the European

---

5 This was the case with UK sex discrimination law following the Court's upholding the Commission's complaints in *Commission of the European Communities* v. *UK*, case 61/81, [1982] ECR 2601; *Commission* v. *UK*, case 165/82, [1983] ECR 3431.
6 *Marleasing* v. *La Commercial Internacional de Alimentation*, case 106/89, [1990] ECR 4135; see B. Fitzpatrick and C. Docksey, 'The Duty of National Courts to Interpret Provisions of National Law in Accordance with Community Law', 20 *Industrial Law Journal* (1990) 113.
7 *Defrenne* v. *SABENA* (II), case 43/75, [1976] ECR 455.
8 *Foster* v. *British Gas plc*, case 188/89, [1989] ECR 3313. For a discussion see B. Bercusson, [1991] *Legal Studies* 351-365.
9 Council Directive of October 20, 1980 on the Approximation of the Laws of the Member States relating to the protection of employees in the event of the insolvency of their employer, OJ 1980, L 283/23.
10 *Francovich and Bonifaci* v. *Italian Republic*, cases 6/90 and 9/90, [1991] ECR 5357.
11 In the case of the UK, see Hepple and Byre, 'EEC Labour Law in the United Kingdom – A New Approach', 18 *Industrial Law Journal* (1989) 129.

Communities to develop initiatives for the implementation of the rights listed in the Charter, using the legal instruments available under the Treaty of Rome. Some of these allow for approval by a qualified majority of Member States, rendering the UK's opposition irrelevant. The Commission's Action Programme for the implementation of the Charter provides, *inter alia*, for a large number of directives to be proposed.[12]

The directives proposed under the Action Programme have been subject to intensive debate as to which Articles of the Treaty should constitute their legal basis. This was highlighted in the aftermath of the Community Charter by the Commission's proposal of three different Directives on 'certain employment relationships', each with a legal basis in a different article of the Treaty.[13] The legal basis selected determines whether they require the unanimous approval of the Member States in the Council of Ministers, or only that of a qualified majority. Despite the expected difficulties in obtaining the requisite approval in some cases, once approved, a directive 'shall be binding, as to the result to be achieved, upon each Member State to which it is addressed, but shall leave to the national authorities the choice of form and methods' (Article 189).

A crucial development was that the Charter, and subsequent Commission proposals, also formally recognized the role of collective bargaining within Member States as a means of implementing fundamental social rights. The role of collective bargaining/social dialogue was later to become generalized in the Maastricht Agreement to all of Community labour law.

C. Collective Bargaining and EC Social Law before Maastricht

The possible implementation of Community labour law through collective bargaining arose first in the case law of the European Court following complaints by the Commission that certain Member States were not complying with the obligation under Article 189 to introduce the measures required to implement directives.[14] Article 189 provides for implementation, leaving to Member States the 'choice of form and methods'. Directives in the area of labour law habitually referred in their concluding provisions to implementation through legislation, regulations or administrative provisions. They did not mention implementation through collective agreements. In a first challenge, the European Court held: 'Member States may leave the implementation ... in the first instance to representatives of management and labour.[15] However, while upholding the principle that collective agreements may be used to implement Community labour law obligations, the Court

---

12 Bercusson, 'The European Community's Charter of Fundamental Social Rights of Workers', 53 *Modern Law Review* (1990) 624.

13 COM (90) 228 final – SYN 280 and SYN 281, Brussels, 21 August 1990.

14 Adinolfi, 'The Implementation of Social Policy Directives through Collective Agreements?', 25 *Common Market Law Review* (1988) 291.

15 *Commission* v. *Denmark*, case 143/83, [1985] ECR 427.

emphasized that there must be adequate coverage by the agreements and that the substantive content of the agreements must coincide with the directive's requirements. Otherwise, there must be a back-up in the form of a State guarantee (usually legislation).[16] Finally, Member States cannot rely on too slow a process of implementation of Community obligations through collective bargaining.[17]

The Community Charter of 1989 marked a major advance in that eleven Member States approved not only a declaration of fundamental social rights of workers, but also explicitly indicated that the implementation of these rights could go beyond the traditional method of legislative, regulatory or administrative measures. The Preamble stated:

> whereas such implementation may take the form of laws, collective agreements or existing practices at the various appropriate levels and whereas it requires in many spheres the active involvement of the two sides of industry.

Further, Article 27:[18]

> It is more particularly the responsibility of the Member States, in accordance with national practices, notably through legislative measures or collective agreements, to guarantee the fundamental social rights in this Charter...

One directive already approved after the Charter provides:[19]

> Member States shall adopt the laws, regulations and administrative provisions necessary to comply with this Directive no later than 30 June 1993, or shall ensure by that date that the employers' and workers' representatives introduce the required provisions by way of agreement, the Member States being obliged to take the necessary steps at all times to guarantee the results imposed by this Directive.

A number of other proposed directives aimed at implementing the Charter also explicitly recognize collective bargaining as one means of implementation.[20]

The implementation of Community labour law through collective bargaining has thus now attained recognition in both the case law of the Court and, following the Community Charter, in the legislative practice of the Commission and Council. A

---

16 *Commission* v. *Italy*, case 235/84, [1986] ECR 2291. The Court reiterated this principle, despite the contrary opinion of the Advocate-General.
17 *Commission* v. *French Republic*, case 312/86, [1989] ECR 6315.
18 The Text of the Charter, earlier drafts and the Commission's Action Programme are published in *Social Europe*, 1/90. For a detailed analysis of the implications of implementation of European Community social rights through collective bargaining, see the discussion in my report to the European Commission submitted during the preparatory stages of the Charter, 'Fundamental Social and Economic Rights in the European Community', reprinted in A. Cassese *et al.* (ed.), *Human Rights in the European Community: Methods of Protection* (1991) 195-294.
19 Council Directive 91/533 of 14 October 1991 on an employer's obligation to inform employees of the conditions applicable to the contract or employment relationship. OJ L 288 of 18 October 1991, Article 9(1).
20 Proposal for a Council Directive on certain employment relationships with regard to distortions of competition, Article 6; COM(90) 228 final – SYN 280, Brussels, 13 August 1990. Proposal for a Council Directive concerning certain aspects of the organisation of working time, Article 14; COM(90) 317 final – SYN 295, Brussels, 20 September 1990.

quantum leap in the role of collective bargaining resulted from the Maastricht negotiations on social policy in the Community.

II. The Maastricht Treaty

A. Europe of the Eleven and Europe of the Twelve

The negotiations at Maastricht produced the Treaty on European Union signed by the Member States of the European Community on 7 February 1992, a Protocol on Social Policy and an Agreement, annexed to the Protocol, between eleven Member States, with the exception of the UK, also on Social Policy. The Protocol notes that eleven Member States 'wish to continue along the path laid down in the 1989 Social Charter [and] have adopted among themselves an Agreement to this end'; accordingly, all twelve Member States:

> 1. Agree to authorise those 11 Member States [excluding the UK] to have recourse to the institutions, procedures and mechanisms of the Treaty for the purposes of taking among themselves and applying as far as they are concerned the acts and decisions required for giving effect to the above mentioned Agreement.

> 2. The [UK] shall not take part in the deliberations and the adoption by the Council of Commission proposals made on the basis of this Protocol and the above mentioned Agreement...

> Acts adopted by the Council ... shall not be applicable to the [UK].

The Agreement comprises a new formulation of some of the Articles on social policy of the Treaty of Rome. The question of whether the Agreement and its consequences are regarded as part of Community law is crucial, since the legal implications for the eleven Member States are very different if the Agreement constitutes only an intergovernmental treaty, and is governed by public international law, not European Community law.

The issue would have been resolved by the (perhaps expected) victory of the Labour Party in the British general election of April 1992, which presumably would have led to the UK becoming party to the Agreement. Its provisions would then have substituted for the provisions in the Treaty. As this did not happen, there continue in existence two parallel sets of provisions: one applicable to the 12 Member States in the Treaty, and one applicable to the 11 Member States in the Agreement. The outcome in practice is that (subject to ratification of the Treaty by national parliaments) the Community institutions and the eleven Member States are to undertake the operation of the new provisions in the expectation that, sooner or later, the UK will accede to the results. The desirability of this outcome depends on whether the UK's contribution to Community social policy is regarded as positive or negative.

The analysis in this chapter of the implications of the Maastricht Treaty on European Union for the social law and policy of the European Community will provide a detailed interpretation of the texts. But it also addresses the dynamics of the Protocol and Agreement on Social Policy – how they may work in practice. This involves, first, an analysis of the legal nature of these instruments. The consequences of their legal status will powerfully influence the way in which the actors involved – Community institutions, Member States and the social partners – plan their strategies. The legal status of the instruments will also have a determining effect on a second issue to be analysed: the scope of potential social policy proposals emanating from the Commission.

It is the interaction between Commission proposals and the social dialogue which constitutes the defining quality of the emergent process of social policy formation in the European Community: what I have called 'bargaining in the shadow of the law'.[21] The social dialogue takes place on many levels. Agreements at Community level, and the process of their articulation with Member State labour laws may encompass many different actors. This multiplicity of actors poses a complex problem of choice of levels for social policy formation and implementation. It can be summed up in the word 'subsidiarity'. This chapter seeks to provide some clarification of this principle as it may be applied in the area of Community social law and policy.

B. The Legal Nature of the Agreement and its Consequences

The Protocol on Social Policy forms an integral part of the EC Treaty.[22] The Agreement is stated in the Protocol to be annexed to the Protocol. The presumption is that both Protocol and Agreement are, therefore, part of Community law. Similarly, any measures adopted using the institutions, procedures and mechanisms of the Treaty will have effects in Community law as far as the 11 Member States are concerned.

Arguments against the Agreement being part of EC law have been elaborated by Eliane Vogel-Polsky.[23] A first argument characterized the Agreement as the result of a diplomatic conference of the Member States within the framework of the European Council. The results of such meetings are not Community law. Against this, it may be argued that, unlike such diplomatic practice, the Agreement on Social Policy is annexed to a Protocol which is part of the Maastricht Treaty, itself the product of the intergovernmental conference and undeniably EC law.

---

21 Bercusson, 'Maastricht: A Fundamental Change in European Labour Law' 23 *Industrial Relations Journal* (1992) 177.
22 Article 239: 'The Protocols annexed to this Treaty by common accord of the Member States shall form an integral part thereof'.
23 E. Vogel-Polsky, 'Evaluation of the Social Provisions of the Treaty on European Union Agreed by the European Summit at Maastricht on 9 and 10 December 1991', Committee on Social Affairs, Employment and the Working Environment of the European Parliament, 7 February 1992, DOC EN/CM/202155, PE 155.405/I.

A second argument compared Protocol No. 14 on Social Policy with Protocol No. 11 on Economic and Monetary Policy, which states that the voting rights of the UK in the Council shall be suspended (Article 7), but allows the UK to later choose to join the economic and monetary union (Article 10). Protocol No. 14 on Social Policy authorizes 11 Member States to 'have recourse to the institutions, procedures and mechanisms of the Treaty for the purpose of taking *among themselves* and applying *as far as they are concerned* the acts and decisions required for giving effect to the above-mentioned Agreement' (emphasis added). As it is relevant only to 11 Member States, it is said not to be Community law.

The claim is that the 11 Member States have made an international agreement regarding exclusively themselves. However, such an argument renders the Protocol meaningless. The UK's consent is not necessary for the 11 Member States to assume mutual obligations to which the UK is not a party. The Protocol only makes sense if EC law is engaged and the UK has to give its consent to such obligations. Without such consent, the agreement would fall foul of the European Court's Opinion 1/76 of 26 April 1977, which condemned international agreements engaging only some Member States in a field of EC competence as 'a change in the internal constitution of the Community ... not compatible with the requirements of unity and solidarity'.[24]

If it was merely an international agreement between the 11 Member States, under it the Commission might propose measures to be adopted by the 11 which would modify, by international agreement, existing EC law – a result contrary to the Commission's duty as 'guardian of the Treaties' for which the UK could even complain to the Court as a violation of the other Member States' Treaty obligations.

As EC law, the acts adopted by the EC institutions under the Protocol could come before the European Court under Article 177 without the problem canvassed in Opinion 1/91 of 14 December 1991 as to the incompatibility between interpretation of an international treaty and the EC Treaty in the context of the Community legal order.[25] The contrast may be made with Protocol 35 of the EEA Treaty, from which it appears that 'without recognizing the principles of direct effect and primacy ... the Contracting Parties undertake merely to introduce into their respective legal orders a statutory provision to the effect that EEA rules are to prevail over contrary legislative provisions'.[26]

Further, it may be argued that both Protocols 11 and 14 have the consequence that the UK simply is excluded from one aspect of the European union. Both Protocols have the same legal status. Both envisage the use by 11 Member States of institutions, procedures and mechanisms of the Community. In both cases, it would seem that the intention of the Member States was that the UK could rejoin economic

---

24   *Re Draft Agreement establishing a European laying-up fund for inland waterway vessels* [1977] ECR 741, para. 27 at 269.
25   *Re the Draft Treaty on a European Economic Area* (1991) CMLR 245.
26   Ibid., para. 27, 269.

and monetary union or the social policy of the other Member States. The problem is that in the case of the former, this was explicit; not so in the case of the latter.

Protocol 11 dealing with economic and monetary union provides in Article 1, paragraph 2 that:

> Unless the United Kingdom notifies the Council that it intends to move to the third stage (of economic and monetary union) it shall be under no obligation to do so.

However, Article 10 allows that the UK:

> may change its notification at any time after the beginning of (the third) stage.

In other words, the procedure under Protocol 11 is that the UK is excluded unless it 'opts in' in one of two ways: either notification of UK intention to move to the third stage, for otherwise there is no obligation (Article 1); or change of its original notification, entailing obligations (Article 10).

Protocol 14 on social policy simply provides in Article 2, paragraph 1, that:

> The United Kingdom of Great Britain and Northern Ireland shall not take part in the deliberations and the adoption by the Council of Commission proposals made on the basis of this Protocol and the above mentioned Agreement.

Protocol 14 contains no explicit mechanism for 'opting in' by way of notification. Paragraph 2 merely goes on to outline the voting procedures in the absence of the UK, and paragraph 3 provides that the:

> Acts adopted by the Council and any financial consequences other than administrative costs entailed for the institutions shall not be applicable to the United Kingdom of Great Britain and Northern Ireland.

At bottom, the issue is whether the Maastricht Treaty provisions on economic and monetary union were intended to allow eventual opting in by the UK, but those on social policy were intended permanently to exclude the UK. I would submit that the latter cannot be seriously contended.

Hence, the Protocol should be read not as an exclusion of the UK forever from the social policy of the EC. Rather, as with economic and monetary union, UK participation is subject to a special procedure for opting-in. The question remains: what procedure?

The issue is particularly acute following the complex Parliamentary history of the Maastricht Bill.

According to the Social Policy Protocol, the UK does not take part in the procedures when the new social policy is invoked, and the outcomes of those procedures do not apply to it. If we assume that this exclusion was not intended to be permanent, three alternative strategies would enable the UK to join the new social policy.

1. Treaty Amendment/Revision:

Opting-in could be achieved by an amendment to Protocol 14, in other words, to the Treaty. This amendment could take two forms:

a. the deletion of the entire Protocol and Agreement and the substitution of the existing EC Treaty provisions with the new formulation of Articles 118 et seq. now in the Agreement.

b. changing the text of the Protocol from '11' to '12' Member States, and including the UK in the list; also in paragraph 1 of the Protocol and similarly in the Agreement; and deleting paragraph 2 of the Protocol entirely.

2. Interpretation of the Protocol

Rather than amend the Protocol, the question can be posed as one of interpretation of the Protocol. Can it be read to allow for the UK to opt in or not? I submit that the Protocol can be read as implying that when the UK does take part in the deliberations of and the adoption by the Council of Commission proposals (assuming also adhesion to the Agreement), the acts adopted shall be applicable to the UK.

3. Adhesion to the Agreement

The Protocol applies so long as the UK does not adhere to the Agreement. This is the precondition for participation in decision-making by the Council. All 12 Member States authorize recourse to EC machinery to give effect to the Agreement. The preamble to the Protocol notes that only 11 Member States have adopted the Agreement. It follows that the UK is excluded and is not bound. What is necessary is that the UK adhere to the Agreement, not to the Protocol. This does not require amendment of the Protocol at all. Following adhesion, it is obvious that all 12 Member States authorize use of EC machinery to give effect to the Agreement through procedures involving also the participation of the UK

In conclusion: as between (1) amendment of the Protocol, (2) interpretation of the Protocol, (3) adhesion to the Agreement, the latter two strategies obviously involve much lighter procedures. The other Member States clearly wished the UK to join the new social policy initiatives. Under any of these procedures, the UK retains the right to refuse to take part until it wishes to join.

These alternative strategies throw an interesting light on the debates over the legal consequences of the itinerary of the Maastricht Bill in the UK Parliament.

The Treaty includes the Protocol (with the annexed Agreement). The Maastricht Bill, as approved by Parliament, does not. Four interrelated questions arise:

- will the Bill be upheld as ratification by the UK courts or the European Court?
- if so, what is it that is being upheld: has the UK opted into the new social policy?

- if not, what is the effect of the Bill in UK law even if it is not ratification of the Treaty?
- what happens if there is a difference of view between the UK courts and the European Court?

The Labour Party amendment deleted the Protocol from the Bill. There are at least two interpretations of the effect of this amendment. First, it could be said to remove all new social competences. These were deleted but were not incorporated into the EC Treaty (as in the first proposed strategy of amendment/ revision of the Treaty).

But, secondly, in light of the background to the amendment deleting the Protocol, it could be said that Parliament intended that the UK accept the new social policy. As such, it is tantamount to the second and third strategies: the UK can participate in Council decision-making under the Agreement.

These issues may come before both the UK courts and the European Court. In a challenge to the government's claim as to ratification, the UK courts might simply reject the view that the Bill constitutes ratification. If the Bill is held by UK courts not to be ratification, it will nonetheless be UK law. How is this law to be interpreted? Again there are two interpretations: either excluding or including new EC social competences.

However, the UK courts might equally agree that the Bill does constitute ratification, but uphold the view that deletion of the Protocol removes all new social competences. Whether upheld by the UK courts as ratification or not, the issue could still come before the European Court.

The European Court might hold that the Bill's approval by Parliament does constitute ratification, and, furthermore, in light of the background to the amendment deleting the Protocol, uphold the view that Parliament intended that the UK adhere to the Agreement on Social Policy.

If so, this would produce a clash between the UK courts and the European Court. If the European Court upholds the Bill as amounting to ratification, and takes the view that the Bill accepts new social competences, UK courts must follow this line.

The timing is delicate. Either court's pronouncements could influence the other. In practice, it is likely that an Article 177 issue would be referred to the European Court (after the other 11 Member States have ratified), pre-empting any UK court decision on the constitutional law issue of ratification. Any appeal to a UK Court would involve questions of European law to be referred to the European Court. First, what constitutes ratification by the 12 Member States? Secondly, what is it that has been ratified?

To hold the UK bound by the new social provisions, the European Court would have to hold, first, that the UK legislation is valid ratification despite deletion of the Protocol, secondly, that deletion of the Protocol is to be read as the UK opting-in to new social provisions, in effect, adhesion to the Agreement.

Consistently with this view, the ratifications of the Treaty, including the Protocol, by the other Member States is to be read in one of the two ways suggested above. Either that when the UK does take part in the deliberations and the adoption by the Council of Commission proposals (assuming also adhesion to the Agreement), the acts adopted shall be applicable to the UK Or that the UK's ratification excluding the Protocol constitutes adhesion to the Agreement, and it is obvious that the 12 Member States authorize use of EC machinery to give effect to the Agreement through procedures involving also the participation of the UK

In conclusion, a similar 'teleological' reading is required both of UK ratification – that deletion of the Protocol in the Bill is to be read as adhesion to the Agreement ('opting in') – and of other Member State ratifications – the Treaty including the Protocol is approved. The argument is that the Protocol always implied that the UK could opt-in whenever it so decided. This having now happened, all Member States implicitly approve UK participation in procedures giving effect to the new social provisions.

A third argument qualifies the Agreement as an intergovernmental agreement between 11 Member States and as such having effect in public international law, not Community law. Against this it may be argued that the 11 Member States appear to have intended the Protocol and Agreement to have an effect equivalent to that of Community law. Hence, the Agreement's effect in public international law would be to create the identical effects to those of Community law, using the institutions, procedures and mechanisms of the Community. This would include also the possibility of the European Court assuming jurisdiction over measures resulting from the Agreement (including the Agreement itself, proposed by the Commission and affirmed by the 11 Member States in the form of an EC measure!), since these, in terms of the Protocol, could be qualified as acts of the institutions of the Community under Article 177.[27] It seems absurd to create this 'shadow' EC law to

---

27 The European Court, in considering its position on the Fund Tribunal provided for in the draft Agreement on the European laying-up fund for inland waterway vessels (Opinion 1/76, *supra* note 24), 'hoped that there is only the smallest possibility of conflicts of interpretations giving rise to conflicts of jurisdiction' between it and the Fund Tribunal'. Nonetheless the Court felt 'obliged to express certain reservations (p. 761, para. 21). These risks, and therefore reservations, would be less in the case of the Court interpreting the EC Treaty and the same Court interpreting the Agreement on Social Policy. On the other hand, in Opinion 1/91 (*supra* note 25), the differences between international law and EC law were such that the Court held 'that homogeneity of the rules of law throughout the EEA is not secured by the fact that the provisions of Community law and those of the corresponding provisions of the (EEA) agreement are identical in their content or wording' (p. 269, para. 22); *a fortiori* in the case of the EC Treaty social provisions and those of the Maastricht Agreement on Social Policy.

avoid the conclusion that it is EC law.[28] [29]

To classify the Agreement as not part of Community law would be to render the Protocol effectively meaningless (by requiring, for example, subsequent repeated ratification by each of the 11 Member States of all measures adopted under it) and to contradict the express intention of the Member States. The argument that it is not EC law is based on the view that, *a priori*, there is an absence of an adequate legal basis for such an Agreement and this frustrates the political will of the Member States. More accurate is the view that the legal power to create the Agreement as part of Community law exists.[30] In a choice between two interpretations, one of which gives rise to practical absurdity, the other should be preferred. This is particularly so where the authors of the document being interpreted strenuously support this other interpretation.

The issue of legal status is of fundamental importance. Its consequences will be apparent in the enforcement of the Agreement and measures (directives, decisions, Community level agreements between management and labour) which result from it. As mentioned above, four methods are available to ensure that the labour law of the Member States reflects Community law: first, a Commission complaint to the Court under Article 189; secondly, references by national courts to the European Court under Article 177 and the requirement that national courts interpret national legislation in line with Community law;[31] thirdly, the possibility of 'direct effect';[32] and, finally, potential claims for compensation in the event of losses suffered due to non-implementation of EC law by Member States.[33]

The question is whether some or all measures which result from the Agreement can utilize these methods of enforcement. In the case of Community level agreements, this would possibly put the Court in the position of interpreting and enforcing such agreements. Other consequences emerge as a result of the new competences attributed to the Community by the Agreement.

---

28 I owe this point to an intervention by Prof. Marie-Ange Moreau at the 'conclave' organized by the *Association Française de Droit du Travail* at Saverne, 11-12 September 1992.
29 As 'shadow EC law', there would remain the problem of the effect of the Agreement and measures adopted under it in national courts in dualist systems, unless national legislation on EC law could be interpreted to include also this 'shadow EC law'.
30 An analogy would be with the adoption of the Social Action Programme of 1974. As put by a former Commissioner for Social Affairs: it 'reflected a political judgment of what was thought to be both desirable and possible, rather than a juridical judgment of what were thought to be the social policy implications of the Rome Treaty'. M. Shanks, *European Community Social Policy* (1977) at 13. The results of that Programme are unquestionably part of EC law.
31 B. Fitzpatrick and C. Docksey, *supra* note 6.
32 *Defrenne* v. *SABENA*, *supra* note 7.
33 *Francovich and Bonifaci* v. *Italian Republic*, *supra* note 10.

C. The Scope of Community Competences and Majority Voting Procedures

Article 1 of the Agreement, the redrafted Article 117 of the Treaty of Rome, has greatly expanded the legal competences of the Community in the field of social policy.

> The Community and the Member States shall have as their objectives the promotion of employment, improved living and working conditions, proper social protection, dialogue between management and labour, the development of human resources with a view to lasting high employment and the combating of exclusion.

Within this new sphere of Community social policy, the Council is authorized, by Article 2, paragraphs 1 and 2 (of the Agreement, the redrafted Article 118 of the Treaty of Rome), to proceed by qualified majority voting to 'adopt, by means of directives, minimum requirements for gradual implementation' in the following five fields: [34]

- improvement in particular of the working environment to protect workers' health and safety;
- working conditions;
- the information and consultation of workers;
- equality between men and women with regard to labour market opportunities and treatment at work;
- the integration of persons excluded from the labour market ...

This is an expansion of the capacity of the Community to act in the social policy area even where one or more Member States are opposed. Article 2, paragraph 3 requires unanimity (among the 11, pending UK adhesion) [35] in the following five 'areas:

- social security and social protection of workers;
- protection of workers where their employment is terminated;
- representation and collective defence of the interests of workers and employers, including co-determination, subject to paragraph 6;
- conditions of employment for third-country nationals legally residing in Community territory;
- financial contributions for promotion of employment and job-creation, without prejudice to the provisions relating to the Social Fund'.

---

34 The Protocol, Article 2, deems the new qualified majority in the Council, given the absence of the UK, to be 44 votes.
35 As to the possibility of the UK 'opting-in', see *supra* II b.

Paragraph 6 of Article 2, however, provides that:

The provisions of this Article shall not apply to pay, the right of association, the right to strike or the right to impose lock-outs. [36]

These provisions expand both the legal scope and the ability of the Community to develop social policy and labour law at European level. In the past, there have been many disputes over whether there was any legal basis for social policy measures, and, if so, whether the legal basis allowed for qualified majority voting or required unanimity in the Council. The new and more complex formulations of competence, and the apparent overlap between those fields allowing for qualified majority voting (Article 2(1)), those areas subjected to unanimity (Article 2(3)), and those excluded altogether (Article 2(6)) will doubtless give rise to much debate when measures are proposed by the Commission. [37]

What is the relation of the new competences in the Agreement to the old competences in Arts. 117-118b of the Treaty? [38] The Protocol and Agreement aim, in the words of the latter's preamble: 'to implement the 1989 Social Charter on the basis of the *acquis communautaire*'. I have elsewhere commented on the ambiguity of the 1989 Charter's objectives as regards consolidation versus development of social rights. In particular, it was noted that in the final Draft of the Charter's Preamble a new clause was added: 'whereas the implementation of the Charter must not entail an extension of the Community's powers as defined by the Treaties'. [39] The Protocol and Agreement comprise a major extension of the Community's powers in the social field as regards the 11 Member States party to the Agreement. This implies the proposal of measures going beyond the present *acquis communautaire*, based on the powers in the EC Treaty to which that *acquis* was restricted, and henceforth engaging the new legal powers. [40]

---

36 This exclusion contradicts the expressed intention in the Protocol that 11 Member States 'wish to continue along the path laid down in the 1989 Social Charter; that they have adopted among themselves an Agreement to this end...'. The Social Charter contained explicit guarantees related to pay, the right to strike and the right of association. The implication must be that the exclusions in this paragraph are to be interpreted narrowly.

37 A notorious example was the Commission's Social Charter Action Programme proposal on 'atypical workers', ultimately divided into three separate proposals, each with its own legal basis and voting procedure.

38 The recital to the Protocol stipulates: 'that this Protocol and the said Agreement are without prejudice to the provisions of this Treaty, particularly those relating to social policy which constitute an integral part of the *acquis communautaire*'. 'This Treaty' refers to the Treaty on European Union, which makes only one change to the relevant parts of the EC Treaty (Arts. 117-121): Art. G (33) replacing the first subparagraph of Art. 118a(2).

39 Bercusson, *supra* note 12, at 625.

40 As put in the Maastricht Treaty's Article B on the objectives of the Union: 'to maintain in full the *acquis communautaire* and build on it...'. Article C again refers to 'respecting and building upon the *acquis communautaire*'.

Manfred Weiss has stated that the Agreement 'imposes an obligation upon the eleven signatory Member States to consider themselves bound by the Protocol, instead of Articles 117-121 of the Treaty'.[41] In my view, this can mean two things. First, that if the 11 Member States wish to adopt a social policy, they are now obliged to pursue the new agreement whenever the old framework fails (either on grounds of alleged lack of competence or voting requirements (UK veto). Secondly, again, if they wish to adopt a social policy, they are precluded from approving proposals narrowly conceived within the old framework, but must pursue the new competences. If these are consistent with the old framework, the UK may participate. If not, the Agreement of the 11 applies.

Like the Community Charter of 1989, the Agreement should be regarded not only as a legal, but also as a political document.[42] It not only defines the new scope of Community social policy, more importantly, it directs the Commission to produce proposals to implement the new competences.

It is not only a legal question of what the competences of the 11 versus 12 Member States are in social policy. In practice, the crucial issue is the Commission's role. Social policy proposals can be conceived in either the old or the new framework of competences. The question is whether the Commission is able to continue in the old pattern, or is obliged to construct a new social policy within the framework of the new competences.

At least three options exist. The Commission could, first, use the Agreement to promote previous proposals which failed to achieve requisite majority/unanimity. Secondly, it could redraft old proposals to fit in with the new parameters between majority/unanimity. For example, an old proposal vetoed by the UK, or confronted by a majority vote including the UK, could be redrafted to achieve requisite unanimity or a sufficient majority of the 11 Member States under the Agreement. Thirdly, it could draft new proposals in light of the new competences of the Agreement.

In my view, the key is the scope of proposals (their approval is secondary as the UK may or may not vote depending on the scope). Are they to be formulated in light of the Agreement or the old framework of competences? Is it satisfactory for the Agreement to constitute only the fall-back competences when the old framework fails because of the UK veto? A more positive vision would be for the Commission to work from the new conception of social policy. In this political rather than legal sense, it is not so much that the Agreement obliges the Member States, as that it obliges the Commission to operate within a new framework.

The position of the Commission probably depends, in part, on the status of the Agreement in EC law. If it is not EC law, the answer is simplest: the new competences are outside the Treaty. If it is EC law, the alternatives seem to be:

41   Weiss, 'The significance of Maastricht for EC social policy', *International Journal of Comparative Labour Law and Industrial Relations* (1992) 3-14, at 6.

42   Bercusson, *supra* note 12.

1. they replace the Treaty provisions – but, presumably, only so far as the 11 Member States are concerned.

2. they are additional to the Treaty – but, again, only so far as the 11 Member States are concerned. This has the disadvantage that it involves overlaps between new and old competences; also, perhaps, contradictions, in addition to those already inherent within Article 2, between paragraphs 2 (majority) and 4 (unanimity).

3. they both replace and are additional. For the 11, the Agreement replaces the old Treaty provisions as the basis for social policy. But where there are overlaps, they are (for the 11) additional to the old Treaty provisions. In the overlapping area, proposals may then be made involving the UK as well. These proposals fit under both rubrics: the old Treaty provisions and the Agreement. Voting can take place with a number of consequences:

    i.   unanimity – all 12 are bound;

    ii. qualified majority – if available under the old provisions, it will bind all 12;

    iii. if qualified majority is not available under the 12, then it may be upheld on unanimity or qualified majority voting among the 11.

This has the procedural consequence that *two* legal bases (the old Treaty provisions and the Agreement) will be invoked when voting on the same proposal. The ultimate legal basis will depend on the result of the voting.

A determining role may be played by the social partners. Under the Maastricht Agreement, they have the right to be consulted and, if they wish, to request that agreement be sought on the issue by way of social dialogue (Articles 3(4) and 4). These rights only operate in the case of social policy proposals under the new competences. Since the Commission has the duty to promote social dialogue (Article 3(1)), there is an implication that the new competences – allowing for social dialogue – should be used. Indeed, the question arises whether the social partners could challenge the legal basis (under the EC Treaty provisions) as excluding them unnecessarily. [43]

The substantive content of the policy, under whatever framework of competences, is to be achieved. But at which level is the requisite action to be taken to achieve the policy? This is to be determined in accordance with the principle of subsidiarity.

D. Subsidiarity

The subsidiarity principle was the subject of explicit elaboration in the Union Treaty agreed at Maastricht, though this does not mean it has necessarily been clarified:

> The Community shall act within the limits of the powers conferred upon it by this Treaty and of the objectives assigned to it therein.

---

43 Could the UK similarly complain if the new competences were used, thereby excluding it? I would submit that the answer is no: the UK always has the possibility of 'opting-in'.

In the areas which do not fall within its exclusive jurisdiction, the Community shall take action, in accordance with the principle of subsidiarity, only if and insofar as the objectives of the proposed action cannot be sufficiently achieved by the Member States and can therefore, by reason of the scale or effects of the proposed action, be better achieved by the Community.

Any action by the Community shall not go beyond what is necessary to achieve the objectives of this Treaty.[44]

1. The Choice among Multiple Levels of Action

The issue has been made rather more complex by the injection of Community level action involving not EC institutions, but the social partners at Community level. The problem is that EC level action can now be undertaken by the social partners as well as by the Commission. Similarly, action at national level can include that by the social partners as well as by Member States.

The question is: How does the principle of subsidiarity apply in the resulting complex of interactions? Formerly it could be said to apply to Community action versus Member State action. But is the same standard applicable as between:

– EC level action by the social partners versus Member State action; or
– EC Community action versus action by the social partners within the Member State; or
– EC level action by the social partners versus action by the social partners within the Member State?

Are any or all of these subject to the same principle of subsidiarity? Or are they subject to a principle of subsidiarity formulated differently?

Finally, there is the question of whether Community action or action by the social partners at EC level is preferable; similarly, at Member State level, whether action by the State or the social partners is preferable. Neither of these choices seems directly governed by the subsidiarity principle, but the choice between them is subject to the same logic as the subsidiarity principle.

The result of the application of the subsidiarity principle to the classic choice between Member State or Community action (but now also between EC social partner action versus Member State action/social partner action at Member State level) will also be determined by the choices made as between Commission/EC social partner level action and Member State/social partner within Member State action.

---

44   Article 3b.

2. Application of the Subsidiarity Principle in Community Social Policy[45]

The principle of subsidiarity only applies when the Community and Member States both have competence. The question is which of the two (Community or Member States) is to exercise the competence. As defined in Article 3b of the Treaty on European Union, there are two conditions for Community action: first, insufficient achievement by Member States of the objectives of the proposed action; and, secondly, better achievement by the Community by reason of the scale or effects of the proposed action.

The issue is to be posed in *relative* terms: which level is better (as in '... cannot be sufficiently achieved by the Member States and can ... be better achieved by the Community'). The Community could argue Member State insufficiency, and the Member States could argue that the Community is no better (or worse). This raises the difficult question of which criteria and standards to adopt to assess sufficiency. The allocation of competences depends on a reliable assessment of relative sufficiency. The terms of the assessment are critical; in particular, what is the role of economic or other criteria and standards?

The debate over subsidiarity is likely to be influenced by the European Economic Community logic of economic rather than political (let alone social) union. Exclusivity/competences is the language of legal/political union. Efficiency ('sufficiently achieved') and scale and effects are the language of economic union. The ambiguity is apparent in the (slippery) terms in which the debate has been conducted: (political-social) objections to centralization are dressed up in (economic) terminology of efficiency. But schools of economics include political and social considerations to varying extents. The neo-classical school of economics which underlies the old conception of the European Economic Community is unlikely to be sustainable in the context of the Treaty on European Union.

On the other hand, efficiency may have to be weighed against fundamental constitutional principles of Member States which include other values. For example, in the specific context of the application of the principle of subsidiarity to the question of whether the social partners at the EC or at Member State level should take action, or whether it should be the Community or the Member States themselves, the principle of the autonomy of the social partners, at Community level as well as at Member State level, should be brought into the equation. 'Efficiency' might dictate EC or Member State action, but long-standing hegemony of the social partners, at one or other levels of bargaining, over certain policy areas may dictate leaving it to management and labour to settle the substance of EC social policy in that area.[46]

---

45 I am grateful to Renaud Dehousse for allowing me to read his draft chapter for this volume, which stimulated my thoughts for much of this section.
46 This principle may underlie the exclusion of competences on the right of association in Article 2(6) of the Agreement – though some competence is allowed for on 'representation and collective defence of the interests of workers and employers' (Article 2(3)).

Subsidiarity being a relative test as between levels, if, for example, the social partners are unable to adopt measures as a result of the intransigence of one side, this will be a sign that the competence may have to be exercised at a different level. Similarly if the Community is unable to adopt measures due to majority or unanimous voting requirements, competence should be exercised by the social partners at the 'better' level.

There is a further point. I believe the subsidiarity principle has been misconceived as implying an allocation of powers to either a higher or lower level. The test of relative sufficiency indicates that it is not a question of exclusive allocation. Instead, deciding which level is better implies that both have something to contribute. Though one may be better overall, the other may be more advantageous in some respects. The solution might be to use the subsidiarity principle to delineate the respective advantages of each level and promote cooperation between them, rather than assign exclusive jurisdiction to one or the other. Within the relevant field of competence, different levels can coordinate their action. This is a familiar problem in labour law and industrial relations: the relative role of legislation and collective bargaining in regulating different policy areas.

This ties up with the problems of criteria and standards for efficiency. The allocation of competences, particularly if cooperation/interdependence rather than exclusivity is the objective, depends on a reliable assessment of relative sufficiency, a concept which should be expanded beyond its narrow economic confines. More than ever it becomes clear that a court of law is ill-equipped to deal with the issue.

The problem of subsidiarity becomes, therefore, one of practical application. What are the procedures and institutional structures appropriate for resolving conflicts over which level or levels take action? What may be required is a body which could adjudicate, mediate, arbitrate, report or whatever in an effort to unfreeze any stalemate, and, more importantly, give guidance aimed at coordination of cooperative action at different levels. Labour law and industrial relations dispute resolution machinery in Member States provides a reservoir of experience.

The Agreement invites the exploitation of this experience precisely because it makes explicit the use of collective bargaining – at EC level and within Member States – in the formulation and implementation of Community social law.

D. Collective Bargaining and Implementation of Community Labour Law – after Maastricht

The first Dutch Presidency draft proposed a new Article 118 which provided in paragraph 4:[47]

---

47 *Europe Documents* No. 1734, 3 October 1991.

A Member State may entrust management and labour with the implementation of all or part of the measures which it has laid down in order to implement the directives adopted in accordance with paragraphs 2 and 3.

It did not seem clear that the social partners were to be entrusted with implementation of directives directly. Rather, the Member State lays down measures to implement directives, and it is the implementation of these measures which may be entrusted to labour and management. I would argue that this first draft was not an accurate rendering of the jurisprudence of the European Court.[48]

In *Commission of the European Communities* v. *the Kingdom of Denmark*, the Danish government's position was explicitly that collective agreements were its choice of form and method for implementation of the obligations of Council Directive 75/117 on equal pay.[49] It was argued that the Danish legislation was but a secondary guarantee of the equality principle in the event that this principle was not guaranteed by collective agreements. An agreement of 1971 made such provision and covered most employment relations in Denmark.[50] The Court held: 'that Member States may leave the implementation of the principle of equal pay in the first instance to representatives of management and labour'.[51] The Court re-affirmed this principle in a second case involving Italy, *Commission of the European Communities* v. *the Italian Republic*, when implementation of Directive 77/187 was at issue.[52]

In light of this jurisprudence, and the Charter and subsequent directives (proposed and approved)[53] it appeared that the meaning of the phrase (the proposed new Article 118(4)):

...may entrust management and labour with the implementation of all or part of the measures which it has laid down in order to implement the directives...

was that State measures are required which delegate to the social partners the task of implementation, and also that there must also be back-up provision to safeguard against loopholes in the agreements.

In my view, however, the jurisprudence did not require an explicit delegation by national measures. Rather, the social partners could directly and independently of State measures implement directives through collective agreements. The State measures necessary only regard the back-up provision where agreements are inadequate.

That this is so is evidenced by the provision which replaced the Dutch presidency's first draft. The sequence of events is important. This first draft was rejected by the Member States as a basis for negotiations at the Maastricht summit.

---

48 If considered part of the *acquis communautaire*, this limitation of the capacity of the social partners to implement directly EC directives might have been challenged.
49 Case 143/83, [1985] ECR 427.
50 Ibid., 434, para. 7.
51 Ibid., 434-435, para. 8.
52 Case 235/84, [1986] ECR 2291.

In the interval between this and the second draft, presented by the Dutch presidency on 8 November,[54] the ETUC, UNICE and CEEP produced their accord of 31 October 1991, including a redrafted Article 118(4):

> On a joint request by the social partners, a Member State may entrust them with the implementation of the directives prepared on the basis of paragraphs 2 and 3.
> In this case, it shall ensure that, by the date of entry into force of a directive at the latest, the social partners have set up the necessary provisions by agreement, the Member State concerned being required to take any necessary provisions enabling it to guarantee the results imposed by the directive.

The substance of this provision became the text of the second Draft of the Dutch presidency, which was rejected by the UK It was adopted by the 11 Member States in their Agreement comprising Annex IV of the Treaty concluded at Maastricht and is now Article 2(4) (proposed revision of Article 118(4)) of the Agreement attached to the Treaty on European Union. It reads:

> A Member State may entrust management and labour, at their joint request, with the implementation of directives adopted pursuant to paragraphs 2 and 3.
> In that case, it shall ensure that, no later than the date on which a directive must be transposed in accordance with Article 189, management and labour have introduced the necessary measures by agreements, the Member State concerned being required to take any necessary measure enabling it at any time to be in a position to guarantee the results imposed by that directive.

A number of observations may be made. As always, it is optional for the Member State to entrust implementation to the social partners. It is not clear whether the Member State may prevent or obstruct the social partners from implementing directives. There is no mention of State measures; direct implementation of directives by management and labour is the issue. It should be noted that the ETUC/UNICE/CEEP accord specified that 'the social partners' were to be entrusted with the implementation of directives. It is not clear whether 'management and labour' signifies a wider choice of representatives of employers and workers, and also of levels of representation, than would be case if 'social partners' had been the term used. This becomes particularly important since States cannot impose the burden upon social partners; it must be at their joint request. This can create problems where there are multiple parties: divided union movements or multiple employer associations. It presumes a level of collective bargaining (national, regional, enterprise) appropriate for this type of implementation.

The result could range from peak organizations requesting block exemption for whole industries (or even multi-industry agreements), to enterprises and works councils requesting authority to implement the directive in their workplaces. The Member State is not obliged to allow this. But one prospect is of legislation flexibly allowing the social partners (but query: (i) what are appropriate levels? and (ii) who

---

53   See *supra* notes 18 to 20.
54   *Europe Documents* No. 1746/1747, 20 November 1991.

are the eligible social partners?) to opt out of State regulation by substituting a collective agreement, providing this guarantees the results imposed by the directive.[55]

This is the end result of the long process described above: first individual Member States, then the European Court, then the 11 Member States in Article 27 of the Community Charter, then the Commission in its proposed directives and now the Maastricht Agreement – all have formally recognized the role of collective bargaining in the implementation of Community labour law.

E. The Role of the European Social Dialogue in Formulating Community Labour Law

At Community level, collective bargaining derives two major impulses – linked to each other – from the Maastricht Agreement. The first is Article 3's alteration of Article 118b regarding the Commission's role in promoting the social dialogue at Community level. The second concerns the role of European level collective bargaining in the formulation of Community labour law.

1. Promotion of Social Dialogue

The first reinforcement of social partner action at EC level emerged, not from the Dutch presidency's first draft, but from the ETUC/UNICE/CEEP accord. This proposed to replace the existing Article 118b:

> The Commission shall endeavour to develop the dialogue between management and labour at European level...

Instead, the new Article 118b proposed by the social partners at EC level was approved at the Maastricht Summit and is now Article 3(1) of the Agreement appended to the Union Treaty:

> The Commission shall have the task of promoting the consultation of management and labour at Community level and shall take any relevant measure to facilitate their dialogue by ensuring balanced support for the parties...

This seems to reinforce the obligation of the Commission regarding the social dialogue at EC level beyond the former 'endeavour to develop'. But it also, I suggest, implicitly reflects on the subsidiarity principle. The most 'relevant measure' which the Commission can take 'to facilitate their dialogue' is to devolve to them the task of formulating and implementing agreements on Community labour law.

---

55 Such a provision is proposed in the Commission's proposal for a Council Directive concerning certain aspects of the organization of working time, Art. 12(3); COM(90) 317 final – SYN 295, Brussels, 20 September 1990.

2. Participation of the Social Partners in the Formulation of EC Labour Law: 'Bargaining in the Shadow of the Law'

(a) Consultation

The second impulse to action by the social partners at EC level surfaced in the Dutch Presidency's first draft. This provided, first, formal recognition for what was already the practice at EC level. The proposed new Article 118a provided:

> Before submitting proposals in the social policy field, the Commission shall consult management and labour on the advisability of Community action.

This, I suggest, also reflects on the subsidiarity principle, requiring its active consideration as it applies not only to the advisability of the substance of Community action, but also on the appropriate level of implementation.

More significant was the proposal which was not in the Dutch Presidency's first draft, but the second draft, which adopted an amended text of Article 118a agreed by the ETUC/UNICE/CEEP. The substance (and virtually the identical wording) of this text agreed by the social partners became Article 3, paragraphs 2-4 of the Agreement. The final text of the Agreement is as follows:

> 2. To this end, before submitting proposals in the social policy field, the Commission shall consult management and labour on the possible direction of Community action.
> 3. If, after such consultation, the Commission considers Community action advisable, it shall consult management and labour on the content of the envisaged proposal. Management and labour shall forward to the Commission an opinion or, where appropriate, a recommendation.
> 4. On the occasion of such consultation, management and labour may inform the Commission of their wish to initiate the process provided for in Article 4. The duration of the procedure shall not exceed nine months, unless the management and labour concerned and the Commission decide jointly to extend it'

One change appears in the Agreement from the text produced by the social partners. This was introduced by the Dutch Presidency and requires Commission consent to a prolongation beyond nine months of the independent procedure of the social partners.

However, a second change also emerged in the Dutch Presidency's second draft, but does not appear in the text of the Union Treaty signed in Maastricht on 7 February 1992. That text provides that the second consultation of the Commission with the social partners is to be 'on the content of the envisaged proposal'. This was also the wording in the social partners' accord. However, the Dutch Presidency's second draft and, astonishingly, also the Agreement made at Maastricht on 9-10 December 1991, both provided for this second consultation to be 'on the envisaged proposal'.

The latter phrase might be interpreted as either wider or narrower. Wider, in that consultations limited to 'the content' might be interpreted as excluding, for example, issues to do with the appropriate legal basis, or even implementation procedures as opposed to 'substantive' content. Narrower, in that consultations 'on the envisaged proposal' might be limited to whether a proposal should be made, and not its substantive content. However, given that the first round of consultations was concerned with 'the advisability of Community action', it seems unlikely that the second round of consultations was to merely repeat the first, though at the stage of an actual proposal.

The original wording of the social partners requiring consultation 'on the content of the envisaged proposal' was reinstated in the final Treaty. However, it is unlikely that this change will affect the practice of the Commission's consultation procedure.

(b) Timing of Consultation: 'Bargaining in the Shadow of the Law'

A major ambiguity arises as to the timing of the initiation of the special procedure referred to in paragraph 4 of Article 3 – the social dialogue and possible agreements at Community level. Article 3(4) states that the procedure may be initiated by the social partners 'on the occasion of such consultation'. The question is which consultation of the two envisaged by Article 3 – before, and/or after the Commission produces its 'envisaged proposal'?

Each possibility has implications for the bargaining tactics of the social partners at Community level. In both cases there occurs a familiar situation of 'bargaining in the shadow of the law'. If the procedure may be initiated at the stage of consultations when only 'the advisability of Community action' is being considered, but *before* the Commission presents its envisaged proposal, the parties have to assess whether the result of their bargaining will be more advantageous than the unknown content of the Community action. Experience from many countries demonstrates that there will be pressures on the social partners to negotiate and agree to avoid an imposed standard which pre-empts their autonomy, and which may be also a less desirable result.

This incentive is lost if the procedure may be initiated only at the stage of consultations *after* the Commission presents its envisaged proposal. The parties may be more or less content with the proposal. They may still judge that the result of further bargaining would be more advantageous than the known content of the proposed Community action, taking into account the possible amendment of the Commission proposal as it goes through the Community institutions. The side less satisfied with the envisaged proposal will have an incentive to negotiate and agree to a different standard. The side more contented may still see advantages in a different agreed standard. Again, experience in many countries demonstrates that the social partners are often able and willing to negotiate derogations from specified standards which allow for flexibility and offer advantages to both sides.

Indeed, the negotiation of the accord which led to the insertion of these provisions into the Maastricht Treaty Protocol can be invoked as a concrete example of the process in action. The combination of expansion of competences and extension of qualified majority voting proposed in the Dutch Presidency's first draft was sufficient to induce UNICE/CEEP to agree to a procedure allowing for pre-emption of what threatened to be Community regulatory standards in a wide range of social policy areas. This despite the potentially obligatory effects of agreements between the social partners proposed by the Dutch Presidency.[56]

(c) A Hypothetical Case of 'Bargaining in the Shadow of the Law'

The possibility is not excluded that the procedure may be initiated at either occasion of consultation – before and/or after the proposal. This would allow for negotiations aimed at pre-empting a proposal; or, if these do not take place, or fail, negotiations allowing for agreed derogations and flexibility.

The tactics involved may be illustrated by a hypothetical case: the Commission, in accordance with Article 3(2) of the Treaty Protocol (the redrafted Article 118a(2)) consults the social partners on the possible direction of Community action regarding a specific aspect of working conditions. The assumption of the case (which I believe reflects the position to date) is that such action is desired by the ETUC – which is willing to negotiate an agreement – and less so by UNICE (though here, as elsewhere, the agglomeration of national interests in each of the social partners at Community level is assumed to be capable of generating a single view).

UNICE may judge that the Commission proposal is likely to set a standard too high and/or too rigid. In this case it will have an incentive to pre-empt this result by agreeing to initiate the procedure under Article 3(4) (the redrafted Article 118a(4)).

Alternatively, UNICE may judge that the Commission proposal is likely to set a standard tolerably low and/or flexible. There will be less incentive to agree to initiate the procedure at this stage. But UNICE might still prefer to avoid any risk by initiating the procedure and trying to avoid the Commission proposing a standard.

If UNICE waits until the Commission produces its envisaged proposal, two scenarios emerge. First, the proposal is too high and/or too rigid. In this case UNICE will have an incentive to avoid this result by agreeing to initiate the procedure under Article 3(4). However, it does so from a weakened position, since the Commission proposal becomes a probable minimum standard. In the second scenario, the proposal is tolerably low and/or flexible. There will be less incentive for UNICE to agree to initiate the procedure, but negotiations may still be desirable to increase flexibility or allow for derogations.

---

56   See *infra* section d. ii.

Given what I believe to be the current positions of the social partners at Community level, the prospects of and incentives for negotiation and agreement are greater the *higher* the social policy standard espoused by the Commission.

(d) The Special Procedure: EC Level Agreements and their Implementation

The procedure referred to in Article 3(4) of the Agreement is the subject of Article 4 (the redrafted Article 118b):

> 1. Should management and labour so desire, the dialogue between them at Community level may lead to contractual relations, including agreements.
> 2. Agreements concluded at Community level shall be implemented either in accordance with the procedures and practices specific to management and labour and the Member States or, in matters covered by Article 2, at the joint request of the signatory parties, by a Council decision on a proposal from the Commission.
> The Council shall act by qualified majority, except where the agreement in question contains one or more provisions relating to one of the areas referred to in Article 2(3), in which case it shall act unanimously.

The procedure outlined here has aspects which are clearly voluntary. First, it cannot be initiated without the consent of both the social partners (Article 3(4). Secondly, Article 4(1)) makes it clear that neither party is obliged to agree. Thirdly, the Commission seems free to produce proposals even when the social partners initiate the procedure, or during it. Finally, extension of the procedure beyond the nine-month period proposed is subject not only to the joint decision of the social partners, but also to the decision of the Commission.

The obligatory pre-emption, if any, by the social partners of Community labour law does not take effect at the point of initiation or for the duration of the procedure. It is not clear whether the Commission is precluded from pursuing its original social policy proposal even when informed by management and labour of their wish to initiate the process under Article 4 which may culminate in an agreement. The nine-month duration (which may be extended) does not explicitly preclude a parallel process of social policy formulation by the Commission. It might even be that such a 'two-track' process would impart a certain dynamism to both Commission and social partners. However, while it is not clear that the Commission is thus pre-empted in the formulation of social policy, it is as regards the successful outcome of the procedure – 'agreements concluded at Community level' – that the potentially obligatory nature of the procedure emerges.

i) 'Agreements Concluded at Community Level'

Since 1985, the Commission has stressed that negotiations between employers' and workers' organizations at Community level were a cornerstone of the European social area which goes hand in hand with the creation of the single European market.[57] These negotiations have come to be known as the 'European social dialogue'. The debate over the potential of European social dialogue which has taken place since the first meetings between the social partners at Val Duchesse in 1985 has posited four types of 'European agreement': (i) an inter-confederal/inter-sectoral agreement between the social partners organized at European level (ETUC/UNICE/CEEP), (ii) a European industry/sectoral/branch agreement between social partners organized on an industry/ sectoral/branch level; (iii) an agreement with a multinational enterprise having affiliates in more than one Member State; and (iv) an agreement covering more than one Member State.

To define the phrase 'agreements concluded at Community level' in Article 4(2) in restrictive terms of geography or of actors seems counterproductive. For example, since the UK does not adhere to the Agreement, 'Community level' agreements may well engage the organizations of British employers and trade union members of the ETUC and UNICE, but not the Member State in which these agreements are to be applied.

If the phrase 'agreements concluded at Community level' were taken to require that agreements must engage all and only Member State organizations of workers and employers, this could eliminate all the four types of European agreements foreseen above as possibly emerging from the European social dialogue. The first two because the social partners at European level are not organized so as to include exclusively organizations of workers and employers of Community Member States. Non-Member State organizations are included, and some organizations within Member States are not included. The last two because the enterprises and regions concerned do not include all Member States.

The 'Community' dimension of 'agreements concluded at Community level' is considerably diluted by the potentially paradoxical fact that, in contrast to the limitations imposed by restricted competences and voting procedures on organs of the Community, such agreements are not subject to any explicit restriction either as to content or to majority or unanimous voting. Nor do the procedures of reaching agreements entail the direct involvement of Community institutions.[58] The European social dialogue is not formally dependent on Community law, whatever benefits it may derive from use of the Community legal framework.[59]

The conclusion proposed is that the phrase 'agreements concluded at Community level' can be understood in terms of the European social dialogue as carried on since 1985. Therefore, at the least, agreements emerging from the

---

57 See *Joint Opinions*, European Social Dialogue Documentary Series, Commission of the European Communities.
58 At a time when the assertions are frequent as to the democratic deficit of measures adopted by Community institutions, this raises important questions of the legitimacy of such agreements. As to the democratic legitimacy of neo-corporatist outcomes, see P.C. Schmitter, *Democratic Theory and Neo-Corporatist Practice*, EUI Working Paper No. 74, 1983.
59 It may be argued that the Accord reached by the ETUC/UNICE/CEEP and later incorporated more or less completely into the Maastricht Agreements could survive the failure of Member States to ratify the Treaty on European Union. However, the utility of the Accord after such a failure is much less of a practical prospect.

European social dialogue should be deemed to fall within the meaning of the phrase. But, in addition, other agreements with a European Community element (geographical, actors) may also be eligible for inclusion within the framework of Article 4(2).

ii) Implementation of 'Agreements Concluded at Community Level'

Once an agreement has been concluded at Community level, there are two methods of implementing the agreement reached.

The first is that 'Agreements concluded at Community level shall be implemented ... in accordance with the procedures and practices specific to management and labour and the Member States...' (Article 4(2)). It should be noted that the reference to management and labour is supplemented by '*and* the Member States'. It seems from this formulation that some degree of obligation is imposed directly on Member States by the word 'shall'. One question is: If such implementation is obligatory, how does such an obligation operate? At least three possibilities exist.

One possibility is that the Member States are obliged to develop procedures and practices (which may be peculiar to themselves) to implement the agreements reached at Community level. This would seem to require some formal machinery of articulation of national standards with those laid down in the agreements. The experience of implementation of Community instruments, such as directives, provides a basis for assessing whether Member States have complied with this obligation.

A second possibility is that the Member States are not obliged to develop new procedures and practices to implement the agreements. But where there exists machinery of articulation of national standards with those laid down in the agreements, this is to be used.

A third possibility is that, given the nature of the authors of the standards (Community level organizations of employers and workers), the procedures and practices peculiar to each Member State may consist of mechanisms of articulation of Community agreements with collective bargaining in the Member State concerned. Member States are not obliged to create such mechanisms, but national law may not interfere with such mechanisms which already exist, or which may be created by the social partners within the Member State to deal with the new development at Community level.

This possibility of a process of articulation of 'agreements concluded at Community level' with 'procedures and practices specific to management and labour' does not detract from the significance of the following words: '*and* the Member States...'. This may be a reflection of the above-mentioned jurisprudence of the European Court of Justice concerned with implementation of Community instruments through collective bargaining, now encapsulated in Article 2(4) of the Agreement.

It is not clear whether, and, if so, how far any of these possibilities allows for Member State discretion regarding the content of the Community level agreements. Do 'practices and procedures specific' to the Member States imply that the content may be adapted to such exigencies? Does it depend on the nature of the agreement: following the pattern of Community directives, the agreement may specify either objectives to be achieved in various ways, or more clear and precise obligations which limit the scope for deviation. The existence of clear and precise obligations even raises the question whether such provisions could have direct effect – at least in vertical form – as regards Member States.

Implementation is particularly affected by the above-mentioned possibility that agreements may be reached without the direct involvement of Community institutions, and are not subject to any explicit restriction either as to content or to majority or unanimous voting. The problem could take at least two forms. First, agreements reached outside the competence of Community institutions – does any obligation to implement apply? Secondly, agreements reached which are opposed by sufficient Member States to block approval had they been presented to the Council under either majority or unanimous voting requirements.

In the latter case, it may be argued that voting requirements do not affect the agreement, as it has been reached in another forum authorized by the 11 Member States. But if so, a double set of Community competences emerges: first, the new scope envisaged by the Agreement applicable to the measures adopted by Community institutions; but also, second, a more extensive scope allotted to the social partners, and carrying with it the obligation to implement 'agreements concluded at Community level'. These latter would thus fall within the scope of Community law, with all the enforcement implications canvassed above.

This may seem a startling proposition. It is argued on the basis of the Agreement's adoption of extraordinary new procedures for the development of Community law, restricting the direct participation of Community institutions, and, in particular, rendering inapplicable the consequent restrictive voting requirements closely tied to specific areas of competence. This new approach to formulating Community labour law may imply that the detailed limits on competences carefully attached to the old institutions and procedures are not necessarily to be carried over to the new institutions and procedures.

For example, Article 2 of the Protocol specifies that the Council may adopt directives by qualified majority vote as regards the fields specified in Article 2(1), but must act unanimously as regards the areas specified in Article 2(3). But, as per Article 2(6):

> The provisions of *this Article* shall not apply to pay, the right of association, the right to strike or the right to impose lock-outs (emphasis added).

The question is whether this exclusion of competences as regards the procedures in Article 2 applies to the radically different procedures laid down in Articles 3 and 4. If not, by implication, under Article 3, the Commission may make a proposal in a social policy field specified in Article 2(6) which, under Article 3(4), is then taken up by management and labour, with the possible result of an agreement on the subject at Community level (Article 4(1) which 'shall be implemented' in one of the ways specified in Article 4(2). This difference in potential competences may be understood because of the particular delicacy of the matters listed in Article 2(6) touching, as they do, upon the area of the autonomy of the social partners (right of association, the rights to strike or impose lock-outs) and the most central of collective bargaining subjects (pay).

If it is possible to justify and understand this difference between Community competences for procedures involving the Commission, Council and Parliament on the one hand, and competences for procedures involving the Commission, management and labour on the other, then it may be that the competences listed generally in Article 2 are not to limit the potential of the social dialogue procedure prescribed in Articles 3 and 4.

To summarize; the starting point is Article 1, which specifies the social policy objectives, and hence competences, of the Community and the Member States in very general terms. Article 2 then lays down certain procedures for achieving such objectives by the usual procedure of Council directives – specifying some of the competences for qualified majority voting, unanimity for others, and excluding still others.

Article 3(2) simply provides for Commission proposals 'in the social policy field' which may be taken up by management and labour in the new procedure of social dialogue. These proposals may go beyond those specified in Article 2, though still within the Community competences specified in Article 1.

Member State obligations to implement agreements at Community level within those competences flow from Article 4(2).[60] Finally, it is interesting to note that Article 4(2) provides for the second method of implementing agreements concluded at Community level – by a Council decision on a proposal from the Commission 'in matters covered by Article 2', with a further paragraph specifying the voting requirements. This reinforces the argument that the range of competences in social policy reserved to the social partners is distinct from that of the Community institutions.

A second method is envisaged to implement Community level agreements at Member State level. The second paragraph of a revised Article 118b proposed in the first Draft of the Dutch Presidency provided:

---

60   Also Article 5 of the Treaty: 'Member States shall take all appropriate measures, whether general or particular, to ensure fulfilment of the obligations arising out of this Treaty or resulting from action taken by the institutions of the Community'.

> In matters falling within Article 118, where management and labour so desire, the Commission may submit proposals to transpose the agreements referred to in paragraph 1 into Community legislation. The Council shall act under the conditions laid down in Article 118.

Unlike paragraph 1, this makes implementation of agreements conditional on a Commission proposal. Moreover, unlike the obligation under the first paragraph to implement agreements, such a proposal of the Commission is made explicitly subject to the conditions of Article 118 as to competences and voting procedures.

In at least one significant respect it appears to differ from the first method: the Commission's proposals are 'to transpose the agreements'. This seems expressly to limit the discretion of the Commission to change the contents of the agreements reached.

However, the nature of the Community legal instrument proposed is left to the Commission's discretion and the Council's action.

The ETUC/UNICE/CEEP accord altered this provision to implementation of 'Agreements concluded at Community level ... in matters covered by Article 2, at the joint request of the signatory parties, by a Council decision on a proposal from the Commission concerning the agreements as they have been concluded' (proposed revision of Article 118b(2)).

As with the Dutch Presidency's proposal, this makes implementation of agreements conditional on a Commission proposal. Again, such a proposal of the Commission is made explicitly subject to conditions as to competences and voting procedures. Finally, while the word 'transpose' is deleted, its substance is retained by the requirement that agreements be implemented 'as they have been concluded'.

The final version adopted as Article 4(2) of the Agreement annexed to the Protocol on Social Policy incorporated the text agreed by the social partners with the exception of the provision that the Commission proposal and Council decision must adopt the agreements reached by the social partners '...as they have been concluded'. This seems to open the way for the Commission possibly to change the content of the agreements. It is contested whether this is so. After all, the wording still is: 'Agreements... shall be implemented... on a proposal from the Commission'. The ambiguity remains a crucial one: how much are the Member States and the Commission entitled to vary the agreements reached at EC level?

Another critical issue is the nature of the instrument to be used to implement the agreement. The first draft of the Dutch Presidency left it to the discretion of the Commission and Council to determine the appropriate instrument. The ETUC/UNICE/CEEP accord and the final Agreement refer to a 'proposal from the Commission' and 'a Council decision'.

A Council Decision is one of the specific instruments of Community legislation listed in Article 189. It is not clear whether the reference in Article 4(2) is to such an instrument, or rather reflects the Dutch Presidency's preference for the Commission and Council to have a choice of instruments. One indication, perhaps, is that the

Agreement in its Danish version uses the term for 'arriving at a decision' (*ved en afgorelse*), not the technical term to 'take decisions' (*ved besltninger*) used in Article 189.[61]

A possible choice of instruments to be decided upon by the Commission and Council is a much more flexible approach. It also avoids some of the technical problems of utilising a Decision which, under Articles 189-192 'shall be binding in its entirety upon those to whom it is addressed', 'shall state the reasons on which they are based and shall refer to the proposals or opinions which were required to be obtained pursuant to this Treaty' and 'shall be notified to those to whom they are addressed and shall take effect upon notification'. Further, on the terms of Article 2(4) of the Agreement (revised Article 118(4)), implementation may be entrusted to management and labour only of Directives. Use of other instruments might preclude such articulation.

On the other hand, leaving it to Commission discretion and Council action to determine the instrument of implementation does leave open the possibility of their choosing non-legally binding instruments. This might be inconsistent with the intention of the social partners that their agreements should have legal effect. It would also contribute to an unequal application of agreements across Member States in some of which these agreements are or are not legally enforceable. Finally, whatever the technical problems, a decision would, given a sufficiently broad definition of a class of addressees, resolve some of the problems of general application and enforcement of agreements.

A further change occurred in the wording in the December agreement. The Council decision was formerly said: 'to be taken according to the voting procedures laid down in Article 118'. The December agreement changed this:

> The Council shall act by qualified majority, except where the agreement in question contains one or more provisions relating to one of the areas referred to in Article 2(3), in which case it shall act unanimously.

Under Article 2(1), certain areas were subject to majority voting. The agreements might: a) cover only such areas; b) cover areas neither within majority nor unanimous voting procedures, i.e. not within the competence of EC institutions[62]; c) cover only areas within the unanimous voting procedure; d) cover areas which fell partly within more than one of the above ('one or more provisions...' (mixed agreements)). Cases a) and c) seem clear. Case b) is problematic as to whether a Council decision can be taken at all. Case d) seems, under the final version of the

---

61   I am grateful to Mr. Tore Hakonsson, a researcher at the European University Institute, for providing this translation. The point is also made with reference to the German translation by the European Trade Union Institute's Working Paper prepared for a conference in Luxembourg, 1-2 June 1992, *The European Dimensions of Collective Bargaining after Maastricht*, Working Documents, Brussels, 1992, at 104, paragraph 19.

62   Though within that of the social partners, see above, section d.i.

Maastricht Agreement (now also in the February Agreement) to subject 'mixed agreements' to unanimity. [63]

(e) Obligatory Implementation of EC Agreements?

The obligatory implementation of agreements reached through the social dialogue at Community level was declared ('shall be implemented') in the first Draft presented by the Dutch Presidency. The ETUC/UNICE/CEEP accord of 31 October 1991 (paragraph 1) repeated the Dutch first draft proposal regarding the voluntary nature of the dialogue which may lead to agreements. However, unlike the Dutch first draft, the second paragraph of the proposed Article 118b stated that: 'Agreements concluded at the Community level *may* be implemented ...'.[64]

The intention was clearly to make implementation of such agreements voluntary also as regards Member State or social partners within them, as well as in the case of action by the Community organs – which under the first Dutch draft was already voluntary in the sense that it was subject to the request of the social partners.

The second Dutch draft which followed the ETUC/UNICE/CEEP accord raised problems because of the differences between the English and French versions. The English version reinstated the wording rendering implementation obligatory via national procedures and practices. The French version, however, did not change the wording relating to the obligatory or voluntary nature. The outcome is not helpful in understanding this key point.

The situation has been further confused by a change which occurred in the French version between the agreement in Maastricht in December and the signing of the Treaty in February. The English version remained the same: a high level of obligation: (Article 4(2)): 'Agreements concluded at Community level shall be implemented...'. The French version changed one key word: instead of the December version: 'La mise en œuvre des accords conclus au niveau communautaire *interviendra*...', there appears in the Union Treaty Accord: 'La mise en œuvre des accords conclus au niveau communautaire *intervient*...'.

The key issue remains the degree of obligation regarding implementation of EC level agreements. The uncertainty is highlighted by a Declaration attached to the Maastricht Treaty Accord:

---

63   A similar argument arose concerning the interpretation of Art. 100A(2) of the Treaty of Rome. This subjects to unanimity proposals related to the rights and interests of workers. It was argued that if the proposal related solely to workers' rights it was subject to unanimity. But if it related only partially to workers' rights, it was eligible for majority voting, even if it affected workers' rights. The problems arose when the proposal affected both workers' rights, but also other matters. See Bercusson, *supra* notes 12 and 18. The issue has been made clearer here: any proposal which 'contains one or more provisions relating to one of the areas referred to in Article 2(3)' becomes subject to unanimity.

64   The French version is not so clearly permissive: 'La mise en œuvre des accords conclus au niveau communautaire *interviendra*...'.

The Conference declares that the first of the arrangements for application of the agreements between management and labour Community-wide – referred to in Article 118b(2) – will consist in developing by collective bargaining according to the rules of each Member State, the content of the agreements, and that consequently this arrangement implies no obligation on the member states to apply the agreements directly or to work out rules for their transposition, nor any obligation to amend national legislation in force to facilitate their implementation.

This Declaration raises a series of difficulties. What is the legal effect of a declaration to an Agreement attached to a Treaty? Such declarations on Community legal instruments are not granted any status before the Court of Justice. If the Agreement's redrafted Articles of the Rome Treaty are subsequently incorporated into the Treaty, what will happen to this Declaration?

How, if at all, does it change and/or reduce the obligation of the Member States regarding implementation? The obligation is transformed from implementation to developing the content of the agreement by domestic bargaining. This is not necessarily implicit in the implementation process; indeed, it goes beyond it. Finally, if there is no obligation to apply agreements directly, or to transpose them, or even to facilitate implementation, what is left of the obligation to implement?

III. Conclusion

Three outcomes of the Maastricht summit are of outstanding importance for the future of Community labour law:

1. The implementation of Community labour law through collective bargaining within Member States is explicitly recognized.
2. A role for the social partners at EC level in formulating Community labour law is introduced. The procedure is that of 'bargaining in the shadow of the law'. The social dialogue is delicately timed to take place during the Commission's procedure of consulting the social partners about social policy proposals. This raises complex issues of subsidiarity.
3. If the social partners at EC level reach agreements, it appears that Member States are obliged to implement these agreements within their national legal orders; it is not clear how this is to be accomplished.

This chapter has explored three issues which arise from the attempt to understand the problems of interpretation and implementation of the Maastricht Agreement.

1. The legal nature of the Agreement and its consequences. The conclusion was that the Agreement is probably part of Community law, as are the likely outcomes of the Agreement (directives, decisions, EC level agreements). The methods of enforcing Community law should be available for these instruments as well.
2. The scope of the new competences and majority voting. The conclusion was that the new competences probably replaced the Treaty of Rome for

the 11 Member States, and that the Commission would play a key role depending on whether it accepted that it was now obliged to produce proposals based on these new competences.

3. Social dialogue and the role of subsidiarity. The conclusion was that social dialogue at EC level was characterized by its tripartite nature, and that the Commission would play a key role. The role of different levels in developing social policy was likely to be influenced by the principle of subsidiarity – understood as a measure of the relative sufficiency of actions by the Community or the social partners. The decision as to relative sufficiency is a highly political one, and requires the development of appropriate procedures and institutional structures.

The future of European labour law lies with the instruments agreed by the Member States at Maastricht: directives and EC level collective agreements, to be implemented within Member States, and enforced, *inter alia*, using the techniques developed to enforce Community law.

The European social dialogue thus emerges as a critical feature of Community social law and policy.[65] It is important to appreciate the novel features of this process and avoid the temptation to chart the future path of European social dialogue following national models, either in detail or even in some of their basic principles. These are the product of much reflection and experience which must be respected. But at the same time their application in a transnational context is quite new, and hence requires new thinking.

For example, the fundamental principle of the autonomy of the social partners is granted almost, if not literally, constitutional status in the legal orders of Member States. This is reflected in the Maastricht Agreement's respect for the requirement that social partners' consent be obtained before their agreements can be transmuted into Community instruments. But once so transmuted, the need arises for enforcement of these instruments, a process which national experience has shown to present dangers to the autonomy of the social partners which challenge even the most experienced labour tribunals. Community institutions will have to respond to these challenges.

Again, the legitimacy of the agreements adopted will raise questions of the legitimacy of the social partners who through them develop fundamental social and economic rights. Decline in membership and proliferation of organizational forms seem to be the dominant characteristics of Western European labour at the present.[66] The implications for the role of the social partners in the European social dialogue are not hard to perceive. They can be summarized by asking two questions:

---

65 My Report for the Commission of October 1989 on *Fundamental Social and Economic Rights in the European Community* proposed that collective bargaining/the social dialogue in Member States and transnationally should be the primary instrument for developing and implementing fundamental social and economic rights in the European Community. See *supra* note 18, at 287-289.

(1) what bodies or organizations claiming representativeness are to benefit from the rights granted by the Maastricht Agreement? and (2) what legal obligations and liabilities are to be imposed upon them?

Traditionally, labour law has been much concerned with the external relations of the actors involved in industrial relations, specifically with their relations to each other through collective bargaining. Increasingly, however, labour law has been forced to grapple with the issue of internal constitutional structures, particularly of the new and changing actors emerging. It is worth recalling the prediction of Simitis that the 'third generation' of labour law would be concerned with this issue.[67] These questions become of the first importance if the process creating Community social policy and law bypasses existing institutions, such as the European Parliament and the Economic and Social Committee, and is based instead on trade union and employer confederations organized at Community level. Similarly, if the legal consequences of the new social rights are to extend beyond the existing membership of trade unions and employers associations.

Finally, collective bargaining/social dialogue within Member States is universally regarded as reflecting a balance of power between labour and capital, exercised traditionally through the weapons of industrial conflict. The Maastricht Agreement does not address even the possibility of industrial conflict at European level. Indeed, Article 2(6) seems explicitly to withhold, at least from the EC institutions, regulatory competences which would be most relevant.

The logic to this auto-exclusion is, perhaps, that the current state of Community level social dialogue is qualitatively different in that the normal means of pressure – strikes – are not (yet) operational at Community level. It may be that the present prospect of the Community social dialogue implies rather a tripartite process – involving the social partners and the Commission/Community as a dynamic factor. This is the scenario canvassed above: 'bargaining in the shadow of the law'.

The argument is that it is for the Commission to give a clear signal that the factor breaking any deadlock in bargaining will not be the classic weapons of class struggle as evident in national contexts, but the stimulus of Commission activity in the form of proposals for social legislation. Given what I believe to be the current positions of the social partners at Community level, the prospects of and incentives for negotiation and agreement are greater the *higher* the social policy standard espoused by the Commission.

This imposes a heavy burden of responsibility on the Commission. But this has been so ever since it launched the new European social dialogue through the Val Duchesse initiative in 1985. The Commission's initiative was crucial to the achievement of the Agreement reached by the social partners on 31 October 1991

---

66   See B. Bercusson, 'Europäisches und nationales Arbeitsrecht – Die gegenwartige Situation', *Zeitschrift für ausländisches und internationales Arbeits– und Sozialrecht* (1991) 1-40.
67   S. Simitis, 'Juridification of Labor Relations', in G. Teubner (ed.), *Juridification of Social Spheres* (1987) 113, at 142-143.

and incorporated into the Maastricht Agreement. It is by furthering such initiatives that the European social dialogue will continue to develop.

Part IV

The External Dimension

Chapter 8

How Common Will Foreign and Security Policies be?

Roger Morgan

I. Introduction

The Maastricht Treaty's provisions on foreign and security policy (Title V) are formulated in very general terms, and combined with a number of clearly-expressed limitations on any rapid development of common policies in this field: in the key stages of the processes envisaged, unanimity prevails, as will be shown in more detail below. Despite these inhibitions, however, the projected Common Foreign and Security Policy (CFSP) has proved, paradoxically, to be one of the sections of the Maastricht Treaty which has led to the greatest redeployment of political and administrative manpower.

In January 1993, when a new Commission took office to guide the affairs of the Community until 1995, it was announced that no fewer than three Commissioners (apart from the President, Jacques Delors) would have responsibilities in the field of foreign relations: as well as Manuel Marin's responsibility for development aid and Third World relations, and Sir Leon Brittan's role as Commissioner for external economic relations more generally, the new Dutch Commissioner Hans van den Broek (a former Foreign Minister) would be responsible for external political relations, for enlargement negotiations, and for the CFSP as a whole.

This upgrading of foreign policy, which, at the level of the Commission, seemed to anticipate that the Maastricht Treaty would indeed be ratified, was paralleled by a restructuring and reinforcement of the Commission's administrative services. Alongside the existing Directorate-General I, responsible for foreign economic relations, a new Directorate-General for CFSP issues was established, working under Hans van den Broek.

Corresponding, and equally radical, changes were meanwhile taking place in other Community institutions. The Council Secretariat made preparations to incorporate the Political Cooperation Secretariat, and the number of its staff concerned with CFSP issues was scheduled to be substantially increased. The European Parliament's Political Affairs Committee renamed itself Committee on Foreign Relations and Security, and devoted considerable attention to the problems of enhancing its capacity to exercise parliamentary control over the operations of the CFSP.

All these preparations suggested that the European Union's foreign policy would indeed be developed in a dynamic and to a large extent a communitarian way, including a substantial role for the Commission and other EC institutions. There may prove to be a strong trend in this direction, but at the same time a close examination of the relevant Title of the Treaty suggests that the Member States may be in a position to raise substantial obstacles to the Commission's more ambitious projects.

II. A New Foreign Policy?

Title V of the Treaty on European Union ('Provisions on a Common Foreign and Security Policy)[1] states the commitment of the parties to achieve this aim, in unprecedentedly firm and ambitious terms: 'A common foreign and security policy is hereby established which shall be governed by the following provisions...'; 'The Union and its Member States shall define and implement a common foreign and security policy ... covering all areas of foreign and security policy.'[2] ; and so forth. After a statement of the general objectives of the common policy – safeguarding the common values, fundamental interests and independence of the Union, preserving peace, strengthening international security, and promoting international cooperation, democracy, and human rights, Article J.1 concludes with a very comprehensive commitment:

> The Member States shall support the Union's external and security policy actively and unreservedly in a spirit of loyalty and mutual solidarity. They shall refrain from any action which is contrary to the interests of the Union or likely to impair its effectiveness as a cohesive force in international relations... [3].

Title V continues with equally sweeping language:

> Member States shall inform and consult one another within the Council on any matter of foreign and security policy of general interest in order to ensure that their combined influence is exerted as effectively as possible by means of concerted and convergent action.[4]

This article also binds the Member States to 'ensure that their national policies conform to common positions' as defined by the Council,[5] to 'coordinate their action in international organizations and international conferences' and to 'uphold the common position in such forums', and (in the case of Member States

---

1   Page references to the Maastricht Treaty on European Union are to the edition published by the Council and Commission of the European Communities (Luxembourg, 1992).
2   Article J.1.
3   Article J.1(4).
4   Article J.2(1).
5   Article J.2(2).

participating in international organizations and conferences where not all Member States are present) to 'uphold the common positions'.[6]

The opening passage of Title V thus commits the Member States, in language which could be qualified as rhetorical, to patterns of behaviour in foreign policy which go well beyond the norms established in the 20-year experience of European Political Cooperation (EPC), and suggests that the CFSP of the European Union aspires to be something qualitatively different from, and much more closely harmonized than, the system of EPC as hitherto practised by the Member States of the Community.

In fact, the remaining nine articles of Title V (Articles J.3-J.11: the whole of Title V runs to only six pages out of the total of 139 pages of the Treaty) consist essentially of procedural provisions and substantive reservations which seem to be designed to set strict limits on the implementation and evolution of the common policy which Title V proclaims as an objective. It is true that if Article J.1(4) (solidarity with the Union) and Article J.2(1) (mandatory and comprehensive consultation) are taken seriously, the existing density of consultation between the Member States, through EPC, will be enhanced. This will no doubt be facilitated by the agreement to merge the Political Cooperation Secretariat with the General Secretariat of the Council.[7] In practice, however, before a foreign or security policy issue can become the subject of joint action, a number of rigorously defined stages have to be accomplished. Firstly, the 'general guidelines' governing the CFSP have to be defined by the European Council,[8] and it is on the basis of these guidelines that 'the Council shall take the decisions necessary for defining and implementing the common foreign and security policy'.[9] The next stage in adopting joint action in 'matters covered by the foreign and security policy'[10] is that 'the Council shall decide on the basis of general guidelines from the European Council that a matter should be the subject of joint action', and that whenever such a decision is taken, the Council 'shall lay down the specific scope, the Union's general and specific objectives in carrying out such action, if necessary its duration, and the means, procedures and conditions for its implementation'.[11] Up to this point, of course, the principle of unanimity applies, so that any Member State could in principle block any decision that a foreign policy matter should be the subject of joint action. Moreover, 'the Council shall when adopting the joint action and at any time during its development, define those matters on which decisions are to be taken by a qualified majority.'[12] It remains to be seen how these procedures will work in practice, but on the face of it they appear to impose fairly stringent limitations on

---

6   Article J.2(3).
7   Final Act, 'Declaration on Practical Arrangements in the Field of the Common Foreign and Security Policy', Treaty on European Union, 240.
8   Article J.8(1).
9   Article J.8(2).
10   Article J.3.
11   Article J.3(2).
12   Article J.3(2).

the evolution of the present EPC system into anything really deserving the title of 'Common Foreign and Security Policy'.

III. Security and Defence Policies

Article J.4(2) of the Treaty, which deals directly with the security aspects of the common policy, contains at least one decisive innovation:

> the Union requests the Western European Union (WEU), which is an integral part of the development of the Union, to elaborate and implement decisions and actions of the Union which have defence implications. The Council shall, in agreement with the institutions of the WEU, adopt the necessary practical arrangements.

These practical arrangements, as we shall see, will not be achieved without some difficulty, and the views of various Member States on what exactly it means to make WEU 'an integral part of the development of the Union' are very far apart on certain key aspects. However, the decision to establish an organic relationship with the WEU represents, as has already been noted, a decisive step forward.

On the other hand the introductory paragraph of Article J.4, which precedes the commitment concerning WEU, is couched in language which indicates that the development of a military role for the European Union, as represented by WEU, may take a very long time indeed:

> The common foreign and security policy shall include all questions related to the security of the Union, including the eventual framing of a common defence policy, which might in time lead to a common defence.

This careful distinction between 'security policy', 'a common defence policy', and 'a common defence', together with the use of the phrases 'the eventual framing' and 'might in time' give an indication of the long distance still to be covered before the points of view of the major Member States can be reconciled. Indeed, the rest of Article J.4 spells out further limitations on the unity and comprehensiveness of the security dimension of the new common policy. For a start, 'issues having defence implications' will not be subject to the procedures governing 'joint action', described earlier.[13] In confirming that 'the policy of the Union in accordance with this Article shall not prejudice the specific character of the security and defence policy of certain Member States', the Treaty recognizes the independent defence posture of France, and when the same Article declares that the policy of the Union 'shall respect the obligations of certain Member States under the North Atlantic Treaty and be compatible with the common security and defence policy established within that framework',[14] the Atlanticist position of certain other NATO member states, as distinct from France, is brought in to balance the equation.

13 Article J.4(3).
14 Article J.4(4).

Again, the declaration in Article J.4(5) that 'the provisions of this article shall not prevent the development of closer cooperation between two or more Member States on a bilateral level' is clearly designed to accommodate the development of Franco-German military cooperation: this is especially important to France. Again, the specific approval of bilateral cooperation is circumscribed by multilateral conditions: this article stipulates that such bilateral cooperation should take place 'in the framework of the WEU and the Atlantic Alliance', and should 'not run counter to or impede that provided for in this Title'.

The elaborate – even contorted – wording of Article J.4 makes it clear that the Member States of the proposed European Union are far from consensus on the way in which the military aspect of this Union is to be developed. On the one hand, WEU is clearly to be regarded as the vehicle for whatever military cooperation the Union may decide to implement, but on the other hand the view that WEU has a distinct function as the organizational framework bringing together the European member states of NATO remains very powerful in some capitals. Is the WEU moving its Secretariat from London to Brussels in order to be near the European Union, or in order to be near NATO? This question not only has deep symbolic connotations: it also, as we shall see, raises very delicate practical issues about how the Council of WEU, in its new rôle, will actually function.

The 'Declaration on Western European Union', issued in the name of the nine member states of WEU on the occasion of the Maastricht summit meeting, goes into considerably more detail on the proposed relationship of WEU with the European Union than the main text of the Treaty: indeed, this declaration contains slightly more words than the whole of Title V of the Treaty itself. This is of course not surprising, since the nine member states of WEU have worked hard in recent years to establish common positions, so that their Declaration of December 1991 represents the culmination of a sort of military equivalent of the work of the intergovernmental conferences which preceded the Maastricht summit. The Nine can also, of course, speak with much more cohesion on defence matters than the Twelve. This WEU Declaration – which in effect represents the programme for a possible development of a military role for the European Union – contains a clear commitment by the WEU member states on the need

> to develop a genuine European security and defence identity and a greater European responsibility on defence matters... WEU Member States agree to strengthen the role of WEU, in the longer term perspective of a common defence policy within the European Union which might in time lead to a common defence, compatible with that of the Atlantic Alliance.[15]

The WEU, in preparing for its role as 'the defence component of the European Union'[16] undertakes to establish a close working relationship with the institutions of the Union, notably the Commission and the Council. This of course will entail

15   Paragraph 1 of the WEU Declaration, Treaty on European Union, 242.
16   WEU Declaration, para. 3.

cooperation between the Secretariat General of WEU on the one hand and the General Secretariat of the Council (including in future the EPC Secretariat) on the other. The cooperation between WEU and the Commission, which is declared to be necessary 'in accordance with the role of the Commission in the Common Foreign and Security Policy' marks a radically new development, as does the proposal for the harmonization of the sequence and duration of the respective Presidencies of WEU and the Union, and the encouragement of closer cooperation between the Parliamentary Assembly of WEU and the European Parliament.

It should again be stressed that the WEU's commitment to acting as the defence agency of the European Union is balanced by a reaffirmation of WEU's continuing role 'as a means to strengthen the European pillar of the Atlantic Alliance'.[17] The various provisions for coordination between WEU and the European Union, just mentioned, are indeed matched by corresponding commitments to synchronization and cooperation between the Secretariats General of WEU and NATO. Further limitations on the role of WEU as the agent of the defence policy of a European union could also be mentioned: for instance, the commitment to establishing a 'WEU planning cell' for military operations is a step forward, but it carefully stops short of the term 'general staff'.[18]

The ambiguous future role of WEU as a component part both of the European Union and of NATO is perfectly illustrated by the provisions of the Declaration concerning the composition of the WEU Council. Ever since the establishment of the WEU as a vehicle for West German rearmament in the 1950s, the Council, located in London, has consisted of the ambassadors of the WEU's member states in London, together with the British Foreign Office Under Secretary responsible for West European affairs. This arrangement, while it has sometimes led to the inclusion in the Council of diplomats of great experience in politico-military affairs, has more often than not produced a Council whose competence was only commensurate with the relatively low-level missions of WEU as a whole. Henceforth, when the WEU's Council and Secretariat operate in Brussels, the composition of the Council will be different, but this composition will in fact vary, from one member state to another, in a highly significant way. Whereas some member states of WEU (notably France) apparently wish to affirm their view that WEU is the defence wing of the European Union by appointing their Permanent Representative to the European Union as their member of the WEU Council, other member states (including the Federal Republic of Germany and United Kingdom) will wish to underline WEU's links with NATO by appointing as their representative to this council their existing representative on the North Atlantic Council. This dichotomy – some members of the WEU Council wearing the 'double hat' of Permanent Representatives to the European Union, and others wearing the 'double hat' of ambassadors to NATO – surely raises serious questions about the viability and the capacity for action of WEU as a whole. Up to the present time, at

17   Ibid., para. 4.
18   Ibid., para. 5.

any rate – that is to say, over nearly 40 years of experience – the Permanent Representatives of Member States to the Communities (now to be called European Union) have been diplomats with special experience in the technicalities of EC affairs, and have had links to the economic, commercial, and agricultural departments of government in their respective capitals. Ambassadors to NATO, in contrast, have been diplomats specialized in politico-military affairs, whose links with their national capitals reach into the ministries of foreign affairs and defence. It is hard to imagine how the WEU Council, composed of a mixture of these two breeds, can achieve the cohesion, *esprit de corps*, and capacity for action of either the Community's Committee of Permanent Representatives (COREPER) on the one hand or of the NATO Council on the other.

It may be that by 1996, when both the European Union and WEU are committed to re-examining the provisions now being made, ways will be found to develop the WEU into an effective defence agency for the European Union, and that the renewal of the WEU Treaty, due in 1998, will be carried through on this basis. As this discussion has shown, however, the situation is full of ambiguities (in the background, we should recall that the whole notion of a military 'threat' to Western Europe is widely perceived as having evaporated with the demise of the Soviet Union, so that the very functions that might be necessary for a West European defence capacity are a matter of fundamental debate). The future development of this dimension of the European Union and of its CFSP inevitably remains very obscure.

IV. The Cohesion between Economic and Political Affairs

If we turn from the military aspects, and consider again the broader political dimensions of the CFSP, the prospect could be summarized by saying that the Treaty on European Union, although it has advanced tentatively towards some of the well-known difficulties arising from the separation between on the one hand EC external relations (Community competence) and on the other hand European Political Cooperation (intergovernmental responsibility), has in the end drawn back from taking any decisive steps to overcome this separation. In some respects, it has even taken steps that may dilute the commitment contained in the Single European Act that the maintenance of 'cohesion' between the two dimensions of the Community's external affairs should have a high priority.

It is true that the Treaty on European Union, and the negotiations which accompanied it, have led to some positive steps. For instance, it now seems to be understood that the Political Committee (a key element in the EPC machinery) will henceforth meet in Brussels, instead of in the capital of the Member State holding the Presidency. It even seems that the Political Committee, as well as meeting in Brussels, will be expected to be more directly involved in the external policies of the Community. The carefully-worded provision to this effect is in Article J.8(5) of the Treaty:

> Without prejudice to Article 151 of the Treaty establishing the European Community, a Political Committee consisting of Political Directors shall monitor the international situation in the areas covered by common foreign and security policy and contribute to the definition of policies by delivering opinions to the Council at the request of the Council or on its own initiative. It shall also monitor the implementation of agreed policies, without prejudice to the responsibility of the Presidency and the Commission.

This disposition (Article 151 of the amended Treaty of Rome refers to the responsibilities of COREPER and the Secretariat of the Council) seems to suggest that the coordination between the Political Committee and the Community institutions will be closer. The fact that the Secretariat of the CFSP (formerly EPC) will merge with the Council Secretariat is a further move in the same direction. It should also be noted that the Treaty on European Union gives the Commission, as well as all Member States, the right to 'refer to the Council any question relating to the common foreign and security policy and ... submit proposals to the Council'.[19]

These changes suggest not only a closer coordination between the 'political' and 'economic' aspects of the Union's external relations: they also suggest the possibility of an enhanced role for the Commission in some respects. In general, however, the old distinction between 'political' and 'economic' aspects of foreign relations remains: the external relations of the Community are firmly within the 'Community' pillar of the new European Union, whereas the CFSP falls squarely within the 'intergovernmental' area. Thus, for instance, it is the responsibility of the Council, rather than the Commission, to ensure that all Member States give full and loyal support to the external and security policy of the Union, and refrain from any action likely to impair its effectiveness.[20] Even though the Council of the Union (the new incarnation of the General Affairs Council of the Community Foreign Ministers) is likely to discuss 'economic' and 'political' aspects of external problems without excessive formal distinction – thus continuing and even extending the practice sanctioned by the Single Act – the fact remains that the preparatory work on these different dossiers will be done by separate sets of officials both in Brussels and in the national capitals, and the Foreign Ministers meeting in the Council will need the support of two distinct sets of personnel. We have only to consider the wording of Article J.8(5), quoted earlier, to see that the possibility of conflict between the Political Committee and COREPER is quite considerable. As the Political Directors normally hold a powerful position in the foreign ministries of the Member States, the Political Committee is likely to be the winner in such conflicts.

19   Article J.8(3).
20   Article J.1(4).

Turning again to the role of the Commission,[21] it should be noted that a further limitation on this is represented by the provision that the Presidency alone will continue to represent the Union as far as CFSP is concerned.[22]

Even within the sphere of EC external relations (i.e. under the Treaty of Rome as now revised), there are certain provisions which might well have the effect of limiting the influence of the Commission, to the benefit of the Member States. In the revised version of Article 228(1), the Commission is not only excluded – as before – from the conclusion of external agreements in the name of the Community: it is now explicitly required to seek the authorization of the Council before the opening of any negotiation. Even though this reflects the existing practice, the new wording may signify a formal limitation of the Commission's role as the chief international negotiator for the Community. It is also possible that further difficulties for the Commission might be created by the wording of the new Article 228(a), which provides for the first time the use of Community (i.e. economic) instruments for foreign policy objectives.

For instance, a 'common action' within the framework of CFSP which had been adopted unanimously by the Member States, and which implied the use of economic instruments, could place the Commission under strong pressure to submit corresponding proposals for action within the EC framework, even against its will. This is of course a hypothetical case, since in general the Commission would presumably be willing, normally, to act as the agent of a Community consensus, but the implications of this undermining of the Commission's exclusive right of initiative could be potentially dangerous for the *acquis communautaire*.

Again, the development of attempts to bring together economic means and foreign policy purposes, although desirable in itself, might in some circumstances constitute a step back rather than forward. One can imagine, for instance, an external economic action which might hitherto have been taken within the EC framework by a majority vote, which might now, within CFSP, be defined as a 'common action', and thus subject to unanimity. Since the European Court of Justice has no jurisdiction over Title V of the Treaty on European Union (any more than over its other intergovernmental components), the retrograde step back to unanimity would presumably not be susceptible to challenge.[23]

A final possible danger for the *acquis communautaire* – it should be emphasized that all these points are hypothetical – concerns the Commission's right of initiative within international organizations. Although on the one hand Articles J.8(3) and J.2(3) of the Treaty on European Union explicitly or implicitly provide the Commission, along with the Member States, with a right of initiative with regard to common positions in such international fora, this may prove to be no compensation for the disappearance of Article 116 of the Treaty of Rome, and with it the

---

21   In the following passage I have drawn extensively on a paper by Professor Jörg Monar, 'The European Union's Foreign Affairs System after the Maastricht Treaty: a preliminary assessment.'
22   Article J.5(1).
23   See however the contribution by Renaud Dehousse, *supra* at 11-12.

Commission's exclusive right of initiative with regard to common action within frameworks of this kind.

V. Conclusion

These indications of possible encroachments of the Member States on the existing prerogatives of the Commission, although minor in themselves, underline the point already made, that the fundamental principle of the CFSP – as of EPC before it – must be said to be intergovernmentalism.

Indeed, the CFSP of the future certainly looks as though it will be accompanied by all the familiar problems of the EPC of the past. Despite the commitment of Article J.2(1) that Member States shall consult one another on any matter of general interest, to ensure 'concerted and convergent action', it should never be forgotten that actions in foreign policy are often an essential ingredient in the domestic politics of Member States. President Mitterrand's surprise visit to Sarajevo in June 1992, immediately after a European Council meeting in Lisbon in which he had failed to inform his colleagues, let alone consult them, was no doubt 'convergent' with the policy positions of other Member States, but it illustrates the fact that 'concerted' action may not always suit individual governments. The admirable principle laid down in the Three Wise Men's report of 1979, and in numerous other EC documents, that the Member States should give each other 'no surprises' in the conduct of their foreign relations, is likely to be breached under the new system of CFSP just as much as under the old system of EPC.

Again, the CFSP is likely to have continued difficulty because foreign policy is only partly 'proactive': a great deal of it consists of reactive measures in response to external pressures. In practice, the great success stories of EPC have been in 'proactive' operations in which the Member States, acting as a group, have been engaged in the process of laying down the ground-rules for a new international regime of some kind: the CSCE, for instance, or in a lesser degree the 'new international economic order' of the mid-1970s. The performance of EPC in terms of creating a united position of a reactive kind, in response to an external stimulus, has always been less successful: one could point to the EPC's unsatisfactory performance at the time of the United States bombing of Libya, for instance, or more recently and more importantly the crisis in Yugoslavia. Do the provisions of the Treaty give us any assurance that the CFSP will be any more successful in this respect than EPC?

Finally, we have to recall that the whole attempt to construct the CFSP has been undertaken at a time when the Community is simultaneously considering, in an active way, its future enlargement. How much of the *acquis politique* which the Twelve can now claim (or rather, in the military field, which they will be able to claim if Denmark, Greece, and Ireland accede to the WEU) would be maintained in a Community or Union which also included Austria, Sweden, Finland and Switzerland, not to mention the Czech Lands, Slovakia, Poland and Hungary?

When measured against the responses to questions such as these, the laborious compromise represented in Title V of the Treaty on European Union, and the related Declaration on WEU, may appear to fall very short of what the situation requires. However, measured against the record of the past, which shows that progress in organizing the external relations of the Community (economic and political) has always been slow and complicated, the achievements of Maastricht may be judged to be not so limited after all.

Conclusion

Fin-de-Siècle Europe

Joseph H.H. Weiler[*]

I

It is not difficult to gauge the public mood in post-1992 Europe.

Brecht's wicked quip may well describe the bitter, vindictive sentiment among the Brussels Mandarins: *The People* have disappointed: a would-be triumph has turned sour. The Maastricht Treaty on European Union, justly hailed as a remarkable diplomatic achievement, has been met in the European street with a sentiment ranging from hostility to indifference. One cannot even derive comfort from those segments of public opinion which have rallied behind 'Europe', such as the agricultural lobby in Ireland, the political Establishment in France, the German Partitocracy. Narrow self-interest, a formidable stake in the status quo, a growing cleavage with the constituents are the respective hallmarks of this support. Maybe *The People* should, indeed, be changed. Even if Maastricht eventually comes into force, as is likely, it will be recalled as a low, anti-climactic moment in the history of contemporary European integration, not as its crowning achievement.

Mandarins' frustration has its comic side too. They got it wrong also last time, on the occasion of the 1986 adoption of the bureaucratically-named Single European Act which consecrated the single market plan. That time the indifference and hostility towards the new instrument were expressed by the Commission, the European Parliament, and even Governments (Mrs. Thatcher called it 'a modest step') and yet public opinion was swept by veritable Euro-mania.

What, then, has 'gone wrong' now (assuming, of course, that being hostile or indifferent to the plans for Europe is 'wrong')? For some, the reason for the current malaise rests with the very process of negotiating the new Treaty, a process emblematic of much that is bad with European governance: secretive, high-handed, paternalistic. For others it is the prolix content of the Treaty, piling compromise upon compromise. For yet others it is the so-called democratic deficit which Maastricht supposedly did not close. To believe that these important factors explain the root cause is to turn away from far more painful truths. After all, was the process of adopting the Single European Act any less secretive and high-handed? Its content any less prolix? Its indifference to the gaping voids in public accountability in the Community any less daunting?

*   This chapter is in the genre of a 'Think Piece'. It is the nature of this genre that the narrative does not acknowledge the intellectual debt owed to many authors whose writing inform the text. I am, however, indebted to Karen Alter, Anne-Marie Burley, Jose de Areilza and Renaud Dehousse for many critical comments and suggestions on an earlier draft.

The attitude to Maastricht brings into sharp relief a pathology far deeper than its specific content. Dare one say it? The Europe of Maastricht is devoid of ideals. The Member States of the European Community are being swept by an electorate which, not unlike its American counterpart, is increasingly frustrated, alienated and angry with politics as usual. Sadly, 'Europe' has become just that – politics as usual.

A subtle change has occurred in the positioning of the idea of European integration in public discourse. To be sure, as the political scientists of the realists school never tire of telling us, the evolution of European integration was driven by national self-interest and cold calculations of cost and benefit to its participating Member States. But in its formative years, and for a considerable while after that, the very idea of the Community was associated with a set of values which could captivate the imagination, mobilize broadly-based political forces, counteract the powerful, even captivating, but often abused, pull of nationalism. Supporting the Community was to 'Do the Right Thing'. It was a happy state in which one could believe that long-term self-interest coincided with higher values. And yet, slowly, inexorably these values were extinguished one by one. The Single European Act, with its single market Back-to-the-Future message, a crude face-lift to the original objective of a Common Market, managed to claim a last twirl with yesteryear's ideals. But it was a dance with a cadaver. The reception by the public of the far more ambitious Maastricht Treaty is the writing on the wall – 'Europe' is an ideal which has lost its mobilizing force, it is a force which has lost its mobilizing ideals.

II

A disquisition focusing explicitly on ideals is not an easy task, and this for two reasons.

First, for some, social science, to be science at all, must be value free. Ideals must be looked at dispassionately and from a distance. For others, to whom the notion of value-free discourse is impossible or in fact value laden, ideals, especially *Ideals* are there to be exposed as sham, debunked, deconstructed. All in all, ideals, like religion and spirituality are almost embarrassing topics, to be reconceptualized as ideology and treated with the reductive methodologies of psychology, sociology and the like.

Second, it is difficult to construct a persuasive 20th century phenomenology of ideals. We should not confuse ideals with ideology or morality. Ideals are usually part of an ideology. Morality is usually part of ideals. But the terms do not conflate. Ideologies, in relation to which theories abound, often include or are premised on some ideals. But they are much more than that. Ideology is in part an epistemology – a way of knowing and understanding reality – in part a programme for changing that reality to achieve certain goals. Ideals, in and of themselves, constitute neither an epistemology nor a programme for realization, and are often the least explained elements of any given ideology. Morality, practical reason, the good life, will inform ideals, but ideals have a social reality which practical reason necessarily does not – though it can be an ideal to live the good life. It is not surprising that, for example, the Macmillan Encyclopedia of Philosophy has no separate entry for ideals.

It is surprising, however, that there appears to be no analysis of the ideals – as distinct from the objectives – of European integration and the European Community. If this, indeed, is the case, one may wonder if there is no good reason for this absence. Could it be that a low 'pay-off' is the explanation? I think not. I think the pay-off could be high and that the reason for the absence lies rather with the disciplinary 'misfit' of ideals as an object for enquiry. What then would be the interest in exploring the ideals of European integration and the European Community?

I propose to answer this question after first describing one of the Community's foundational ideals, which, in turn, will serve as a means for a general phenomenological reflection and as a tool to explain the utility of exploring the ideals of European Integration.

Peace, in the immediate wake of World War II, was the most explicit and evocative of ideals for which the would-be-polity was to be an instrument. Nowhere is this captured better than in the oft repeated phraseology of the Schuman Declaration of 9 May 1950: 'The gathering of the nations of Europe requires the elimination of the age-old opposition of France and the Federal Republic of Germany'. The Schuman Declaration is to the Treaties establishing the European Communities what, say, the American Declaration of Independence is to the subsequent Articles of Confederation and, eventually, to the Constitution.

Peace, at all times an attractive desideratum, would have had its appeal in purely utilitarian terms. But it is readily apparent that in the historical context in which the Schuman Plan was put forward the notion of *peace as an ideal* probes a far deeper stratum than simple swords into ploughshares, sitting under one's vine and fig tree, lambs and wolves.

These were, after all, the early 50s with the horrors of War still fresh in the mind and, in particular, the memory of the unspeakable savagery of German occupation. It would take many years for the hatred in countries such as the Netherlands, Denmark or France to subside fully. The idea, then, in 1950, of a Community of Equals as providing the structural underpinning for long-term peace among yesteryear's enemies, represented more than the wise counsel of experienced statesmen.

It was also a call for forgiveness, a challenge to overcome an understandable hatred. In that particular historical context the Schumanian notion of Peace resonates with, is evocative of, the distinct discourse, imagery and values of Christian Love – not, I think, a particularly astonishing evocation given the personal backgrounds of the Founding Fathers – Adenauer, De Gasperi, Schuman himself, Monnet himself.

III

I will use Peace as a spring board for a more general reflection on ideals. In the phenomenology I would like to develop there are four principal considerations which inform ideals as a concept and as a social construct: the idyllic, the demonic, the virtuous and the idolatrous. If my understanding of peace as an ideal is valid and typical it would enable us to illustrate these considerations.

The idyllic

In upholding or subscribing to an ideal, one is in part putting forward a desired state of affairs (material or spiritual) in which one would like to exist. It can be peace, it can be justice, it can be power or grandeur. It is usually, but not necessarily, futuristic. It is usually a state of affairs the desirability or appeal of which are self-evident either because they are essentialist and/or because they correspond to deep-seated social constructs.

The demonic

A simple desirable state of affairs – an idyllic state: 'if I were a rich man' – does not in and of itself qualify as an ideal. Often it can be almost a counter-ideal. What prevents us from making all our fantasies of desired-idyllic states *ideals* – is that so often they are selfish, self-serving. We perceive these desiderata, in fact, as an expression of desire, greed, jealousy, our Hobbesian side (whether essentialist or socially constructed). In the words of Genesis: for the imagination of man's heart is evil from his youth. [1]

Ideals then involve not simply putting forward a desired state of affairs – material or spiritual – but a recognition of our demonic tendencies. Ideals must represent a challenge to the demonic in us, a call to our better half. Ideals contain an altruistic allure.

In my view, this challenge accounts for the huge appeal of the great ideals. First, there is the *per se* attractiveness and satisfaction of sacrifice: things that demand sacrifice are cherished more than things that come easily. Sacrifice invests things with value. Additionally, the *combination* of the idyllic and the demonic in ideals explain their abiding centrality to all human culture: the call to overcome the demonic ennobles our self-interest – it legitimates our desires.

The desire for peace is frequently not an ideal. Like riches it is a very comfortable state of affairs – for the sake of peace I will not fight my battles, not stand up for my values, turn my gaze, avert my eyes, and so on.

What brings the message of peace in the formation of the Community into the realm of ideals, what connects it to so deep a fountain as Christian Love, is the historical context of justified hatred and fear. Chamberlain's infamous 'Peace in our

---

1   Gen: VIII.21.

time' speech of 1938 was a counter-ideal: the idyllic without the demonic. In the EC of the early 50s and somewhat beyond, there is a context where peace has both the idyllic and the demonic – we have to overcome our feelings of revenge, which were given full vent after World War I, but at the same time the comfort of peace is being offered.

The virtuous

The idyllic and the demonic elements in this phenomenology of ideals have been explained in linguistic and behaviouristic terms: they correspond to what we normally mean when we use the word, or think of, ideals; they imply a certain understanding of the human psyche and what appeals and motivates us.

They are also value-free and ahistorical. They do not differentiate between the 'ideals' of Adolph Hitler or Mother Theresa. One can, after all, desire evil or mistake it for virtue, and make great sacrifices to achieve it.

I would add therefore a third consideration: the grounding of ideals in ethics. I can justify this consideration in two ways. First, as a reflection of social reality: when ideals have been put forward as a social phenomenon, as part of a programme of action, they have always been presented as being so grounded. But, I would also add this consideration as an unashamedly normative layer to ideals discourse: a refusal on my part to discuss ideals in purely behaviouristic terms, even if I am mindful of the fashionability of moral relativism, and the manipulability of ethics. Even peace can pose considerable ethical dilemmas. Few of us, after all, are total pacifists.

I shall explain the fourth and final consideration later in this chapter.

IV

Before we turn to examine the other ideals of European integration in its formative years, I shall reflect now more deliberately on the interest in exploring ideals in general and European integration ideals in particular.

I see three distinct interests.

First, a large, the largest, part of EC studies is instrumentalist: actor-interest-outcome, structure-power-process. Trying to explain why things are the way they are. The disciplines – political science, economics, law – will shift the 'thing' which is being explained, and will privilege one kind of explanation over another, or, alternatively, try to be interdisciplinary or even challenge the disciplinary divide altogether and adopt a holistic approach.

From this instrumental perspective, the value of looking at ideals is evident: ideals can be part of the matrix which explains socialization, mobilization and legitimacy. In an analysis as to why certain élites, or masses support, or tolerate or oppose European Integration in general or this or that policy in particular, ideals should clearly have a place. To deny the mobilizing force of ideals is folly.

Second, ideals (and the ideals of European integration) can be looked at from a perspective which is more indifferent to the specific story of European Integration but acknowledges it, and its rhetoric, as part (important or otherwise) of social intercourse. This perspective has as its focus the individual as such and 'society' (national society, regional society, transnational society). The interest here then is in the 'social'.

Ideals are a principal vehicle through which individuals and groups interpret reality, give meaning to their life, and *define their identity* – positively and negatively. The idyllic in ideals refers in this context to social space, the demonic to individual self. In what kind of society do I live, what does our society 'stand for' – can only be given an answer by reference to ideals. What kind of person am I, can only be given an answer by reference to ideals. What kind of society should I live in, aspire to; what kind of person should I be are similarly premised on the existence of ideals. Even the rejection of ideals (a pseudo-Machiavellian approach to life) is just that: a rejection of ideals. You cannot do without them as a referent for value and meaning.

If we are, then, interested in the European persona, in a European polity, we will profit by understanding the world of ideals which is part of the polity. Can there be a psychological understanding of the individual without a reference to one's conflict with ideals? Can there be an appreciation of the political culture of a polity without reference to its values and ideals? In the tension between eros and civilization, our discourse of civilization is in substantial part a discourse of values and ideals.

There is a third interest in ideals – an interest in ideals for their own sake. They are part (and with the passage of time an important part) of cultural history and cultural identity of an epoch. They are, sometimes, the deepest residue – or at least the most visible – which history leaves. Even educated women and men will probably be more fluent with the values of antiquity, or of the age of enlightenment than with their respective political or social histories.

It appears to me that it is a totally serious, and possibly longer lasting enterprise, to try and define European integration in terms of its ideals and not only in terms of its structural, processual and material components. It is an enterprise which will help locate the idea of the Community in the flow of European intellectual history.

V

We may return now to the history of the Community. In its foundational period, alongside peace, I would identify two other principal ideals: prosperity and supranationalism.

Prosperity is the second value for which the Community was to be instrumental. Max Kohnstamm used to say that the twin dilemmas for Monnet were 'What do we do with Germany?' – I translated the answer given as the Peace Ideal in the European Construct – and 'How to rebuild Europe' – and I translate that as the ideal of Prosperity. This is captured in, among other places, Article 2 of the Treaty of Rome. After all, the economic reconstruction of the devastated continent was intimately connected with the notion of peace. Each was the means for the other. Indeed in the biblical passage, frequent in the Book of Judges, peace and prosperity are linked: the vineyard and the fig tree being a symbol for both.

The idyllic, the desired state of affairs, is self-evident. But at first blush it is hard to capture the idealistic, non-utilitarian dimension of the quest for prosperity. Are we not here in the presence of pure self-interest, something to be almost ashamed of – the very antithesis of altruism, challenge, sacrifice which are essential parts of idealistic narrative? Where is the virtuous and where is the challenge to the demonic which, I argued were essential components of the phenomenology of ideals?

There was an idealistic dimension, nuanced to be sure, to the quest for prosperity which mediated its utilitarian aspects. Its virtue appears when set against a backdrop of destruction and poverty. In these conditions (individual and social) prosperity assumed an altogether different meaning: dignity – both personal and collective. Poverty resonates with the embarrassment of dependence on others, with the humiliation bred by helplessness, with the degradation of lack of autonomy. There is, thus, nothing shameful in aspiring for prosperity when it comes to mean dignity. There, then, is its virtue.

Second, the Community's quest for prosperity in its formative years took place in a period which inextricably linked it with widespread (re)construction, with visible (re)generation, with palpable effort and toil. Bread gained with the sweat of one's brow is a matter for pride rather than embarrassment, shame and degradation.

Last but not least, linking prosperity to a cooperative enterprise inevitably blunted the sharp edges of avidity feelings. The Community in its reconstructive effort was about collective responsibility: it attempted to constrain an unchecked search for economic prosperity by one Member States at the expense of others. To be sure, there was an economic theory of open markets, level playing field and all the rest which informed the Common Market. But the elements of transnational economic solidarity are an undeniable part of the discourse of the time and of the Treaty itself. This solidarity is the element which appeals to the better self. It is the control of the demonic at the statal economic level.

Put in this way, we also detect the deeper roots of the Prosperity ideal: it links up with and is evocative of, a different but no less central strand of European idealism since the mid-19th century: be it socialism, fabianism, communism, Welfare Statism all sharing an underlying ethos of collective societal responsibility for the welfare of individuals and the community as a whole.

The third ideal is that of *supranationalism* – for want of a better word.

Supranationalism is cast as a counter to nationalism (also a powerful ideal). It encapsulates two notions – separate but interlinked: at the statal level supranationalism replaces a kind of 'liberal' premise of international society with a communitarian one: the Community as a supranational regime will not simply be a neutral arena in which states will seek to maximize their benefits but will create a tension between the national self and the collective self. Crucially, the Community idea is not meant to eliminate the national state but to create a regime which seeks to tame the national interest with a new discipline. The idyllic is a state of affairs which eliminates the excesses of nationalism. The challenge is to control at societal level reflexes of national interest that are often uncontrolled in the international sphere.

This may seem very much a play on the theme of the first ideals – peace and prosperity through solidarity – for is war (and trade wars) not the worst excess of nationalism?

But there is another dimension to supranationalism which will help define more sharply its differences from peace.

Supranationalism at the societal and individual, rather than the statal level, embodies an ideal which diminishes the importance of nationality – the most powerful signifier of groupness – as the principal referent for transnational human intercourse. That is the value side of non-discrimination on grounds of nationality, of free movement provisions and the like.

It is not difficult to identify the idyllic and the demonic and the deep idealistic wellspring with which this ideal resonates.

Hermann Cohen, the great neo-Kantian, tried to explain the meaning of the Mosaic law which calls for non-oppression of the stranger.

According to him, the alien is to be protected, not because he is a member of one's family, clan, religious community or people, but because he is a human being. In the alien, therefore, man discovered the idea of humanity.[2] That, indeed, is a Neo-Kantian gloss on Jewish law of 4000 years ago.

But we see through this exquisite exegesis that in the curtailment of the totalistic claim of the nation-state (Britannia Rules the Waves, Deutschland *über Alles*), and the reduction of nationality – of groupness – as the principle referent for human intercourse, the Community ideal of Supranationality is evocative of, and resonates with, Enlightenment ideas, with the privileging of the individual, with a different aspect of liberalism which has its progeny today in human rights.

---

2   J.H. Hertz, *Commentary to the Pentateuch* (1980 end ed.) 313 explicating H. Cohen, 'Religion der Vernunft aus den Quellen des Judentums', translated as 'Religion of Reason, Out of the Sources of Judaism', Chapters 5, 8 and 9 esp. at 125 et seq.

VI

The ideals of peace, prosperity, supranationalism which animated the Community in its foundational period are, on my reading, a new expression to the three principal strands of European idealism which the 20th century inherits. They tap into core values of Christianity, social responsibility and the Enlightenment.

At this point a critical proviso would be in order. My claim is not, decidedly not, that the Community in its foundational period actually lived these ideals, realized their virtues, vindicated their promise. I am agnostic on this issue. To explain the ideals of the French revolution, of the American revolution or of the October revolution is not to claim that post-monarchist France, republican America or the Soviet Union lived up to the aspirations which animated these social revolutions. Analyses such as that by Milward and his collaborators tell a very different story of the ensuing reality.[3]

But the reality of the ideals themselves works, nonetheless, at all three levels I explained before.

First, mobilization, socialization and legitimacy. European integration, it has often been claimed, was élite driven. Ideals discourse may be part of the explanation of the mobilization of these élites. It was a construct which was safe, appealing to values inculcated deeply in a generation which grew up in this century.

The idea of Europe and the ideals of Europe may also be a partial explanation for mobilization at mass level, through national party structures. All principal political forces and parties in post-World War II Europe regard themselves as the true inheritors of European idealism as explained above. The Socialists and Social-Democrats, the lay parties, decidedly do not turn their back to the Church. Christian Democrats embrace the Welfare State.

The vision of European integration as explicated above, may explain, in part, how it was that the Community only rarely becomes the focus of party politics in continental Europe. All parties can embrace it, because of, if you want, the appeal, or the blandness, (take your pick) of its idealistic superstructure. Historically, one cannot speak of mass mobilization for Europe. But as years of Eurobarometer surveys show, it was an acceptable idea always easy to support.

At a second level we may turn to ideals as a vehicle for the constitution of the self – individual and social. Consider first the generation of the so-called Founding Fathers who saw their world fall apart in the horrors of World War II – a negation of the very values of Christian love, of solidarity, of the Enlightenment project. European Integration presents itself on my analysis as very alluring: it is not only a new political and economic architecture for postwar Europe which radically supplants the old Versailles model of Post-World War I. It is a vision which whilst being innovative and radical, is also deeply conservative, since it reaffirms their old

---

3   See, e.g., A.S. Milward, *The European Rescue of the Nation-State* (1993).

Weltanschauung; indeed, it gives a new lease of life to ideals for which there are no available (meaning acceptable) substitutes at the time.

It was a *par excellence* way of affirming one's identity on well-known terrain and avoiding the deep dislocations which the breakdown of civility in the War may have created.

It provided, for individuals and societies, a comfortable way of dealing with the recent past: this Past need not call into question fundamental values and ideals; only the political structure and technology for their realization. Europe could (re)define itself as a Christian, socially responsible, worthy successor of the Enlightenment.

As for the history of ideas – we can evaluate European Integration in that epoch as being at the cusp, the very end brink of modernism. The Community idea on this reading is quintessentially European, embracing the core of European idealism. But, it was not only a reflection of these ideals, but, as explained above, it became a vehicle for their rejuvenation, lending them a new, temporary perhaps, credibility and outlet. More importantly, indeed crucially, it places Europe and the Community not as an end in itself, but as a means for the realization of higher ennobling values.

VII

What has become of ideals discourse in the Europe of Maastricht? What values, as opposed to interests, can be associated with European Union 1993?

The narrative is short, a form of sudden death: Maastricht, emblematic of the current stage of European Integration can no longer serve as a vehicle for the foundational ideals; and not much has been offered in replacement.

Peace, reconciliation between France and Germany 'and all that' has been achieved, thanks in large part to the Community. To continue to posit peace as a Maastricht ideal is simply not real. If peace has any place in European discourse today, it is the peace of Munich, of Chamberlain, of peace in our time, which saw 50 years ago the dismemberment of Czechoslovakia and sees today the destruction of Bosnia. Peace can mobilize: who in Europe wants war unless it is Americans who do the fighting? But one can hardly evoke peace as a mobilizing ideal.

Prosperity too has been achieved, thanks in large part to the Community. It was the move from poverty to prosperity which was virtuous. Today the move is from prosperity to even more prosperity. This too can capture votes and support – pocket-book politics always has. But there is no pretence even at casting this discourse in the language of ideals.

The obsolescence of the Community as a vehicle for the foundational ideals is personified in the figures of two leading European politicians. There is something altogether pathetic in the aging figure of Mr Mitterand preaching Franco-German peace to an incredulous electorate in 1992. But is there not something equally pathetic in Mr Major's technocratic 'what's in it for us' approach as his justification for Maastricht?

What then of supranationalism: is not Maastricht, at least in its aspirations and rhetoric a definite clarion cry for further supranationalism? To believe that is to misunderstand supranationalism. From this perspective Maastricht is a deception. It may or may not advance the structure and processes of European integration. One has learnt to be cautious and non-dismissive of these steps in Community evolution. But its symbolism is very clear. In its rhetoric Maastricht appropriates the deepest symbols of statehood: European citizenship, defence, foreign policy – the rhetoric of a superstate. We all know that these are the emptiest and weakest provisions of the Treaty, but they undermine the ethics of supranationalism. In its statal aspect supranationalism was a move away from statism to a new uneasy relationship between Community and its Member States. Community was a fine word to capture that value. Now the operational rhetoric is Union, not Community. We have come full circle.

In its individual aspect supranationalism was about the diminution of nationality as a referent for transnational intercourse. Under the rhetoric of Maastricht, the 'Us' is no longer Germans or French or Italians and the 'Them' is no longer British, or Dutch or Irish. The 'Us' has become European and the 'Them', non-European. If Europe embraces so earnestly at the symbolic level European citizenship, on what moral ground can one turn against French National Fronts, German Republicans and their brethren elsewhere who embrace Member State nationalism. On the ground that they chose to embrace the wrong nationalism? The irony, if it needs spelling out, is that whilst the idealistic moral ground has been shattered, perhaps even lost, in reality, in these areas, Maastricht offers very little by way of tangible prospects. Maastricht has thrown out the supranational water without waiting for the baby to get in the bath.

VIII

The Europe of Maastricht no longer serves, as did its grandparents the Europe of Paris and Rome, as a vehicle for the original foundational values. This, if my analysis is correct, represents too a rupture with an earlier pre-modern and modern historical continuity of ideas.

The explanation for rupture may not however lie simply at the feet of the Community, and at the changed historical conditions which have rendered the Community an obsolescent vehicle for the foundational ideals. It may, too, be a reflection of a rupture in European society as such. On this reading Maastricht becomes the mirror of the society which it is supposed to serve, a reflection of *fin-de-siècle* Europe.

Consider afresh the Maastricht Treaty and its double structure: EMU and Political Union. There is a symbolism in this double structure and the relative weight given to each. It is a commonplace that Economic and Monetary Union constitute the heart of the Treaty; that the intergovernmental conference on Political

Union was more rhetorical than substantive, lip-service paid to the need to increase accountability and strengthen the powers of the European Parliament. The symbolism is that of the Roman *panem et circenses*: a scale of values which privileges the economic: wealth and prosperity; which deprivileges control, autonomy and responsibility.

The language of symbols is just that – symbolic. And thus not too much should be read into it. But the notion that the problem of Maastricht is in the drafting, in its prolix style, in its incomprehensibility should perhaps be questioned – maybe its message is all too apparent. And, to the extent that Maastricht is a reflection, a mirror of its polity, the interesting datum is not in the size of the opposition, but in the impressive support the Treaty has evoked. In this respect, Maastricht is simply a creature of its time.

The personification of this symbolism is to be found in the Commission. It is no secret that there is a deep crisis of morale in that institution, emblematic of the fortunes of Europe. To be sure, the cool reception of Maastricht is part of the explanation. But the low morale may have an additional explanation in sync with the theme of this essay, namely the loss of the deeper *raison d'être* of the enterprise, the disconcerting realization that Europe has become an end in itself – no longer a means for higher human end. No measure of information, explanation or even structural change can remedy this.

IX

Assuming that there is some merit to my analysis, there could be a tendency to take it as an indication of a bleak future for Europe. That tendency should be resisted. Europe may or may not have a bleak future, but a causal nexus to the theme of this essay is tenuous. Pragmatic and utilitarian politics can be highly successful, in both mobilization and result. Providing welfare and security may be all we wish from public authority in the post-modernist age. Indeed, this is the place to mention the fourth and last element in the phenomenology of ideals – ideals as idolatry. An unstated premise of this narrative was that ideals give meaning, ennoble existence, refine materialism. But, as Halbertal and Margalit demonstrate in an altogether remarkable new book,[4] and as our own experience will often indicate, ideals are not only a promise but always, at the same time, a danger. For the move from, the change of, ideals to idolatry – a blinding enslavement to supposedly higher values in the name of which all manner of barbarism is committed, is almost predetermined. European history is replete with such examples: the savagery of the Crusaders was committed in the name of Christian love, collective responsibility was the justification for the ghastliness of the Gulags, and the brutality of European colonialism was committed under the flag of the Enlightenment.

---

4   M. Halbertal and A. Margalit, *Idolatry* (1992).

Fin-de-Siècle Europe may, thus, be not a reflection of emptiness, but the sign of a healthy suspicion of ideals as idolatry.

X

Even with this danger in mind, there may be an unease at a conclusion which left such stark choices with which to think of the future of Europe. By way of conclusion I would like to offer three alternative perspectives for, to use a new *en vogue* term, a politics-of-meaning for Europe.

One approach, explored by a Danish civil servant, Jørgen Østrom-Møller, in a dichotomy between technology and culture,[5] and echoed in the writings of Giandomenico Majone on regulatory Europe,[6] repositions, indeed reconceptualizes, the Community not as a new polity for European citizens, but as a technological instrument, an agency, for the resolution of post-industrial problems such as environmental protection, transnational trade, transport and the like which transcend national boundaries. According to this vision, one should not look for meaning and value at all in the Community, but regard it as a device which liberates people to develop a myriad of culture communities expressing local values at the level of localities and workplace. A huge payoff, according to this vision, is the undermining of national boundaries as the prime delimitation of political culture and the nation-state as the prime vehicle for political and social expression.

There is much that is alluring in this reconceptualization. I do not propose to explore it in detail, but one should note its weak points: to regard the Community as a technological instrument is, in the first place, to underestimate the profound political choice and cultural impact which the single market involves – a politics of efficiency, a culture of market. Historically we know the flattening impact which markets have on local cultural diversity. Consequently, it underestimates the critical value choices involved in technocratic regulatory regimes.

A second approach, deeply historical, would find a new politics of meaning for the Community in its putative responsibility towards the East. We could take Western Europe 1951 and impose it without change to Eastern Europe 1991. Does Eastern Europe, awakened like sleeping beauty into the nationalist ethos of pre-1939 Europe, not need, above all, new structures for peace, prosperity and a supranational ethos which would blunt the excesses of nationalism run amok? Could not this be the prime historical mission of the Community? Sure it could, but it will not, if the new mean-spirited arrangements offered by the Community to Eastern Europe are a sign of things to come.

---

5   J. Østrom-Møller, Technology and Culture in a European Context (1991).
6   G. Majone, 'Preservation of Cultural Diversity in a Federal System: The Role of the Regions', in M. Tushnet (ed.), *Comparative Constitutional Federalism – Europe and America Compared* (1990) 67.

A third and final approach would be one which would explore the communitarian, as opposed to liberal, strand in the European Community ethos. This, of course, is not the place to expound the communitarian, republican, political theory and ethos, which emphasizes at all levels of social organization, not only rights and liberties, but civic responsibility and solidarity. By espousing this ethos as the guiding principle for its ever expanding socio-economic legislative agenda, the European Community could become a vehicle for this type of politics of meaning. This would not be an artificial graft: it is not difficult, as Francis Snyder has shown, to find communitarian strands in much of Community discourse.[7] But, even if communitarianism is there it is in strong opposition to the deeply-rooted liberal ethic. It is not difficult to find – but would be hugely difficult to realize.

Whatever choices are put forward, if any at all, Europe would be served if the debate about its future moved from structures and processes, from means to ends.

---

7   F. Snyder, *New Directions in European Community Law* (1990), Ch. 3.

Annex

Treaty on European Union
(including the consolidated EC Treaty)

His Majesty the King of the Belgians,

Her Majesty the Queen of Denmark,

The President of the Federal Republic of Germany,

The President of the Hellenic Republic,

His Majesty the King of Spain,

The President of the French Republic,

The President of Ireland,

The President of the Italian Republic,

His Royal Highness the Grand Duke of Luxembourg,

Her Majesty the Queen of the Netherlands,

The President of the Portuguese Republic,

Her Majesty the Queen of the United Kingdom of Great Britain and Northern Ireland,

RESOLVED to mark a new stage in the process of European integration undertaken with the establishment of the European Communities,

RECALLING the historic importance of the ending of the division of the European continent and the need to create firm bases for the construction of the future Europe,

CONFIRMING their attachment to the principles of liberty, democracy and respect for human rights and fundamental freedoms and the rule of law,

DESIRING to deepen the solidarity between their peoples while respecting their history, their culture and their traditions,

DESIRING to enhance further the democratic and efficient functioning of the institutions so as to enable them better to carry out, within a single institutional framework, the tasks entrusted to them,

RESOLVED to achieve the strengthening and the convergence of their economies and to establish an economic and monetary union including, in accordance with the provisions of this Treaty, a single and stable currency,

DETERMINED to promote economic and social progress for their peoples, within the context of the accomplishment of the internal market and of reinforced cohesion and environmental protection, and to implement policies ensuring that advances in economic integration are accompanied by parallel progress in other fields,

RESOLVED to establish a citizenship common to nationals of their countries,

RESOLVED to implement a common foreign and security policy including the eventual framing of a common defence policy, which might in time lead to a common defence, thereby reinforcing the European identity and its independence in order to promote peace, security and progress in Europe and in the world,

REAFFIRMING their objective to facilitate the free movement of persons, while ensuring the safety and security of their peoples, by including provisions on justice and home affairs in this Treaty,

RESOLVED to continue in the process of creating an ever closer union among the peoples of Europe, in which decisions are taken as closely as possible to the citizen in accordance with the principle of subsidiarity,

IN VIEW of further steps to be taken in order to advance European integration,

HAVE DECIDED to establish a European Union and to this end have designated as their plenipotentiaries:

His Majesty the King of the Belgians: Mark Eyskens, Minister for Foreign Affairs, Philippe Maystadt, Minister for Finance;

Her Majesty the Queen of Denmark: Uffe Ellemann-Jensen, Minister for Foreign Affairs, Anders Fogh Rasmussen, Minister for Economic Affairs;

The President of the Federal Republic of Germany: Hans-Dietrich Genscher, Federal Minister for Foreign Affairs, Theodor Waigel, Federal Minister for Finance;

The President of the Hellenic Republic: Antonios Samaras, Minister for Foreign Affairs, Efthymios Christodoulou, Minister for Economic Affairs;

His Majesty the King of Spain: Francisco Fernández Ordóñez, Minister for Foreign Affairs; Carlos Solchaga Catalán, Minister for Economic Affairs and Finance;

The President of the French Republic: Roland Dumas, Minister for Foreign Affairs, Pierre Bérégovoy, Minister for Economic and Financial Affairs and the Budget;

The President of Ireland: Gerard Collins, Minister for Foreign Affairs, Bertie Ahern, Minister for Finance;

The President of the Italian Republic: Gianni De Michelis, Minister for Foreign Affairs, Guido Carli, Minister for the Treasury;

His Royal Highness the Grand Duke of Luxembourg: Jacques F. Poos, Deputy Prime Minister, Minister for Foreign Affairs, Jean-Claude Juncker, Minister for Finance;

Her Majesty the Queen of the Netherlands: Hans van den Broek, Minister for Foreign Affairs, Willem Kok, Minister for Finance;

The President of the Portuguese Republic: Joao de Deus Pinheiro, Minister for Foreign Affairs, Jorge Braga de Macedo, Minister for Finance,

Her Majesty the Queen of the United Kingdom of Great Britain and Northern Ireland: The Rt. Hon. Douglas Hurd, Secretary of State for Foreign and Commonwealth Affairs, The Hon. Francis Maude, Financial Secretary to the Treasury;

WHO, having exchanged their full powers, found in good and due form,

have agreed as follows:

Title I

Article A

By this Treaty, the High Contracting Parties establish among themselves a European Union, hereinafter called 'the Union'.

This Treaty marks a new stage in the process of creating an ever closer union among the peoples of Europe, in which decisions are taken as closely as possible to the citizen.

The Union shall be founded on the European Communities, supplemented by the policies and forms of cooperation established by this Treaty. Its task shall be to organize, in a manner demonstrating consistency and solidarity, relations between the Member States and between their peoples.

Article B

The Union shall set itself the following objectives:

–   to promote economic and social progress which is balanced and sustainable, in particular through the creation of an area without internal frontiers, through the strengthening of economic and social cohesion and through the establishment of economic and monetary union, ultimately including a single currency in accordance with the provisions of this Treaty;

- to assert its identity on the international scene, in particular through the implementation of a common foreign and security policy including the eventual framing of a common defence policy, which might in time lead to a common defence;
- to strengthen the protection of the rights and interests of the nationals of its Member States through the introduction of a citizenship of the Union;
- to develop close cooperation on justice and home affairs;
- to maintain in full the 'acquis communautaire' and build on it with a view to considering, through the procedure referred to in Article N (2), to what extent the policies and forms of cooperation introduced by this Treaty may need to be revised with the aim of ensuring the effectiveness of the mechanisms and the institutions of the Community.

The objectives of the Union shall be achieved as provided in this Treaty and in accordance with the conditions and the timetable set out therein while respecting the principle of subsidiarity as defined in Article 3b of the Treaty establishing the European Community.

Article C

The Union shall be served by a single institutional framework which shall ensure the consistency and the continuity of the activities carried out in order to attain its objectives while respecting and building upon the 'acquis communautaire'.

The Union shall in particular ensure the consistency of its external activities as a whole in the context of its external relations, security, economic and development policies. The Council and the Commission shall be responsible for ensuring such consistency. They shall ensure the implementation of these policies, each in accordance with its respective powers.

Article D

The European Council shall provide the Union with the necessary impetus for its development and shall define the general political guidelines thereof.

The European Council shall bring together the Heads of State or Government of the Member States and the President of the Commission. They shall be assisted by the Ministers of Foreign Affairs of the Member States and by a Member of the Commission. The European Council shall meet at least twice a year, under the chairmanship of the Head of State or Government of the Member State which holds the Presidency of the Council.

The European Council shall submit to the European Parliament a report after each of its meetings and a yearly written report on the progress achieved by the Union.

Article E

The European Parliament, the Council, the Commission and the Court of Justice shall exercise their powers under the conditions and for the purposes provided for, on the one hand, by the provisions of the Treaties establishing the European Communities and of the subsequent Treaties and Acts modifying and supplementing them and, on the other hand, by the other provisions of this Treaty.

Article F

1. The Union shall respect the national identities of its Member States, whose systems of government are founded on the principles of democracy.

2. The Union shall respect fundamental rights, as guaranteed by the European Convention for the Protection of Human Rights and Fundamental Freedoms signed in Rome on 4 November 1950 and as they result from the constitutional traditions common to the Member States, as general principles of Community law.

3. The Union shall provide itself with the means necessary to attain its objectives and carry through its policies.

Annex

Title II

Provisions Amending The Treaty Establishing The European Economic Community With A View To Establishing The European Community

Article G

The Treaty establishing the European Economic Community shall be amended in accordance with the provisions of this Article, in order to establish a European Community.

A – Throughout the Treaty:

1. The term "European Economic Community" shall be replaced by the term "European Community".

B – ... [the following amendments have been incorporated in the text of the EEC Treaty. The present text is thus what will in the future be the EC Treaty; amendments appear in italics.]

Part One: Principles

Article 1

By this Treaty, the High Contracting Parties establish among themselves a *European Community*.

Article 2 [1]

The Community shall have as its task, by establishing a common market *and an economic and monetary union and by implementing the common policies or activities referred to in Articles 3 and 3a*, to promote throughout the Community a harmonious *and balanced* development of economic activities, *sustainable and non-inflationary growth respecting the environment, a high degree of convergence of economic performance, a high level of employment and of social protection, the raising of the standard of living and quality of life, and economic and social cohesion and solidarity among Member States.*

Article 3 [2]

For the purposes set out in Article 2, the activities of the Community shall include, as provided in this Treaty and in accordance with the timetable set out therein:

(a) the elimination, as between Member States, of customs duties and quantitative restrictions on the import and export of goods, and of all other measures having equivalent effect;

(b) *a common commercial policy*;

(c) *an internal market characterised by* the abolition, as between Member States, of obstacles to the free movement of goods, persons, services and capital;

(d) *measures concerning the entry and movement of persons in the internal market as provided for in Article 100c*;

(e) *a common policy in the sphere of agriculture and fisheries*;

(f) *a common policy in the sphere of transport*;

(g) *a system ensuring that competition in the internal market is not distorted*;

(h) the approximation of the laws of Member States to the extent required for the functioning of the common market;

(i) *a policy in the social sphere comprising a European Social Fund*;

(j) *the strengthening of economic and social cohesion*;

(k) *a policy in the sphere of the environment*;

(l) *the strengthening of the competitiveness of Community industry*;

(m) *the promotion of research and technological development*;

(n) *encouragement for the establishment and development of trans-European networks*;

(o) *a contribution to the attainment of a high level of health protection*;

1   As amended by Article G(2) TEU.
2   As amended by Article G(3) TEU.

(p) *a contribution to education and training of quality and to the flowering of the cultures of the Member States*;

(q) *a policy in the sphere of development cooperation*;

(r) *the association of the overseas countries and territories in order to increase trade and promote jointly economic and social development*;

(s) *a contribution to the strengthening of consumer protection*;

(t) *measures in the spheres of energy, civil protection and tourism.*

Article 3a[3]

1. For the purposes set out in Article 2, the activities of the Member States and the Community shall include, as provided in this Treaty and in accordance with the timetable set out therein, the adoption of an economic policy which is based on the close co-ordination of Member States' economic policies, on the internal market and on the definition of common objectives, and conducted in accordance with the principle of an open market economy with free competition.

2. Concurrently with the foregoing, and as provided in this Treaty and in accordance with the timetable and the procedures set out therein, these activities shall include the irrevocable fixing of exchange rates leading to the introduction of a single currency, the ECU, and the definition and conduct of a single monetary policy and exchange rate policy the primary objective of both of which shall be to maintain price stability and, without prejudice to this objective, to support the general economic policies in the Community, in accordance with the principle of an open market economy with free competition.

3. These activities of the Member States and the Community shall entail compliance with the following guiding principles: stable prices, sound public finances and monetary conditions and a sustainable balance of payments.

Article 3b[4]

The Community shall act within the limits of the powers conferred upon it by this Treaty and of the objectives assigned to it therein.

In areas which do not fall within its exclusive competence, the Community shall take action, in accordance with the principle of subsidiarity, only if and in so far as the objectives of the proposed action cannot be sufficiently achieved by the Member States and can therefore, by reason of the scale or effects of the proposed action, be better achieved by the Community.

Any action by the Community shall not go beyond what is necessary to achieve the objectives of this Treaty.

Article 4[5]

1. The tasks entrusted to the Community shall be carried out by the following institutions:

    – a European Parliament,
    – a Council,
    – a Commission,
    – a Court of Justice,
    – *a Court of Auditors.*

Each institution shall act within the limits of the powers conferred upon it by this Treaty.

2. The Council and the Commission shall be assisted by an Economic and Social Committee and a Committee of the Regions acting in an advisory capacity.

---

3   As amended by G(4) TEU.
4   As amended by G(5) TEU.
5   As amended by G(6) TEU.

Annex

Article 4a[6]

A European System of Central Banks (hereafter referred to as "ESCB") and a European Central Bank (hereinafter referred to as "ECB") shall be established in accordance with the procedures laid down in this Treaty; they shall act within the limits of the powers conferred upon them by this Treaty and by the Statute of the ESCB and of the ECB (hereinafter referred to as "Statute of the ESCB") annexed thereto.

Article 4b[7]

A European Investment Bank is hereby established, which shall act within the limits of the powers conferred upon it by this Treaty and the Statute annexed thereto.

Article 5

Member States shall take all appropriate measures, whether general or particular, to ensure fulfilment of the obligations arising out of this Treaty or resulting from action taken by the institutions of the Community. They shall facilitate the achievement of the Community's tasks.

They shall abstain from any measure which could jeopardize the attainment of the objectives of this Treaty.

Article 6[8]

Within the scope of application of this Treaty, and without prejudice to any special provisions contained therein, any discrimination on grounds of nationality shall be prohibited.

The Council, acting in accordance with the procedure referred to in Article 189c, may adopt rules designed to prohibit such discrimination.

Article 7[9]

1.   The common market shall be progressively established during a transitional period of twelve years.

This transitional period shall be divided into three stages of four years each; the length of each stage may be altered in accordance with the provisions set out below.

2.   To each stage there shall be assigned a set of actions to be initiated and carried through concurrently.

3.   Transition from the first to the second stage shall be conditional upon a finding that the objectives specifically laid down in this treaty for the first stage have in fact been attained in substance and that, subject to the exceptions and procedures provided for in this Treaty, the obligations have been fulfilled.

This finding shall be made at the end of the fourth year by the Council, acting unanimously on a report from the Commission. A Member State may not, however, prevent unanimity by relying upon the non-fulfilment of its own obligations. Failing unanimity, the first stage shall automatically be extended for one year.

At the end of the fifth year, the Council shall make its finding under the same conditions. Failing unanimity, the first stage shall automatically be extended for a further year.

At the end of the sixth year, the Council shall make its finding, acting by a qualified majority on a report from the Commission.

4.   Within one month of the last-mentioned vote any Member State which voted with the minority or, if the required majority was not obtained, any Member State shall be entitled to call upon the Council to appoint an arbitration board whose decision shall be binding upon all Member States and upon the institutions of the Community. The arbitration board shall consist of three members appointed by the Council acting unanimously on a proposal from the Commission.

If the Council has not appointed the members of the arbitration board within one month of being called upon to do so, they shall be appointed by the Court of Justice within a further period of one month.

---

6   As amended by G(7) TEU.
7   As amended by G(7) TEU.
8   As amended by G(8) TEU.
9   Articles 7, 7a, 7b and 7c: Former Articles 8, 8a, 8b and 8c (Article G(9) TEU).

The arbitration board shall elect its own Chairman.

The board shall make its award within six months of the date of the Council vote referred to in the last subparagraph of paragraph 3.

5. The second and third stages may not be extended or curtailed except by a decision of the Council, acting unanimously on a proposal from the Commission.

6. Nothing in the preceding paragraphs shall cause the transitional period to last more than fifteen years after the entry into force of this Treaty.

7. Save for the exceptions or derogations provided for in this Treaty, the expiry of the transitional period shall constitute the latest date by which all the rules laid down must enter into force and all the measures required for establishing the common market must be implemented.

Article 7a

The Community shall adopt measures with the aim of progressively establishing the internal market over a period expiring on 31 December 1992, in accordance with the provisions of this Article and of Articles 7b, 7c, 28, 57 (2), 59, 70 (1), 84, 99, 100a and 100b and without prejudice to the other provisions of this Treaty.

The internal market shall comprise an area without internal frontiers in which the free movement of goods, persons, services and capital is ensured in accordance with the provisions of this Treaty.

Article 7b

The Commission shall report to the Council before 31 December 1988 and again before 31 December 1990 on the progress made towards achieving the internal market within the time limit fixed in Article 7a.

The Council, acting by a qualified majority on a proposal from the Commission, shall determine the guidelines and conditions necessary to ensure balanced progress in all the sectors concerned.

Article 7c

When drawing up its proposals with a view to achieving the objectives set out in Article 7a, the Commission shall take into account the extent of the effort that certain economies showing differences in development will have to sustain during the period of establishment of the internal market and it may propose appropriate provisions.

If these provisions take the form of derogations, they must be of a temporary nature and must cause the least possible disturbance to the functioning of the Common Market.

Part Two: Citizenship of the Union [10]

Article 8

1. *Citizenship of the Union is hereby established.*

Every person holding the nationality of a Member State shall be a citizen of the Union.

2. *Citizens of the Union shall enjoy the rights conferred by this Treaty and shall be subject to the duties imposed thereby.*

Article 8a

1. *Every citizen of the Union shall have the right to move and reside freely within the territory of the Member States, subject to the limitations and conditions laid down in this Treaty and by the measures adopted to give it effect.*

2. *The Council may adopt provisions with a view to facilitating the exercise of the rights referred to in paragraph 1; save as otherwise provided in this Treaty, the Council shall act unanimously on a proposal from the Commission and after obtaining the assent of the European Parliament.*

10   Part Two as inserted by Article G.C TEU.

Article 8b

1. Every citizen of the Union residing in a Member State of which he is not a national shall have the right to vote and to stand as a candidate at municipal elections in the Member State in which he resides, under the same conditions as nationals of that State. This right shall be exercised subject to detailed arrangements to be adopted before 31 December 1994 by the Council, acting unanimously on a proposal from the Commission and after consulting the European Parliament; these arrangements may provide for derogations where warranted by problems specific to a Member State.

2. Without prejudice to Article 138 (3) and to the provisions adopted for its implementation, every citizen of the Union residing in a Member State of which he is not a national shall have the right to vote and to stand as a candidate in elections to the European Parliament in the Member State in which he resides, under the same conditions as nationals of that State. This right shall be exercised subject to detailed arrangements to be adopted before 31 December 1993 by the Council, acting unanimously on a proposal from the Commission and after consulting the European Parliament; these arrangements may provide for derogations where warranted by problems specific to a Member State.

Article 8c

Every citizen of the Union shall, in the territory of a third country in which the Member State of which he is a national is not represented, be entitled to protection by the diplomatic or consular authorities of any Member State, on the same conditions as the nationals of that State. Before 31 December 1993, Member States shall establish the necessary rules among themselves and start the international negotiations required to secure this protection.

Article 8d

Every citizen of the Union shall have the right to petition the European Parliament in accordance with Article 138d.

Every citizen of the Union may apply to the Ombudsman established in accordance with Article 138e.

Article 8e

The Commission shall report to the European Parliament, to the Council and to the Economic and Social Committee before 31 December 1993 and then every three years on the application of the provisions of this Part. This report shall take account of the development of the Union.

On this basis, and without prejudice to the other provisions of this Treaty, the Council, acting unanimously on a proposal from the Commission and after consulting the European Parliament, may adopt provisions to strengthen or to add to the rights laid down in this Part, which it shall recommend to the Member States for adoption in accordance with their respective constitutional requirements.

Part Three: Community Policies [11]

Title I – Free Movement of Goods

Article 9

1. The Community shall be based upon a customs union which shall cover all trade in goods and which shall involve the prohibition between Member States of customs duties on imports and exports and of all charges having equivalent effect, and the adoption of a common customs tariff in their relations with third countries.

2. The provisions of Chapter 1, Section 1, and of Chapter 2 of this Title shall apply to products originating in Member States and to products coming from third countries which are in free circulation in Member States.

---

11   Part Three, regrouping former Parts Two and Three (Article G.D TEU).

Article 10

1. Products coming from a third country shall be considered to be in free circulation in a Member State if the import formalities have been complied with and any customs duties or charges having equivalent effect which are payable have been levied in that Member State, and if they have not benefited from a total or partial drawback of such duties or charges.

2. The Commission shall, before the end of the first year after the entry into force of this Treaty, determine the methods of administrative co-operation to be adopted for the purpose of applying Article 9 (2), taking into account the need to reduce as much as possible formalities imposed on trade.

Before the end of the first year after the entry into force of this Treaty, the Commission shall lay down the provisions applicable, as regards trade between Member States, to goods originating in another Member State in whose manufacture products have been used on which the exporting Member State has not levied the appropriate customs duties or charges having equivalent effect, or which have benefited from a total or partial drawback of such duties or charges.

In adopting these provisions, the Commission shall take into account the rules for the elimination of customs duties within the Community and for the progressive application of the common customs tariff.

Article 11

Member States shall take all appropriate measures to enable Governments to carry out, within the periods of time laid down, the obligations with regard to customs duties which devolve upon them pursuant to the Treaty.

Chapter 1. The Customs Union

Section 1. Elimination of customs duties between Member States

Article 12

Member States shall refrain from introducing between themselves any new customs duties on imports or exports or any charges having equivalent effect, and from increasing those which they already apply in their trade with each other.

Article 13

1. Customs duties on imports in force between Member States shall be progressively abolished by them during the transitional period in accordance with Articles 14 and 15.

2. Charges having an effect equivalent to customs duties on imports, in force between Member States, shall be progressively abolished by them during the transitional period. The Commission shall determine by means of directives the timetable for such abolition. It shall be guided by the rules contained in Article 14 (2) and (3) and by the directives issued by the Council pursuant to Article 14 (2).

Article 14

1. For each product, the basic duty to which the successive reductions shall be applied shall be the duty applied on 1 January 1957.

2. The timetable for the reductions shall be determined as follows:

(a) during the first stage, the first reduction shall be made one year after the date when this Treaty enters into force; the second reduction, eighteen months later; the third reduction, at the end of the fourth year after the date when this Treaty enters into force;

(b) during the second stage, reduction shall be made eighteen months after that stage begins; a second reduction, eighteen months after the preceding one; a third reduction, one year later;

(c) any remaining reductions shall be made during the third stage; the Council shall, acting by a qualified majority on a proposal from the Commission, determine the timetable therefor by means of directives.

3. At the time of the first reduction, Member States shall introduce between themselves a duty on each product equal to the basic duty minus 10%.

At the time of each subsequent reduction, each Member State shall reduce its customs duties as a whole in such manner at to lower by 10% its total customs receipts as defined in paragraph 4 and to reduce the duty on each product by at least 5% of the basic duty.

In the case, however, of products on which the duty is still in excess of 30%, each reduction must be at least 10% of the basic duty.

4. The total customs receipts of each Member States, as referred to in paragraph 3, shall be calculated by multiplying the value of its imports from other Member States during 1956 by the basic duties.

5. Any special problems raised in applying paragraphs 1 to 4 shall be settled by directives issued by the Council acting by a qualified majority on a proposal from the Commission.

6. Member States shall report to the Commission on the manner in which effect has been given to the proceeding rules for the reduction of duties. They shall endeavour to ensure that the reduction made in the duties on each product shall mount:

– at the end of the first stage, to at least 25% of the basic duty;

– at the end of the second stage, to at least 50% of the basic duty.

If the Commission finds that there is a risk that the objectives laid down in Article 13, and the percentages laid down in this paragraph, can not be attained, it shall make all appropriate recommendations to Member States.

7. The provisions of this Article may be amended by the Council, acting unanimously on a proposal from the Commission and after consulting the European Parliament.

Article 15

1. Irrespective of the provisions of Article 14, any Member state may, in the course of the transitional period, suspend in whole or in part the collection of duties applied by it to products imported from other Member States. It shall inform the other Member States and the Commission thereof.

2. The Member States declare their readiness to reduce customs duties against the other Member States more rapidly than is provided for in Article 14 if their general economic situation and the situation of the economic sector concerned so permit.

To this end, the Commission shall make recommendations to the Member States concerned.

Article 16

Member States shall abolish between themselves customs duties on exports and charges having equivalent effect by the end of the first stage at the latest.

Article 17

1. The provisions of Articles 9 to 15 (1) shall also apply to customs duties of a fiscal nature. Such duties shall not, however, be taken into consideration for the purpose of calculating either total customs receipts or the reduction of customs duties as a whole as referred to in Article 14 (3) and (4).

Such duties shall, at each reduction, be lowered by not less than 10% of the basic duty. Member States may reduce such duties more rapidly than is provided for in Article 14.

2. Member States shall, before the end of the first year after the entry into force of this Treaty, inform the Commission of their customs duties of a fiscal nature.

3. Member States shall retain the right to substitute for these duties an internal tax which complies with the provisions of Article 95.

4. If the Commission finds that substitution for any customs duty of a fiscal nature meets with serious difficulties in a Member State, it shall authorize that State to retain the duty on condition that it shall abolish it not later than six years after the entry into force of this Treaty. Such authorization must be applied for before the end of the first year after the entry into force of this Treaty.

Section 2. Setting up of the common customs tariff

Article 18

The Member States declare their readiness to contribute to the development of international trade and the lowering of barriers to trade by entering into agreements designed, on a basis of reciprocity and mutual advantage, to reduce customs duties below the general level of which they could avail themselves as a result of the establishment of a customs union between them.

Article 19

1. Subject to the conditions and within the limits provided for hereinafter, duties in the common customs tariff shall be at the level of the arithmetical average of the duties applied in the four customs territories comprised in the Community.

2. The duties taken as the basis for calculating this average shall be those applied by Member States on 1 January 1957.

In the case of the Italian tariff, however, the duty applied shall be that without the temporary 10% reduction. Furthermore, with respect to items on which the Italian tariff contains a conventional duty, this duty shall be substituted for the duty applied as defined above, provided that it does not exceed the latter by more than 10%. Where the conventional duty exceed the duty applied as defined above by more than 10%, the latter duty plus 10% shall be taken as the basis for calculating the arithmetical average.

With regard to the tariff headings in List A, the duties shown in that List shall, for the purpose of calculating the arithmetical average, be substituted for the duties applied.

3. The duties in the common customs tariff shall not exceed:

(a) 3% for products within the tariff headings in List B;

(b) 10% for products within the tariff headings in list C;

(c) 15% for products within the tariff headings in List D;

(d) 25% for products within the tariff headings in List E; where in respect of such products, the tariff of the Benelux countries contains a duty not exceeding 3%, such duty shall, for the purpose of calculating the arithmetical average, be raised to 12%.

4. List F prescribes the duties applicable to the products listed therein.

5. The lists of tariff headings referred to in this Article and in Article 20 are set out in Annex I to this Treaty.

Article 20

The duties applicable to the products in List G shall be determined by negotiations between the Member States. Each Member State may add further products to this List to a value not exceeding 2% of the total value of its imports from third countries in the course of the year 1956.

The Commission shall take all appropriate steps to ensure that such negotiations shall be undertaken before the end of the second year after the entry into force of this Treaty and be concluded before the end of the first stage.

If, for certain products, no agreement can be reached within these periods, the Council shall, on a proposal from the Commission, acting unanimously until the end of the second stage and by a qualified majority thereafter, determine the duties in the common customs tariff.

Article 21

1. Technical difficulties which may arise in applying Articles 19 and 20 shall be resolved, within two years of the entry into force of this Treaty, by directives issued by the Council acting by a qualified majority on a proposal from the Commission.

2. Before the end of the first stage, or at latest when the duties are determined, the Council shall, acting by a qualified majority on a proposal from the Commission, decide on any adjustments required in the interests of the internal consistency of the common customs tariff as a result of applying the rules set out

in Articles 19 and 20, taking account in particular of the degree of processing undergone by the various goods to which the common tariff applies.

Article 22

The Commission shall, within two years of the entry into force of this Treaty, determine the extent to which the customs duties of a fiscal nature referred to in Article 17 (2) shall be taken into account in calculating the arithmetical average provided for in Article 19 (1). The Commission shall take account of any protective character which such duties may have.

Within six months of such determination, any Member State may request that the procedure provided for in Article 20 should be applied to the product in question, but in this event the percentage limit provided in that Article shall not be applicable to that State.

Article 23

1. For the purpose of the progressive introduction of the common customs tariff, Member States shall amend their tariffs applicable to third countries as follows:

(a) in the case of tariff headings on which the duties applied in practice on 1 January 1957 do not differ by more than 15% in either direction from the duties in the common customs tariff, the latter duties shall be applied at the end of the fourth year after the entry into force of this Treaty;

(b) in any other case, each Member State shall, as from the same date, apply a duty reducing by 30% the difference between the duty applied in practice on 1 January 1957 and the duty in the common customs tariff;

(c) at the end of the second stage this difference shall again be reduced by 30%;

(d) in the case of tariff headings for which the duties in the common customs tariff are not yet available at the end of the first stage, each Member States shall, within six months of the Council's action in accordance with Article 20, apply such duties as would result from application of the rules contained in this paragraph.

2. Where a Member States has been granted an authorization under Article 17 (4), it need not, for as long as that authorization remains valid, apply the preceding provisions to the tariff headings to which the authorization applies. When such authorization expires, the Member State concerned shall apply such duty as would have resulted from application of the rules contained in paragraph 1.

3. The common customs tariff shall be applied in its entirety by the end of the transitional period at the latest.

Article 24

Member States shall remain free to change their duties more rapidly than is provided for in Article 23 in order to bring them into line with the common customs tariff.

Article 25

1. If the Commission finds that the production in Member States of particular products contained in Lists B, C and D is insufficient to supply the demands of one of the Member States, and that such supply traditionally depends to a considerable extent on imports from third countries, the Council shall, acting by a qualified majority on a proposal from the Commission, grant the Member States concerned tariff quotas at a reduced rate of duty or duty free.

Such quotas may not exceed the limits beyond which the risk might arise of activities being transferred to the detriment of other Member States.

2. In the case of the products in List E, and of those in List G for which the rates of duty have been determined in accordance with the procedures provided for in the third paragraph of Article 20, the Commission shall, where a change in sources of supply or shortage of supplies within the Community is such as to entail harmful consequences for the processing industries of a Member State, at the request of that Member States, grant it tariff quotas at a reduced rate of duty or duty free.

Such quotas may not exceed the limits beyond which the risk might arise of activities being transferred to the detriment of other Member States.

3.   In the case of the products listed in Annex II to this Treaty, the Commission may authorize any Member State to suspend, in whole or in part, collection of the duties applicable or may grant such Member State tariff quotas at a reduced rate of duty or duty free, provided that no serious disturbance of the market of the products concerned results therefrom.

4.   The Commission shall periodically examine tariff quotas granted pursuant to this Article.

Article 26

The Commission may authorize any Member State encountering special difficulties to postpone the lowering or raising of duties provided for in Article 23 in respect of particular headings in its tariff.

Such authorization may only be granted for a limited period and in respect of tariff headings which, taken together, represent for such State not more than 5% of the value of its imports from third countries in the course of the latest year for which statistical data are available.

Article 27

Before the end of the first stage, Member States shall, in so far as may be necessary, take steps to approximate their provisions laid down by law, regulation or administrative action in respect of customs matters. To this end, the Commission shall make all appropriate recommendations to Member States.

Article 28

Any autonomous alteration or suspension of duties in the common customs tariff shall be decided by the Council acting by a qualified majority on a proposal from the Commission.

Article 29

In carrying out the tasks entrusted to it under this Section the Commission shall be guided by:

(a) the need to promote trade between Member Sates and third countries;

(b) developments in conditions of competition within the Community in so far as they lead to an improvement in the competitive capacity of undertakings;

(c) the requirements of the Community as regards the supply of raw materials and semi-finished goods; in this connection the Commission shall take care to avoid distorting conditions of competition between Member States in respect of finished goods;

(d) the need to avoid serious disturbances in the economies of Member States and to ensure rational development of production and an expansion of consumption within the Community.

Chapter 2. Elimination of Quantitative Restrictions Between Member States

Article 30

Quantitative restrictions on imports and all measures having equivalent effect shall, without prejudice to the following provisions, be prohibited between Member States.

Article 31

Member States shall refrain from introducing between themselves any new quantitative restrictions or measures having equivalent effect.

This obligation shall, however, relate only to the degree of liberalization attained in pursuance of the decisions of the Council of the Organization for European Economic Co-operation of 14 January 1955. Member States shall supply the Commission, not later than six months after the entry into force of this Treaty, with lists of the products liberalized by them in pursuance of these decisions. These lists shall be consolidated between Member States.

Annex

Article 32

In their trade with one another Member States shall refrain from making more restrictive the quotas and measures having equivalent effect existing at the date of the entry into force of this Treaty.

These quotas shall be abolished by the end of the transitional period at the latest. During that period, they shall be progressively abolished in accordance with the following provisions.

Article 33

1. One year after the entry into force of this Treaty, each Member State shall convert any bilateral quotas open to any other Member States into global quotas open without discrimination to all other Member States.

On the same date, Member States shall increase the aggregate of the global quotas so established in such a manner as to bring about an increase of not less than 20% in their total value as compared with the preceding year.

The global quota for each product, however, shall be increased by not less than 10%. The quotas shall be increased annually in accordance with the same rules and in the same proportions in relation to the preceding year.

The fourth increase shall take place at the end of the fourth year after the entry into force of this Treaty; the fifth, one year after the beginning of the second stage.

2. Where, in the case of a product which has not been liberalized, the global quota does not amount to 3% of the national production of the State concerned, a quota equal to not less than 3% of such national production shall be introduced not later than one year after the entry into force of this Treaty. This quota shall be raised to 4% at the end of the second year, and to 5% at the end of the third. Thereafter, the Member State concerned shall increase the quota by not less than 15% annually.

Where there is no such national production, the Commission shall take a decision establishing an appropriate quota.

3. At the end of the tenth year, each quota shall be equal to not less than 20% of the national production.

4. If the Commission finds by means of a decision that during two successive years the imports of any product have been below the level of the quota opened, this global quota shall not be taken into account in calculating the total value of the global quotas. In such case, the Member State shall abolish quota restrictions on the product concerned.

5. In the case of quotas representing more than 20% of the national production of the product concerned, the Council may, acting by a qualified majority on a proposal from the Commission, reduce the minimum percentage of 10% laid down in paragraph 1. This alteration shall not, however, affect the obligation to increase the total value of global quotas by 20% annually.

6. Member States which have exceeded their obligations as regards the degree of liberalization attained in pursuance of the decisions of the Council of the Organization for European Economic Co-operation of 14 January 1955 shall be entitled, when calculating the annual total increase of 20% provided for in paragraph 1, to take into account the amount of imports liberalized by autonomous action. Such calculation shall be submitted to the Commission for its prior approval.

7. The Commission shall issue directives establishing the procedure and timetable in accordance with which Member States shall abolish, as between themselves, any measures in existence, when this Treaty enters into force which have an effect equivalent to quotas.

8. If the Commission finds that the application of the provisions of this Article, and in particular of the provisions concerning percentages, makes it impossible to ensure that the abolition of quotas provided for in the second paragraph of ArtArticle32 is carried out progressively, the Council may, on a proposal from the Commission, acting unanimously during the first stage and by a qualified majority thereafter, amend the procedure laid down in this Article and may, in particular, increase the percentages fixed.

Annex

Article 34

1. Quantitative restrictions on exports, and all measures having equivalent effect, shall be prohibited between Member States.

2. Member States shall, by the end of the first stage at the latest, abolish all quantitative restrictions on exports and any measures having equivalent effect which are in existence when this Treaty enters into force.

Article 35

The Member States declare their readiness to abolish quantitative restrictions on imports from and exports to other Member States more rapidly than is provided for in the preceding Articles, if their general economic situation and the situation of the economic sector concerned so permit.

To this end, the Commission shall make recommendations to the Member State concerned.

Article 36

The provisions of Article 30 to 34 shall not preclude prohibitions or restrictions on imports, exports or goods in transit justified on grounds of public morality, public policy or public security; the protection of health and life of humans, animals or plants; the protection of national treasures possessing artistic, historic or archaeological value; or the protection of industrial and commercial property. Such prohibitions or restrictions shall not, however, constitute a means of arbitrary discrimination or a disguised restriction on trade between Member States.

Article 37

1. Member States shall progressively adjust any State monopolies of a commercial character so as to ensure that when the transitional period has ended no discrimination regarding the conditions under which goods are procured and marketed exists between nationals of Member States.

The provisions of this Article shall apply to any body through which a Member State, in law or in fact, either directly or indirectly supervises, determines or appreciably influences imports or exports between Member States. These provisions shall likewise apply to monopolies delegated by the State to others.

2. Member States shall refrain from introducing any new measure which is contrary to the principles laid down in paragraph 1 or which restricts the scope of the Articles dealing with the abolition of customs duties and quantitative restrictions between Member States.

3. The timetable for the measures referred to in paragraph 1 shall be harmonized with the abolition of quantitative restrictions on the same products provided for in Articles 30 to 34.

If a product is subject to a State monopoly of a commercial character in only one or some Member States, the Commission may authorize the other Member States to apply protective measures until the adjustment provided for in paragraph 1 has been effected; the Commission shall determine the conditions and details of such measures.

4. If a State monopoly of a commercial character has rules which are designed to make it easier to dispose of agricultural products or obtain for them the best return, steps should be taken in applying the rules contained in this Article to ensure equivalent safeguards for the employment and standard of living of the producers concerned, account being taken of the adjustments that will be possible and the specialization that will be needed with the passage of time.

5. The obligations on Member States shall be binding only in so far as they are compatible with existing international agreements.

6. With effect from the first stage the Commission shall make recommendations as to the manner in which and the timetable according to which the adjustment provided for in this Article shall be carried out.

Annex

Title II – Agriculture

Article 38

1. The common market shall extend to agriculture and trade in agricultural products. "Agricultural products" means the products of the soil, of stockfarming and of fisheries and products of first-stage processing directly related to these products.

2. Save as otherwise provided in Articles 39 to 46, the rules laid down for the establishment of the common market shall apply to agricultural products.

3. The products subject to the provisions of Article 39 to 46 are listed in Annex II to this Treaty. Within two years of the entry into force of this Treaty, however, the Council shall, acting by a qualified majority on a proposal from the Commission, decide what products are to be added to this list.

4. The operation and development of the common market for agricultural products must be accompanied by the establishment of a common agricultural policy among the Member States.

Article 39

1. The objectives of the common agricultural policy shall be:

(a) to increase agricultural productivity by promoting technical progress and by ensuring the rational development of agricultural production and the optimum utilisation of the factors of production, in particular labour;

(b) thus, to ensure a fair standard of living for the agricultural community, in particular by increasing the individual earnings of persons engaged in agriculture.

(c) to stabilise markets;

(d) to assure the availability of supplies;

(e) to ensure that supplies reach consumers at reasonable prices.

2. In working out the common agricultural policy and the special methods for its application, account shall be taken of:

(a) the particular nature of agricultural activity, which results from the social structure of agriculture and from structural and natural disparities between the various agricultural regions;

(b) the need to effect the appropriate adjustments by degrees;

(c) the fact that in the Member States agriculture constitutes a sector closely linked with the economy as a whole.

Article 40

1. Member States shall develop the common agricultural policy by degrees during the transitional period and shall bring it into force by the end of that period at the latest.

2. In order to attain the objectives set out in Article 39 a common organization of agricultural markets shall be established.

This organization shall taken one of the following forms, depending on the product concerned.

(a) common rules on competition;

(b) compulsory co-ordination of the various national market organizations;

(c) a European market organization.

3. The common organization established in accordance with paragraph 2 may include all measures required to attain the objectives set out in Article 39, in particular regulation of prices, aids for the production and marketing of the various products, storage and carryover arrangements and common machinery for stabilising imports or exports.

The common organization shall be limited to pursuit of the objectives set out in Article 39 and shall exclude any discrimination between producers or consumers within the Community.

Any common price policy shall be based on common criteria and uniform methods of calculation.

4. In order to enable the common organization referred to in paragraph 2 to attain its objectives, one or more agricultural guidance and guarantee funds may be set up.

Article 41

To enable the objectives set out in Article 39 to be attained, provision may be made within the framework of the common agricultural policy for measures such as:

(a) an effective co-ordination of efforts in the spheres of vocational training, of research and of the dissemination of agricultural knowledge; this may include joint financing of projects or institutions.

(b) joint measures to promote consumption of certain products.

Article 42

The provisions of the Chapter relating to rules on competition shall apply to production of and trade in agricultural products only to the extent determined by the Council within the framework of Article 43 (2) and (3) and in accordance with the procedure laid down therein, account being taken of the objectives set out in Art. 39.

The Council may, in particular, authorize the granting of aid:

(a) for the protection of enterprises handicapped by structural or natural conditions;

(b) with the framework of economic development programmes.

Article 43

1. In order to evolve the broad lines of a common agricultural policy, the Commission shall, immediately this Treaty enters into force, convene a conference of the Member States with a view to making a comparison of their agricultural policies, in particular by producing a statement of their resources and needs.

2. Having taken into account the work of the conference provided for in paragraph 1, after consulting the Economic and Social Committee and within two years of the entry into force of this Treaty, the Commission shall submit proposals for working out and implementing the common agricultural policy, including the replacement of the national organization by one of the forms of common organization provided for in Article 40 (2), and for implementing the measures specified in this Title.

These proposals shall take account of the interdependence of the agricultural matters mentioned in this Title.

The Council shall, on a proposal from the Commission and after consulting the European Parliament, acting unanimously during the first two stages and by a qualified majority thereafter, make regulation issue directives, or take decisions without prejudice to any recommendations it may also make.

3. The Council may, acting by a qualified majority and in accordance with paragraph 2, replace the national market organizations by the common organization provided for in Article 40 (2) if:

(a) the common organization offers Member States which are opposed to this measure and which have an organization of their own for the production in question equivalent safeguards for the employment and standard of living of the producers concerned, account being taken of the adjustments that will be possible and the specialization that will be needed with the passage of time;

(b) such an organization ensures conditions for trade within the Community similar to those existing in a national market.

4. If a common organization for certain raw materials is established before a common organization exists for the corresponding processed products, such raw materials as are used for processed products intended for export to third countries may be imported from outside the Community.

Article 44

1. In so far as progressive abolition of customs duties and quantitative restrictions between Member States may result in prices likely to jeopardize the attainment of the objectives set out in Article 39, each Member State shall, during the transitional period, be entitled to apply to particular products, in a non-discriminatory manner and in substitution for quotas and to such an extent as shall not impede the

expansion of the volume of trade provided for in Article 45 (2), a system of minimum prices below which imports may be either:

– temporarily suspended or reduced; or
– allowed, but subjected to the condition that they are made at a price higher than the minimum price for the product concerned.

In the latter case the minimum prices shall not include customs duties.

2.   Minimum prices shall neither cause a reduction of the trade existing between Member States where this Treaty enters into force nor form an obstacle to progressive expansion of this trade. Minimum prices shall not be applied so as to form an obstacle to the development of a natural preference between Member States.

3.   As soon as this Treaty enters into force the Council shall, on a proposal from the Commission, determine objective criteria for the establishment of minimum price systems and for the fixing of such prices.

These criteria shall in particular take account of the average national production costs in the Member State applying the minimum price, of the position of the various undertakings concerned in relation to such average production costs, and of the need to promote both the progressive improvement of agricultural practice and the adjustments and specialization needed within the common market.

The Commission shall further propose a procedure for revising these criteria in order to allow for and speed up technical progress and to approximate prices progressively within the common market.

These criteria and the procedure for revising them shall be determined by the Council acting unanimously within three years of the entry into force of this Treaty.

4.   Until the decision of the Council takes effect Member States may fix minimum prices on condition that these are communicated beforehand to the Commission and to the other Member States so that they may submit their comments.

Once the Council has taken its decision, Member States shall fix minimum prices on the basis of the criteria determined as above.

The Council may, acting by a qualified majority on a proposal from the Commission, rectify any decisions taken by Member States which do not conform to the criteria defined above

5.   If it does not prove possible to determine the said objective criteria for certain products by the beginning of the third stage, the Council may, acting by a qualified majority on a proposal from the Commission, vary the minimum prices applied to these products.

6.   At the end of the transitional period, a table of minimum prices still in force shall be drawn up. The Council shall, acting on a proposal from the Commission and by a majority of nine votes in accordance with the weighting laid down in the first subparagraph of Art. 148 (2), determine the system to be applied within the framework of the common agricultural policy.

Article 45

1.   Until national market organizations have been replaced by one of the forms of common organization referred to in Article 40 (2), trade in products in respect of which certain Member States:

-   have arrangements designed to guarantee national producers a market for their products;
–   and are in need of imports,

shall be developed by the conclusion of long-term agreements or contracts between importing and exporting Member States.

These agreements or contracts shall be directed towards the progressive abolition of any discrimination in the application of these arrangements to the various producers within the Community.

Such agreements or contracts shall be concluded during the first stage; account shall be taken of the principle or reciprocity.

2. As regards quantities, these agreements or contracts shall be based on the average volume of trade between Member States in the products concerned during the three years before the entry into force of this Treaty and shall provide for an increase in the volume of trade within the limits of existing requirements, account being taken of traditional patterns of trade.

As regards prices, these agreements or contracts shall enable producers to dispose of the agreed quantities at prices which shall be progressively approximated to those paid to national producers on the domestic market of the purchasing country.

This approximation shall proceed as steadily as possible and shall be completed by the end of the transitional period at the latest.

Prices shall be negotiated between the parties concerned within the framework of directives issued by the Commission for the purpose of implementing the two preceding subparagraphs.

If the first stage is extended, these agreements or contracts shall continue to be carried out in accordance with the conditions applicable at the end of the fourth year after the entry into force of this Treaty, the obligation to increase quantities and to approximate prices being suspended until the transition to the second stage.

Member States shall avail themselves of any opportunity open to them under their legislation, particularly in respect of import policy, to ensure the conclusion and carrying out of these agreements or contracts.

3. To the extent that Member States require raw materials for the manufacture of products to be exported outside the Community in competition with products of third countries, the above agreements or contracts shall not form an obstacle to the importation of raw materials for this purpose from third countries. This provision shall not, however, apply if the Council unanimously decides to make provision for payments required to compensate for the higher price paid on goods imported for this purpose on the basis of these agreements or contracts in relation to the delivered price of the same goods purchased on the world market.

Article 46

Where in a Member State a product is subject to a national market organization or to internal rules having equivalent effect which affect the competitive position of similar production in another Member States, a countervailing charge shall be applied by Member States to imports of this product coming from the Member State where such organization or rules exist, unless that State applies a countervailing charge on export.

The Commission shall fix the amount of these charges at the level required to redress the balance; it may also authorize other measures, the conditions and details of which it shall determine.

Article 47

As to the functions to be performed by the Economic and Social Committee in pursuance of this Title, its agricultural section shall hold itself at the disposal of the Commission to prepare, in accordance with the provisions of Articles 197 and 198, the deliberations of the Committee.

Title III – Free Movement of Persons, Services and Capital

Chapter 1. Workers

Article 48

1. Freedom of movement for workers shall be secured within the Community by the end of the transitional period at the latest.

2. Such freedom of movement shall entail the abolition of any discrimination based on nationality between workers of the Member States as regards employment, remuneration and other conditions of work and employment.

3. It shall entail the right, subject to limitations justified on grounds of public policy, public security or public health:

(a) to accept offers of employment actually made;

(b) to move freely within the territory of Member States for this purpose;

(c) to stay in a Member State for the purpose of employment in accordance with the provisions, governing the employment of nationals of that State laid down by law, regulation or administrative action;

(d) to remain in the territory of a Member State after having been employed in that State, subject to conditions which shall be embodied in implementing regulations to be drawn up by the Commission.

4. The provisions of this Article shall not apply to employment in the public service.

Article 49

As soon as this Treaty enters into force, the Council shall, *acting in accordance with the procedure referred to in Article 189b* and after consulting the Economic and Social Committee, issue directives or make regulations setting out the measures required to bring about, by progressive stages, freedom of movement for workers, as defined in Article 48, in particular:[12]

(a) by ensuring close co-operation between national employment services;

(b) by systematically and progressively abolishing those administrative procedures and practices and those qualifying periods in respect of eligibility for available employment, whether resulting from national legislation or from agreements previously concluded between Member States, the maintenance of which would form an obstacle to liberalization of the movement of workers;

(c) by systematically and progressively abolishing all such qualifying periods and other restrictions provided for either under national legislation or under agreements previously concluded between Member States as imposed on workers of other Member States conditions regarding the free choice of employment other than those imposed on workers of the State concerned;

(d) by setting up appropriate machinery to bring offers of employment into touch with applications for employment and to facilitate the achievement of a balance between supply and demand in the employment market in such a way as to avoid serious threats to the standard of living and level of employment in the various regions and industries

Article 50

Member States shall, within the framework of a joint programme, encourage the exchange of young workers.

Article 51

The Council shall, acting unanimously on a proposal from the Commission, adopt such measures in the field of social security as are necessary to provide freedom of movement for workers; to this end, it shall make arrangements to secure for migrant workers and their dependants:

(a) aggregation, for the purpose of acquiring and retaining the right to benefit and of calculating the amount of benefit, of all periods taken into account under the laws of the several countries;

(b) payment of benefits to persons resident in the territories of Member States.

Chapter 2. Right of Establishment

Article 52

Within the framework of the provisions set out below, restrictions on the freedom of establishment of nationals of a Member State in the territory of another Member State shall be abolished by progressive stages in the course of the transitional period. Such progressive abolition shall also apply to restrictions on the setting up of agencies, branches or subsidiaries by nationals of any Member State established in the territory of any Member State.

---

12   Introductory words amended by Article G(10) TEU.

Freedom of establishment shall include the right to take up and pursue activities as self-employed persons and to set up and manage undertakings, in particular companies or firms within the meaning of the second paragraph of Article 58, under the conditions laid down for its own nationals by the law of the country where such establishment is effected, subject to the provisions of the Chapter relating to capital.

Article 53

Member States shall not introduce any new restrictions on the right of establishment in their territories of nationals of other Member States, save as otherwise provided in this Treaty.

Article 54

1. Before the end of the first stage, the Council shall, acting unanimously on a proposal from the Commission and after consulting the Economic and Social Committee and the European Parliament, draw up a general programme for the abolition of existing restrictions on freedom of establishment within the Community. The Commission shall submit its proposal to the Council during the first two years of the first stage.

The programme shall set out the general conditions under which freedom of establishment is to be attained in the case of each type of activity and in particular the stages by which it is to be attained.

2. In order to implement this general programme or, in the absence of such programme, in order to achieve a stage in attaining freedom of establishment as regards a particular activity, the Council, *acting in accordance with the procedure referred to in Article 189b* and after consulting the Economic and Social Committee, shall act by means of directives.[13]

3. The Council and the Commission shall carry out the duties devolving upon them under the preceding provisions, in particular;

(a) by according, as a general rule, priority treatment to activities where freedom of establishment makes a particularly valuable contribution to the development of production and trade;

(b) by ensuring close co-operation between the competent authorities in the Member States in order to ascertain the particular situation within the Community of the various activities concerned;

(c) by abolishing those administrative procedures and practices, whether resulting from national legislation or from agreements previously concluded between Member States, the maintenance of which would form an obstacle to freedom of establishment;

(d) by ensuring that workers of one Member State employed in the territory of another Member State may remain in that territory for the purpose of taking up activities therein as selfemployed persons, where they satisfy the conditions which they would be required to satisfy if they were entering that State at the time when they intended to take up such activities;

(e) by enabling a national of one Member State to acquire and use land and buildings situated in the territory of another Member State, in so far as this does not conflict with the principles laid down in Article 39 (2);

(f) by effecting the progressive abolition of restrictions on freedom of establishment in every branch of activity under consideration, both as regards the conditions for setting up agencies, branches or subsidiaries in the territory of a Member State and as regards the subsidiaries in the territory of a Member State and as regards the conditions governing the entry of personnel belonging to the main establishment into managerial or supervisory posts in such agencies, branches or subsidiaries;

(g) by coordinating to the necessary extent the safeguards which, for the protection of the interests of Members and others, are required by Member States of companies or firms within the meaning of the second paragraph of Article 58 with a view to making such safeguards equivalent throughout the Community;

(h) by satisfying themselves that the conditions of establishment are not distorted by aids granted by Member States.

13   Paragraph 2 as amended by Article G(11) TEU.

Article 55

The provisions of this Chapter shall not apply, so far as any given Member State is concerned, to activities which in that State are connected, even occasionally, with the exercise of official authority.

The Council may, acting by a qualified majority on a proposal from the Commission, rule that the provisions of this Chapter shall not apply to certain activities.

Article 56

1. The provisions of this Chapter and measures taken in pursuance thereof shall not prejudice the applicability of provisions laid down by law, regulation or administrative action providing for special treatment for foreign nations on grounds of public policy, public security or public health.

2. Before the end of the transitional period, the Council shall, acting unanimously on a proposal from the Commission and after consulting the European Parliament, issue directives for the co-ordination of the abovementioned provisions laid down by law, regulation or administrative action. After the end of the second stage, however, the Council shall, *acting in accordance with the procedure referred to in Article 189b*, issue directives for the coordination of such provisions as, in each Member State, are a matter for regulation or administrative action.[14]

Article57 [15]

1. In order to make it easier for persons to take up and pursue activities as self-employed persons, the Council shall, *acting in accordance with the procedure referred to in Article 189b*, issue directives for the mutual recognition of diplomas, certificates and other evidence of formal qualifications.

2. *For the same purpose, the Council shall, before the end of the transitional period, issue directives for the co-ordination of the provisions laid down by law, regulation or administrative action in Member States concerning the taking up and pursuit of activities as self-employed persons. The Council, acting unanimously on a proposal from the Commission and after consulting the European Parliament, shall decide on directives the implementation of which involves in at least one Member State amendment of the existing principles laid down by law governing the professions with respect to training and conditions of access for natural persons. In other cases the Council shall act in accordance with the procedure referred to in Article 189b.*

3. In the case of the medical and allied and pharmaceutical professions, the progressive abolition of restrictions shall be dependent upon co-ordination of the conditions for their exercise in the various Member States.

Article 58

Companies or firms formed in accordance with the law of a Member State and having their registered office, central administration or principal place of business within the Community shall, for the purposes of this Chapter, be treated in the same way as natural persons who are nationals of Member States.

'Companies or firms' means companies or firms constituted under civil or commercial law, including cooperative societies, and other legal persons governed by public or private law, save for those which are non-profit making.

Chapter 3. Services

Article 59

Within the framework of the provisions set out below, restrictions on freedom to provide services within the Community shall be progressively abolished during the transitional period in respect of nationals of Member States who are established in a State of the Community other than that of the person for whom the services are intended.

---

14   Paragraph 2 as amended by Article G(12) TEU.
15   As amended by Article G(13) TEU.

Annex

The Council may, acting by a qualified majority on a proposal from the Commission, extend the provisions of the Chapter to nationals of a third country who provide services and who are established within the Community.

Article 60

Services shall be considered to be "services" within the meaning of the Treaty where they are normally provided for remuneration, in so far as they are not governed by the provisions relating to freedom of movement for goods, capital and persons.

"Services" shall in particular include:

(a) activities of an industrial character;

(b) activities of a commercial character;

(c) activities of craftsmen;

(d) activities of the professions.

Without prejudice to the provisions of the Chapter relating to the right of establishment, the person providing a service may, in order to do so, temporarily pursue his activity in the State where the service is provided, under the same conditions as are imposed by that State on its own nationals.

Article 61

1. Freedom to provide services in the field of transport shall be governed by the provisions of the Title relating to transport.

2. The liberalization of banking and insurance services connected with movements of capital shall be effected in step with the progressive liberalization of movement of capital.

Article 62

Save as otherwise provided in this Treaty, Member States shall not introduce any new restrictions on the freedom to provide services which have in fact been attained in the date of the entry into force of this Treaty.

Article 63

1. Before the end of the first stage, the Council shall, acting unanimously on a proposal from the Commission and after consulting the Economic and Social Committee and the European Parliament, draw up a general programme for the abolition of existing restrictions on freedom to provide services within the Community. The Commission shall submit its proposal to the Council during the first two years of the first stage.

The programme shall set out the general conditions under which and the stages by which each type of service is to be liberalized.

2. In order to implement this general programme or, in the absence of such programme, in order to achieve a stage in the liberalization of a specific service the Council shall, on a proposal from the Commission and after consulting the Economic and Social Committee and the European Parliament, issue directives acting unanimously until the end of the first stage and by a qualified majority thereafter.

3. As regards the proposals and decisions referred to in paragraphs 1 and 2, priority shall as a general rule be given to those services which directly affect production costs or the liberalization of which helps to promote trade in goods.

Article 64

The Member States declare their readiness to undertake the liberalization of services beyond the extent required by the directives issued pursuant to Article 63 (2), if their general economic situation and the situation of the economic sector concerned so permit.

To this end, the Commission shall make recommendations to the Member States concerned.

Article 65

As long as restrictions on freedom to provide services have not been abolished, each Member State shall apply such restrictions without distinction on grounds of nationality or residence to all persons providing services within the meaning of the first paragraph of Article 59.

Article 66

The provisions of Articles 55 to 58 shall apply to the matters covered by this Chapter.

Chapter 4. Capital and Payments[16]

Article 67

1. During the transitional period and to the extent necessary to ensure the proper functioning of the common market, Member States shall progressively abolish between themselves all restrictions on the movement of capital belonging to persons resident in Member States and any discrimination based on the nationality or on the place of residence of the parties or on the place where such capital is invested.

2. Current payments, connected with the movement of capital between Member States, shall be freed from all restrictions by the end of the first stage at the latest.

Article 68

1. Member States shall, as regards the matters dealt with in this Chapter, be as liberal as possible in granting such exchange authorization as are still necessary after the entry into force of this Treaty.

2. Where a Member State applies to the movements of capital liberalized in accordance with the provisions of this Chapter the domestic rules governing the capital market and the credit system, it shall do so in a non-discriminatory manner.

3. Loans for the direct or indirect financing of a Member State or its regional or local authorities shall not be issued or placed in other Member States unless the States concerned have reached agreement thereon. This provision shall not preclude the application of Article 22 of the Protocol on the Statute of the European Investment bank.

Article 69

The Council shall, on a proposal from the Commission, which for this purpose shall consult the Monetary Committee provided for in Article 105, issue the necessary directives for the progressive implementation of the provisions of Article 67, acting unanimously during the first two stages and by a qualified majority thereafter.

Article 70

1. The Commission shall propose to the Council measures for the progressive co-ordination of the exchange policies of Member States in respect of the movement of capital between those States and third countries. For this purpose the Council shall issue directives, acting by a qualified majority. It shall endeavour to attain the highest possible degree of liberalization. Unanimity shall be required for measures which constitute a step back as regards the liberalization of capital movements.

2. Where the measures taken in accordance with paragraph 1 do not permit the elimination of differences between the exchange rules of Member States and where such differences could lead persons resident in one of the Member States to use the freer transfer facilities within the Community which are provided for in Article 67 in order to evade the rules of one of the Member States concerning the movement of capital to or from third countries, that State may, after consulting the other Member States and the Commission, take appropriate measures to overcome these difficulties.

Should the Council find that these measures are restricting the free movement of capital within the Community to a greater extent than is required for the purpose of overcoming the difficulties, it may, acting by a qualified majority on a proposal from the Commission, decide that the State concerned shall amend or abolish these measures.

16   Title as amended by Article G(14) TEU.

Annex

Article 71

Member States shall endeavour to avoid introducing within the Community any new exchange restrictions on the movement of capital and current payments connected with such movements, and shall endeavour not to make existing rules more restrictive.

They declare their readiness to go beyond the degree of liberalization of capital movements provided for in the preceding Articles in so far as their economic situation, in particular the situation of their balance of payments, so permits.

The Commission may, after consulting the Monetary Committee, make recommendations to Member States on this subject.

Article 72

Member States shall keep the Commission informed of any movements of capital to and from third countries which come to their knowledge. The Commission may deliver to Member States any opinions which it considers appropriate on this subject.

Article 73

1. If movements of capital lead to disturbances in the functioning of the capital market in any Member State, the Commission shall, after consulting the Monetary Committee, authorize that State to take protective measures in the field of capital movements, the conditions and details of which the Commission shall determine.

The Council may, acting by a qualified majority, revoke this authorization or amend the conditions or details thereof.

2. A Member State which is in difficulties may, however, on grounds of secrecy or urgency, take the measures mentioned above, where this proves necessary, on its own initiative. The Commission and the other Member States shall be informed of such measures by the date of their entry into force at the latest. In this event the Commission may, after consulting the Monetary Committee, decide that the State concerned shall amend or abolish the measures.

Article 73a[17]

From 1 January 1994, Articles 67 to 73 shall be replaced by Articles 73b, c, d, e, f and g.

Article 73b

1. Within the framework of the provisions set out in this Chapter, all restrictions on the movement of capital between Member States and between Member States and third countries shall be prohibited.

2. Within the framework of the provisions set out in this Chapter, all restrictions on payments between Member States and between Member States and third countries shall be prohibited.

Article 73c

1. The provisions of Article 73c shall be without prejudice to the application to third countries of any restrictions which exist on 31 December 1993 under national or Community law adopted in respect of the movement of capital to or from third countries involving direct investment -including investment in real estate-, [sic] establishment, the provision of financial services or the admission of securities to capital markets.

2. Whilst endeavouring to achieve the objective of free movement of capital between Member States and third countries to the greatest extent possible and without prejudice to the other Chapters of this Treaty, the Council may, acting by a qualified majority on a proposal from the Commission, adopt measures on the movement of capital to or from third countries involving direct investment -including investment in real estate-, [sic] establishment, the provision of financial services or the admission of securities to capital markets. Unanimity shall be required for measures under this paragraph which

17   Articles 73a to 73h as inserted by G(15) TEU.

constitute a step back in Community law as regards the liberalization of the movement of capital to or from third countries.

Article 73d

1. The provisions of Article 73b shall be without prejudice to the right of Members States:

(a) to apply the relevant provisions of their tax law which distinguish between tax-payers who are not in the same situation with regard to their place of residence or with regard to the place where their capital is invested; .

(b) to take all requisite measures to prevent infringements of national law and regulations, in particular in the field of taxation and the prudential supervision of financial institutions, or to lay down procedures for the declaration of capital movements for purposes of administrative or statistical information, or to take measures which are justified on grounds of public policy or public security.

2. The provisions of this Chapter shall be without prejudice to the applicability of restrictions on the right of establishment which are compatible with this Treaty.

3. The measures and procedures referred to in paragraphs 1 and 2 shall not constitute a means of arbitrary discrimination or a disguised restriction on the free movement of capital and payments as defined in Article 73b.

Article 73e

By way of derogation from Article 73b, Member States which, on 31 December 1993, enjoy a derogation on the basis of existing Community law, shall be entitled to maintain, until 31 December 1995 at the latest, restrictions on movements of capital authorized by such derogations as exist on that date.

Article 73f

Where, in exceptional circumstances, movements of capital to or from third countries cause, or threaten to cause, serious difficulties for the operation of economic and monetary union, the Council, acting by a qualified majority on a proposal from the Commission and after consulting the ECB, may take safeguard measures with regard to third countries for a period not exceeding six months if such measures are strictly necessary.

Article 73g

1. If, in the cases envisaged in Article 228a, action by the Community is deemed necessary, the Council may, in accordance with the procedure provided for in Article 228a, take the necessary urgent measures on the movement of capital and on payments as regards third countries concerned.

2. Without prejudice to Article 224 and as long as the Council has not taken measures pursuant to paragraph 1, a Member State may, for serious political reasons and on grounds of urgency, take unilateral measures against a third country with regard to capital movements and payments. The Commission and the other Member States shall be informed of such measures by the date of their entry into force at the latest.

The Council may, acting by a qualified majority on a proposal from the Commission, decide that the Member State concerned shall amend or abolish such measures. The President of the Council shall inform the European Parliament of any such decision taken by the Council.

Article 73h

Until 1 January 1994, the following provisions shall be applicable:

1. Each Member State undertakes to authorize, in the currency of the Member State in which the creditor or the beneficiary resides, any payments connected with the movement of goods, services or capital, and any transfers of capital and earnings, to the extent that the movement of goods, services, capital and persons between Member States has been liberalized pursuant to this Treaty.

The Member States declare their readiness to undertake the liberalization of payments beyond the extent provided in the preceding subparagraph, in so far as their economic situation in general and the state of their balance of payments in particular so permit.

2. In so far as movements of goods, services and capital are limited only by restrictions on payments connected therewith, these restrictions shall be progressively abolished by applying, mutatis mutandis, the provisions of this Chapter and the Chapters relating to the abolition of quantitative restrictions and to the liberalization of services.

3. Member States undertake not to introduce between themselves any new restrictions on transfers connected with the invisible transactions listed in Annex III to this Treaty.

The progressive abolition of existing restrictions shall be effected in accordance with the provisions of Articles 63 to 65, in so far as such abolition is not governed by the provisions contained in paragraphs 1 and 2 or by the other provisions of this Chapter.

4. If need be, Member States shall consult each other on the measures to be taken to enable the payments and transfers mentioned in this Article to be effected; such measures shall not prejudice the attainment of the objectives set out in this Treaty.

Title IV – Transport

Article 74

The objectives of this Treaty shall, in matters governed by this Title, be pursued by Member States within the framework of a common transport policy.

Article 75 [18]

1. For the purpose of implementing Article 74, and taking into account the distinctive features of transport, the Council shall, *acting in accordance with the procedure referred to in Article 189c* and after consulting the Economic and Social Committee, lay down:

(a) common rules applicable to international transport to or from the territory of a Member State or passing across the territory of one or more Member States;

(b) the conditions under which non-resident carriers may operate transport services within a Member State;

(c) measures to improve transport safety;

(d) any other appropriate provisions.

2. The provisions referred to in (a) and (b) of paragraph 1 shall be laid down during the transitional period.

3. By way of derogation from the procedure provided for in paragraph 1, where the application of provisions concerning the principles of the regulatory system for transport would be liable to have a serious effect on the standard of living and on employment in certain areas and on the operation of transport facilities, they shall be laid down by the Council acting unanimously *on a proposal from the Commission, after consulting the European Parliament and the Economic and Social Committee.* In so doing, the Council shall take into account the need for adaptation to the economic development which will result from establishing the common market.

Article 76

Until the provisions referred to in Article 75 (1) have been laid down, no Member State may, without the unanimous approval of the Council, make the various provisions governing the subject when this Treaty enters into force less favourable in their direct or indirect effect on carriers of other Member States as compared with carriers who are nationals of that State.

Article 77

Aids shall be compatible with this Treaty if they meet the needs of co-ordination of transport or if they represent reimbursement for the discharge of certain obligations inherent in the concept of a public service.

18   As amended by Article G(16) TEU.

Annex

Article 78

Any measures taken within the framework of this Treaty is respect of transport rates and conditions shall take account of the economic circumstances of carriers.

Article 79

1. In the case of transport within the Community, discrimination which takes the form of carriers charging different rates and imposing different conditions for the carriage of the same goods over the same transport links on grounds of the country of origin or of destination of the goods in question, shall be abolished, at the latest, before the end of the second stage.

2. Paragraph 1 shall not prevent the Council from adopting other measures in pursuance of Article 75 (1).

3. Within two years of the entry into force of this Treaty, the Council shall, acting by a qualified majority on a proposal from the Commission and after consulting the Economic and Social Committee, lay down rules for implementing the provisions of paragraph 1.

The Council may in particular lay down the provisions needed to enable the institutions of the Community to secure compliance with the rule laid down in paragraph 1 and to ensure that users benefit from it to the full.

4. The Commission shall, acting on its own initiative or on application by a Member State, investigate any cases of discrimination falling within paragraph 1 and, after consulting any Member State concerned, shall take the necessary decisions, within the framework of the rules laid down in accordance with the provisions of paragraph 3.

Article 80

1. The imposition by a Member State, in respect of transport operations carried out within the Community, of rates and conditions involving any element of support or protection in the interest of one or more particular undertakings or industries shall be prohibited as from the beginning of the second stage, unless authorized by the Commission.

2. The Commission shall, acting on its own initiative or on application by a Member State, examine the rates and conditions referred to in paragraph 1, taking account in particular of the requirements of an appropriate regional economic policy, the needs of underdeveloped areas and the problems of areas seriously affected by political circumstances on the one hand, and of the effects of such rates and conditions on competition between the different modes of transport on the other.

After consulting each Member State concerned, the Commission shall take the necessary decisions.

3. The prohibition provided for in paragraph 1 shall not apply to tariffs fixed to meet competition.

Article 81

Charges or dues in respect of the crossing of frontiers which are charged by a carrier in addition to the transport rates shall not exceed a reasonable level after taking the costs actually incurred thereby into account.

Member States shall endeavour to reduce these costs progressively.

The Commission may make recommendations to Member States for the application of this Article.

Article 82

The provisions of this title shall not form an obstacle to the application of measures taken in the Federal Republic of Germany to the extent that such measures are required in order to compensate for the economic disadvantages caused by the division of Germany to the economy of certain areas of the Federal Republic affected by that division.

Article 83

An Advisory Committee consisting of experts, designated by the Governments of Member States, shall be attached to the Commission. The Commission, whenever it considers it desirable, shall consult the

Committee on transport matters without prejudice to the powers of the transport section of the Economic and Social Committee.

Article 84

1. The provisions of this Title shall apply to transport by rail, road, and inland waterway.

2. The Council may, acting by a qualified majority, decide whether, to what extent and by what procedure appropriate provisions may be laid down for sea and air transport.

The procedural provisions of Article 75 (1) and (3) shall apply.

Title V – Common Rules on Competition, Taxation and Approximation of Laws[19]

Chapter 1. Rules on Competition

Section 1. Rules applying to undertakings

Article 85

1. The following shall be prohibited as incompatible with the common market: all agreements between undertakings, decisions by associations of undertakings and concerted practices which may affect trade between Member States and which have as their object or effect the prevention, restriction or distortion of competition within the common market, and in particular those which:

(a) directly or indirectly fix purchase or selling prices or any other trading conditions;

(b) limit or control production, markets, technical development, or investment;

(c) share market or sources of supply;

(d) apply dissimilar conditions to equivalent transactions with other trading parties, thereby placing them at a competitive disadvantage;

(e) make the conclusion of contracts subject to acceptance by the other parties of supplementary obligations which, by their nature or according to commercial usage, have no connection with the subject of such contracts.

2. Any agreements or decisions prohibited pursuant to this Article shall be automatically void.

3. The provisions of paragraph 1 may, however, be declared inapplicable in the case of:

–   any agreement or category of agreements between undertakings;

–   any decision or category of decisions by associations of undertakings;

–   any concerted practice or category of concerted practices;

which contributes to improving the production or distribution of goods or to promoting technical or economic progress, while allowing consumers a fair share of the resulting benefit, and which does not:

(a) impose on the undertakings concerned restrictions which are not indispensable to the attainment of these objectives;

(b) afford such undertakings the possibility of eliminating competition in respect of a substantial part of the products in question.

Article 86

Any abuse by one or more undertakings of a dominant position within the common market or in a substantial part of it shall be prohibited as incompatible with the common market in so far as it may affect trade between Member States.

Such abuse may, in particular, consist in:

(a) directly or indirectly imposing unfair purchase or selling prices or other unfair trading conditions;

(b) limiting production, markets or technical development to the prejudice of consumers;

---

19   Title introduced by Article G(17) TEU.

(c) applying dissimilar conditions to equivalent transactions with other trading parties, thereby placing them at a competitive disadvantage;

(d) making the conclusion of contracts subject to acceptance by the other parties of supplementary obligations which, by their nature or according to commercial usage, have no connection with the subject of such contracts.

Article 87

1. Within three years of the entry into force of this Treaty the Council shall, acting unanimously on a proposal from the Commission and after consulting the European Parliament, adopt any appropriate regulations or directives to give effect to the principles set out in Articles 85 and 86.

If such provisions have not been adopted within the period mentioned, they shall be laid down by the Council, acting by a qualified majority on a proposal from the Commission and after consulting the European Parliament.

2. The regulations or directives referred to in paragraph 1 shall be designed in particular:

(a) to ensure compliance with the prohibitions laid down in Article 85 (1) and in Article 86 by making provision for fines and periodic penalty payments;

(b) to lay down detailed rules for the application of Article 85 (3), taking into account the need to ensure effective supervision on the one hand, and to simplify administration to the greatest possible extent on the other;

(c) to define, if need be, in the various branches of the economy, the scope of the provisions of Articles 85 and

(d) to define the respective functions of the Commission and of the Court of Justice in applying the provisions laid down in this paragraph;

(e) to determine the relationship between national laws and the provisions contained in this Section or adopted pursuant to this Article.

Article 88

Until the entry into force of the provisions adopted in pursuance of Article 87, the authorities in Member States shall rule on the admissibility of agreements, decisions and concerted practices and on abuse of a dominant position in the common market in accordance with the law of their country and with the provisions of Article 85, in particular paragraph 3, and of Article 86.

Article 89

1. Without prejudice to Article 88, the Commission shall, as soon as it takes up its duties, ensure the application of the principles laid down in Articles 85 and 86. On application by a Member State or on its own initiative, and in co-operation with the competent authorities in the Member States, who shall give it their assistance, the Commission shall investigate cases of suspected infringement of these principles. If it finds that there has been an infringement, it shall propose appropriate measures to bring it to an end.

2. If the infringement is not brought to an end, the Commission shall record such infringement of the principles of a reasoned decision. The Commission may publish its decision and authorize Member States to take the measures, the conditions and details of which it shall determine, needed to remedy the situation.

Article 90

1. In the case of public undertakings and undertakings to which Member States grant special or exclusive rights, Member States shall neither enact nor maintain in force any measure contrary to those rules contained in this Treaty in particular to those rules provided for in Article 7 and Articles 85 to 94.

2. Undertakings entrusted with the operation of services of general economic interest or having the character of a revenue-producing monopoly shall be subject to the rules contained in this Treaty, in particular to the rules on competition, in so far as the application of such rules does not obstruct the performance, in law or in fact, of the particular tasks assigned to them. The development of trade must not be affected to such an extent as would be contrary to the interests of the Community.

3. The Commission shall ensure the application of the provisions of this Article and shall, where necessary, address appropriate directives or decisions to Member States.

Section 2. Dumping

Article 91

1. If during the transitional period, the Commission, on application by a Member State or by any other interested party, finds that dumping is being practised within the common market, it shall address recommendations to the person or persons with whom such practices originate for the purpose of putting an end to them.

Should the practices continue, the Commission shall authorize the injured Member State to take protective measures, the conditions and details of which the Commission shall determine.

2. As soon as this Treaty enters into force, products which originate in or are in free circulation in one Member State and which have been exported to another Member State shall, on reimportation, be admitted into the territory of the first-mentioned State free of all customs duties, quantitative restrictions or measures having equivalent effect. The Commission shall lay down appropriate rules for the application of this paragraph.

Section 3. Aids granted by States

Article 92

1. Save as otherwise provided in this Treaty, any aid granted by a Member State or through State resources in any form whatsoever which distorts or threatens to distort competition by favouring certain undertakings or the production of certain goods shall, in so far as it affects trade between Member States, be incompatible with the common market.

2. The following shall be compatible with the common market:

(a) aid having a social character, granted to individual consumers, provided that such aid is granted without discrimination related to the origin of the products concerned;

(b) aid to make good the damage caused by natural disasters or exceptional occurrences;

(c) aid granted to the economy of certain areas of the Federal Republic of Germany affected by the division of Germany, in so far as such aid is required in order to compensate for the economic disadvantages caused by that division.

3. The following may be considered to be compatible with the common market:

(a) aid to promote the economic development of areas where the standard of living is abnormally low or where there is serious underemployment;

(b) aid to promote the execution of an important project of common European interest or to remedy a serious disturbance in the economy of a Member State;

(c) aid to facilitate the development of certain economic activities or of certain economic areas, where such aid does not adversely affect trading conditions to an extent contrary to the common interest. However, the aids granted to shipbuilding as of 1 January 1957 shall, in so far as they serve only to compensate for the absence of customs protection, be progressively reduced under the same conditions as apply to the elimination of customs duties, subject to the provisions of this Treaty concerning common commercial policy towards third countries;

(d) aid to promote culture and heritage conservation where such aid does not affect trading conditions and competition in the Community to an extent that is contrary to the common interest;[20]

(e) such other categories of aid as may be specified by decision of the Council acting by a qualified majority on a proposal from the Commission.

---

20 Point (d) as inserted by Article G(18) TEU.

Article 93

1. The Commission shall, in co-operation with Member States, keep under constant review all systems of aid existing in those States. It shall propose to the latter any appropriate measures required by the progressive development or by the functioning of the common market.

2. If, after giving notice to the parties concerned to submit their comments, the Commission finds that aid granted by a State or through State resources is not compatible with the common market having regard to Article 92, or that such aid is being misused, it shall decide that the State concerned shall abolish such aid within a period of time to be determined by the Commission.

If the State concerned does not comply with this decision within the prescribed time, the Commission or any other interested State may, in derogation from the provisions of Articles 169 and 170, refer the matter to the Court of Justice direct.

On application by a Member State, the Council, may, acting unanimously, decide that aid which that State is granting or intends to grant shall be considered to be compatible with the common market, in derogation from the provisions of Article 92 or from the regulations provided for in Article 94, if such a decision is justified by exceptional circumstances. If, as regards the aid in question, the Commission has already initiated the procedure provided for in the first subparagraph of this paragraph, the fact that the State concerned has made its application to the Council shall have the effect of suspending that procedure until the Council has made its attitude known.

If, however, the Council has not made its attitude known within three months of the said application being made, the Commission shall give its decision on the case.

3. The Commission shall be informed, in sufficient time to enable it to submit its comments, of any plans to grant or alter aid. If it considers that any such plan is not compatible with the common market having regard to Article 92, it shall without delay initiate the procedure provided for in paragraph 2. The Member State concerned shall not put its proposed measures into effect until this procedure has resulted in a final decision.

Article 94 [21]

The Council, acting by a qualified majority on a proposal from the Commission *and after consulting the European Parliament*, may make any appropriate regulations for the application of Arts. 92 and 93 and may in particular determine the conditions in which Art. 93 (3) shall apply and the categories of aid exempted from this procedure.

Chapter 2. Tax Provisions

Article 95

No Member State shall impose, directly or indirectly, on the products of other Mernber States any internal taxation of any kind in excess of that imposed directly or indirectly on similar domestic products.

Furthermore, no Member State shall impose on the products of other Member States any internal taxation of such a nature as to afford indirect protection to other products.

Member States shall, not later than at the beginning of the second stage, repeal or amend any provisions existing when this Treaty enters into force which conflict with the preceding rules.

Article 96

Where products are exported to the territory of any Member State, any repayment of internal taxation shall not exceed the internal taxation imposed on them whether directly or indirectly.

Article 97

Member States which levy a turnover tax calculated on a cumulative multi-stage tax system may, in the case of internal taxation imposed by them on imported products or of repayments allowed by them on

---

21   As amended by Article G(19) TEU.

exported products, establish average rates for products or groups of products, provided that there is no infringement of the principles laid down in Articles 95 and 96.

Where the average rates established by a Member State do not conform to these principles, the Commission shall address appropriate directives or decisions to the State concerned.

Article 98

In the case of charges other than turnover taxes, excise duties and other forms of indirect taxation, remissions and repayments in respect of exports to other Member States may not be granted and countervailing charges in respect of imports from Member States may not be imposed unless the measures contemplated have been previously approved for a limited period by the Council acting by a qualified majority on a proposal from the Commission.

Article 99 [22]

The Council shall, acting unanimously on a proposal from the Commission and after consulting the European Parliament *and the Economic and Social Committee*, adopt provisions for the harmonization of legislation concerning turnover taxes, excise duties and other forms of indirect taxation to the extent that such harmonization is necessary to ensure the establishment and the functioning of the internal market within the time limit laid down in Article 7a.

Chapter 3. Approximation of Laws

Article 100 [23]

The Council shall, acting unanimously on a proposal from the Commission and after consulting the European Parliament and the Economic and Social Committee, issue directives for the approximation of such laws, regulations or administrative provisions of the Member States as directly affect the establishment or functioning of the common market.

Article 100a

1. By way of derogation from Article 100 and save where otherwise provided in this Treaty, the following provisions shall apply for the achievement of the objectives set out in Article 7a. The Council shall, acting in accordance with the procedure referred to in Article 189b and after consulting the Economic and Social Committee, adopt the measures for the approximation of the provisions laid down by law, regulation or administrative action in Member States which have as their object the establishment and functioning of the internal market. [24]

2. Paragraph 1 shall not apply to fiscal provisions, to those relating to the free movement of persons nor to those relating to the rights and interests of employed persons.

3. The Commission, in its proposals envisaged in paragraph 1 concerning health, safety, environmental protection and consumer protection, will take as a base a high level of protection.

4. If, after the adoption of a harmonization measure by the Council acting by a qualified majority, a Member State deems it necessary to apply national provisions on grounds of major needs referred to in Article 36, or relating to protection of the environment or the working environment, it shall notify the Commission of these provisions.

The Commission shall confirm the provisions involved after having verified that they are not a means of arbitrary discrimination or a disguised restriction on trade between Member States. By way of derogation from the procedure laid down in Articles 169 and 170, the Commission or any Member State may bring the matter directly before the Court of Justice if it considers that another Member State is making improper use of the powers provided for in this Article.

---

22 As amended by Article G(20) TEU.
23 As amended by Article G(21) TEU.
24 Paragraph 1 as amended by Article G(22) TEU.

5.   The harmonization measures referred to above shall, in appropriate cases, include a safeguard clause authorising the Member States to take for one or more of the non-economic reasons referred to in Article 36, provisional measures subject to a Community control procedure.

Article 100b

1.   During 1992, the Commission shall, together with each Member State draw up an inventory of national laws, regulations and administrative provisions which fall under Article at and which have not been harmonized pursuant to that Article. The Council, acting in accordance with the provisions of Article at may decide that the provisions in force in a Member State must be recognized as being equivalent to those applied by another Member State.

2.   The provisions of Article 100a (4) shall apply by analogy.

3.   The Commission shall draw up the inventory referred to in the first subparagraph of paragraph 1 and shall submit appropriate proposals in good time to allow the Council to act before the end of 1992.

Article 100c[25]

1.   The Council, acting unanimously on a proposal from the Commission and after consulting the European Parliament, shall determine the third countries whose nationals must be in possession of a visa when crossing the external borders of the Member States.

2.   However, in the event of an emergency situation in a third country posing a threat of a sudden inflow of nationals from that country into the Community, the Council, acting by a qualified majority on a recommendation from the Commission, may introduce, for a period not exceeding six months, a visa requirement for nationals from the country in question. The visa requirement established under this paragraph may be extended in accordance with the procedure referred to in paragraph 1.

3.   From 1 January 1996, the Council shall adopt the decisions referred to in paragraph 1 by a qualified majority. The Council shall, before that date, acting by a qualified majority on a proposal from the Commission and after consulting the European Parliament, adopt measures relating to a uniform format for visas.

4.   In the areas referred to in this Article, the Commission shall examine any request made by a Member State that it submit a proposal to the Council.

5.   This Article shall be without prejudice to the exercise of the responsibilities incumbent upon the Member States with regard to the maintenance of law and order and the safeguarding of internal security.

6.   This Article shall apply to other areas if so decided pursuant to Article K.9 of the provisions of the Treaty on European Union which relate to co-operation in the fields of justice and home affairs, subject to the voting conditions determined at the same time.

7.   The provisions of the conventions in force between the Member States governing areas covered by this Article shall remain in force until their content has been replaced by directives or measures adopted pursuant to this Article.

Article 100d[26]

The Coordinating Committee consisting of senior officials set up by Article K.4 of the Treaty on European Union shall contribute, without prejudice to the provisions of Article 151, to the preparation of the proceedings of the Council in the fields referred to in Article 100c.

Article 101

Where the Commission finds that a difference between the provisions laid down by law, regulation or administrative action in Member States is distorting the conditions of competition in the common market and that the resultant distortion needs to be eliminated, it shall consult the Member States concerned.

---

25   As inserted by Article G(23) TEU.
26   As inserted by Article G(24) TEU.

If such consultation does not result in an agreement eliminating the distortion in question, the Council shall, on a proposal from the Commission, acting unanimously during the first stage and by a qualified majority thereafter, issue the necessary directives. The Commission and the Council may take any other appropriate measures provided for in this Treaty.

Article 102

1. Where there is reason to fear that the adoption or amendment of a provision laid down by law, regulation or administrative action may cause distortion within the meaning of Article 101, a Member State desiring to proceed therewith shall consult the Commission. After consulting the Member States, the Commission shall recommend to the States concerned such measures as may be appropriate to avoid the distortion in question.

2. If a State desiring to introduce or amend its own provisions does not comply with the recommendation addressed to it by the Commission, other Member States shall not be required, in pursuance of Article 101, to amend their own provisions in order to eliminate such distortion. If the Member State which has ignored the recommendation of the Commission causes distortion detrimental only to itself, the provisions of Article 101 shall not apply.

Title VI – Economic and Monetary Policy [27]

Chapter 1. Economic Policy

Article 102a

Member States shall conduct their economic policies with a view to contributing to the achievement of the objectives of the Community, as defined in Article 2, and in the context of the broad guidelines referred to in Article 103 (2). The Member States and the Community shall act in accordance with the principle of an open market economy with free competition, favouring an efficient allocation of resources, and in compliance with the principles set out in Article 3a.

Article 103

1. Member States shall regard their economic policies as a matter of common concern and shall co-ordinate them within the Council, in accordance with the provisions of Article 102a.

2. The Council shall, acting by a qualified majority on a recommendation from the Commission, formulate a draft for the broad guidelines of the economic policies of the Member States and of the Community, and shall report its findings to the European Council.

The European Council shall, acting on the basis of the report from the Council, discuss a conclusion on the broad guidelines of the economic policies of the Member States and of the Community.

On the basis of this conclusion, the Council shall, acting by a qualified majority, adopt a recommendation setting out these broad guidelines. The Council shall inform the European Parliament of its recommendation.

3. In order to ensure closer co-ordination of economic policies and sustained convergence of the economic performances of the Member States, the Council shall, on the basis of reports submitted by the Commission, monitor economic developments in each of the Member States and in the Community as well as the consistency of economic policies with the broad guidelines referred to in paragraph 2, and regularly carry out an overall assessment.

For the purposes of this multilateral surveillance, Member States shall forward information to the Commission about important measures taken by them in the field of their economic policy and such other information as they deem necessary.

4. Where it is established, under the procedure referred to in paragraph 3, that the economic policies of a Member State are not consistent with the broad guidelines referred to in paragraph 2 or that they risk jeopardizing the proper functioning of economic and monetary union, the Council may, acting by a

27   New title as inserted by Article G(28) TEU, replacing Title II, Articles 102a to 109.

qualified majority on a recommendation from the Commission, make the necessary recommendations to the Member State concerned. The Council may, acting by a qualified majority on a proposal from the Commission, decide to make its recommendations public.

The President of the Council and the Commission shall report to the European Parliament on the results of multilateral surveillance. The President of the Council may be invited to appear before the competent Committee of the European Parliament if the Council has made its recommendations public.

5. The Council, acting in accordance with the procedure referred to in Article 189c, may adopt detailed rules for the multilateral surveillance procedure referred to in paragraphs 3 and 4 of this Article.

Article 103a

1. Without prejudice to any other procedures provided for in this Treaty, the Council may, acting unanimously on a proposal from the Commission, decide upon the measures appropriate to the economic situation, in particular if severe difficulties arise in the supply of certain products.

2. Where a Member State is in difficulties or is seriously threatened with severe difficulties caused by exceptional occurrences beyond its control, the Council may, acting unanimously on a proposal from the Commission, grant, under certain conditions, Community financial assistance to the Member State concerned. Where the severe difficulties are caused by natural disasters, the Council shall act by qualified majority. The President of the Council shall inform the European Parliament of the decision taken.

Article 104

1. Overdraft facilities or any other type of credit facility with the ECB or with the central banks of the Member States (hereinafter referred to as "national central banks") in favour of Community institutions or bodies, central governments, regional, local or other public authorities, other bodies governed by public law, or public undertakings of Member States shall be prohibited, as shall the purchase directly from them by the ECB or national central banks of debt instruments.

2. Paragraph 1 shall not apply to publicly-owned credit institutions which, in the context of the supply of reserves by central banks, shall be given the same treatment by national central banks and the ECB as private credit institutions.

Article 104a

1. Any measure, not based on prudential considerations, establishing privileged access by Community institutions or bodies, central governments, regional, local or other public authorities, other bodies governed by public law, or public undertakings of Member States to financial institutions shall be prohibited.

2. The Council, acting in accordance with the procedure referred to in Article 189c, shall, before 1 January 1994, specify definitions for the application of the prohibition referred to in paragraph 1.

Article 104b

1. The Community shall not be liable for or assume the commitments of central governments, regional, local or other public authorities, other bodies governed by public law, or public undertakings of any Member State, without prejudice to mutual financial guarantees for the joint execution of a specific project. A Member State shall not be liable for or assume the commitments of central governments, regional, local or other public authorities, other bodies governed by public law or public undertakings of another Member State, without prejudice to mutual financial guarantees for the joint execution of a specific project.

2. If necessary, the Council, acting in accordance with the procedure referred to in Article 189c, may specify definitions for the application of the prohibitions referred to in Article 104 and in this Article.

Annex

Article 104c

1. Member States shall avoid excessive government deficits.

2. The Commission shall monitor the development of the budgetary situation and of the stock of government debt in the Member States with a view to identifying gross errors. In particular it shall examine compliance with budgetary discipline on the basis of the following two criteria:

(a) whether the ratio of the planned or actual government deficit to gross domestic product exceeds a reference value, unless

- either the ratio has declined substantially and continuously and reached a level that comes close to the reference value;

- or, alternatively, the excess over the reference value is only exceptional and temporary and the ratio remains close to the reference value;

(b) whether the ratio of government debt to gross domestic product exceeds a reference value, unless the ratio is sufficiently diminishing and approaching the reference value at a satisfactory pace.

The reference values are specified in the Protocol on the excessive deficit procedure annexed to this Treaty.

3. If a Member State does not fulfil the requirements under one or both of these criteria, the Commission shall prepare a report. The report of the Commission shall also take into account whether the government deficit exceeds government investment expenditure and take into account all other relevant factors, including the medium term economic and budgetary position of the Member State.

The Commission may also prepare a report if, notwithstanding the fulfilment of the requirements under the criteria, it is of the opinion that there is a risk of an excessive deficit in a Member State.

4. The Committee provided for in Article 109c shall formulate an opinion on the report of the Commission.

5. If the Commission considers that an excessive deficit in a Member State exists or may occur, the Commission shall address an opinion to the Council.

6. The Council shall, acting by a qualified majority on a recommendation from the Commission, and having considered any observations which the Member State concerned may wish to make, decide after an overall assessment whether an excessive deficit exists.

7. Where the existence of an excessive deficit is decided according to paragraph 6, the Council shall make recommendations to the Member State concerned with a view to bringing that situation to an end within a given period. Subject to the provisions of paragraph 8, these recommendations shall not be made public.

8. Where it establishes that there has been no effective action in response to its recommendations within the period to remedy the situation.

Ilaid down, the Council may make its recommendations public.

9. If a Member State persists in failing to put into practice the recommendations of the Council, the Council may decide to give notice to the Member State to take, within a specified time limit, measures for the deficit reduction which is judged necessary by the Council in order n such a case, the Council may request the Member State concerned to submit reports in accordance with a specific timetable in order to examine the adjustment efforts of that Member State.

10. The rights to bring actions provided for in Articles 169 and 170 may not be exercised within the framework of paragraphs 1 to 9 of this article.

11. As long as a Member State fails to comply with a decision taken in accordance with paragraph 9, the Council may decide to apply or, as the case may be, intensify one or more of the following measures:

- to require the Member State concerned to publish additional information, to be specified by the Council, before issuing bonds and securities;

- to invite the European Investment Bank to reconsider its lending policy towards the Member State concerned;

— to require the Member State concerned to make a non-interest-bearing deposit of an appropriate size with the Community until the excessive deficit has, in the view of the Council, been corrected;

— to impose fines of an appropriate size.

The President of the Council shall inform the European Parliament of the decisions taken.

12. The Council shall abrogate any or all of its decisions referred to in paragraphs 6 to 9 and 11 to the extent that the excessive deficit in the Member State concerned has, in the view of the Council, been corrected. If the Council has previously made public recommendations, it shall, as soon as the decision under paragraph 8 has been abrogated, make a public statement that an excessive deficit in the Member State concerned no longer exists.

13. When taking decisions referred to in paragraphs 7 to 9, 11 and 12, the Council shall act on a recommendation from the Commission by a majority of two thirds of the votes of its members weighted in accordance with Article 148(2)), excluding the votes of the representative of the Member State concerned.

14. Further provisions relating to the implementation of the procedure described in this Article are set out in the Protocol on the excessive deficit procedure annexed to this Treaty.

The Council shall, acting unanimously on a proposal from the Commission and after consulting the European Parliament and the ECB, adopt the appropriate provisions which shall then replace the said Protocol.

Subject to the other provisions of this paragraph the Council shall, before 1 January 1994, acting by a qualified majority on a proposal from the Commission and after consulting the European Parliament, lay down detailed rules and definitions for the application of the provisions of the said Protocol.

Chapter 2. Monetary Policy

Article 105

1. The primary objective of the ESCB shall be to maintain price stability. Without prejudice to the objective of price stability, the ESCB shall support the general economic policies in the Community with a view to contributing to the achievement of the objectives of the Community as laid down in Article 2. The ESCB shall act in accordance with the principle of an open market economy with free competition, favouring an efficient allocation of resources, and in compliance with the principles set out in Article 3a.

2. The basic tasks to be carried out through the ESCB shall be:

— to define and implement the monetary policy of the Community;

— to conduct foreign exchange operations consistent with the provisions of Article 109;

— to hold and manage the official foreign reserves of the Member States;

— to promote the smooth operation of payment systems.

3. The third indent of paragraph 2 shall be without prejudice to the holding and management by the governments of Member States of foreign exchange working balances.

4. The ECB shall be consulted:

— on any proposed Community act in its fields of competence;

— by national authorities regarding any draft legislative provision in its fields of competence, but within the limits and under the conditions set out by the Council in accordance with the procedure laid down in Article 106 (6).

The ECB may submit opinions to the appropriate Community institutions or bodies or to national authorities on matters in its fields of competence.

5. The ESCB shall contribute to the smooth conduct of policies pursued by the competent authorities relating to the prudential supervision of credit institutions and the stability of the financial system.

6. The Council may, acting unanimously on a proposal from the Commission and after consulting the ECB and after receiving the assent of the European Parliament, confer upon the ECB specific tasks

concerning policies relating to the prudential supervision of credit institutions and other financial institutions with the exception of insurance undertakings.

Article 105a

1. The ECB shall have the exclusive right to authorize the issue of bank notes within the Community. The ECB and the national central banks may issue such notes. The bank notes issued by the ECB and the national central banks shall be the only such notes to have the status of legal tender within the Community.

2. Member States may issue coins subject to approval by the ECB of the volume of the issue. The Council may, acting in accordance with the procedure referred to in Article 189c and after consulting the ECB, adopt measures to harmonize the denominations and technical specifications of all coins intended for circulation to the extent necessary to permit their smooth circulation within the Community.

Article 106

1. The ESCB shall be composed of the ECB and of the national central banks.

2. The ECB shall have legal personality.

3. The ESCB shall be governed by the decision-making bodies of the ECB which shall be the Governing Council and the Executive Board.

4. The Statute of the ESCB is laid down in a Protocol annexed to this Treaty.

5. Articles 5.1, 5.2, 5.3, 17, 18, 19.1, 22, 23, 24, 26, 32.2, 32.3, 32.4, 32.6, 33.1 (a) and 36 of the Statute of the ESCB may be amended by the Council, acting either by a qualified majority on a recommendation from the ECB and after consulting the Commission or unanimously on a proposal from the Commission and after consulting the ECB. In either case, the assent of the European Parliament shall be required.

6. The Council, acting by a qualified majority either on a proposal from the Commission and after consulting the European Parliament and the ECB or on a recommendation from the ECB and after consulting the European Parliament and the Commission, shall adopt the provisions referred to in Articles 4, 5.4, 19.2, 20, 28.1, 29.2, 30.4 and 34.3 of the Statute of the ESCB.

Article 107

When exercising the powers and carrying out the tasks and duties conferred upon them by this Treaty and the Statute of the ESCB, neither the ECB, nor a national central bank, nor any member of their decision-making bodies shall seek or take instructions from Community institutions or bodies, from any government of a Member State or from any other body. The Community institutions and bodies and the governments of the Member States undertake to respect this principle and not to seek to influence the members of the decision-making bodies of the ECB or of the national central banks in the performance of their tasks.

Article 108

Each Member State shall ensure, at the latest at the date of the establishment of the ESCB, that its national legislation including the statutes of its national central bank is compatible with this Treaty and the Statute of the ESCB.

Article 108a

1. In order to carry out the tasks entrusted to the ESCB, the ECB shall, in accordance with the provisions of this Treaty and under the conditions laid down in the Statute of the ESCB:

– make regulations to the extent necessary to implement the tasks defined in Article 3.1, first indent, Articles 19.1, 22 and 25.2 of the Statute of the ESCB and in cases which shall be laid down in the acts of the Council referred to in Article 106 (6);

– take decisions necessary for carrying out the tasks entrusted to the ESCB under this Treaty and the Statute of the ESCB;

– make recommendations and deliver opinions.

2. A regulation shall have general application. It shall be binding in its entirety and directly applicable in all Member States.

Recommendations and opinions shall have no binding force.

A decision shall be binding in its entirety upon those to whom it is addressed.

Articles 190 to 192 shall apply to regulations and decisions adopted by the ECB.

The ECB may decide to publish its decisions, recommendations and opinions.

3. Within the limits and under the conditions adopted by the Council under the procedures laid down in Article 106 (6), the ECB shall be entitled to impose fines or periodic penalty payments on undertakings for failure to comply with obligations under its regulations and decisions.

Article 109

1. By way of derogation from Article 228, the Council may, acting unanimously on a recommendation from the ECB or from the Commission, and after consulting the ECB in an endeavour to reach a consensus consistent with the objective of price stability, after consulting the European Parliament, in accordance with the procedure in paragraph 3 for determining the arrangements, conclude formal agreements on an exchange rate system for the ECU in relation to non-Community currencies. The Council may, acting by a qualified majority on a recommendation from the ECB or from the Commission, and after consulting the ECB in an endeavour to reach a consensus consistent with the objective of price stability, adopt, adjust or abandon the central rates of the ECU within the exchange rate system. The President of the Council shall inform the European Parliament of the adoption, adjustment or abandonment of the ECU central rates.

2. In the absence of an exchange rate system in relation to one or more non-Community currencies as referred to in paragraph 1, the Council, acting by a qualified majority either on a recommendation from the Commission and after consulting the ECB or on a recommendation from the ECB, may formulate general orientations for exchange rate policy in relation to these currencies. These general orientations shall be without prejudice to the primary objective of the ESCB to maintain price stability.

3. By way of derogation from Article 228, where agreements concerning monetary or foreign exchange regime matters need to be negotiated by the Community with one or more States or international organizations, the Council, acting by a qualified majority on a recommendation from the Commission and after consulting the ECB, shall decide the arrangements for the negotiation and for the conclusion of such agreements. These arrangements shall ensure that the Community expresses a single position. The Commission shall be fully associated with the negotiations.

Agreements concluded in accordance with this paragraph shall be binding on the institutions of the Community, on the ECB and on Member States.

4. Subject to paragraph 1, the Council shall, on a proposal from the Commission and after consulting the ECB, acting by a qualified majority decide on the position of the Community at international level as regards issues of particular relevance to economic and monetary union and, acting unanimously, decide its representation in compliance with the allocation of powers laid down in Articles 103 and 105.

5. Without prejudice to Community competence and Community agreements as regards economic and monetary union, Member States may negotiate in international bodies and conclude international agreements.

Chapter 3. Institutional Provisions

Article 109a

1. The Governing Council of the ECB shall comprise the members of the Executive Board of the ECB and the Governors of the national central banks.

2. (a)   The Executive Board shall comprise the President, the Vice-President and four other members.

(b)   The President, the Vice-President and the other members of the Executive Board shall be appointed from among persons of recognized standing and professional experience in monetary or banking matters by common accord of the Governments of the Member States at the level of Heads of State or of Government, on a recommendation from the Council, after it has consulted the European Parliament and the Governing Council of the ECB.

Their term of office shall be eight years and shall not be renewable.

Only nationals of Member States may be members of the Executive Board.

Article 109b

1.   The President of the Council and a member of the Commission may participate, without having the right to vote, in meetings of the Governing Council of the ECB.

The President of the Council may submit a motion for deliberation to the Governing Council of the ECB.

2.   The President of the ECB shall be invited to participate in Council meetings when the Council is discussing matters relating to the objectives and tasks of the ESCB.

3.   The ECB shall address an annual report on the activities of the ESCB and on the monetary policy of both the previous and current year to the European Parliament, the Council and the Commission, and also to the European Council. The President of the ECB shall present this report to the Council and to the European Parliament, which may hold a general debate on that basis.

The President of the ECB and the other members of the Executive Board may, at the request of the European Parliament or on their own initiative, be heard by the competent Committees of the European Parliament.

Article 109c

1.   In order to promote co-ordination of the policies of Member States to the full extent needed for the functioning of the internal market, a Monetary Committee with advisory status is hereby set up.

It shall have the following tasks:

– *to keep under review the monetary and financial situation of the Member States and of the Community and the general payments system of the Member States and to report regularly thereon to the Council and to the Commission;*

– *to deliver opinions at the request of the Council or of the Commission, or on its own initiative for submission to these institutions;*

– *without prejudice to Article 151, to contribute to the preparation of the work of the Council referred to in Articles 73f, 73g, 103 (2), (3), (4) and (5), 103a, 104a, 104b, 104c, 109e (2), 109f (6), 109h, 109i, 109j (2) and 109k (1);*

– *to examine, at least once a year, the situation regarding the movement of capital and the freedom of payments, as they result from the application of this Treaty and of measures adopted by the Council; the examination shall cover all measures relating to capital movements and payments; the Committee shall report to the Commission and to the Council on the outcome of this examination.*

The Member States and the Commission shall each appoint two members of the Monetary Committee.

2.   At the start of the third stage, an Economic and Financial Committee shall be set up. The Monetary Committee provided for in paragraph 1 shall be dissolved.

The Economic and Financial Committee shall have the following tasks:

– *to deliver opinions at the request of the Council or of the Commission, or on its own initiative for submission to these institutions;*

– *to keep under review the economic and financial situation of the Member States and of the Community and to report regularly thereon to the Council and to the Commission, in particular on financial relations with third countries and international institutions;*

– *without prejudice to Article 151, to contribute to the preparation of the work of the Council referred to in Articles 73f, 73g, 103 (2), (3), (4) and (5), 103a, 104a, 104b, 104c, 105 (6), 105a (2), 106 (5) and (6), 109, 109h, 109i (2) and (3), 109k (2), 109l (4) and (5), and to carry out other advisory and preparatory tasks assigned to it by the Council;*

– *to examine, at least once a year, the situation regarding the movement of capital and the freedom of payments, as they result from the application of this Treaty and of measures adopted by the Council; the examination shall cover all measures relating to capital movements and payments; the Committee shall report to the Commission and to the Council on the outcome of this examination.*

The Member States, the Commission and the ECB shall each appoint no more than two members of the Committee.

3. The Council shall, acting by a qualified majority on a proposal from the Commission and after consulting the ECB and the Committee referred to in this Article, lay down detailed provisions concerning the composition of the Economic and Financial Committee. The President of the Council shall inform the European Parliament of such a decision.

4. In addition to the tasks set out in paragraph 2, if and as long as there are Member States with a derogation as referred to in Article 109k and 109l, the Committee shall keep under review the monetary and financial situation and the general payments systems of those Member States and report regularly thereon to the Council and to the Commission.

Article 109d

For matters within the scope of Articles 103 (4), 104c with the exception of paragraph 14, 109, 109j, 109k and 109l (4) and (5), the Council or a Member State may request the Commission to make a recommendation or a proposal as appropriate. The Commission shall examine this request and submit its conclusions to the Council without delay.

Chapter 4. Transitional Provisions

Article 109e

1. The second stage for achieving economic and monetary union shall begin on 1 January 1994.

2. Before that date

(a) each Member State shall

– *adopt, where necessary, appropriate measures to comply with the prohibitions laid down in Article 73b, without prejudice to Article 73e, and in Articles 104 and 104a (1);*

– *adopt, if necessary, with a view to permitting the assessment provided for in subparagraph (b), multiannual programmes intended to ensure the lasting convergence necessary for the achievement of economic and monetary union, in particular with regard to price stability and sound public finances;*

(b) the Council shall, on the basis of a report from the Commission, assess the progress made with regard to economic and monetary convergence, in particular with regard to price stability and sound public finances, and the progress made with the implementation of Community law concerning the internal market.

3. The provisions of Articles 104, 104a (1), 104b (1) and 104c with the exception of paragraphs 1, 9, 11 and 14 shall apply from the beginning of the second stage.

The provisions of Articles 103a (2), 104c (1), (9) and (11), 105, 105a, 107, 109, 109a, 109b and 109c (2) and (4) shall apply from the beginning of the third stage.

4. In the second stage, Member States shall endeavour to avoid excessive government deficits.

5. During the second stage, each Member State shall, as appropriate, start the process leading to the independence of its central bank, in accordance with Article 108.

Article 109f

1. At the start of the second stage, a European Monetary Institute (hereinafter referred to as "EMI") shall be established and take up its duties; it shall have legal personality and be directed and managed by a Council, consisting of a President and the Governors of the national central banks, one of whom shall be Vice-President.

The President shall be appointed by common accord of the Governments of the Member States at the level of Heads of State or of Government, on a recommendation from, as the case may be, the Committee of Governors of the central banks of the Member States (hereinafter referred to as "Committee of Governors") or the Council of the EMI, and after consulting the European Parliament and the Council. The President shall be selected from among persons of recognized standing and professional experience in monetary or banking matters. Only nationals of Member States may be president of the EMI. The Council of the EMI shall appoint the Vice-President.

The Statute of the EMI is laid down in a Protocol annexed to this Treaty.

The Committee of Governors shall be dissolved at the start of the second stage.

2. *The EMI shall:*

–   *strengthen co-operation between the national central banks;*

–   *strengthen the co-ordination of the monetary policies of the Member States, with the aim of ensuring price stability;*

–   *monitor the functioning of the European Monetary System;*

–   *hold consultations concerning issues falling within the competence of the national central banks and affecting the stability of financial institutions and markets;*

–   *take over the tasks of the European Monetary Cooperation Fund, which shall be dissolved; the modalities of dissolution are laid down in the Statute of the EMI;*

–   *facilitate the use of the ECU and oversee its the development, including the smooth functioning of the ECU clearing system.*

3. *For the preparation of the third stage, the EMI shall:*

–   *prepare the instruments and the procedures necessary for carrying out a single monetary policy in the third stage;*

–   *promote the harmonization, where necessary, of the rules and practices governing the collection, compilation and distribution of statistics in the areas within its field of competence;*

–   *prepare the rules for operations to be undertaken by the national central banks within the framework of the ESCB;*

–   *promote the efficiency of cross-border payments;*

–   *supervise the technical preparation of ECU banknotes.*

At the latest by 31 December 1996, the EMI shall specify the regulatory, organizational and logistical framework necessary for the ESCB to perform its tasks in the third stage. This framework shall be submitted for decision to the ECB at the date of its establishment.

4. *The EMI, acting by a majority of two-thirds of the members of its Council, may:*

–   *formulate opinions or recommendations on the overall orientation of monetary policy and exchange rate policy as well as on related measures introduced in each Member State;*

–   *submit opinions or recommendations to Governments and to the Council on policies which might affect the internal or external monetary situation in the Community and, in particular, the functioning of the European Monetary System;*

–   *make recommendations to the monetary authorities of the Member States concerning the conduct of their monetary policy.*

5. *The EMI, acting unanimously, may decide to publish its opinions and its recommendations.*

6. *The EMI shall be consulted by the Council regarding any proposed Community act within its field of competence.*

Within the limits and under the conditions set out by the Council, acting by a qualified majority on a proposal from the Commission and after consulting the European Parliament and the EMI, the EMI shall be consulted by the authorities of the Member States on any draft legislative provision within its field of competence.

7.   The Council may, acting unanimously on a proposal from the Commission and after consulting the European Parliament and the EMI, confer upon the EMI other tasks for the preparation of the third stage.

8.   Where this Treaty provides for a consultative role for the ECB, references to the ECB shall be read as referring to the EMI before the establishment of the ECB.

Where this Treaty provides for a consultative role for the EMI, references to the EMI shall be read, before 1 January 1994, as referring to the Committee of Governors.

9.   During the second stage, the term "ECB" used in Articles 173,175,176,177,180 and 215 shall be read as referring to the EMI.

Article 109g

The currency composition of the ECU basket shall not be changed.

From the start of the third stage, the value of the ECU shall be irrevocably fixed in accordance with Article 109l (4)

Article 109h

1.   Where a Member State is in difficulties or is seriously threatened with difficulties as regards its balance of payments either as a result of an overall disequilibrium in its balance of payments, or as a result of the type of currency at its disposal, and where such difficulties are liable in particular to jeopardize the functioning of the common market or the progressive implementation of the common commercial policy, the Commission shall immediately investigate the position of the State in question and the action which, making use of all the means at its disposal, that State has taken or may take in accordance with the provisions of this Treaty. The Commission shall state what measures it recommends the State concerned to take.

If the action taken by a Member State and the measures suggested by the Commission do not prove sufficient to overcome the difficulties which have arisen or which threaten, the Commission shall, after consulting the Committee referred to in Article 109c, recommend to the Council the granting of mutual assistance and appropriate methods therefor.

The Commission shall keep the Council regularly informed of the situation and of how it is developing.

2.   The Council, acting by a qualified majority, shall grant such mutual assistance; it shall adopt directives or decisions laying down the conditions and details of such assistance, which may take such forms as:

(a) a concerted approach to or within any other international organizations to which Member States may have recourse;

(b) measures needed to avoid deflection of trade where the State which is in difficulties maintains or reintroduces quantitative restrictions against third countries;

(c) the granting of limited credits by other Member States, subject to their agreement.

3.   If the mutual assistance recommended by the Commission is not granted by the Council or if the mutual assistance granted and the measures taken are insufficient, the Commission shall authorize the State which is in difficulties to take protective measures, the conditions and details of which the Commission shall determine.

Such authorization may be revoked and such conditions and details may be changed by the Council acting by a qualified majority.

4.   Subject to Article 109k (6), this Article shall cease to apply from the beginning of the third stage.

Article 109i

1.   Where a sudden crisis in the balance of payments occurs and a decision within the meaning of Article 109h (2) is not immediately taken, the Member State concerned may, as a precaution, take the

necessary protective measures. Such measures must cause the least possible disturbance in the functioning of the common market and must not be wider in scope than is strictly necessary to remedy the sudden difficulties which have arisen.

2. *The Commission and the other Member States shall be informed of such protective measures not later than when they enter into force. The Commission may recommend to the Council the granting of mutual assistance under Article 109h.*

3. *After the Commission has delivered an opinion and the Committee referred to in Article 109c has been consulted, the Council may, acting by a qualified majority, decide that the State concerned shall amend, suspend or abolish the protective measures referred to above.*

4. *Subject to Article 109k (6), this Article shall cease to apply from the beginning of the third stage.*

Article 109j

1. *The Commission and the EMI shall report to the Council on the progress made in the fulfilment by the Member States of their obligations regarding the achievement of economic and monetary union. These reports shall include an examination of the compatibility between each Member State's national legislation, including the statutes of its national central bank, and Articles 107 and 108 of this Treaty and the Statute of the ESCB. The reports shall also examine the achievement of a high degree of sustainable convergence by reference to the fulfilment by each Member State of the following criteria:*

– *the achievement of a high degree of price stability; this will be apparent from a rate of inflation which is close to that of, at most, the three best performing Member States in terms of price stability;*

– *the sustainability of the government financial position; this will be apparent from having achieved a government budgetary position without a deficit that is excessive as determined in accordance with Article 104c (6);*

– *the observance of the normal fluctuation margins provided for by the Exchange Rate Mechanism of the European Monetary System, for at least two years, without devaluing against the currency of any other Member State;*

– *the durability of convergence achieved by the Member State and of its participation in the Exchange Rate Mechanism of the European Monetary System being reflected in the long-term interest rate levels.*

The four criteria mentioned in this paragraph and the relevant periods over which they are to be respected are developed further in a Protocol annexed to this Treaty. The reports of the Commission and the EMI shall also take account of the development of the ECU, the results of the integration of markets, the situation and development of the balances of payments on current account and an examination of the development of unit labour costs and other price indexes.

2. *On the basis of these reports, the Council, acting by a qualified majority on a recommendation from the Commission, shall assess:*

– *for each Member State, whether it fulfills the necessary conditions for the adoption of a single currency;*

– *whether a majority of the Member States fulfil the necessary conditions for the adoption of a single currency,*

   and recommend its findings to the Council, meeting in the composition of the Heads of State or of Government. The European Parliament shall be consulted and forward its opinion to the Council, meeting in the composition of Heads of State or of Government.

3. *Taking due account of the reports as referred to in paragraph 1 and the opinion of the European Parliament referred to in paragraph 2, the Council, meeting in the composition of Heads of State or of Government, shall, acting by a qualified majority, not later than 31 December 1996:*

– *decide, on the basis of the recommendations of the Council referred to in paragraph 2, whether a majority of the Member States fulfil the necessary conditions for the adoption of a single currency;*

– *decide whether it is appropriate for the Community to enter the third stage, and if so*

– set the date for the beginning of the third stage.

4. If by the end of 1997 the date for the beginning of the third stage has not been set, the third stage shall start on 1 January 1999. Before 1 July 1998, the Council, meeting in the composition of Heads of State or of Government, after a repetition of the procedure provided for in paragraphs 1 and 2, with the exception of the second indent of paragraph 2, taking into account the reports as referred to in paragraph 1 and the opinion of the European Parliament, shall, acting by a qualified majority and on the basis of the recommendations of the Council referred to in paragraph 2, confirm which Member States fulfil the necessary conditions for the adoption of a single currency.

Article 109k

1. If the decision has been taken to set the date in accordance with Article 109j (3), the Council shall, on the basis of recommendations referred to in Article 109j (2), acting by a qualified majority on a recommendation from the Commission, decide whether any, and if so which, Member States shall have a derogation as defined in paragraph 3 of this Article. Such Member States shall in this Treaty be referred to as "Member States with a derogation".

If the Council has confirmed which Member States fulfil the necessary conditions for the adoption of a single currency, in accordance with Article 109j (4), those Member States which do not fulfil the conditions shall have a derogation as defined in paragraph 3 of this Article. Such Member States shall in this Treaty be referred to as "Member States with a derogation".

2. At least once every two years, or at the request of a Member State with a derogation, the Commission and the ECB shall report to the Council in accordance with the procedure laid down in Article 109j (1). After consulting the European Parliament and after discussion in the Council, meeting in the composition of the Heads of State or of Government, the Council shall, acting by a qualified majority on a proposal from the Commission, decide which Member States with a derogation fulfil the necessary conditions on the basis of the criteria set out in Article 109j (1), and abrogate the derogations of the Member States concerned.

3. A derogation referred to in paragraph 1 shall entail that the following Articles do not apply to the Member State concerned: Articles 104c (9) and (11), 105 (1), (2), (3) and (5), 105a, 108a, 109 and 109a (2)(b). The exclusion of such a Member State and its national central bank from rights and obligations within the ESCB is laid down in Chapter IX of the Statute of the ESCB.

4. In Articles 105 (1), (2) and (3), 105a, 108a, 109 and 109a (2)(b), "Member States" shall be read as "Member States without a derogation".

5. The voting rights of Member States with a derogation shall be suspended for the Council decisions referred to in the Articles of this Treaty mentioned in paragraph 3. In that case, by way of derogation from Articles 148 and 189a (1), a qualified majority shall be defined as two thirds of the votes of the representatives of the Member States without a derogation weighted in accordance with Article 148 (2), and unanimity of those Member States shall be required for an act requiring unanimity.

6. Articles 109h and 109i shall continue to apply to a Member State with a derogation.

Article 109l

1. Immediately after the decision on the date for the beginning of the third stage has been taken in accordance with Article 109j (3), or, as the case may be, immediately after 1 July 1998:

– the Council shall adopt the provisions referred to in Article 106 (6);

– the governments of the Member States without a derogation shall appoint, in accordance with the procedure set out in Article 50 of the Statute of the ESCB, the President, the Vice-President and the other members of the Executive Board of the ECB. If there are Member States with a derogation, the number of members of the Executive Board may be smaller than provided for in Article 11.1 of the Statute of the ESCB, but in no circumstances shall it be less than four.

As soon as the Executive Board is appointed, the ESCB and the ECB shall be established and shall prepare for their full operation as described in this Treaty and the Statute of the ESCB. The full exercise of their powers shall start from the first day of the third stage.

2.   As soon as the ECB is established, it shall, if necessary, take over tasks of the EMI. The EMI shall go into liquidation upon the establishment of the ECB; the modalities of liquidation are laid down in the Statute of the EMI.

3.   If and as long as there are Member States with a derogation, and without prejudice to Article 106 (3) of this Treaty, the General Council of the ECB referred to in Article 45 of the Statute of the ESCB shall be constituted as a third decision-making body of the ECB.

4.   At the starting date of the third stage, the Council shall, acting with the unanimity of the Member States without a derogation, on a proposal from the Commission and after consulting the ECB, adopt the conversion rates at which their currencies shall be irrevocably fixed and at which irrevocably fixed rate the ECU shall be substituted for these currencies, and the ECU will become a currency in its own right. This measure shall by itself not modify the external value of the ECU. The Council shall, acting according to the same procedure, also take the other measures necessary for the rapid introduction of the ECU as the single currency of those Member States.

5.   If it is decided, according to the procedure set out in Article 109k (2), to abrogate a derogation, the Council shall, acting with the unanimity of the Member States without a derogation and the Member State concerned, on a proposal from the Commission and after consulting the ECB, adopt the rate at which the ECU shall be substituted for the currency of the Member State concerned, and take the other measures necessary for the introduction of the ECU as the single currency in the Member State concerned.

Article 109m

1.   Until the beginning of the third stage, each Member State shall treat its exchange rate policy as a matter of common interest. In so doing, Member States shall take account of the experience acquired in co-operation within the framework of the European Monetary System (EMS) and in developing the ECU, and shall respect existing powers in this field.

2.   From the beginning of the third stage and for as long as a Member State has a derogation, paragraph 1 shall apply by analogy to the exchange rate policy of that Member State.

Title VII – Common Commercial Policy [28]

Article 110

By establishing a customs union between themselves Member States aim to contribute, in the common interest, to the harmonious development of world trade, the progressive abolition of restrictions on international trade and the lowering of customs barriers.

The common commercial policy shall take into account the favourable effect which the abolition of customs duties between Member States may have on the increase in the competitive strength of undertakings in those States.

Article 111

(repealed)

Article 112

1.   Without prejudice to obligations undertaken by them within the framework of other international organizations, Member States shall, before the end of the transitional period, progressively harmonize the systems where by they grant aid for exports to third countries, to the extent necessary to ensure that competition between undertakings of the Community is not distorted.

---

28   New title as inserted by Article G(26) TEU, replacing Chapter 4 of Title II, Articles 110 to 116.

On a proposal from the Commission, the Council, shall, acting unanimously until the end of the second stage and by a qualified majority thereafter, issue any directives needed for this purpose.

2. The preceding provisions shall not apply to such drawback of customs duties or charges having equivalent effect nor to such repayment of indirect taxation including turnover taxes, excise duties and other indirect taxes as is allowed when goods are exported from a Member State to a third country, in so far as such drawback or repayment does not exceed the amount imposed, directly or indirectly, on the products exported.

Article 113[29]

1. *The* common commercial policy shall be based on uniform principles, particularly in regard to changes in tariff rates, the conclusion of tariff and trade agreements, the achievement of uniformity in measures of liberalization, export policy and measures to protect trade such as those to be taken in the event of dumping or subsidies.

2. The Commission shall submit proposals to the Council for implementing the common commercial policy.

3. Where agreements with *one or more States or international organizations* need to be negotiated, the Commission shall make recommendations to the Council, which shall authorize the Commission to open the necessary negotiations.

The Commission shall conduct these negotiations in consultation with a special committee appointed by the Council to assist the Commission in this task and within the framework of such directives as the Council may issue to it.

The relevant provisions of Article 228 shall apply.

4. In exercising the powers conferred upon it by this Article, the Council shall act by a qualified majority.

Article 114

(repealed)

Article 115[30]

In order to ensure that the execution of measures of commercial policy taken in accordance with this Treaty by any Member State is not obstructed by deflection of trade, or where differences between such measures lead to economic difficulties in one or more Member States, the Commission shall recommend the methods for the requisite co-operation between Member States. Failing this, the Commission *may authorize* Member States to take the necessary protective measures, the conditions and details of which it shall determine.

In the case of urgency, Member States shall request authorization to take the necessary measures themselves from the Commission, which shall take a decision as soon as possible; the Member States concerned shall then notify the measures to the other Member States. The Commission may decide at any time that the Member States concerned shall amend or abolish the measures in question.

In the selection of such measures, priority shall be given to those which cause the least disturbance to the functioning of the common market.

Article 116

(repealed)

---

29   As amended by Article G(28) TEU.
30   As amended by Article G(30) TEU.

Title VIII – Social Policy, Education, Vocational Training and Youth[31]
Chapter 1. Social Provisions

Article 117

Member States agree upon the need to promote improved working conditions and an improved standard of living for workers, so as to make possible their harmonization while the improvement is being maintained.

They believe that such a development will ensue not only from the functioning of the common market, which will favour the harmonization of social systems, but also from the procedures provided for in this Treaty and from the approximation of provisions laid down by law, regulation or administrative action.

Article 118

Without prejudice to the other provisions of this Treaty and in conformity with its general objectives, the Commission shall have the task of promoting close co-operation between Member States in the social field, particularly in matters relating to:

– employment;
– labour law and working conditions;
– basic and advanced vocational training;
– social security;
– prevention of occupational accidents and diseases;
– occupational hygiene;
– the right of association, and collective bargaining between employers and workers.

To this end, the Commission shall act in close contact with Member States by making studies, delivering opinions and arranging consultations both on problems arising at national level and on those of concern to international organizations.

Before delivering the opinions provided for in this Article, the Commission shall consult the Economic and Social Committee.

Article 118a

1. Member States shall pay particular attention to encouraging improvements, especially in the working environment, as regards the health and safety workers, and shall set as their objective the harmonization of conditions in this area, while maintaining the improvements made.

2. In order to help achieve the objective laid down in the first paragraph, the Council, *acting in accordance with the procedure referred to in Article 189c* and after consulting the Economic and Social Committee, shall adopt by means of directives, minimum requirements for gradual implementation, having regard to the conditions and technical rules obtaining in each of the Member States.[32]

Such directives shall avoid imposing administrative, financial and legal constraints in a way which would hold back the creation and development of small and medium-sized undertakings.

3. The provisions adopted pursuant to this Article shall not prevent any Member States from maintaining or introducing more stringent measures for the protection of working conditions compatible with this Treaty.

Article 118b

The Commission shall endeavour to develop the dialogue between management and labour at European level which could, if the two sides consider it desirable, lead to relations based on agreement.

31   Title as introduced by Article G(32) TEU.
32   First subparagraph as amended by Article G(33) TEU.

Article 119

Each Member State shall during the first stage ensure and subsequently maintain the application of the principle that men and women should receive equal pay for equal work.

For the purpose of this Article, "pay" means the ordinary basic or minimum wage or salary and any other consideration, whether in cash or in kind, which the worker receives, directly or indirectly, in respect of his employment from his employer.

Equal pay without discrimination based on sex means:

(a) that pay for the same work at piece rates shall be calculated on the basis of the same unit of measurement;

(b) that pay for work at time rates shall be the same for the same job.

Article 120

Member States shall endeavour to maintain the existing equivalence between paid holiday schemes.

Article 121

The Council may, acting unanimously and after consulting the Economic and Social Committee, assign to the Commission tasks in connection with the implementation of common measures, particularly as regards social security for the migrant workers referred to in Articles 48 to 51.

Article 122

The Commission shall include a separate chapter on social developments within the Community in its annual report to the European Parliament.

The European Parliament may invite the Commission to draw up reports on any particular problems concerning social conditions.

Chapter 2. The European Social Fund

Article 123 [33]

In order to improve employment opportunities for workers in the *internal* market and to contribute thereby to raising the standard of living, a European Social Fund is hereby established in accordance with the provisions set out below; *it shall aim to* render the employment of workers easier and to increase their geographical and occupational mobility within the Community, *and to facilitate their adaptation to industrial changes and to changes in production systems, in particular through vocational training and retraining.*

Article 124

The Fund shall be administered by the Commission.

The Commission shall be assisted in this task by a Committee presided over by a member of the Commission and composed of representatives of Governments, trade unions and employers' organizations.

Article 125

The Council, acting in accordance with the procedure referred to in Article 189c, and after consulting the Economic and Social Committee, shall adopt implementing decisions relating to the European Social Fund.

---

33   As amended by Article G(34) TEU.

Chapter 3. Education, Vocational Training and Youth

Article 126[34]

1.   The Community shall contribute to the development of quality education by encouraging co operation between Member States and, if necessary, by supporting and supplementing their action, while fully respecting the responsibility of the Member States for the content of teaching and the organization of education systems and their cultural and linguistic diversity.

2.   Community action shall be aimed at:

–   developing the European dimension in education, particularly through the teaching and dissemination of the languages of the Member States;

–   encouraging mobility of students and teachers, inter alia by encouraging the academic recognition of diplomas and periods of study;

–   promoting co-operation between educational establishments;

–   developing exchanges of information and experience on issues common to the education systems of the Member States;

–   encouraging the development of youth exchanges and of exchanges of socio educational instructors;

–   encouraging the development of distance education.

3.   The Community and the Member States shall foster co-operation with third countries and the competent international organizations in the field of education, in particular the Council of Europe.

4.   In order to contribute to the achievement of the objectives referred to in this Article, the Council:

–   in accordance with the procedure in Article 189b, after consulting the Economic and Social Committee and the Committee of the Regions, shall adopt incentive measures, excluding any harmonization of the laws and regulations of the Member States;

–   acting by a qualified majority on a proposal from the Commission, shall adopt recommendations.

Article 127

1.   The Community shall implement a vocational training policy which shall support and supplement the action of the Member States, while fully respecting the responsibility of the Member States for the content and organization of vocational training.

2.   Community action shall aim to:

–   facilitate adaptation to industrial changes, in particular through vocational training and retraining;

–   improve initial and continuing vocational training in order to facilitate vocational integration and reintegration into the labour market;

–   facilitate access to vocational training and encourage mobility of instructors and trainees and particularly young people;

–   stimulate co-operation on training between educational or training establishments and firms;

–   develop exchanges of information and experience on issues common to the training systems of the Member States.

3.   The Community and the Member States shall foster co-operation with third countries and the competent international organizations in the sphere of vocational training.

4.   The Council, acting in accordance with the procedure referred to in Article 189c and after consulting the Economic and Social Committee, shall adopt measures to contribute to the achievement of the objectives referred to in this Article, excluding any harmonization of the laws and regulations of the Member States.

34   As amended by Article G(35) TEU.

Title IX – Culture[35]

Article 128

1. The Community shall contribute to the flowering of the cultures of the Member States, while respecting their national and regional diversity and at the same time bringing the common cultural heritage to the fore.

2. Action by the Community shall be aimed at encouraging co-operation between Member States and, if necessary, supporting and supplementing their action in the following areas:

– improvement of the knowledge and dissemination of the culture and history of the European peoples;

– conservation and safeguarding of cultural heritage of European significance;

– non-commercial cultural exchanges;

– artistic and literary creation, including in the audiovisual sector.

3. The Community and the Member States shall foster co-operation with third countries and the competent international organizations in the sphere of culture, in particular the Council of Europe.

4. The Community shall take cultural aspects into account in its action under other provisions of this Treaty.

5. In order to contribute to the achievement of the objectives referred to in this Article, the Council:

– acting in accordance with the procedure referred to in Article 189b and after consulting the Committee of the Regions, shall adopt incentive measures, excluding any harmonization of the laws and regulations of the Member States. The Council shall act unanimously throughout the procedures referred to in Article 189b;

– acting unanimously on a proposal from the Commission, shall adopt recommendations.

Title X– Public Health[36]

Article 129

1. The Community shall contribute towards ensuring a high level of human health protection by encouraging co-operation between the Member States and, if necessary, lending support to their action.

Community action shall be directed towards the prevention of diseases, in particular the major health scourges, including drug dependence, by promoting research into their causes and their transmission, as well as health information and education.

Health protection requirements shall form a constituent part of the Community's other policies.

2. Member States shall, in liaison with the Commission, co-ordinate among themselves their policies and programmes in the areas referred to in paragraph 1. The Commission may, in close contact with the Member States, take any useful initiative to promote such coordination.

3. The Community and the Member States shall foster co-operation with third countries and the competent international organizations in the sphere of public health.

4. In order to contribute to the achievement of the objectives referred to in this Article, the Council:

– acting in accordance with the procedure referred to in Article 189b, after consulting the Economic and Social Committee and the Committee of the Regions, shall adopt incentive measures, excluding any harmonization of the laws and regulations of the Member States;

– acting by a qualified majority on a proposal from the Commission, shall adopt recommendations.

---

35   As inserted by Article G(37) TEU. Former Article 128 null and void. Former Articles 129 and 130
      have become Articles 198d and 198e.
36   As inserted by Article G(38) TEU.

Annex

Title XI– Consumer Protection[37]

Article 129a

1. The Community shall contribute to the attainment of a high level of consumer protection through:

(a) measures adopted pursuant to Article 100a in the context of the completion of the internal market;

(b) specific action which supports and supplements the policy pursued by the Member States to protect the health, safety and economic interests of consumers and to provide adequate information to consumers.

2. The Council, acting in accordance with the procedure referred to in Article 189b and after consulting the Economic and Social Committee, shall adopt the specific action referred to in paragraph 1 (b).

3. Action adopted pursuant to paragraph 2 shall not prevent any Member State from maintaining or introducing more stringent protective measures. Such measures must be compatible with this Treaty. The Commission shall be notified of them.

Title XII– Trans-European Networks[38]

Article 129b

1. To help achieve the objectives referred to in Articles 7a and 130a and to enable citizens of the Union, economic operators and regional and local communities to derive full benefit from the setting up of an area without internal frontiers, the Community shall contribute to the establishment and development of trans-European networks in the areas of transport, telecommunications and energy infrastructures.

2. Within the framework of a system of open and competitive markets, action by the Community shall aim at promoting the interconnection and inter-operability of national networks as well as access to such networks. It shall take account in particular of the need to link island, landlocked and peripheral regions with the central regions of the Community.

Article 129c

1. In order to achieve the objectives referred to in Article 129b, the Community:

– shall establish a series of guidelines covering the objectives, priorities and broad lines of measures envisaged in the sphere of trans-European networks; these guidelines shall identify projects of common interest;

– shall implement any measures that may prove necessary to ensure the inter-operability of the networks, in particular in the field of technical standardization;

– may support the financial efforts made by the member States for projects of common interest financed by Member States, which are identified in the framework of the guidelines referred to in the first indent, particularly through feasibility studies, loan guarantees or interest rate subsidies; the Community may also contribute, through the Cohesion Fund to be set up no later than 31 December 1993 pursuant to Article 130d, to the financing of specific projects in Member States in the area of transport infrastructure.

The Community's activities shall take into account the potential economic viability of the projects.

2. Member States shall, in liaison with the Commission, co-ordinate among themselves the policies pursued at national level which may have a significant impact on the achievement of the objectives referred to in Article 129b. The Commission may, in close co-operation with the Member States, take any useful initiative to promote such co-ordination.

3. The Community may decide to co-operate with third countries to promote projects of mutual interest and to ensure the inter-operability of networks.

---

37   As inserted by Article G(38) TEU.
38   As amended by Article G(38) TEU.

Article 129d

The guidelines referred to in Article 129c (1) shall be adopted by the Council, acting in accordance with the procedure referred to in Article 189b and after consulting the Economic and Social Committee and the Committee of the Regions.

Guidelines and projects of common interest which relate to the territory of a Member State shall require the approval of the Member State concerned.

The Council, acting in accordance with the procedure referred to in Article 189c and after consulting the Economic and Social Committee and the Committee of the Regions, shall adopt the other measures provided for in Article 129c (1).

Title XIII– Industry[39]

Article 130

1. The Community and the Member States shall ensure that the conditions necessary for the competitiveness of the Community's industry exist.

For that purpose, in accordance with a system of open and competitive markets, their action shall be aimed at:

- *speeding up the adjustment of industry to structural changes;*
- *encouraging an environment favourable to initiative and to the development of undertakings throughout the Community, particularly small and medium-sized undertakings;*
- *encouraging an environment favourable to co-operation between undertakings;*
- *fostering better exploitation of the industrial potential of policies of innovation, research and technological development.*

2. The Member States shall consult each other in liaison with the Commission and, where necessary, shall co-ordinate their action. The Commission may take any useful initiative to promote such co-ordination.

3. The Community shall contribute to the achievement of the objectives set out in paragraph 1 through the policies and activities it pursues under other provisions of this Treaty. The Council, acting unanimously on a proposal from the Commission, after consulting the European Parliament and the Economic and Social Committee, may decide on specific measures in support of action taken in the Member States to achieve the objectives set out in paragraph 1.

This Title shall not provide a basis for the introduction by the Community of any measure which could lead to a distortion of competition.

Title XIV – Economic and Social Cohesion[40]

Article 130a

In order to promote its overall harmonious development, the Community shall develop and pursue its actions leading to the strengthening of its economic and social cohesion.

In particular, the Community shall aim at reducing disparities between *the levels of development* of the various regions and the backwardness of the least-favoured regions, *including rural areas.*

Article 130b

Member States shall conduct their economic policies and shall co-ordinate them in such a way as, in addition, to attain the objectives set out in Article 130a. *The formulation* and implementation of the Community's policies and actions and the implementation of the internal market shall take into account the objectives set out in Article 130a and shall contribute to their achievement. The Community shall also

39   As inserted by Article G(38) TEU.
40   As inserted by Article G(38) TEU.

support the achievement of these objectives by the action it takes through the Structural Funds (European Agricultural Guidance and Guarantee Fund, Guidance Section; European Social Fund; European Regional Development Fund), the European Investment Bank and the other existing financial instruments.

The Commission shall submit a report to the European Parliament, the Council, the Economic and Social Committee and the Committee of the Regions every three years on the progress made towards achieving economic and social cohesion and on the manner in which the various means provided for in this Article have contributed to it. This report shall, if necessary, be accompanied by appropriate proposals.

If specific actions prove necessary outside the Funds and without prejudice to the measures decided upon within the framework of the other Community policies, such actions may be adopted by the Council acting unanimously on a proposal from the Commission and after consulting the European Parliament, the Economic and Social Committee and the Committee of the Regions.

Article 130c

The European Regional Development Fund is intended to help to redress the main regional imbalances in the Community through participation in the development and structural adjustment of regions whose development is lagging behind and in the conversion of declining industrial regions.

Article 130d

Without prejudice to Article 130e, the Council, acting unanimously on a proposal from the Commission and after obtaining the assent of the European Parliament and consulting the Economic and Social Committee and the Committee of the Regions, shall define the tasks, priority objectives and the organization of the Structural Funds, which may involve grouping the Funds. The Council, acting by the same procedure, shall also define the general rules applicable to them and the provisions necessary to ensure their effectiveness and the co-ordination of the Funds with one another and with the other existing financial instruments.

The Council, acting in accordance with the same procedure, shall before 31 December 1993 set up a Cohesion Fund to provide a financial contribution to projects in the fields of environment and trans-European networks in the area of transport infrastructure.

Article 130e

Implementing decisions relating to the European Regional Development Fund shall be taken by the Council, acting in accordance with the procedure referred to in Article 189c and after consulting the Economic and Social Committee and the Committee of the Regions.

With regard to the European Agricultural Guidance and Guarantee Fund, Guidance Section, and the European Social Fund, *Articles 43 and 125* respectively shall continue to apply.

Title XV– Research and Technological Development [41]

Article 130f

1. The Community *shall have* the objective of strengthening the scientific and technological bases of Community industry and encouraging it to become more competitive at international level, *while promoting all the research activities deemed necessary by virtue of other Chapters of this Treaty.*

2. *For this purpose* the Community shall, throughout the Community, encourage undertakings, including small and medium-sized undertakings, research centres and universities in their research and technological development activities of *high quality*; it shall support their efforts to co-operate with one another, aiming, notably, at enabling undertakings to exploit the internal market potential to the full, in particular through the opening up of national public contracts, the definition of common standards and the removal of legal and fiscal obstacles to that co-operation.

---

41   Former Title VI, as amended by Article G(38) TEU.

3. All Community activities under this Treaty in the area of research and technological development, including demonstration projects, shall be decided on and implemented in accordance with the provisions of this Title.

Article 130g

In pursuing these objectives, the Community shall carry out the following activities, complementing the activities carried out in the Member States:

(a) implementation of research, technological development and demonstration programmes, by promoting co-operation with and between undertakings, research centres and universities;

(b) promotion of co-operation in the field of Community research, technological development, and demonstration with third countries and international organizations;

(c) dissemination and optimization of the results of activities in Community research, technological development and demonstration;

(d) stimulation of the training and mobility of researchers in the Community.

Article 130h

1. The Community and the Member States shall co-ordinate their research and technological development activities so as to ensure that national policies and Community policy are mutually consistent.

2. In close co-operation with the Member States, the Commission may take any useful initiative to promote the co-ordination referred to in paragraph 1.

Article 130i

1. A multiannual framework programme, setting out all the activities of the Community, shall be adopted by the Council, acting in accordance with the procedure referred to in Article 189b after consulting the Economic and Social Committee. The Council shall act unanimously throughout the procedures referred to in Article 189b.

The framework programme shall:

–   establish the scientific and technological objectives to be achieved by the activities provided for in Article 130g and fix the relevant priorities;

–   indicate the broad lines of such activities;

–   fix the maximum overall amount and the detailed rules for Community financial participation in the framework programme and the respective shares in each of the actions provided for.

2. The framework programme shall be adapted or supplemented as the situation changes.

3. The framework programme shall be implemented through specific programmes developed within each activity. Each specific programme shall define the detailed rules for implementing it, fix its duration and provide for the means deemed necessary. The sum of the amounts deemed necessary, fixed in the specific programmes, may not exceed the overall maximum amount fixed for the framework programme and each activity.

4. The Council, acting by a qualified majority on a proposal from the Commission and after consulting the European Parliament and the Economic and Social Committee, shall adopt the specific programmes.

Article 130j

For the implementation of the multiannual framework programme the Council shall:

–   determine the rules for the participation of undertakings, research centres and universities;

–   lay down the rules governing the dissemination of research results.

Article 130k

In implementing the multiannual framework programme, supplementary programmes may be decided on involving the participation of certain Member States only, which shall finance them subject to possible Community participation.

The Council shall adopt the rules applicable to supplementary programmes, particularly as regards the dissemination of knowledge and access by other Member States.

Article 130l

In implementing the multiannual framework programme the Community may make provision, in agreement with the Member States concerned, for participation in research and development programmes undertaken by several Member States, including participation in the structures created for the execution of those programmes.

Article 130m

In implementing the multiannual framework programme the Community may make provision for co-operation in Community research, technological development and demonstration with third countries or international organizations.

The detailed arrangements for such co-operation may be the subject of agreements between the Community and the third parties concerned, which shall be negotiated and concluded in accordance with Article 228.

Article 130n

The Community may set up joint undertakings or any other structure necessary for the efficient execution of Community research, technological development and demonstration programmes.

Article 130o

The Council, acting unanimously on a proposal from the Commission and after consulting the European Parliament and the Economic and Social Committee, shall adopt the provisions referred to in Article 130n.

The Council, acting in accordance with the procedure referred to in Article 189c and after consulting the Economic and Social Committee, shall adopt the provisions referred to in Articles 130j to l. Adoption of the supplementary programmes shall require the agreement of the Member States concerned.

Article 130p

At the beginning of each year the Commission shall send a report to the European Parliament and the Council. The report shall include information on research and technological development activities and dissemination of results during the previous year, and the work programme for the current year.

Article 130q

(repealed)

Title XVI– Environment[42]

Article 130r

1. Community policy on the environment *shall contribute to pursuit of the following objectives:*

– *preserving, protecting and improving the quality of the environment;*

– *protecting human health;*

– *prudent and rational utilization of natural resources;*

– *promoting measures at international level to deal with regional or worldwide environmental problems.*

2. *Community policy on the environment shall aim at a high level of protection taking into account the diversity of situations in the various regions of the Community. It shall be based on the precautionary principle and on the principles that preventive action should be taken, that environmental damage should as a priority be rectified at source and that the polluter should pay. Environmental protection requirements must be integrated into the definition and implementation of other Community policies.*

42   Former Title VII, as amended by Article G(38) TEU.

In this context, harmonization measures answering these requirements shall include, where appropriate, a safeguard clause allowing Member States to take provisional measures, for non-economic environmental reasons, subject to a Community inspection procedure.

3. *In preparing its policy relating to the environment, the Community shall take account of:*

– *available scientific and technical data;*

– *environmental conditions in the various regions of the Community;*

– *the potential benefits and costs of action or lack of action;*

– *the economic and social development of the Community as a whole and the balanced development of its regions.*

4. Within their respective spheres of competence, the Community and the Member States shall co-operate with third countries and with the competent international organizations. The arrangements for Community co-operation may be the subject of agreements between the Community and the third parties concerned, which shall be negotiated and concluded in accordance with Article 228.

The previous subparagraph shall be without prejudice to Member States' competence to negotiate in international bodies and to conclude international agreements.

Article 130s

1. *The Council, acting in accordance with the procedure referred to in Article 189c and after consulting the Economic and Social Committee, shall decide what action is to be taken by the Community in order to achieve the objectives referred to in Article 130r.*

2. *By way of derogation from the decision-making procedure provided for in paragraph 1 and without prejudice to Article 100a, the Council, acting unanimously on a proposal from the Commission and after consulting the European Parliament and the Economic and Social Committee, shall adopt:*

– *provisions primarily of a fiscal nature;*

– *measures concerning town and country planning, land use with the exception of waste management and measures of a general nature, and management of water resources;*

– *measures significantly affecting a Member State's choice between different energy sources and the general structure of its energy supply.*

The Council may, under the conditions laid down in the preceding subparagraph, define those matters referred to in this paragraph on which decisions are to be taken by a qualified majority.

3. *In other areas, general action programmes setting out priority objectives to be attained shall be adopted by the Council, acting in accordance with the procedure referred to in Article 189b and after consulting the Economic and Social Committee.*

The Council, acting under the terms of paragraph 1 or paragraph 2 according to the case, shall adopt the measures necessary for the implementation of these programmes.

4. *Without prejudice to certain measures of a Community nature, the Member States shall finance and implement the environment policy.*

5. *Without prejudice to the principle that the polluter should pay, if a measure based on the provisions of paragraph 1 involves costs deemed disproportionate for the public authorities of a Member State, the Council shall, in the act adopting that measure, lay down appropriate provisions in the form of:*

– *temporary derogations and/or*

– *financial support from the Cohesion Fund to be set up no later than 31 December 1993 pursuant to Article 130d.*

Article 130t

The protective measures adopted pursuant to Article 130s shall not prevent any Member State from maintaining or introducing more stringent protective measures. *Such measures must be compatible with this Treaty. They shall be notified to the Commission.*

Title XVII– Development Cooperation [43]

Article 130u

1. Community policy in the sphere of development co-operation, which shall be complementary to the policies pursued by the Member States, shall foster:

– the sustainable economic and social development of the developing countries, and more particularly the most disadvantaged among them;

– the smooth and gradual integration of the developing countries into the world economy;

– the campaign against poverty in the developing countries.

2. Community policy in this area shall contribute to the general objective of developing and consolidating democracy and the rule of law, and to that of respecting human rights and fundamental freedoms.

3. The Community and the Member States shall comply with the commitments and take account of the objectives they have approved in the context of the United Nations and other competent international organizations.

Article 130v

The Community shall take account of the objectives referred to in Article 130u in the policies that it implements which are likely to affect developing countries.

Article 130w

1. Without prejudice to the other provisions of this Treaty the Council, acting in accordance with the procedure referred to in Article 189c, shall adopt the measures necessary to further the objectives referred to in Article 130u. Such action may take the form of multiannual programmes.

2. The European Investment Bank shall contribute, under the terms laid down in its Statute, to the implementation of the measures referred to in paragraph 1.

3. The provisions of this Article shall not affect co-operation with the African, Caribbean and Pacific countries in the framework of the ACP-EEC Convention.

Article 130x

1. The Community and the Member States shall co-ordinate their policies on development co operation and shall consult each other on their aid programmes, including in international organizations and during international conferences. They may undertake joint action. Member States shall contribute if necessary to the implementation of Community aid programmes.

2. The Commission may take any useful initiative to promote the co-ordination referred to in paragraph 1.

Article 130y

Within their respective spheres of competence, the Community and the Member States shall co operate with third countries and with the international organizations. The arrangements for Community co-operation may be the subject of agreements between the Community and the third parties concerned, which shall be negotiated and concluded in accordance with Article 228.

The previous paragraph shall be without prejudice to Member States' competence to negotiate in international bodies and to conclude international agreements.

Part Four: Association of the Overseas Countries and Territories

Article 131

The Member States agree to associate with the Community the non-European countries and territories which have special relations with Belgium, Denmark, France, Italy, the Netherlands and the United

---

43   As inserted by Article G(38) TEU.

Kingdom. These countries and territories (hereinafter called the "countries and territories") are listed in Annex IV to this Treaty.

The purpose of association shall be to promote the economic and social development of the countries and territories and to establish close economic relations between them and the Community as a whole.

In accordance with the principles set out in the Preamble to this Treaty, association shall serve primarily to further the interests and prosperity of the inhabitants of these countries and territories in order to lead them to the economic, social and cultural development to which they aspire.

Article 132

Association shall have the following objectives:

1. Member States shall apply to their trade with the countries and territories the same treatment as they accord each other pursuant to this Treaty.

2. Each country or territory shall apply to its trade with Member States and with the other countries and territories the same treatment as that which it applies to the European State with which it has special relations.

3. The Member States shall contribute to the investments required for the progressive development of these countries and territories.

4. For investments financed by the Community, participation in tenders and supplies shall be open on equal terms to all natural and legal persons who are nationals of a Member State or of one of the countries and territories.

5. In relations between Member States and the countries and territories the right of establishment of nationals and companies or firms shall be regulated in accordance with the provisions and procedures laid down in the Chapter relating to the right of establishment and one a non-discriminatory basis, subject to any special provisions laid down pursuant to Article 136.

Article 133

1. Customs duties on imports into the Member States of goods originating in the countries and territories shall be completely abolished in conformity with the progressive abolition of customs duties between Member States in accordance with the provisions of this Treaty.

2. Customs duties on imports into each country or territory from Member States or from the other countries or territories shall be progressively abolished in accordance with the provisions of Articles 12, 13, 14, 15 and 17.

3. The countries and territories may, however, levy customs duties which meet the needs of their developments and industrialisation or produce revenue for their budgets. The duties referred to in the preceding subparagraph shall nevertheless be progressively reduced to the level of those imposed on imports of products from the Member State with which each country or territory has special relations. The percentages and the timetable of the reductions provided for under this Treaty shall apply to the difference between the duty imposed on a product coming from the Member State which has special relations with the country or territory concerned and the duty imposed on the same product coming from within the Community on entry into the importing country or territory.

4. Paragraph 2 shall not apply to countries and territories which, by reason of the particular international obligations by which they are bound, already apply a non-discriminatory customs tariff when this Treaty enters into force.

5. The introduction of or any change in customs duties imposed on goods imported into the countries and territories shall not, either in law or in fact, give rise to any direct or indirect discrimination between imports from the various Member States.

Article 134

If the level of the duties applicable to goods from a third country on entry into a country or territory is liable, when the provisions of Article 133 (1) have been applied, to cause deflections of trade to the detriment of any Member State, the latter may request the Commission to propose to the other Member States the measures needed to remedy the situation.

Article 135

Subject to the provisions relating to public health, public security or public policy, freedom of movement within Member States for workers from the countries and territories, and within the countries and territories for workers from Member States, shall be governed by agreements to be concluded subsequently with the unanimous approval of Member States.

Article 136

For an initial period of five years after the entry into force of this Treaty, the details of and procedure for the association of the countries and territories with the Community shall be determined by an implementing Convention annexed to this Treaty.

Before the Convention referred to in the preceding paragraph expires, the Council shall, acting unanimously, lay down provisions for a further period, on the basis of the experience acquired and of the principles set out in this Treaty.

Article 136a

The provisions of Articles 131 to 136 shall apply to Greenland, subject to the specific provisions for Greenland set out in the Protocol on special arrangements for Greenland, annexed to this Treaty.

Part Five: Institutions of the Community

Title I – Provisions Governing the Institutions

Chapter 1. The Institutions

Section 1. The European Parliament

Article 137[44]

The European Parliament, which shall consist of representatives of the peoples of the States brought together in the Community, shall exercise the powers conferred upon it by this Treaty.

Article 138

1. The representatives in the European Parliament of the peoples of the States brought together in the Community shall be elected by direct universal suffrage.

2. The number of representatives elected in each Member States is as follows:

Belgium	24
Denmark	16
Germany	81
Greece	24
Spain	60
France	81
Ireland	15
Italy	81
Luxembourg	6
The Netherlands	25
Portugal	24
United Kingdom	81

44   As amended by Article G(39) TEU.

3. The European Parliament shall draw up proposals for elections by direct universal suffrage in accordance with a uniform procedure in all Member States.

The Council shall, acting unanimously after obtaining the assent of the European Parliament, which shall act by a majority of its component members, lay down the appropriate provisions, which it shall recommend to Member States for adoption in accordance with their respective constitutional requirements.[45]

Article 138a[46]

Political parties at European level are important as a factor for integration within the Union. They contribute to forming a European awareness and to expressing the political will of the citizens of the Union.

Article 138b[47]

In so far as provided in this Treaty, the European Parliament shall participate in the process leading up to the adoption of Community acts by exercising its powers under the procedures laid down in Articles 189b and 189c and by giving its assent or delivering advisory opinions.

The European Parliament may, acting by a majority of its members, request the Commission to submit any appropriate proposal on matters on which it considers that a Community act is required for the purpose of implementing this Treaty.

Article 138c[48]

In the course of its duties, the European Parliament may, at the request of a quarter of its members, set up a temporary Committee of Inquiry to investigate, without prejudice to the powers conferred by this Treaty on other institutions or bodies, alleged contraventions or maladministration in the implementation of Community law, except where the alleged facts are being examined before a court and while the case is still subject to legal proceedings.

The temporary Committee of Inquiry shall cease to exist on the submission of its report.

The detailed provisions governing the exercise of the right of inquiry shall be determined by common agreement of the European Parliament, the Council and the Commission.

Article 138d[49]

Any citizen of the Union, and any natural or legal person residing or having its registered office in a Member State of the Community, shall have the right to address, individually or in association with other citizens or persons, a petition to the European Parliament on a matter which comes within the Community's fields of activity and which affects him, her or it directly.

Article 138e[50]

1. The European Parliament shall appoint an Ombudsman empowered to receive complaints from any citizen of the Union or any natural or legal person residing or having its registered office in a Member State concerning instances of maladministration in the activities of the Community institutions or bodies, with the exception of the Court of Justice and the Court of First Instance acting in their judicial role.

In accordance with his duties, the Ombudsman shall conduct inquiries for which he finds grounds, either on his own initiative on the basis of complaints submitted to him direct or through a member of the European Parliament, except where the alleged facts are or have been the subject of legal proceedings. Where the Ombudsman establishes an instance of maladministration, he shall refer the matter to the institution concerned, which shall have a period of three months in which to inform him of its views. The

---

45   Second paragraph as amended by Article G(40) TEU.
46   As inserted by Article G(41) TEU.
47   As inserted by Article G(41) TEU.
48   As inserted by Article G(41) TEU.
49   As inserted by Article G(41) TEU.
50   As inserted by Article G(41) TEU.

Ombudsman shall then forward a report to the European Parliament and the institution concerned. The person lodging the complaint shall be informed of the outcome of such inquiries.

The Ombudsman shall submit an annual report to the European Parliament on the outcome of his inquiries.

2. The Ombudsman shall be appointed after each election of the European Parliament for the duration of its term of office. The Ombudsman shall be eligible for reappointment.

The Ombudsman may be dismissed by the Court of Justice at the request of the European Parliament if he no longer fulfils the conditions required for the performance of his duties or if he is guilty of serious misconduct.

3. The Ombudsman shall be completely independent in the performance of his duties. In the performance of those duties he shall neither seek nor take instructions from any body. The Ombudsman may not, during his term of office, engage in any other occupation, whether gainful or not.

4. The European Parliament shall, after seeking an opinion from the Commission and with the approval of the Council acting by a qualified majority, lay down the regulations and general conditions governing the performance of the Ombudsman's duties.

Article 139

The European Parliament shall hold an annual session. It shall meet, without requiring to be convened, on the second Tuesday in March.[51]

The European Parliament may meet in extraordinary session at the request of a majority of its members or at the request of the Council or of the Commission.

Article 140

The European Parliament shall elect its President and its officers from among its members.

Members of the Commission may attend all meetings and shall, at their request, be heard on behalf of the Commission.

The Commission shall reply orally or in writing to questions put to it by the European Parliament or by its members.

The Council shall be heard by the European Parliament in accordance with the conditions laid down by the Council in its rules of procedure.

Article 141

Save as otherwise provided in this Treaty, the European Parliament shall act by an absolute majority of the votes cast.

The rules of procedure shall determine the quorum.

Article 142

The European Parliament shall adopt its rules of procedure, acting by a majority of its members.

The proceedings of the European Parliament shall be published in the manner laid down in its rules of procedure.

Article 143

The European Parliament shall discuss in open session the annual general report submitted to it by the Commission.

Article 144

If a motion of censure on the activities of the Commission is tabled before it, the European Parliament shall not vote thereon until at least three days after the motion has been tabled and only by open vote.

---

51   With regard to the second sentence of this subparagraph, see also Article 10(3) of the Act concerning the election of the representatives of the European Parliament.

If the motion of censure is carried by a two-thirds majority of the votes cast, representing a majority of the members of the European Parliament, the members of the Commission shall resign as a body. They shall continue to deal with current business until they are replaced in accordance with Article 158. *In this case, the term of office of the members of the Commission appointed to replace them shall expire on the date on which the term of office of the members of the Commission obliged to resign as a body would have expired.*[52]

Section 2. The Council

Article 145

To ensure that the objectives set out in this Treaty are attained, the Council shall, in accordance with the provisions of this Treaty:

– *ensure co-ordination of the general economic policies of the Member States;*

– *have power to take decisions;*

– *confer on the Commission, in the acts which the Council adopts, powers for the implementation of the rules which the Council lays down. The Council may impose certain requirements in respect of the exercise of these powers. The Council may also reserve the right, in specific cases, to excise directly implementing powers itself. The procedures referred to above must be consonant with principles and rules to be laid down in advance by the Council, acting unanimously on a proposal from the Commission and after obtaining the opinion of the European Parliament.*

Article 146[53]

The Council shall consist of a representative of each Member State at ministerial level, authorized to commit the government of that Member State.

The office of President shall be held in turn by each Member State in the Council for a term of six months, in the following order of Member States:

– *for a first cycle of six years: Belgium, Denmark, Germany, Greece, Spain, France, Ireland, Italy, Luxembourg, Netherlands, Portugal, United Kingdom;*

– *for the following cycle of six years: Denmark, Belgium, Greece, Germany, France, Spain, Italy, Ireland, Netherlands, Luxembourg, United Kingdom, Portugal.*

Article 147

The Council shall meet when convened by its President on his own initiative or at the request of one of its members or of the Commission.

Article 148

1.   Save as otherwise provided in this Treaty, the Council shall act by a majority of its members.

2.   Where the Council is required to act by a qualified majority, the votes of its members shall be weighted as follows:

Belgium	5
Denmark	3
Germany	10
Greece	5
Spain	8
France	10
Ireland	3
Italy	10

52   Third sentence of the second paragraph as inserted by Article G(42) TEU.
53   As amended by Article G(43) TEU.

Luxembourg	2
The Netherlands	5
Portugal	5
United Kingdom	10

For their adoption, acts of the Council shall require at least:

– *fifty-four votes in favour where this Treaty requires them to be adopted on a proposal from the Commission.*

– *fifty-four votes in favour, cast by at least eight members, in other cases.*

3. Abstentions by members present in person or represented shall not prevent the adoption by the Council of acts which require unanimity.

Article 149

(repealed)

Article 150

Where a vote is taken, any member of the Council may also act on behalf of not more than one other member.

Article 151 [54]

1. A committee consisting of the Permanent Representatives of the Member States shall be responsible for preparing the work of the Council and for carrying out the tasks assigned to it by the Council.

2. The Council shall be assisted by a General Secretariat, under the direction of a Secretary-General. The Secretary-General shall be appointed by the Council acting unanimously.

The Council shall decide on the organization of the General Secretariat.

3. The Council shall adopt its rules of procedure.

Article 151a

1. The Council shall be assisted by a General Secretariat, under the direction of a Secretary-General. The Secretary-General shall be appointed by the Council acting unanimously. The Council shall decide on the organization of the General Secretariat.

2. The Council shall adopt its rules of procedure.

Article 152

The Council may request the Commission to undertake any studies the Council considers desirable for the attainment of the common objectives, and to submit it to any appropriate proposals.

Article 153

The Council shall, after receiving an opinion from the Commission, determine the rules governing the committees provided for in this Treaty.

Article 154

The Council shall, acting by a qualified majority, determine the salaries, allowances and pensions of the President and members of the Commission, and of the President, Judges, Advocates-General and Registrar of the Court of Justice. It shall also, again by a qualified majority, determine any payment to be made instead of remuneration.

54   As amended by Article G(46) TEU.

Section 3. The Commission

Article 155

In order to ensure the proper functioning and development of the common market, the Commission shall:

- *ensure that the provisions of this Treaty and the measures taken by the institutions pursuant thereto are applied;*
- *formulate recommendations or deliver opinions on matters, dealt with in this Treaty, if it expressly so provides or if the Commission considers it necessary;*
- *have its own power of decision and participate in the shaping of measures taken by the Council and by the European Parliament in the manner provided for in this Treaty;*
- *exercise the powers conferred on it by the Council for the implementation of the rules laid down by the latter.*

Article 156

The Commission shall publish annually, not later than one month before the opening of the session of the European Parliament, a general report on the activities of the Communities.

Article 157

1. The Commission shall consist of seventeen members, who shall be chosen on the grounds of their general competence and whose independence is beyond doubt.

The number of members of the Commission may be altered by the Council, acting unanimously.

Only nationals of the Member States may be members of the Commission.

The Commission must include at least one national of each of the Member States, but may not include more than two members having the nationality of the same State.

2. The members of the Commission shall, in the general interest of the Community, be completely independent in the performance of their duties.

In the performance of these duties, they shall neither seek nor take instructions from any Government or from any other body. They shall refrain from any action incompatible with their duties. Each Member State undertakes to respect this principle and not to seek to influence the members of the Commission in the performance of their tasks.

The members of the Commission may not, during their term of office, engage in any other occupation, whether gainful or not. When entering upon their duties they shall give a solemn undertaking that, both during and after their term of office, they will respect the obligations arising therefrom and in particular their duty to behave with integrity and discretion as regards the acceptance, after they have ceased to hold office, of certain appointment or benefits. In the event of any breach of these obligations, the Court of Justice may, on application by the Council or the Commission, rule that the member concerned be, according to the circumstance, either compulsorily retired in accordance with Article 160 or deprived of his right to a pension or other benefits in its stead.

Article 158[55]

1.   The members of the Commission shall be appointed, in accordance with the procedure referred to in paragraph 2, for a period of five years, subject, if need be, to Article 144.

Their term of office shall be renewable.

2.   The governments of the Member States shall nominate by common accord, after consulting the European Parliament, the person they intend to appoint as President of the Commission.

The governments of the Member States shall, in consultation with the nominee for President, nominate the other persons whom they intend to appoint as members of the Commission.

---

55   As amended by Article G(48) TEU.

The President and the other members of the Commission thus nominated shall be subject as a body to a vote of approval by the European Parliament. After approval by the European Parliament, the President and the other members of the Commission shall be appointed by common accord of the governments of the Member States.

3. Paragraphs 1 and 2 shall be applied for the first time to the President and the other members of the Commission whose term of office begins on 7 January 1995.

The President and the other members of the Commission whose term of office begins on 7 January 1993 shall be appointed by common accord of the governments of the Member States. Their term of office shall expire on 6 January 1995.

Article 159[56]

Apart from normal replacement, or death, the duties of a member of the Commission shall end when he resigns or is compulsorily retired.

The vacancy thus caused shall be filled for the remainder of the member's term of office by a new member appointed by common accord of the governments of the Member States. The Council may, acting unanimously, decide that such a vacancy need not be filled.

In the event of resignation, compulsory retirement or death, the President shall be replaced for the remainder of his term of office. The procedure laid down in Article 158 (2) shall be applicable for the replacement of the President.

Save in the case of compulsory retirement under Article 160, members of the Commission shall remain in office until they have been replaced.

Article 160

If any member of the Commission no longer fulfils the conditions required for the performance of his duties or if he has been guilty of serious misconduct, the Court of Justice may, on application by the Council or the Commission, compulsorily retire him.

Article 161[57]

The Commission may appoint a Vice-President or two Vice-Presidents from among its members.

Article 162

1. The Council and the Commission shall consult each other and shall settle by common accord their methods of co-operation.

2. The Commission shall adopt its rules of procedure so as to ensure that both it and its departments operate in accordance with the provisions of this Treaty. It shall ensure that these rules are published.

Article 163

The Commission shall act by a majority of the number of members provided for in Article 157.

A meeting of the Commission shall be valid only if the number of members laid down in its rules of procedure is present.

Section 4. The Court of Justice

Article 164

The Court of Justice shall ensure that in the interpretation and application of this Treaty the law is observed.

---

56   As amended by Article G(48) TEU.
57   As amended by Article G(48) TEU.

Annex

Article 165[58]

The Court of Justice shall consist of thirteen judges.

The Court of Justice shall sit in plenary session. It may, however, form chambers, each consisting of three or five judges, either to undertake certain preparatory inquiries or to adjudicate on particular categories of cases in accordance with rules laid down for these purposes.

The Court of Justice shall sit in plenary session when a Member State or a Community institution that is a party to the proceedings so requests.

Should the Court of Justice so request, the Council may, acting unanimously, increase the number of judges and make the necessary adjustments to the second and third paragraphs of this Article and to the second paragraph of Article 167.

Article 166

The Court of Justice shall be assisted by six Advocates-General.

It shall be the duty of the Advocate-General, acting with complete impartiality and independence, to make, in open court, reasoned submissions on cases brought before the Court of Justice, in order to assist the Court in the performance of the task assigned to it in Article 164.

Should the Court of Justice so request, the Council may, acting unanimously, increase the number of Advocates-General and make the necessary adjustments to the third paragraph of Article 167.

Article 167

The Judges and Advocates-General shall be chosen from persons whose independence is beyond doubt and who possess the qualifications required for appointment to the highest judicial offices in their respective countries or who are jurisconsults of recognized competence; they shall be appointed by common accord of the Governments of the Member States for a term of six years.

Every three years there shall be a partial replacement of the Judges. Seven and six Judges shall be replaced alternately.

Every three years there shall be a partial replacement of the Advocates-General. Three Advocates-General shall be replaced on each occasion.

Retiring Judges and Advocates-General shall be eligible for reappointment.

The Judges and Advocates-General shall elect the President of the Court from among the Judges for a term of three years. He may be re-elected.

Article 168

The Court of Justice shall appoint its Registrar and lay down the rules governing his service.

Article 168a[59]

1. A Court of First Instance shall be attached to the Court of Justice with jurisdiction to hear and determine at first instance, subject to a right of appeal to the Court of Justice on points of law only and in accordance with the conditions laid down by the Statute, certain classes of action or proceeding defined in accordance with the conditions laid down in paragraph 2. The Court of First Instance shall not be competent to hear and determine questions referred for a preliminary ruling under Article 177.

2. At the request of the Court of Justice and after consulting the European Parliament and the Commission, the Council, acting unanimously, shall determine the classes of action or proceeding referred to in paragraph 1 and the composition of the Court of First Instance and shall adopt the necessary adjustments and additional provisions to the Statute of the Court of Justice. Unless the Council decides otherwise, the provisions of this Treaty relating to the Court of Justice, in particular the provisions of the Protocol on the Statute of the Court of Justice, shall apply to the Court of First Instance.

---

58 As amended by Article G(49) TEU.
59 As amended by Article G(50) TEU.

Annex

3. The Members of the Court of First Instance shall be chosen from persons whose independence is beyond doubt and who possess the ability required for appointment to judicial office; they shall be appointed by common accord of the governments of the Member States for a term of six years. The membership shall be partially renewed every three years. Retiring members shall be eligible for re-appointment.

4. The Court of First Instance shall establish its rules of procedure in agreement with the Court of Justice. Those rules shall require the unanimous approval of the Council.

Article 169

If the Commission considers that a member State has failed to fulfil an obligation under this Treaty, it shall deliver a reasoned opinion on the matter after giving the State concerned the opportunity to submit its observations.

If the State concerned does not comply with the opinion within the period laid down by the Commission, the latter may bring the matter before the Court of Justice.

Article 170

A Member State which considers that another Member State has failed to fulfil an obligation under this Treaty may bring the matter before the Court of Justice.

Before a Member State brings an action against another Member State for an alleged infringement of an obligation under this Treaty, it shall bring matter before the Commission.

The Commission shall deliver a reasoned opinion after each of the States concerned has been given the opportunity to submit its own case and its observations on the other party's case both orally and in writing.

If the Commission has not delivered an opinion within three months of the date on which the matter was brought before it, the absence of such opinion shall not prevent the matter from being brought before the Court of Justice.

Article 171[60]

1. If the Court of Justice finds that a Member State has failed to fulfil an obligation under this Treaty, the State shall be required to take the necessary measures to comply with the judgment of the Court of Justice.

2. If the Commission considers that the Member State concerned has not taken such measures it shall, after giving that State the opportunity to submit its observations, issue a reasoned opinion specifying the points on which the Member State concerned has not complied with the judgment of the Court of Justice.

If the Member State concerned fails to take the necessary measures to comply with the Court's judgment within the time-limit laid down by the Commission, the latter may bring the case before the Court of Justice. In so doing it shall specify the amount of the lump sum or penalty payment to be paid by the Member State concerned which it considers appropriate in the circumstances.

If the Court of Justice finds that the Member State concerned has not complied with its judgment it may impose a lump sum or penalty payment on it.

This procedure shall be without prejudice to Article 170.

Article 172[61]

Regulations adopted jointly by the European Parliament and the Council, and by the Council, pursuant to the provisions of this Treaty, may give the Court of Justice unlimited jurisdiction with regard to the penalties provided for in such regulations.

60   As amended by Article G(51) TEU.
61   As amended by Article G(52) TEU.

Annex

Article 173 [62]

The Court of Justice shall review the legality of acts adopted jointly by the European Parliament and the Council, of acts of the Council, of the Commission and of the ECB, other than recommendations and opinions, and of acts of the European Parliament intended to produce legal effects vis-a-vis third parties.

It shall for this purpose have jurisdiction in actions brought by a Member State, the Council or the Commission on grounds of lack of competence, infringement of an essential procedural requirement, infringement of this Treaty or of any rule of law relating to its application, or misuse of powers.

The Court shall have jurisdiction under the same conditions in actions brought by the European Parliament and by the ECB for the purpose of protecting their prerogatives.

Any natural or legal person may, under the same conditions, institute proceedings against a decision addressed to that person or against a decision which, although in the form of a regulation or a decision addressed to another person, is of direct and individual concern to the former.

The proceedings provided for in this Article shall be instituted within two months of the publication of the measure, or of its notification to the plaintiff, or, in the absence thereof, of the day on which it came to the knowledge of the latter, as the case may be.

Article 174

If the action is well founded, the Court of Justice shall declare the act concerned to be void.

In the case of a regulation, however, the Court of Justice shall, if it considers this necessary, state which of the effects of the regulation which it has declared void shall be considered as definitive.

Article 175 [63]

Should *the European Parliament*, the Council or the Commission, in infringement of this Treaty, fail to act, the Member States and the other institutions of the Community may bring an action before the Court of Justice to have the infringement established.

The action shall be admissible only if the institution concerned has first been called upon to act. If, within two months of being so called upon, the institution concerned has not defined its position, the action may be brought within a further period of two months.

Any natural or legal person may, under the conditions laid down in the preceding paragraphs, complain to the Court of Justice that an institution of the Community has failed to address to that person any act other than a recommendation or an opinion.

The Court of Justice shall have jurisdiction, under the same conditions, in actions or proceedings brought by the ECB in the areas falling within the latter's field of competence and in actions or proceedings brought against the latter.

Article 176 [64]

The institution or institutions whose act has been declared void or whose failure to act has been declared contrary to this Treaty shall be required to take the necessary measures to comply with the judgment of the Court of Justice.

This obligation shall not affect any obligation which may result from the application of the second paragraph of Article 215.

This Article shall also apply to the ECB.

Article 177 [65]

The Court of Justice shall have jurisdiction to give preliminary rulings concerning:

(a) the interpretation of this Treaty;

---

62   As amended by Article G(53) TEU.
63   As amended by Article G(54) TEU.
64   As amended by Article G(55) TEU.
65   As amended by Article G(56) TEU.

(b) the validity and interpretation of acts of the institutions of the Community *and of the ECB*;

(c) the interpretation of the statutes of bodies established by an act of the Council, where those statutes so provide.

Where such a question is raised before any court or tribunal of a Member State, that court or tribunal may, if it considers that a decision on the question is necessary to enable it to give judgment, request the Court of Justice to give a ruling thereon.

Where any such question is raised in a case pending before a court or tribunal of a Member State against whose decisions there is no judicial remedy under national law, that court or tribunal shall bring the matter before the Court of Justice.

Article 178

The Court of Justice shall have jurisdiction in disputes relating to compensation for damage provided for in the second paragraph of Article 215.

Article 179

The Court of Justice shall have jurisdiction in any dispute between the Community and its servants within the limits and under the conditions laid down in the Staff Regulations or the Conditions of Employment.

Article 180 [66]

The Court of Justice shall, within the limits hereinafter laid town, have jurisdiction in disputes concerning:

(a) the fulfilment by Member States of obligations under the Statute of the European Investment Bank. In this connection, the Board of Directors of the Bank shall enjoy the powers conferred upon the Commission by Article 169;

(b) measures adopted by the Board of Governors of the European Investment Bank. In this connection, any Member State, the Commission or the Board of Directors of the Bank may institute proceedings under the conditions laid down in Article 173;

(c) measures adopted by the Board of Directors of the European Investment Bank. Proceedings against such measures may be instituted only by Member States or by the Commission, under the conditions laid down in Article 173, and solely on the grounds of non-compliance with the procedure provided for in Article 21 (2), (5), (6) and (7) of the Statute of the Bank;

(d) the fulfilment by national central banks of obligations under this Treaty and the Statute of the ESCB. In this connection the powers of the Council of the ECB in respect of national central banks shall be the same as those conferred upon the Commission in respect of Member States by Article 169. If the Court of Justice finds that a national central bank has failed to fulfil an obligation under this Treaty, that bank shall be required to take the necessary measures to comply with the judgment of the Court of Justice.

Article 181

The Court of Justice shall have jurisdiction to give judgment pursuant to any arbitration clause contained in a contract concluded by or on behalf of the Community, whether that contract be governed by public or private law.

Article 182

The Court of Justice shall have jurisdiction in any dispute between Member States which relates to the subject matter of this Treaty if the dispute is submitted to it under a special agreement between the parties.

---

66   As amended by Article G(57) TEU.

Article 183

Save where jurisdiction is conferred on the Court of Justice by this Treaty, disputes to which the Community is a party shall not on that ground be excluded from the jurisdiction of the courts or tribunals of the Member States.

Article 184[67]

Notwithstanding the expiry of the period laid down in *the fifth paragraph of* Article 173, any party may, in proceedings in which *a regulation adopted jointly by the European Parliament and the Council, or* a regulation of the Council, of the Commission, or of the ECB is at issue, plead the grounds specified in *the second paragraph of* Article 173 in order to invoke before the Court of Justice the inapplicability of that regulation.

Article 185

Actions brought before the Court of Justice shall not have suspensory effect. The Court of Justice may, however, if it considers that circumstances so require, order that application of the contested act be suspended.

Article 186

The Court of Justice may in any cases before it prescribe any necessary interim measures.

Article 187

The judgments of the Court of Justice shall be enforceable under the conditions laid down in Article 192.

Article 188

The Statute of the Court of Justice is laid down in a separate Protocol.

The Council may, acting unanimously at the request of the Court of Justice and after consulting the Commission and the European Parliament amend the provisions of Title III of the Statute.

The Court of Justice shall adopt its rules of procedure. These shall require the unanimous approval of the Council.

Section 5. The Court of Auditors[68]

Article 188a

The Court of Auditors shall carry out the audit.

Article 188b

1. The Court of Auditors shall consist of twelve members.

2. The members of the Court of Auditors shall be chosen from among persons who belong or have belonged in their respective countries to external audit bodies or who are especially qualified for this office. Their independence must be beyond doubt.

3. The members of the Court of Auditors shall be appointed for a term of six years by the Council, acting unanimously after consulting the European Parliament.

However, when the first appointments are made, four members of the Court of Auditors, chosen by lot, shall be appointed for a term of office of four years only.

The members of the Court of Auditors shall be eligible for reappointment.

They shall elect the President of the Court of Auditors from among their number for a term of three years. The President may be re-elected.

4. The members of the Court of Auditors shall, in the general interest of the Community, be completely independent in the performance of their duties.

---

67   As amended by Article G(58) TEU.
68   Section 5 (Articles 188a to 188c) formerly Articles 206 and 206a as inserted by Article G(59) TEU.

In the performance of these duties, they shall neither seek nor take instructions from any government or from any other body. They shall refrain from any action incompatible with their duties.

5.   The members of the Court of Auditors may not, during their term of office, engage in any other occupation, whether gainful or not. When entering upon their duties they shall give a solemn undertaking that, both during and after their term of office, they will respect the obligations arising therefrom and in particular their duty to behave with integrity and discretion as regards the acceptance, after they have ceased to hold office, of certain appointments or benefits.

6.   Apart from normal replacement, or death, the duties of a member of the Court of Auditors shall end when he resigns, or is compulsorily retired by a ruling of the Court of Justice pursuant to paragraph 7.

The vacancy thus caused shall be filled for the remainder of the member's term of office.

Save in the case of compulsory retirement, members of the Court of Auditors shall remain in office until they have been replaced.

7.   A member of the Court of Auditors may be deprived of his office or of his right to a pension or other benefits in its stead only if the Court of Justice, at the request of the Court of Auditors, finds that he no longer fulfils the requisite conditions or meets the obligations arising from his office.

8.   The Council, acting by a qualified majority, shall determine the conditions of employment of the President and the members of the Court of Auditors and in particular their salaries, allowances and pensions. It shall also, by the same majority, determine any payment to be made instead of remuneration.

9.   The provisions of the Protocol on the Privileges and Immunities of the European Communities applicable to the Judges of the Court of Justice shall also apply to the members of the Court of Auditors.

Article 188c

1.   The Court of Auditors shall examine the accounts of all revenue and expenditure of the Community. It shall also examine the accounts of all revenue and expenditure of all bodies set up by the Community in so far as the relevant constituent instrument does not preclude such examination.

The Court of Auditors shall provide the European Parliament and Council with a statement of assurance as to the reliability of the accounts and the legality and regularity of the underlying transactions.

2.   The Court of Auditors shall examine whether all revenue has been received and all expenditure incurred in a lawful and regular manner and whether the financial management has been sound.

The audit of revenue shall be carried out on the basis both of the amounts established as due and the amounts actually paid to the Community.

The audit of expenditure shall be carried out on the basis both of commitments undertaken and payments made.

These audits may be carried out before the closure of accounts for the financial year in question.

3.   The audit shall be based on records and, if necessary, performed on the spot in the other institutions of the Community and in the Member States. In the Member States the audit shall be carried out in liaison with the national audit bodies or, if these do not have the necessary powers, with the competent national departments. These bodies or departments shall inform the Court of Auditors whether they intend to take part in the audit.

The other institutions of the Community and the national audit bodies or, if these do not have the necessary powers, the competent national departments, shall forward to the Court of Auditors, at its request, any document or information necessary to carry out its task.

4.   The Court of Auditors shall draw up an annual report after the close of each financial year. It shall be forwarded to the other institutions of the Community and shall be published, together with the replies of these institutions to the observations of the Court of Auditors, in the Official Journal of the European Communities.

The Court of Auditors may also, at any time, submit observations, particularly in the form of special reports, on specific questions and deliver opinions at the request of one of the other institutions of the Community.

It shall adopt its annual reports, special reports or opinions by a majority of its members.

It shall assist the European Parliament and the Council in exercising their powers of control over the implementation of the budget.

Chapter 2. Provisions Common to Several Institutions

Article 189[69]

In order to carry out their task and in accordance with the provisions of this Treaty, *the European Parliament together with the Council*, the Council or the Commission shall make regulations and issue directives, take decisions, make recommendations or deliver opinions.

A regulation shall have general application. It shall be binding in its entirety and directly applicable in all Member States.

A directive shall be binding, as to the result to be achieved, upon each Member State to which it is addressed, but shall leave to the national authorities the choice of form and methods.

A decision shall be binding in its entirety upon those to whom it is addressed.

Recommendations and opinion shall have no binding force.

Article 189a[70]

1. Where, in pursuance of this Treaty, the Council acts on a proposal from the Commission, unanimity shall be required for an act constituting an amendment to that proposal, subject to Article 189b (4) and (5).

2. As long as the Council has not acted, the Commission may alter its proposal at any time during the procedures leading to the adoption of a Community act.

Article 189b[71]

1. Where reference is made in this Treaty to this Article for the adoption of an act, the following procedure shall apply.

2. The Commission shall submit a proposal to the European Parliament and the Council.

The Council, acting by a qualified majority after obtaining the opinion of the European Parliament, shall adopt a common position. The common position shall be communicated to the European Parliament. The Council shall inform the European Parliament fully of the reasons which led it to adopt its common position. The Commission shall inform the European Parliament fully of its position.

If, within three months of such communication, the European Parliament:

(a) approves the common position, the Council shall definitively adopt the act in question in accordance with that common position;

(b) has not taken a decision, the Council shall adopt the act in question in accordance with its common position;

(c) indicates, by an absolute majority of its component members, that it intends to reject the common position, it shall immediately inform the Council. The Council may convene a meeting of the Conciliation Committee referred to in paragraph 4 to explain further its position. The European Parliament shall thereafter either confirm, by an absolute majority of its component members, its rejection of the common position, in which event the proposed act shall be deemed not to have been subparagraph (d) of this paragraph;

(d) proposes amendments to the common position by an absolute majority of its component members, the amended text shall be forwarded to the Council and to the Commission, which shall deliver an opinion on those amendments.

---

69 As amended by Article G(60) TEU.
70 As inserted by Article G(61) TEU.
71 As inserted by Article G(61) TEU.

3. If, within three months of the matter being referred to it, the Council, acting by a qualified majority, approves all the amendments of the European Parliament, it shall amend its common position accordingly and adopt the act in question; however, the Council shall act unanimously on the amendments on which the Commission has delivered a negative opinion. If the Council does not approve the act in question, the President of the Council, in agreement with the President of the European Parliament, shall forthwith convene a meeting of the Conciliation Committee.

4. The Conciliation Committee, which shall be composed of the members of the Council or their representatives and an equal number of representatives of the European Parliament, shall have the task of reaching agreement on a joint text, by a qualified majority of the members of the Council or their representatives and by a majority of the representatives of the European Parliament. The Commission shall take part in the Conciliation Committee's proceedings and shall take all the necessary initiatives with a view to reconciling the positions of the European Parliament and the Council.

5. If, within six weeks of its being convened, the Conciliation Committee approves a joint text, the European Parliament, acting by an absolute majority of the votes cast, and the Council, acting by a qualified majority, shall have a period of six weeks from that approval in which to adopt the act in question in accordance with the joint text. If one of the two institutions fails to adopt the proposed act, it shall be deemed not to have been adopted.

6. Where the Conciliation Committee does not approve a joint text, the proposed act shall not be deemed not to have been adopted unless the Council, acting by a qualified majority within six weeks of expiry of the period granted to the Conciliation Committee, confirms the common position to which it agreed before the conciliation procedure was initiated, possibly with amendments proposed by the European Parliament. In this case, the act in question shall be finally adopted unless the European Parliament, within six weeks of the date of confirmation by the Council, rejects the text by an absolute majority of its component members, in which case the proposed act shall be deemed not to have been adopted.

7. The periods of three months and six weeks referred to in this Article may be extended by a maximum of one month and two weeks respectively by common accord of the European Parliament and the Council. The period of three months referred to in paragraph 2 shall be automatically extended by two months where paragraph 2 (c) applies.

8. The scope of the procedure under this Article may be widened, in accordance with the procedure provided for in Article N (2) of the Treaty on European Union, on the basis of report to be submitted to the Council by the Commission by 1996 at the latest.

Article 189c[72]

Where reference is made in this Treaty to this Article for the adoption of an act, the following procedure shall apply:

(a) The Council, acting by a qualified majority on a proposal from the Commission and after obtaining the opinion of the European Parliament, shall adopt a common position.

(b) The Council's common position shall be communicated to the European Parliament. The Council and the Commission shall inform the European Parliament fully of the reasons which led the Council to adopt its common position and also of the Commission's position.

If, within three months of such communication, the European Parliament approves this common position or has not taken a decision within that period, the Council shall definitively adopt the act in question in accordance with the common position.

(c) The European Parliament may, within the period of three months referred to in point (b), by an absolute majority of its component members, propose amendments to the Council's common position. The European Parliament may also, by the same majority, reject the Council's common position. The result of the proceedings shall be transmitted to the Council and the Commission.

72   As inserted by Article G(61) TEU.

Annex

If the European Parliament has rejected the Council's common position, unanimity shall be required for the Council to act on a second reading.

(d) The Commission shall, within a period of one month, re-examine the proposal on the basis of which the Council adopted its common position, by taking into account the amendments proposed by the European Parliament.

The Commission shall forward to the Council, at the same time as its re-examined proposal, the amendments of the European Parliament which it has not accepted, and shall express its opinion on them. The Council may adopt these amendments unanimously.

(e) The Council, acting by a qualified majority, shall adopt the proposal as re-examined by the Commission.

Unanimity shall be required for the Council to amend the proposal as re-examined by the Commission.

(f) In the cases referred to in points (c), (d) and (e), the Council shall be required to act within a period of three months. If no decision is taken within this period, the Commission proposal shall be deemed not to have been adopted.

(g) The periods referred to in points (b) and (f) may be extended by a maximum of one month by common accord between the Council and the European Parliament.

Article 190[73]

Regulations, directives and decisions adopted jointly by the European Parliament and the Council, and such acts adopted by the Council or the Commission, shall state the reasons on which they are based and shall refer to any proposals or opinions which were required to be obtained pursuant to this Treaty.

Article 191[74]

1. *Regulations, directives and decisions adopted in accordance with the procedure referred to in Article 189b shall be signed by the President of the European Parliament and by the President of the Council and published in the Official Journal of the Community. They shall enter into force on the date specified in them or, in the absence thereof, on the twentieth day following that of their publication.*

2. *Regulations of the Council and of the Commission, as well as directives of those institutions which are addressed to all Member States, shall be published in the Official Journal of the Community. They shall enter into force on the date specified in them or, in the absence thereof, on the twentieth day following that of their publication.*

3. *Other directives, and decisions, shall be notified to those to whom they are addressed and shall take effect upon such notification.*

Article 192

Decisions of the Council or of the Commission which impose a pecuniary obligation on persons other than States, shall be enforceable.

Enforcement shall be governed by the rules of civil procedure in force in the State in the territory of which it is carried out. The order for its enforcement shall be appended to the decision, without other formality than verification of the authenticity of the decision, by the national authority which the Government of each Member State shall designate for this purpose and shall make known to the Commission and to the Court of Justice.

When these formalities have been completed on application by the party concerned, the latter may proceed to enforcement in accordance with the national law, by bringing the matter directly before the competent authority.

Enforcement may be suspended only by a decision of the Court of Justice. However, the courts of the country concerned shall have jurisdiction over complaints that enforcement is being carried out in an irregular manner.

73   As amended by Article G(62) TEU.
74   As amended by Article G(63) TEU.

Chapter 3. The Economic and Social Committee

Article 193

An Economic and Social Committee is hereby established. It shall have advisory status.

The Committee shall consist of representatives of the various categories of economic activity, in particular, representatives of producers, farmers, carriers, workers, dealers, craftsmen, professional occupations and representatives of the general public.

Article 194[75]

The number of members of the Economic and Social Committee shall be as follows:

Belgium	12
Denmark	9
Germany	24
Greece	12
Spain	21
France	24
Ireland	9
Italy	24
Luxembourg	6
Netherlands	12
Portugal	12
United Kingdom	24

The members of the Committee shall be appointed by the Council, acting unanimously, for four years. Their appointments shall be renewable.

The members of the Committee may not be bound by any mandatory instructions. They shall be completely independent in the performance of their duties, in the general interest of the Community.

The Council, acting by a qualified majority, shall determine the allowances of members of the Committee.

Article 195

1. For the appointment of the members of the Committee, each Member State shall provide for Council with a list containing twice as many candidates as there are seats allotted to its nationals.

The composition of the Committee shall take account of the need to ensure adequate of the various categories of economic and social activity.

2. The Council shall consult the Commission. It may obtain the opinion of European bodies which are representative of the various economic and social sectors to which the activities of the Community are of concern.

Article 196[76]

The Committee shall elect its chairman and officers from among its members for a term of two years.

It shall adopt its rules of procedure.

The Committee shall be convened by its chairman at the request of the Council or of the Commission. *It may also meet on its own initiative.*

---

75 As amended by Article G(64) TEU.
76 As amended by Article G(65) TEU.

Article 197

The Committee shall include specialized sections for the principle fields covered by this Treaty.

In particular, it shall contain an agricultural section and a transport section, which are the subject of special provisions in the Titles relating to agriculture and transport.

These specialized sections shall operate within the general terms of reference of the Committee. They may not be consulted independently of the Committee.

Sub-committees may also be established within the Committee to draft opinions to be submitted to the Committee for its consideration.

The rules of procedure shall lay down the methods of composition and the terms of reference of the specialized sections and of the sub-committees.

Article 198 [77]

The Committee must be consulted by the Council or by the Commission where this Treaty so provides. The Committee may be consulted by these institutions in all cases in which they consider it appropriate. *It may issue an opinion on its own initiative in cases in which it considers such action appropriate.*

The Council or the Commission shall, if it considers it necessary, set the Committee, for the submission of its opinion, a time limit which may not be less than one month from the date on which the Chairman receives notification to this effect. Upon expiry of the time limit, the absence of an opinion shall not prevent further action.

The opinion of the Committee and that of the specialized section, together with a record of the proceedings, shall be forwarded to the Council and to the Commission.

Chapter 4. The Committee of the Regions [78]

Article 198a

A Committee consisting of representatives of regional and local bodies, hereinafter referred to as "the Committee of the Regions", is hereby established with advisory status.

The number of members of the Committee of the Regions shall be as follows:

Belgium	12
Denmark	9
Germany	24
Greece	12
Spain	21
France	24
Ireland	9
Italy	24
Luxembourg	6
Netherlands	12
Portugal	12
United Kingdom	24

The members of the Committee and an equal number of alternate members shall be appointed for four years by the Council acting unanimously on proposals from the respective Member States. Their terms of office shall be renewable.

The members of the Committee may not be bound by any mandatory instructions. They shall be dependent in the performance of their duties, in the general interest of the Community.

---

77   As amended by Article G(66) TEU.
78   Chapter 4 (Articles 198a to 198c) as inserted by Article G(67) TEU.

Article 198b

The Committee of the Regions shall elect its chairman and officers from among its members for a term of two years.

It shall adopt its rules of procedure and shall submit them for approval to the Council, acting unanimously.

The Committee shall be convened by its chairman at the request of the Council or of the Commission. It may also meet on its own initiative.

Article 198c

The Committee of the Regions shall be consulted by the Council or by the Commission where this Treaty so provides and in all other cases in which one of these two institutions considers it appropriate.

The Council or the Commission shall, if it considers it necessary, set the Committee, for the submission of its opinion, a time-limit which may not be less than one month from the date on which the chairman receives notification to this effect. Upon expiry of the time-limit, the absence of an opinion shall not prevent further action.

Where the Economic and Social Committee is consulted pursuant to Article 198, the Committee of the Regions shall be informed by the Council or the Commission of the request for an opinion. Where it considers that specific regional interests are involved, the Committee of the Regions may submit an opinion on the matter.

It may issue an opinion on its own initiative in cases in which it considers such action appropriate.

The opinion of the Committee, together with a record of the proceedings, shall be forwarded to the Council and to the Commission.

Chapter 5. European Investment Bank [79]

Article 198d

The European Investment Bank shall have legal personality.

The members of the European Investment Bank shall be the Member States.

The Statute of the European Investment Bank is laid down in a Protocol annexed to this Treaty.

Article 198e

The tasks of the European Investment Bank shall be to contribute, by having recourse to the capital market and utilizing its own resources, to the balanced and steady development of the common market in the interest of the Community. For this purpose the Bank shall, operating on a non profit-making basis, grant loans and give guarantees which facilitate the financing of the following projects in all sectors of the economy:

(a) projects for developing less-developed regions;

(b) projects for modernizing or converting undertakings or for developing fresh activities called for by the progressive establishment of the common market, where these projects are of such a size or nature that they cannot be entirely financed by the various means available in the individual Member States;

(c) projects of common interest to several Member States which are of such a size or nature that they cannot be entirely financed by the various means available in the individual Member States.

In carrying out its task, the Bank shall facilitate the financing of investment programmes in conjunction with assistance from the structural Funds and other Community financial instruments.

---

79   Chapter 5 (Articles 198d and 198 e, formerly Articles 129 and 130) as inserted by Article G(68) TEU.

Title II – Financial Provisions

Article 199[80]

All items of revenue and expenditure of the Community, including those relating to the European Social Fund, shall be included in estimates to be drawn up for each financial year and shall be shown in the budget.

Administrative expenditure occasioned for the institutions by the provisions of the Treaty on European Union relating to common foreign and security policy and to co-operation in the fields of justice and home affairs shall be charged to the budget. The operational expenditure occasioned by the implementation of the said provisions may, under the conditions referred to therein, be charged to the budget.

The revenue and expenditure shown in the budget shall be in balance.

Article 200

(repealed)

Article 201[81]

Without prejudice to other revenue, the budget shall be financed wholly from own resources.

The Council, acting unanimously on a proposal from the Commission and after consulting the European Parliament, shall lay down provisions relating to the system of own resources of the Community, which it shall recommend to the Member States for adoption in accordance with their respective constitutional requirements.

Article 201a[82]

With a view to maintaining budgetary discipline, the Commission shall not make any proposal for a Community act, or alter its proposals, or adopt any implementing measure which is likely to have appreciable implications for the budget without providing the assurance that that proposal or that measure is capable of being financed within the limit of the Community's own resources arising under provisions laid down by the Council pursuant to Article 201.

Article 202

The expenditure shown in the budget shall be authorized for one financial year, unless the regulations made pursuant to Article 209 provide otherwise.

In accordance with conditions to be laid down pursuant to Article 209, any appropriations, other than those relating to staff expenditure, that are unexpended at the end of the financial year may be carried forward to the next financial year only.

Appropriations shall be classified under different chapters grouping items of expenditure according to their nature or purpose and subdivided, as far as may be necessary, in accordance with the regulations made pursuant to Article 209.

The expenditure of the European Parliament, the Council, the Commission and the Court of Justice shall be set out in separate parts of the budget, without prejudice to special arrangements for certain common items of expenditure.

Article 203

1. The financial year shall run from 1 January to 31 December.

2. Each institution of the Community shall, before 1 July, draw up estimates of its expenditure. The Commission shall consolidate these estimates in a preliminary draft budget. It shall attach thereto an opinion which may contain different estimates.

The preliminary draft budget shall contain an estimate of revenue and an estimate of expenditure.

---

80 As amended by Article G(69) TEU.
81 As amended by Article G(71) TEU.
82 As inserted by Article G(72) TEU.

3. The Commission shall place the preliminary draft budget before the Council not later than 1 September of the year preceding that in which the budget is to be implemented.

The Council shall consult the Commission and, where appropriate, the other institutions concerned whenever it intends to depart from the preliminary draft budget.

The Council, acting by a qualified majority, shall establish the draft budget and forward it to the European Parliament.

4. The draft budget shall be placed before the European Parliament not later than 5 October of the year preceding that in which the budget is to be implemented.

The European Parliament shall have the right to amend the draft budget, acting by a majority of its members, and to propose to the Council, acting by an absolute majority of the votes cast, modifications to the draft budget relating to expenditure necessarily resulting from this Treaty or from acts adopted in accordance therewith.

If, within 45 days of the draft budget being placed before it, the European Parliament has given its approval, the budget shall stand as finally adopted. If within this period the European Parliament has not amended the draft budget nor proposed any modifications thereto, the budget shall be deemed to be finally adopted.

If within this period the European Parliament has adopted amendments or proposed modifications, the draft budget together with the amendments or proposed modifications shall be forwarded to the Council.

5. After discussing the draft budget with the Commission and, where appropriate, with the other institutions concerned, the Council shall act under the following conditions:

(a) The Council may, acting by a qualified majority, modify any of the amendments adopted by the European Parliament:

(b) With regard to the proposed modifications:

– where a modification proposed by the European Parliament does not have the effect of increasing the total amount of the expenditure of an institution, owing in particular to the fact that the increase in expenditure which it would involve would be expressly compensated by one or more proposed modifications correspondingly reducing expenditure, the Council may, acting by a qualified majority, reject the proposed modification. In the absence of a decision to reject it, the proposed modification shall stand as accepted:

– where a modification proposed by the European Parliament has the effect of increasing the total amount of the expenditure of an institution, the Council may, acting by a qualified majority, accept this proposed modification. In the absence of a decision to accept it, the proposed modification shall stand as rejected:

– where, in pursuance of one of the two preceding subparagraphs, the Council has rejected a proposed modification, it may, acting by a qualified majority, either retain the amount shown in the draft budget or fix another amount.

The draft budget shall be modified on the basis of the proposed modifications accepted by the Council.

If, within 15 days of the draft being placed before it, the Council has not modified any of the amendments adopted by the European Parliament and if the modifications proposed by the latter have been accepted, the budget shall be deemed to be finally adopted. The Council shall inform the European Parliament that it has not modified any of the amendments and that the proposed modifications have been accepted.

If within this period the Council has modified one or more of the amendments adopted by the European Parliament or if the modifications proposed by the latter have been rejected or modified, the modified draft budget shall again be forwarded to the European Parliament. The Council shall inform the European Parliament of the results of its deliberations.

6. Within 15 days of the draft budget being placed before it, the European Parliament, which shall have been notified of the action taken on its proposed modifications, may, acting by a majority of its members and three-fifths of the votes cast, amend or reject the modifications to its amendments made by the

Council and shall adopt the budget accordingly. If within this period the European Parliament has not acted, the budget shall be deemed to be finally adopted.

7. When the procedure provided for in this Article has been completed, the President of the European Parliament shall declare that the budget has been finally adopted.

8. However, the European Parliament, acting by a majority of its members and two-thirds of the votes cast, may, if there are important reasons, reject the draft budget and ask for a new draft to be submitted to it.

9. A maximum rate of increase in relation to the expenditure of the same type to be incurred during the current year shall be fixed annually for the total expenditure other than that necessarily resulting from this Treaty or from acts adopted in accordance therewith.

The Commission shall, after consulting the Economic Policy Committee, declare what this maximum rate is as it results from:

- the trend, in terms of volume, of the gross national product within the Community;
- the average variation in the budgets of the Member States; and
- the trend of the cost of living during the preceding financial year.

The maximum rate shall be communicated, before 1 May, to all the institutions of the Community. The latter shall be required to conform to this during the budgetary procedure, subject to the provisions of the fourth and fifth subparagraphs of this paragraph.

If, in respect of expenditure other than that necessarily resulting from this Treaty or from acts adopted in accordance therewith, the actual rate of increase in the draft budget, established by the Council is over half the maximum rate, the European Parliament may, exercising its right of amendment, further increase the total amount of that expenditure to a limit not exceeding half the maximum rate.

Where the European Parliament, the Council or the Commission consider that the activities of the Communities require that the rate determined according to the procedure laid down in this paragraph should be exceeded, another rate may be fixed by agreement between the Council, acting by a qualified majority, and the European Parliament, acting by a majority of its members and three-fifths of the votes cast.

10. Each institution shall exercise the powers conferred upon it by this Article, with due regard for the provisions of the Treaty and for acts adopted in accordance therewith, in particular those relating to the Communities own resources and to the balance between revenue and expenditure.

Article 204

If at the beginning of a financial year the budget has not yet been voted, a sum equivalent to not more than one-twelfth of the budget appropriations for the preceding financial year may be spent each month in respect of any chapter or other subdivision of the budget in accordance with the provisions of the Regulations made pursuant to Article 209; this arrangement shall not, however, have the effect of placing at the disposal of the Commission appropriations in excess of one-twelfth of those provided for in the draft budget in course of preparation.

The Council may, acting by a qualified majority, provided that the other conditions laid down in the first subparagraph are observed, authorize expenditure in excess of one-twelfth.

If the decision relates to expenditure which does not necessarily result from this Treaty or from acts adopted in accordance therewith, the Council shall forward it immediately to the European Parliament; within 30 days the European Parliament, acting by a majority of its members and three-fifths of the votes cast, may adopt a different decision on the expenditure in excess of the one-twelfth referred to in the first subparagraph. This part of the decision of the Council shall be suspended until the European Parliament has taken its decision. If within the said period the European Parliament has not taken a decision which differs from the decision of the Council, the latter shall be deemed to be finally adopted.

The decisions referred to in the second and third subparagraphs shall lay down the necessary measures relating to resources to ensure application of this Article.

Annex

Article 205[83]

The Commission shall implement the budget, in accordance with provisions of the regulations made pursuant to Article 209, on its own responsibility and within the limits of the appropriations, *having regard to the principles of sound financial management.*

The regulations shall lay down detailed rules for each institution concerning its part in effecting its own expenditure.

Within the budget, the Commission may, subject to the limits and conditions laid down in the regulations made pursuant to Article 209, transfer appropriations from one chapter to another or from one subdivision to another.

Article 205a

The Commission shall submit annually to the Council and to the European Parliament the accounts of the preceding financial year relating to the implementation of the budget. The Commission shall also forward to them a financial statement of the assets and liabilities of the Community.

Article 206[84]

1.   The European Parliament, acting on a recommendation from the Council which shall act by a qualified majority, shall give a discharge to the Commission in respect of the implementation of the budget. To this end, the Council and the European Parliament in turn shall examine the accounts and the financial statement referred to in Article 205a, the annual report by the Court of Auditors together with the replies of the institutions under audit to the observations of the Court of Auditors and any relevant special reports by the Court of Auditors.

2.   Before giving a discharge to the Commission, or for any other purpose in connection with the exercise of its powers over the implementation of the budget, the European Parliament may ask to hear the Commission give evidence with regard to the execution of expenditure or the operation of financial control systems. The Commission shall submit any necessary information to the European Parliament at the latter's request.

3.   The Commission shall take all appropriate steps to act on the observations in the decisions giving discharge and on other observations by the European Parliament relating to the execution of expenditure, as well as on comments accompanying the recommendations on discharge adopted by the Council.

At the request of the European Parliament or the Council, the Commission shall report on the measures taken in the light of these observations and comments and in particular on the instructions given to the departments which are responsible for the implementation of the budget. These reports shall also be forwarded to the Court of Auditors.

Article 206a

(repealed)

Article 206b

(repealed)

Article 207

The budget shall be drawn up in the unit of account determined in accordance with the provisions of the regulations made pursuant to Article 209.

The financial contributions provided for in Article 200(1) shall be placed at the disposal of the Community by the Member States in their national currencies.

---

83   As amended by Article G(73) TEU.
84   Former Article 206b, as amended by Article G(74) TEU.

The available balances of these contributions shall be deposited with the Treasuries of Member States or with bodies designated by them. While on deposit, such funds shall retail the value corresponding to the parity, at the date of deposit, in relation to the unit of account referred to in the first paragraph.

The balances may be invested on terms to be agreed between the Commission and the Member State concerned.

The regulations made pursuant to Article 209 shall lay down the technical conditions under which financial operations relating to the European Social Fund shall be carried out.

Article 208

The Commission may, provided it notifies the competent authorities of the Member States concerned, transfer into the currency of one of the Member States its holdings in the currency of another Member State, to the extent necessary to enable them to be used for purposes which come within the scope of this Treaty. The Commission shall as far as possible avoid making such transfer if it possesses cash or liquid assets in the currencies which it needs.

The Commission shall deal with each Member State through the authority designated by the State concerned. In carrying out financial operations the Commission shall employ the services of the bank of issue of the Member State concerned or of any other financial institution approved by that State.

Article 209 [85]

The Council, acting unanimously on a proposal from the Commission and after consulting the European Parliament and obtaining the opinion of the Court of Auditors, shall:

(a) make Financial Regulations specifying in particular the procedure to be adopted for establishing and implementing the budget and for presenting and auditing accounts;

(b) determine the methods and procedure whereby the budget revenue provided under the arrangements relating to the Community's own resources shall be made available to the Commission, and determine the measures to be applied, if need be, to meet cash requirements;

(c) lay down rules concerning the responsibility of *financial controllers*, authorizing officers and accounting officers, and concerning appropriate arrangements for inspection.

Article 209a [86]

Member States shall take the same measures to counter fraud affecting the financial interests of the Community as they take to counter fraud affecting their own financial interests.

Without prejudice to other provisions of this Treaty, Member States shall co-ordinate their actions aimed at protecting the financial interests of the Community against fraud. To this end they shall organize, with the help of the Commission, close and regular co-operation between the competent services of their administrations.

Part Six: General Provisions

Article 210

The Community shall have legal personality.

Article 211

In each of the Member States, the Community shall enjoy the most extensive legal capacity accorded to legal persons under their laws; it may, in particular, acquire or dispose of movable and immovable property and may be a party to legal proceedings. To this end, the Community shall be represented by the Commission.

Article 212

[deleted]

---

85 As amended by Article G(76) TEU.
86 As inserted by Article G(77) TEU.

Annex

Article 213

The Commission may, within the limits and under conditions laid down by the Council in accordance with the provisions of this Treaty, collect any information and carry out any checks required for the performance of the tasks entrusted to it.

Article 214

The members of the institutions of the Community, the members of committees, and the officials and other servants of the Community shall be required, even after their duties have ceased, not to disclose information of the kind covered by the obligation of professional secrecy, in particular information about undertakings, their business relations or their cost components.

Article 215[87]

The contractual liability of the Community shall be governed by the law applicable to the contract in question.

In the case of non-contractual liability, the Community shall, in accordance with the general principles common to the laws of the Member States, make good any damage caused by its institutions or by its servants in the performance of their duties.

The preceding paragraph shall apply under the same conditions to damage caused by the ECB or by its servants in the performance of their duties.

The personal liability of its servants towards the Community shall be governed by the provisions laid down in their Staff Regulations or in the Conditions of Employment applicable to them.

Article 216

The seat of the institutions of the Community shall be determined by common accord of the Governments of the Member States.

Article 217

The rules governing the languages of the institutions of the Community shall, without prejudice to the provisions contained in the rules of procedure of the Court of Justice, be determined by the Council, acting unanimously.

Article 218

(Article repealed by the second paragraph of Article 28 of the Merger Treaty)

[See the first paragraph of Article 28 of the Merger Treaty, which reads as follows:

The European Communities shall enjoy in the territories of the Member States such privileges and immunities as are necessary for the performance of their backs, under the conditions laid down in the Protocol annexed to this treaty. The same shall apply to the European Investment Bank.]

Article 219

Member States undertake not to submit a dispute concerning the interpretation or application of this Treaty to any method of settlement other than those provided for therein.

Article 220

Member States shall, so far as is necessary, enter into negotiations with each other with a view to securing for the benefit of their nationals:

- the protection of persons and the enjoyment and protection of rights under the same conditions as those accorded by each State to its own nationals;
- the abolition of double taxation within the Community;
- the mutual recognition of companies or firms within the meaning of the second paragraph of Article 48, the retention of legal personality in the event of transfer of their seat from one country to another,

---

87   As amended by Article G(78) TEU.

and the possibility of mergers between companies or firms governed by the laws of different countries;

- the simplification of formalities governing the reciprocal recognition and enforcement of judgments of courts or tribunals and of arbitration awards.

Article 221

Within three years of the entry into force of this Treaty, Member States shall accord nationals of the other Member States the same treatment as their own nationals as regards participation in the capital of companies or firms within the meaning of Article 58, without prejudice to the application of the other provisions of this Treaty.

Article 222

This Treaty shall in no way prejudice the rules in Member States governing the system of property ownership.

Article 223

1. The provisions of this Treaty shall not preclude the application of the following rules:

(a) No Member State shall be obliged to supply information the disclosure of which it consider contrary to the essential interest of its security;

(b) Any Member State may take such measures as it considers necessary for the protection of the essential interests of its security which are connected with the production of or trade in arms, ammunitions and war material; such measures shall not adversely affect the conditions of competition in the common market regarding products which are not intended for specifically military purposes.

2. During the first year after the entry into force of this Treaty, the Council shall, acting unanimously, draw up a list of products to which the provisions of paragraph 1 (b) shall apply.

3. The Council may, acting unanimously on a proposal from the Commission, make changes in this list.

Article 224

Member States shall consult each other with a view to taking together the steps needed to prevent the functioning of the common market being affected by measures which a Member States may be called upon to take in the event of serious internal disturbances affecting the maintenance of law and order, in the event of war, serious international tension constituting a threat of war, or in order to carry out obligations it has accepted for the purpose of maintaining peace and international security.

Article 225

If measures taken in the circumstances referred to in Articles 223 and 224 have the effect of distorting the conditions of competition in the common market, the Commission shall, together with the State concerned, examine how these measures can be adjusted to the rules laid down in this Treaty.

By way of derogation from the procedure laid down in Articles 169 and 170, the Commission or any Member State may bring the matter directly before the Court of Justice if it considers that another Member State is making improper use of the powers provided for in Arts. 223 and 224. The Court of Justice shall give its ruling in camera.

Article 226

1. If, during the transitional period, difficulties arise which are serious and liable to persist in any sector of the economy or which could bring about serious deterioration in the economic situation of a given area, a Member State may apply for authorization to take protective measures in order to rectify the situation and adjust the sector concerned to the economy of the common market.

2. On application by the State concerned, the Commission shall, by emergency procedure, determine without delay the protective measures which it considers necessary, specifying the circumstances and the manner in which they are to be put into effect.

3. The measures authorized under paragraph 2 may involve derogations from the rules of this Treaty, to such an extent and for such periods as are strictly necessary in order to attain the objectives referred to in

paragraph 1. Priority shall be given to such measures as will least disturb the functioning of the common market.

Article 227 [88]

1.   This Treaty shall apply to the Kingdom of Belgium, the Kingdom of Denmark, the Federal Republic of Germany, the Hellenic Republic, the Kingdom of Spain, the French Republic, Ireland, the Italian Republic, the Grand Duchy of Luxembourg, the Kingdom of the Netherlands, the Portuguese Republic and the United Kingdom of Great Britain and Northern Ireland.

2.   *With regard and the French overseas departments, the general and particular provisions of this Treaty relating to:*

–   *the free movement of goods;*

–   *the agriculture, save for Article 40 (4);*

–   *the liberalization of services;*

–   *the rules on competition;*

–   *the protective measures provided for in Articles 108h, 109i and 226;*

–   *the institutions,*

shall apply as soon as this Treaty enters into force.

The conditions under which the other provisions of this Treaty are to apply shall be determined, within two years of the entry into force of this Treaty, by decisions of the Council acting unanimously on a proposal from the Commission.

The institutions of the Community will, within the framework of the procedures provided for in this Treaty, in particular Article 226, take care that economic and social development of these areas is made possible.

3.   The special arrangements for association set out in Part Four of this Treaty shall apply to the overseas countries and territories listed in Annex IV to this Treaty.

This Treaty shall not apply to those overseas countries and territories having special relations with the United Kingdom of Great Britain and Northern Ireland which are not included in the aforementioned list.

4.   The provisions of this Treaty shall apply to the European territories for whose external relations a Member State is responsible.

5.   Notwithstanding the preceding paragraphs:

(a)   This Treaty shall not apply to the Faroe Islands.

(b)   This Treaty shall not apply to the Sovereign Base Area of the United Kingdom of Great Britain and Northern Ireland in Cyprus.

(c)   This Treaty shall apply to the Channel Islands and the Isle of Man only to the extent necessary to ensure the implementation of the arrangements for those islands set out in the Treaty concerning the accession of new Member States to the European Community and to the European Atomic Energy Community signed on 22 January 1972.

Article 228 [89]

1.   *Where this Treaty provides for the conclusion of agreements between the Community and one or more States or international organizations, the Commission shall make recommendations to the Council, which shall authorize the Commission to open the necessary negotiations. The Commission shall conduct these negotiations in consultation with special committees appointed by the Council to assist it in this task and within the framework of such directives as the Council may issue to it.*

---

88   As amended by Article G(79) TEU.
89   As amended by Article G(80) TEU.

In exercising the powers conferred upon it by this paragraph, the Council shall act by a qualified majority, except in the cases provided for in the second sentence of paragraph 2, for which it shall act unanimously.

2. *Subject to the powers vested in the Commission in this field, the agreements shall be concluded by the Council, acting by a qualified majority on a proposal from the Commission. The Council shall act unanimously when the agreement covers a field for which unanimity is required for the adoption of internal rules, and for the agreements referred to in Article 238.*

3. *The Council shall conclude agreements after consulting the European Parliament, except for the agreements referred to in Article 113 (3), including cases where the agreement covers a field for which the procedure referred to in Article 189b or that referred to in Article 189c is required for the adoption of internal rules. The European Parliament shall deliver its opinion within a time limit which the Council may lay down according to the urgency of the matter. In the absence of an opinion within that time limit, the Council may act.*

By way of derogation from the previous subparagraph, agreements referred to in Article 238, other agreements establishing a specific institutional framework by organizing co-operation procedures, agreements having important budgetary implications for the Community and agreements entailing amendment of an act adopted under the procedure referred to in Article 189b shall be concluded after the assent of the European Parliament has been obtained.

The Council and the European Parliament may, in an urgent situation, agree upon a time limit for the assent.

4. *When concluding an agreement, the Council may, by way of derogation from paragraph 2, authorize the Commission to approve modifications on behalf of the Community where the agreement provides for them to be adopted by a simplified procedure or by a body set up by the agreement; it may attach specific conditions to such authorization.*

5. *When the Council envisages concluding an agreement which calls for amendments to this Treaty, the amendments must first be adopted in accordance with the procedure laid down in Article N of the Treaty on European Union.*

6. *The Council, the Commission or a Member State may obtain the opinion of the Court of Justice as to whether the agreement envisaged is compatible with the provisions of this Treaty. Where the opinion of the Court of Justice is adverse, the agreement may enter into force only in accordance with Article N of the Treaty on European Union.*

7. *Agreements concluded under the conditions set out in this Article shall be binding on the institutions of the Community and on Member States.*

Article 228a[90]

Where it is provided, in a common position or in a joint action adopted according to the provisions of the Treaty on the Union relating to the common foreign and security policy, for an action by the Community to interrupt or to reduce, in part or completely, economic relations with one or more third countries, the Council shall take the necessary urgent measures. The Council shall act by a qualified majority on a proposal from the Commission.

Article 229

It shall be for the Commission to ensure the maintenance of all appropriate relations with the organs of the United Nations, of its specialized agencies and of the General Agreement on Tariffs and Trade.

The Commission shall also maintain such relations as are appropriate with all international organizations.

Article 230

The Community shall establish all appropriate forms of co-operation with the Council of Europe.

---

90   As inserted by Article G(81) TEU.

Annex

Article 231 [91]

The Community shall establish close co-operation with *the Organisation for Economic Co-operation and Development*, the details of which shall be determined by common accord.

Article 232

1. The provisions of this Treaty shall not affect the provisions of the Treaty establishing the European Coal and Steel Community, in particular as regards the rights and obligations of Member States, the powers of the institutions of that Community and the rules laid down by that Treaty for the functioning of the common market in coal and steel.

2. The provisions of this Treaty shall not derogate from those of the Treaty establishing the European Atomic Energy Community.

Article 233

The provisions of this Treaty shall not preclude the existence or completion of regional unions between Belgium and Luxembourg, or between Belgium, Luxembourg and the Netherlands, to the extent that the objectives of these regional unions are not attained by application of this Treaty.

Article 234

The rights and obligations arising from agreements concluded before the entry into force of this Treaty between one or more Member States on the one hand, and one or more third countries on the other, shall not be affected by the provisions of this Treaty.

To the extent that such agreements are not compatible with this Treaty, the Member State or States concerned shall take all appropriate steps to eliminate the incompatibilities established. Member States shall, when necessary, assist each other to this end and shall, where appropriate, adopt a common attitude.

In applying the agreements referred to in the first paragraph, Member States shall take into account the fact that the advantages accorded under this Treaty by each Member State form an integral part of the establishment of the Community and are thereby inseparably linked with the creation of common institutions, the conferring of powers upon them and the granting of the same advantages by all the other Member States.

Article 235

If action by the Community should prove necessary to attain, in the course of the operation of the common market, one of the objectives of the Community and this Treaty has not provided the necessary powers, the Council shall, acting unanimously on a proposal from the Commission and after consulting the European Parliament, take the appropriate measures.

Article 236

(repealed)

Article 237

(repealed)

Article 238 [92]

The Community may conclude *with one or more states or international organizations* agreements establishing an association involving reciprocal rights and obligations, common action and special procedures.

Article 239

The Protocols annexed to this Treaty by common accord of the Member States shall form an integral part thereof.

---

91   As amended by Article G(82) TEU.
92   As amended by Article G(84) TEU.

Annex

Article 240

This Treaty is concluded for an unlimited period.

Setting up of the Institutions

Article 241

The Council shall meet within one month of the entry into force of this Treaty.

Article 242

The Council shall, within three months of its first meeting, take all appropriate measures to constitute the Economic and Social Committee.

Article 243

The Assembly shall meet within two months of the first meeting of the Council, having been convened by the President of the Council, in order to elect its officers and draw up its rules of procedure. Pending the election of its officers, the oldest member shall take the chair.

Article 244

The Court of Justice shall take up its duties as soon as its members have been appointed. Its first President shall be appointed for three years in the same manner as its members.

The Court of Justice shall adopt its rules of procedure within three months of taking up its duties.

No matter may be brought before the Court of Justice until its rules of procedure have been published. The time within which an action must be brought shall run only from the date of-this publication.

Upon his appointment, the President of the Court of Justice shall exercise the powers conferred upon him by this Treaty.

Article 245

The Commission shall take up its duties and assume the responsibilities conferred upon it by this Treaty as soon as its members have been appointed.

Upon taking up its duties, the Commission shall undertake the studies and arrange the contacts needed for making an overall survey of the economic situation of the Community.

Article 246

1. The first financial year shall run from the date on which this Treaty enters into force until 31 December following. Should this Treaty, however, enter into force during the second half of the year, the first financial year shall run until 31 December of the following year.

2. Until the budget for the first financial year has been established, Member States shall make the Community interest-free advances which shall be deducted from their financial contributions to the implementation of the budget.

3. Until the Staff Regulations of officials and the Conditions of Employment of other servants of the Community provided for in Art. 212 have been laid down, each institution shall recruit the staff it needs and to this end conclude contracts of limited duration.

Each institution shall examine together with the Council any question concerning the number, remuneration and distribution of posts.

Final Provisions

Article 247

This Treaty shall be ratified by the High Contracting Parties in accordance with their respective constitutional requirements. The instruments of ratification shall be deposited with the Government of the Italian Republic.

This Treaty shall enter into force on the first day of the month following the deposit of the instrument of ratification by the last signatory State to take this step. If, however, such deposit is made less than fifteen

306

days before the beginning of the following month, this Treaty shall not enter into force until the first day of the second month after the date of such deposit.

Article 248

This Treaty, drawn up in a single original in the Dutch, French, German and Italian languages, all four texts being equally authentic, shall be deposited in the archives of the Government of the Italian Republic, which shall transmit a certified copy to each of the Governments of the other signatory States.

Title III

Provisions Amending the Treaty Establishing the European Coal and Steel Community

Article H

The Treaty establishing the European Coal and Steel Community shall be amended in accordance with the provisions of this Article.

Title IV

Provisions Amending the Treaty Establishing the European Atomic Energy Community

Article I

The Treaty establishing the European Atomic Energy Community shall be amended in accordance with the provisions of this Article.

Title V

Provisions on a Common Foreign and Security Policy

Article J

A common foreign and security policy is hereby established which shall be governed by the following provisions.

Article J.1

1. The Union and its Member States shall define and implement a common foreign and security policy, governed by the provisions of this Title and covering all areas of foreign and security policy.
2. The objectives of the common foreign and security policy shall be:
- to safeguard the common values, fundamental interests and independence of the Union;
- to strengthen the security of the Union and its Member States in all ways;
- to preserve peace and strengthen international security, in accordance with the principles of the United Nations Charter as well as the principles of the Helsinki Final Act and the objectives of the Paris Charter;
- to promote international cooperation;
- to develop and consolidate democracy and the rule of law, and respect for human rights and fundamental freedoms.
3. The Union shall pursue these objectives:
- by establishing systematic cooperation between Member States in the conduct of policy, in accordance with Article J.2;
- by gradually implementing, in accordance with Article J.3, joint action in the areas in which the Member States have important interests in common.
4. The Member States shall support the Union's external and security policy actively and unreservedly in a spirit of loyalty and mutual solidarity. They shall refrain from any action which is contrary to the interests of the Union or likely to impair its effectiveness as a cohesive force in international relations. The Council shall ensure that these principles are complied with.

Article J.2

1.   Member States shall inform and consult one another within the Council on any matter of foreign and security policy of general interest in order to ensure that their combined influence is exerted as effectively as possible by means of concerted and convergent action.

2.   Whenever it deems it necessary, the Council shall define a common position.

Member States shall ensure that their national policies conform to the common positions.

3.   Member States shall coordinate their action in international organizations and at international conferences. They shall uphold the common positions in such forums.

In international organizations and at international conferences where not all the Member States participate, those which do take part shall uphold the common positions.

Article J.3

The procedure for adopting joint action in matters covered by the foreign and security policy shall be the following:

1.   The Council shall decide, on the basis of general guidelines from the European Council, that a matter should be the subject of joint action.

Whenever the Council decides on the principle of joint action, it shall lay down the specific scope, the Union's general and specific objectives in carrying out such action, if necessary its duration, and the means, procedures and conditions for its implementation.

2.   The Council shall, when adopting the joint action and at any stage during its development, define those matters on which decisions are to be taken by a qualified majority.

Where the Council is required to act by a qualified majority pursuant to the preceding subparagraph, the votes of its members shall be weighted in accordance with Article 148 (2) of the Treaty establishing the European Community, and for their adoption, acts of the Council shall require at least 54 votes in favour, cast by at least eight members.

3.   If there is a change in circumstances having a substantial effect on a question subject to joint action, the Council shall review the principles and objectives of that action and take the necessary decisions. As long as the Council has not acted, the joint action shall stand.

4.   Joint actions shall commit the Member States in the positions they adopt and in the conduct of their activity.

5.   Whenever there is any plan to adopt a national position or take national action pursuant to a joint action, information shall be provided in time to allow, if necessary, for prior consultations within the Council. The obligation to provide prior information shall not apply to measures which are merely a national transposition of Council decisions.

6.   In cases of imperative need arising from changes in the situation and failing a Council decision, Member States may take the necessary measures as a matter of urgency having regard to the general objectives of the joint action. The Member State concerned shall inform the Council immediately of any such measures.

7.   Should there be any major difficulties in implementing a joint action, a Member State shall refer them to the Council which shall discuss them and seek appropriate solutions. Such solutions shall not run counter to the objectives of the joint action or impair its effectiveness.

Article J.4

1.   The common foreign and security policy shall include all questions related to the security of the Union, including the eventual framing of a common defence policy, which might in time lead to a common defence.

2.   The Union requests the Western European Union (WEU), which is an integral part of the development of the Union, to elaborate and implement decisions and actions of the Union which have defence implications. The Council shall, in agreement with the institutions of the WEU, adopt the necessary practical arrangements.

3. Issues having defence implications dealt with under this Article shall not be subject to the procedures set out in Article J.3.

4. The policy of the Union in accordance with this Article shall not prejudice the specific character of the security and defence policy of certain Member States and shall respect the obligations of certain Member States under the North Atlantic Treaty and be compatible with the common security and defence policy established within that framework.

5. The provisions of this Article shall not prevent the development of closer cooperation between two or more Member States on a bilateral level, in the framework of the WEU and the Atlantic Alliance, provided such cooperation does not run counter to or impede that provided for in this Title.

6. With a view to furthering the objective of this Treaty, and having in view the date of 1998 in the context of Article XII of the Brussels Treaty, the provisions of this Article may be revised as provided for in Article N (2) on the basis of a report to be presented in 1996 by the Council to the European Council, which shall include an evaluation of the progress made and the experience gained until then.

Article J.5

1. The Presidency shall represent the Union in matters coming with the common foreign and security policy.

2. The Presidency shall be responsible for the implementation of common measures; in that capacity it shall in principle express the position of the Union in international organizations and international conferences.

3. In the tasks referred to in paragraphs 1 and 2, the Presidency shall be assisted if need be by the previous and next Member States to hold the Presidency. The Commission shall be fully associated in these tasks.

4. Without prejudice to Article J.2 (3) and Article J.3 (4), Member States represented in international organizations or international conferences where not all the Member States participate shall keep the latter informed of any matter of common interest.

Member States which are also members of the United Nations Security Council will concert and keep the other Member States fully informed. Member States which are permanent members of the Security Council will, in the execution of their functions, ensure the defence of the positions and the interests of the Union, without prejudice to their responsibilities under the provisions of the United Nations Charter.

Article J.6

The diplomatic and consular missions of the Member States and the Commission Delegations in third countries and international conferences, and their representations to international organizations, shall cooperate in ensuring that the common positions and common measures adopted by the Council are complied with and implemented.

They shall step up cooperation by exchanging information, carrying out joint assessments and contributing to the implementation of the provisions referred to in Article 8c of the Treaty establishing the European Community.

Article J.7

The Presidency shall consult the European Parliament on the main aspects and the basic choices of the common foreign and security policy and shall ensure that the views of the European Parliament are duly taken into consideration. The European Parliament shall be kept regularly informed by the Presidency and the Commission of the development of the Union's foreign and security policy.

The European Parliament may ask questions of the Council or make recommendations to it. It shall hold an annual debate on progress in implementing the common foreign and security policy.

Article J.8

1. The European Council shall define the principles of and general guidelines for the common foreign and security policy.

2. The Council shall take the decisions necessary for defining and implementing the common foreign and security policy on the basis of the general guidelines adopted by the European Council. It shall ensure the unity, consistency and effectiveness of action by the Union.

The Council shall act unanimously, except for procedural questions and in the case referred to in Article J.3 (2).

3. Any Member State or the Commission may refer to the Council any question relating to the common foreign and security policy and may submit proposals to the Council.

4. In cases requiring a rapid decision, the Presidency, of its own motion, or at the request of the Commission or a Member State, shall convene and extraordinary Council meeting within 48 hours or, in an emergency, within a shorter period.

5. Without prejudice to Article 151 of the Treaty establishing the European Community, a Political Committee consisting of Political Directors shall monitor the international situation in the areas covered by common foreign and security policy and contribute to the definition of policies by delivering opinions to the Council at the request of the Council or on its own initiative. It shall also monitor the implementation of agreed policies, without prejudice to the responsibility of the Presidency and the Commission.

Article J.9

The Commission shall be fully associated with the work carried out in the common foreign and security policy field.

Article J.10

On the occasion of any review of the security provisions under Article J.4, the Conference which is convened to that effect shall also examine whether any other amendments need to be made to provisions relating to the common foreign and security policy.

Article J.11

1. The provisions referred to in Articles 137, 138, 139 to 142, 146, 147, 150 to 153, 157 to 163 and 217 of the Treaty establishing the European Community shall apply to the provisions relating to the areas referred to in this Title.

2. Administrative expenditure which the provisions relating to the areas referred to in this Title entail for the institutions shall be charged to the budget of the European Communities.

The Council may also:

– either decide unanimously that operational expenditure to which the implementation of those provisions gives rise is to be charged to the budget of the European Communities; in that event, the budgetary procedure laid down in the Treaty establishing the European Community shall be applicable;

– or determine that such expenditure shall be charged to the Member States, where appropriate in accordance with a scale to be decided.

Title VI

Provisions on Cooperation in the Fields of Justice and Home Affairs

Article K

Cooperation in the fields of justice and home affairs shall be governed by following provisions.

Article K.1

For the purposes of achieving the objectives of the Union, in particular the movement of persons, and without prejudice to the powers of the European Community, Member States shall regard the following areas as matters of common interest:

1. asylum policy;

2. rules governing the crossing by persons of the external borders of the Member States and the exercise of controls thereon;

3. immigration policy and policy regarding nationals of third countries:

(a) conditions of entry and movement by nationals of third countries on the territory of Member States;

(b) conditions of residence by nationals of third countries on the territory of Member States, including family reunion and access to employment;

(c) combating unauthorized immigration, residence and work by nationals of third countries on the territory of Member States;

4. combating drug addiction in so far as this is not covered by (7) to (9);

5. combating fraud on an international scale in so far as this is not covered (7) to (9);

6. judicial cooperation in civil matters;

7. judicial cooperation in criminal matters;

8. customs cooperation;

9. police cooperation for the purposes of preventing and combating terrorism, unlawful drug trafficking and other serious forms of international crime, including if necessary certain aspects of customs cooperation, in connection with the organization of a Union-wide system for exchanging information within a European Police Office (Europol).

Article K.2

1. The matters referred to in Article K.1 shall be dealt with in compliance with European Convention for the Protection of Human Rights and Fundamental Freedoms of 4 November 1950 and the Convention relating to the Status of Refugees of 28 July 1951 and having regard to the protection afforded by Member States to persons persecuted on political grounds.

2. This Title shall not affect the exercise of the responsibilities incumbent upon Member States with regard to the maintenance of law and order and the safeguarding of internal security.

Article K.3

1. In the areas referred to in Article K.1, Member States shall inform and consult one another within the Council with a view to coordinating their action. To that end, they shall establish collaboration between the relevant departments of their administrations.

2. The Council may:

– on the initiative of any Member State or of the Commission, in the areas referred to in Article K.1 (1) to (6);

– on the initiative of any Member State, in the areas referred to in Article K.1 (7) to (9):

(a) adopt joint positions and promote, using the appropriate form and procedures, any cooperation contributing to the pursuit of the objectives of the Union;

(b) adopt joint action in so far as the objectives of the Union can be attained better by joint action than by the Member States acting individually on account of the scale or effects of the action envisaged; it may decide that measures implementing joint action are to be adopted by a qualified majority;

(c) without prejudice to Article 220 of the Treaty establishing the European Community, draw up conventions which it shall recommend to the Member States for adoption in accordance with their respective constitutional requirements.

Unless otherwise provided by such conventions, measures implementing them shall be adopted within the Council by a majority of two-thirds of the High Contracting Parties.

Such conventions may stipulate that the Court of Justice shall have jurisdiction to interpret their provisions and to rule on any disputes regarding their application, in accordance with such arrangements as they may lay down.

Annex

Article K.4

1.   A Coordinating Committee shall be set up consisting of senior officials. In addition to its coordinating role, it shall be the task of the Committee to:

– give opinions for the attention of the Council, either at the Council's request or on its own initiative;

– contribute, without prejudice to Article 151 of the Treaty establishing the European Community, to the preparation of the Council's discussions in the areas referred to in Article K.1 and, in accordance with the conditions laid down in Article 100d of the Treaty establishing the European Community, in the areas referred to in Article 100c of that Treaty.

2.   The Commission shall be fully associated with the work in the areas referred to in this Title.

3.   The Council shall act unanimously, except on matters of procedure and in cast where Article K.3 expressly provides for other voting rules.

Where the Council is required to act by a qualified majority, the votes of its members shall be weighted as laid down in Article 148 (2) of the Treaty establishing the European Community, and for their adoption, acts of the Council shall require at least 54 votes in favour, cast by at least eight members.

Article K.5

Within international organizations and at international conferences in which they take part, Member States shall defend the common positions adopted under the provisions of this Title.

Article K.6

The Presidency and the Commission shall regularly inform the European Parliament of discussions in the areas covered by this Title.

The Presidency shall consult the European Parliament on the principal aspects of activities in the areas referred to in this Title and shall ensure that the views of the European Parliament are duly taken into consideration.

The European Parliament may ask questions of the Council or make recommendations to it. Each year, it shall hold a debate on the progress made in implementation of the areas referred to in this Title.

Article K.7

The provisions of this Title shall not prevent the establishment or development of closer cooperation between two or more Member States in so far as such cooperation does not conflict with, or impede, that provided for in this Title.

Article K.8

1.   The provisions referred to in Articles 137, 138, 139 to 142, 146, 147, 150 to 153, 157 to 163 and 217 of the Treaty establishing the European Community shall apply to the provisions relating to the areas referred to in this Title.

2.   Administrative expenditure which the provisions relating to the areas referred to in this Title entail for the institutions shall be charged to the budget of the European Communities.

The Council may also:

– either decide unanimously that operational expenditure to which the implementation of those provisions gives rise is to be charged to the budget of the European Communities; in that event, the budgetary procedure laid down in the Treaty establishing the European Community shall be applicable;

– or determine that such expenditure shall be charged to the Member States, where appropriate in accordance with a scale to be decided.

Annex

Article K.9

The Council, acting unanimously on the initiative of the Commission or a Member State, may decide to apply Article 1OOc of the Treaty establishing the European Community to action in areas referred to in Article K.1 (1) to (6), and at the same time determine the relevant voting conditions relating to it. It shall recommend the Member States to adopt that decision in accordance with their respective constitutional requirements.

TitleVII

Final Provisions

Article L

The provisions of the Treaty establishing the European Community, the Treaty establishing the European Coal and Steel Community and the Treaty establishing the European Atomic Energy Community concerning the powers of the Court of Justice of the European Communities and the exercise of those powers shall apply only to the following provisions of this Treaty:

(a) provisions amending the Treaty establishing the European Economic Community with a view to establishing the European Community, the Treaty establishing the European Coal and Steel Community and the Treaty establishing the European Atomic Energy Community;

(b) the third subparagraph of Article K.3 (2)(c);

(c) Articles L to S.

Article M

Subject to the provisions amending the Treaty establishing the European Economic Community with a view to establishing the European Community, the Treaty establishing the European Coal and Steel Community and the Treaty establishing the European Atomic Energy Community, and to these final provisions, nothing in this Treaty shall affect the Treaties establishing the European Communities or the subsequent Treaties and Acts modifying or supplementing them.

Article N

1. The government of any Member State or the Commission may submit to the Council proposals for the amendment of the Treaties on which the Union is founded.

If the Council, after consulting the European Parliament and, where appropriate, the Commission, delivers an opinion in favour of calling a conference of representatives of the governments of the Member States, the conference shall be convened by the President of the Council for the purpose of determining by common accord the amendments to be made to those Treaties. The European Central Bank shall also be consulted in the case of institutional changes in the monetary area.

The amendments shall enter into force after being ratified by all the Member States in accordance with their respective constitutional requirements.

2. A conference of representatives of the governments of the Member States shall be convened in 1996 to examine those provisions of this Treaty for which revision is provided, in accordance with the objectives set out in Articles A and B.

Article O

Any European State may apply to become a Member of the Union. It shall address its application to the Council, which shall act unanimously after consulting the Commission and after receiving the assent of the European Parliament, which shall act by an absolute majority of its component members.

The conditions of admission and the adjustments to the Treaties on which the Union is founded which such admission entails shall be the subject of an agreement between the Member States and the applicant State. This agreement shall be submitted for ratification by all the contracting States in accordance with their respective constitutional requirements.

Article P

1. Articles 2 to 7 and 10 to 19 of the Treaty establishing a Single Council and a Single Commission of the European Communities, signed in Brussels on 8 April 1965, are hereby repealed.

2. Article 2, Article 3 (2) and Title III of the Single European Act signed in Luxembourg on 17 February 1986 and in The Hague on 28 February 1986 are hereby repealed.

Article Q

This Treaty is concluded for an unlimited period.

Article R

1. This Treaty shall be ratified by the High Contracting Parties in accordance with their respective constitutional requirements. The instruments of ratification shall be deposited with the government of the Italian Republic.

2. This Treaty shall enter into force on 1 January 1993, provided that all the instruments of ratification have been deposited, or, failing that, on the first day of the month following the deposit of the instrument of ratification by the last signatory State to take this step.

Article S

This Treaty, drawn up in a single original in the Danish, Dutch, English, French, German, Greek, Irish, Italian, Portuguese and Spanish languages, the texts in each of these languages being equally authentic, shall be deposited in the archives of the government of the Italian Republic, which will transmit a certified copy to each of the governments of the other signatory States.

IN WITNESS WHEREOF the undersigned Plenipotentiaries have signed this Treaty.

DONE at Maastricht on the seventh day of February in the year one thousand nine hundred and ninety-two.

Index

Law Books in Europe came into being on the initiative of some of the best known European publishing houses specialized in the field of law. Its purpose is to offer professional people, scholars, libraries, business concerns and public and private bodies timely information about the most significant publications available on legal questions, and to provide quick delivery at favourable conditions for the purchaser.

EDITIONS TECHNIQUES - Paris
Rue d'Alésia 123
75678 Paris Cedex 14
Tel. 33-1-44122050
Telex Editec 270737F
Telefax 33-1-44122097

C. H. BECK - Munich
Wilhelmstrasse 9
80801 München
Tel. 49-89-38 18 90
Telex 5215085 beck d
Telefax 49-89-381 89-398

GIUFFRÈ EDITORE - Milan
Via Busto Arsizio 40
20151 Milano
Tel. 39-2-380891
Telefax 39-2-38009582

KLUWER - Deventer
Staverenstraat 15
7418 CJ Deventer
Tel. 31-5700-47261
Telex 49295
Telefax 31-5700-22244

SWEET & MAXWELL - London
South Quay Plaza, 183 Marsh Wall
London E14 9FT
Tel. 44-71-5388686
Telex 929089 ITPINFG
Telefax 44-71-5389508

BRUYLANT - Brussels
Rue de la Régence 67
1000 Bruxelles
Tel. 32-2-5129845
Telefax 32-2-5117202

MANZ - Vienna
Kohlmarkt 16, P.O.B. 163
1014 Wien
Tel. 43-1-531610
Telex 75310631 manz a
Telefax 43-1-5316181

**EDITORIAL
ARANZADI** - Pamplona
Ctra. Aoiz Km. 3,5
31486 Elcano (Navarra) SPAIN
Tel. 48-330226-331811
Telefax 48-330919

**Graphisches Unternehmen
Stämpfli** - **Berne**
Hallerstrasse 7
3012 Berne
Tel. 4131-3006311
Telefax 4131-3006688